CASES IN INTERNATIONAL ENTREPRENEURSHIP

Robert D. Hisrich
Case Western Reserve University

Patricia P. McDougall
Georgia Institute of Technology

Benjamin M. Oviatt
Georgia State University

IRWIN

Chicago • Bogotá • Boston • Buenos Aires • Caracas
London • Madrid • Mexico City • Sydney • Toronto

© Richard D. Irwin, a Times Mirror Higher Education Group, Inc. company, 1997

Irwin Book Team

Publisher: *Rob Zwettler*
Executive editor: *Craig S. Beytien*
Editorial assistant: *Kimberly Kanakes*
Marketing manager: *Michael Campbell*
Project supervisor: *Paula M. Buschman*
Production supervisor: *Bob Lange*
Designer: *Larry J. Cope*
Director, prepress purchasing: *Kimberly Meriwether David*
Compositor: *Interactive Composition Corporation*
Typeface: *10/12 Palatino*
Printer: R. R. Donnelley & Sons

⬛ Times Mirror
Ⓜ Higher Education Group

Library of Congress Cataloging-in-Publication Data

Hisrich, Robert D.
    Cases in international entrepreneurship/Robert D. Hisrich, Patricia P. McDougall, Benjamin M.
Oviatt.
        p. cm.
    ISBN 0-256-19183-2
    1. Entrepreneurship—Case studies.   2. International business enterprises—Case studies.   3.
Joint ventures—Case studies.   I. McDougall, Patricia P.   II. Oviatt, Benjamin M.   III. Title.
HB615.H575   1997
658.4'21—dc20   96-31158

Printed in the United States of America
1 2 3 4 5 6 7 8 9 0 DO 3 2 1 0 9 8 7 6

The last decade has seen an ever-increasing emphasis on international activity in a hypercompetitive business environment. This has sparked an increasing interest in international entrepreneurship, international business, and international economics by academics, business leaders, and government officials. This book assists in understanding and addressing international opportunities and how international entrepreneurs respond to them. It is unique because each of the entrepreneurs and their entrepreneurial companies are attempting to profit from opportunities in countries that are not their home. International entrepreneurship focuses on how new and small ventures conduct business across national borders. The topic is especially timely because entrepreneurs and small business owners are often reluctant to become involved in international business activities. This book provides a resource of experiences that will assist students, professors, managers, executives, government officials, and other interest groups as well as international entrepreneurs themselves in overcoming the inevitable problems of venturing across country borders. This casebook brings alive both the opportunities and the problems with vitality, relevance, and richness of detail.

The variety of experiences in *Cases in International Entrepreneurship* is significant. The cases demonstrate that entrepreneurs can find the resources to take virtually any type of business international. Most people would think of "high-tech" industries, such as computer software, as being naturally global and several of the cases in this book indicate the struggles of software ventures in various stages of international development. Yet there are also several cases on service businesses, such as a temporary employment agency for scientists and technicians; agricultural ventures, such as a mushroom cooperative; and various manufactured products, all of which have or are attempting to have international operations. Even the performing arts, like the Irish *Riverdance*, offer international entrepreneurial opportunities. From capitalism in China to bricks in Botswana, *Cases in International Entrepreneurship* demonstrates that entrepreneurs can span virtually any international boundary. It is a book about adventurous venturing, providing readers an opportunity to learn from the experiences of creative, enterprising pioneers.

Many of the resources required by entrepreneurs are now available around the world. For example, both wired and wireless communication is available in almost every country, and the Internet virtually ignores country borders. International financial transfers take place at the touch of a computer key. Air transportation can move goods and people halfway around the world in less than a day at prices that most often seem to be steadily decreasing. With these and other efficiencies, people are beginning to realize that international business is no longer the exclusive domain of large multinational enterprises like Matsushita, Ford, and Siemens. As the significant extent and increasing activity of international entrepreneurship is recognized, more and more students and teachers will demand education on the topic, at first as part of other management education, international business, or entrepreneurship courses, and then as a distinct course. *Cases in International Entrepreneurship* is useful in all of these situations. Instructors may supplement the domestic cases they already use with the variety of international cases in this book. Many of the dilemmas that students are asked to resolve in *Cases in International Entrepreneurship*—starting-up, financing, and managing growth—are the same problems they encounter in domestic cases. As more students choose an entrepreneurial orientation, this book offers instructors of traditional international business courses the opportunity to broaden their focus from primarily large multinational firms to include smaller, entrepreneurial ventures. Today, a course in entrepreneurship that is exclusively domestic is losing its relevance in a world where in seconds one can be virtually transported to a foreign culture in 256, full-motion, worldwide-web colors. To the familiar domestic issues, the cases in this book add the increasingly important complexity of international exchange rates, foreign competition, and exotic cultural differences. As entire courses in international entrepreneurship are developed, *Cases in International Entrepreneurship* will be an extremely useful resource.

The book is also easy to use. Instructors and students can find topics and cases of interest in one of three ways. First, broad topics covered by the cases are identified by the chapter titles in the Table of Contents. Second, below each chapter title, the name of each case in a chapter is listed, and below the names are shown the industries, the main countries involved, and the primary developmental stage—opportunity identification, start-up, growth, or maturity—of the main business. Third, the introductory page of each chapter provides a summary of the situation that will be encountered in each case in the chapter.

Many people—professors, entrepreneurs, business executives, research assistants, reviewers, and the publishing staff—have made this book possible. Of great assistance were the inciteful comments of our reviewers,

Harold P. Welsch,   DePaul University
Gary M. Cadenhead,   University of Texas at Austin

Paul R. Johnson,   The American Graduate School of International
                         Management
Gerhardt Plaschka,   DePaul University

Special thanks to each of our contributing authors, from a wide variety of institutions and countries:

Kimberly Abell,   Stanford University, United States
Ibrahim Al-Fahim,   Eastern Washington University, United States
Ismael Al-Fahim,   Eastern Washington University, United States
Zakhar Bolshakov,   Zelenograd Business College, Russia
Barra O'Cinneide,   University of Limerick, Ireland
Nicole Coviello,   University of Auckland, New Zealand
James Chrisman,   University of Calgary, Canada
George Danforth,   GulfNet, Inc., United States
Robert DeFillippi,   Suffolk University, United States
Aditya Dehejia,   Stanford University, United States
Scott Field,   University of Washington, United States
Mikhail Gratchev,   Case Western Reserve University,
                         United States
Walter Good,   University of Manitoba, Canada
Thomas Hellmann,   Stanford University, United States
Don Hopkins,   Temple University, United States
Alexei Ilyin,   Zelenograd Business College, Russia
A. Qayyum Khan,   University of North Carolina at Charlotte,
                         United States
Richard Linowes,   American University, United States
Michael Lamb,   Georgia State University, United States
Kris Opalinski,   University of Manitoba, Canada
David Osgood,   George Washington University,
                         United States
Dmitri Popov,   Zelenograd Business College, Russia
Rajib Sanyal,   Trenton State College, United States
Richard Scamehorn,   Ohio University, United States
David Schweiger,   University of South Carolina,
                         United States
Mark Simon,   Oakland University, United States
Rodney Shrader,   University of Alberta, Canada
Janos Vecsenyi,   International Management Center, Hungary
Charles Wankel,   St. John's University, United States
Diane Welsh,   Eastern Washington University, United States.

Without each of their contributions, cases of such quality, diversity, and different cultural origins would not have been possible.

Our institutions, Case Western Reserve University, Georgia Institute of Technology, and Georgia State University, have generously provided assistance throughout this project. Thanks also to Jason Barone, Steve Barnett, and Philip Hilton for providing research and editorial assistance, and to Georgia Tech's Center for International Business Education and Research for its support. And to Craig Beytien, our editor, who shared a vision for this first-of-its-kind effort in international entrepreneurship.

Finally, it is to our spouses Tina, Jeff, and Judy, whose support and understanding helped bring this effort to closure, and to the future entrepreneurs—our children Kelly, Kary, Katy, and Chris, and the generation they represent—that this book is dedicated. May you always transcend the boundaries of national borders and think internationally.

Robert Hisrich
Patricia McDougall
Ben Oviatt

CHAPTER III

CROSS-BORDER ALLIANCES

CHAPTER IV

MANAGING INTERNATIONAL GROWTH

CHAPTER V

CULTURAL, ETHICAL, AND LEGAL ISSUES

CHAPTER VI

CROSS-BORDER FINANCIAL ISSUES

CHAPTER VII

HUMAN RESOURCE ISSUES

1 STARTING THE INTERNATIONAL NEW VENTURE

CASE SUMMARIES

CASE 1: CHINA INTERNATIONAL TRADE ASSOCIATES, LIMITED: A NEW VENTURE'S JOURNEY INTO CHINA (A)

By Mark Simon (Oakland University, USA)
and Michael Lamb (Georgia State University, USA)

The case describes the struggles of three young entrepreneurs as they strive over five turbulent years to make their newly formed trading company profitable. CITA is a family business that imports ceramic floor tile from the People's Republic of China (PRC). Part A explores the company's formation, the principals, the process by which they decided upon a product line, and the complexity of conducting business with the PRC. Mr. Richard Altwarg, one of the founders, had learned several Chinese dialects and was one of the first American students to visit the PRC. However, at the end of the case, CITA is having difficulties with distribution of their tiles in the United States, and the founders are even questioning whether they are in the right business. The reader is asked to determine an appropriate strategy.

CASE 2: HEARTWARE INTERNATIONAL CORPORATION: A MEDICAL EQUIPMENT COMPANY "BORN INTERNATIONAL" (A)

By Benjamin M. Oviatt (Georgia State University, USA),
Patricia Phillips McDougall (Georgia Institute of Technology, USA),
Mark Simon (Oakland University, USA),
and Rodney C. Shrader (University of Alberta, Canada)

The case explores the founding and initial problems of a new venture in the medical equipment industry. Mr. Gerald Seery starts the venture in New York in 1988 (later moving to Atlanta) with personal and family financing. The cardiac technology and its production come from Holland,

and from inception the plan is to sell in the United States, Europe and, to a lesser extent, in other countries. Although some early sales come from Europe and South America, Mr. Seery's efforts to sell and raise financing in the United States are disappointing. Part A describes the founding and asks the reader to suggest the next moves.

CASE 3:   PROFESSIONAL STAFF LIMITED: TAKING A VENTURE ABROAD

By Thomas Hellmann, Kimberly Abell, and Aditya Dehejia,
(all of Stanford University, USA)

Backed by venture capital, Mr. Bruce Culver starts a successful company in the United States that supplies laboratory scientists and technicians for temporary assignment. After failing to convince his board that similar opportunities are available in Europe, Mr. Culver resigns and forms a similar company in the United Kingdom, also backed by venture capital. It is successful and a related firm headquartered in Paris is acquired, but it turns out to have significant management problems. In late 1994, further European expansion is being considered and the venture anticipates a public offering in 1996. ■

Case 1
China International Trade Associates, Limited

A New Venture's Journey into China (A)

In December 1988, the management of China International Trade Associates, Limited (CITA) held an impromptu meeting in their three-room Atlanta headquarters. CITA, an importer of ceramic floor tile from the People's Republic of China (PRC), was managed by three people: Lisa Tosi, chief executive officer (CEO), age 26; Lisa's husband Richard Altwarg, the company president, age 27; and Lisa's sister, Kathy Tosi, chief financial officer (CFO), age 25. In addition, Du Wei Ping, a citizen of the PRC, handled much of the day-to-day business in China.

The principals of CITA were concerned because customers were reluctant to purchase their floor tile, even though many of these very same customers had given positive feedback when they evaluated earlier product prototypes. The CITA management team had spent a year and a half exploring different trade opportunities between the United States and the PRC, and were reluctant to change products now.

CITA'S EARLY HISTORY

Richard's Background.   It was not altogether unexpected that CITA personnel were interested in trade with the PRC. Richard's intense fascination with China began in the late 1970s when he chose Oriental Studies electives in high school. Later, at Oberlin College, Richard pursued a B.A. in East Asian Studies, majoring in Chinese history, and learned the Mandarin, Cantonese, and Shanghainese dialects. By age 23, he had translated a novel from Chinese to English, interpreted various materials for Taiwanese companies, and taught English to Taiwanese nationals. In addition, he spent his junior year of college in Shanghai, becoming one of the first seven American students to visit the PRC in decades. While there, he noticed a rising standard of living and the demand for many goods that simply were not available.

After returning to the States, Richard finished his college education. Late in 1983, he began working as an assistant traffic manager for Block Industries, a U.S.-based importer of shirts. At Block, he gained experience in international trade fundamentals by tracking shipments and expediting the flow of paperwork for banks, steamship lines, trucking companies, and governments. After learning the fundamentals of the job, Richard complained of boredom.

Less than a year after starting at Block, in 1984 Richard accepted a job offer from a new venture called China Trade Promotions (CTP). The company's founder was trying to organize a trade show in the PRC for U.S. medical equipment companies

Source: This case was prepared by Mark Simon (Oakland University, USA) and Michael Lamb (Georgia State University, USA). The authors would like to thank Richard Altwarg, Kathleen Tosi, and Lisa Tosi for their willingness to share time and information. This case is intended as a basis for class discussion rather than to illustrate either effective or ineffective handling of an administrative situation.

who were interested in exporting. The company consisted of the owner, a secretary, and three recently hired employees who would start work soon after Richard. During Richard's first week of work, the owner left for the PRC to handle some details of the show's setup. Although the trip was only supposed to be for 10 days, it ended up being for four months.

Richard took on the role of managing the office, convincing bill collectors not to cut off the phone, selling additional booth spaces, and developing new promotional material. His 18-hour days paid off and by the time the owner returned, Richard had sold 53 booths. Only three spaces had been purchased before the owner's trip. In recalling his boss's return Richard said,

> 'The Boss' wanted his job back even though he had no relationship with the people. As soon as he came back he started questioning everything I had done and double-checking every decision I was making. However, I was proud of what I had accomplished. I had done a good job and had a lot of ego invested. My father, who was a self-employed attorney, used to tout the benefits of not having to please a boss. Now I knew why.

After a series of arguments, Richard was fired in June 1985, one week before the trade show opened in China.

CITA Is Started.   Without a job in hand, Richard debated whether to start his own company, an idea that had been incubating since his days at Block Industries. He began lengthy discussions with Lisa Tosi, his girlfriend and soon-to-be wife. Together they decided to take the entrepreneurial leap, agreeing to little more than the fact that the company would be called China International Trade Associates and would somehow involve trade with the PRC. Until the company became-profitable, the couple planned to live on Lisa's income from General Motors (GM) and the $10,000 dollars Richard had managed to save. While she worked at GM, Lisa nonetheless played a part in all of CITA's major decisions.

Encouraged by the changing economic conditions in the PRC (see Exhibit 1), Richard and Lisa spent the remainder of 1985 and all of 1986 exploring possibilities for trade with China. Given China's large population and the pent-up consumer demand Richard had observed while abroad, Lisa and Richard decided initially to export goods to China, as opposed to importing goods from China. Specifically, they hunted for products or industries where trading channels between the United States and the PRC had not already been established.

As time progressed, the couple began to use an increasing percentage of Lisa's earnings and Richard's savings to finance their search. Together, they began to write and call any personal contacts and companies in both the United States and China that might lead to opportunities. In addition to reviewing many available publications including the *China Business Review,* Richard flew to China on three occasions to learn more about the market.

One of CITA's first opportunities occurred when Richard was approached by a Chinese army general who wanted to buy U.S. tanks. The general had heard from relatives that there was a Westerner interested in exporting goods to China. After Richard met with the general, Lisa proceeded to telephone General Dynamics. The salesperson on the other end of the line showed little wariness about supplying military equipment to China and immediately began to solicit information such as the make and model number of the tanks. After 10 minutes of gathering information, the General Dynamic's sales representative proceeded to quote prices. However, Richard and Lisa decided not to forward the information, becoming uncomfortable with the idea of dealing in arms. The ethical considerations outweighed potential sales commissions.

EXHIBIT 1   Changing Economic Conditions in the People's Republic of China

In recent decades the People's Republic of China took several steps to increase economic productivity, raise the standard of living, modernize production facilities, and increase exports. Many of these steps marked a departure from the country's previous policies of economic isolation and central government planning of economic activities. Some of the changes included supporting trade and investment with foreign nations, allowing economic incentives to permeate businesses, and relying to a greater extent on the market for allocation of resources and determination of prices. Government loans were granted to business enterprises and favorable treatment of state-owned enterprises was diminished. Government authority began to shift from the central government to provinces.

Perhaps one of the biggest changes was the formation of industrial organizations which were not directly run by the state, although state-run enterprises were responsible for over 85 percent of employment and output as of 1988. Enterprises run by provinces and by holding companies comprised of several local businesses, usually in the same industry, had grown twice as fast as state industrial enterprises, especially in rural areas. Often, these enterprises were given a large degree of autonomy from the state and were, to an extent, able to determine their own prices and management practices.

Much of the second half of the 1980s could be described as a period of unbridled industrial expansion, unprecedented rise in entrepreneurship, growth in household disposable income, and increases in pent-up demand. In part these dramatic results were caused by the establishment of the Special Economic Zones created after 1979. There were four primary zones, including Shenzhen in the Guangdong province, next to Hong Kong. Specifically these zones were established to promote the exporting of Chinese manufactured goods and to become a model for other coastal areas. To an extent, the zones were self-ruling and less answerable to the central government in Beijing. Many of the enterprises within a zone were motivated by profit, an idea formerly foreign to the PRC. Furthermore, foreigners interested in trade had a greater degree of autonomy than anywhere else in China. The Special Zone policy had dramatic local results, most notably in Shenzhen where hundreds of new buildings were constructed and tens of thousands of new jobs were created.

However, the very success of many of the PRC's programs caused difficulties. The lack of tight centralized control created inflationary pressures and the loosening of the trade restrictions worsened China's balance of payments. Also a disproportionate share of the growing economic well-being was concentrated in the Special Economic Zones, a disturbing development in a society still basically committed to socialism.

In the second half of the 1980s, the government began to take some steps to alleviate some of these problems. Concurrent with the general atmosphere of loosening controls, some selective central controls were put in place to repress demand, and the Chinese currency was often devalued in order to promote exports and raise the price of imports. The adoption of new business methods in the pursuit of economic strength did not mean that China accepted the notion of liberal free trade and capitalist ownership.

Sources: J. K. Fairbanks, *China: A New History* (Cambridge, MA: Harvard University Press, 1992); R. Terrill, *China in Our Time: The Epic Saga of the People's Republic from the Communist Victory to Tiananmen Square and Beyond* (New York: Simon & Schuster, 1992).

During the year and a half search period, Richard and Lisa unsuccessfully tried to exploit many trade opportunities, including selling booth space at Chinese trade shows to U.S. exporters, exporting factory equipment, and consulting with companies interested in establishing business relations with China. Most of the projects failed to come to fruition because of China's lack of foreign exchange to pay for U.S. goods.

To overcome the foreign exchange problem, CITA explored countertrade, a form of international trade that takes place when merchandise, not hard currency, is exchanged between companies of different countries. Through the father of a former classmate, Richard learned of a carpet factory in China interested in obtaining tufting machines, used in the production of carpeting, from a U.S. equipment manufacturer. However, the factory did not have access to U.S. currency to pay the manufacturer. Therefore Richard and Lisa arranged a way for the factory to receive the machinery without using U.S. dollars. The equipment manufacturer would ship the tufting machines to the factory in China while the factory simultaneously shipped carpet to a third party, a U.S. carpet wholesaler. The U.S. wholesaler would then in effect "pay" the equipment manufacturer instead of the Chinese factory. U.S. and Chinese banks would guarantee the whole transaction and CITA would receive a commission based on the selling price of the equipment and the selling price of the carpeting.

The deal fell through when the factory's cost of certain raw materials rose due to national shortages, effectively increasing the factory's price of providing carpet to the U.S. wholesalers. According to Lisa and Richard, the deal still made sense in the long run, because the tufting equipment would lower the cost of making carpet in the future. Therefore the "loss" incurred on the carpet shipped to the United States could be subsidized by future sales within China because the new equipment would result in a higher margin. However, they were unsuccessful in convincing the Chinese factory manager that one side of his operations could be used to subsidize another.

Lisa Joins CITA Full Time.   By the end of 1986, the young couple had witnessed project after project fall through and had invested over $30,000 of Richard's savings and Lisa's current earnings trying to make CITA work. After a year and half of living as frugally as possible, Richard was seriously considering getting a traditional job.

Meanwhile, after almost two years of working for GM, in a program for high-potential employees, Lisa was ready to leave corporate America. Although working on a variety of different job rotations, Lisa found most of her work boring or her bosses second-rate. The one rotation she looked forward to fell through because of what Lisa described as "behind the scene political maneuvering." Lisa recalls her feelings at the time:

> I decided that this was a little too arbitrary. One person could totally wreck your whole career, like if he had a bad tamale for lunch or something. I don't usually get upset but this scared me.

---

*Names that are disguised are marked with an asterisk the first time they appear.

Ironically, after arguing with her task force that the inducements in the voluntary separation incentive package they were developing were much too high, in October of 1986, Lisa became one of the first to leave. Although Richard had doubts about continuing CITA, after prolonged debates with Lisa, the couple decided to forge ahead. Lisa, at age 24, started working at CITA full-time.

The Search for Direction and Funds.   Without income, Lisa and Richard now confronted the necessity of quickly obtaining outside funds. To do so the couple had to clarify their strategy. During this process Lisa constantly wrote and rewrote the company's business plan. Exhibit 2 contains excerpts, capturing the essence of CITA's proposed strategy.

Exhibit 2   Excerpts from CITA's Business Plan

CITA Ltd. is a wholesale trading company that specializes in developing *long-term* trading relationships with contacts in the Far East, particularly in the People's Republic of China (PRC). The Company will work closely with Chinese factories and U.S. distributors to develop quality, low-cost ceramic tile lines for sale in North America . . .

CITA was founded by its current president, Richard Altwarg. Having spent a number of years living and working in the PRC, Mr. Altwarg understands the cultural, political, and economic conditions under which manufacturing and trading concerns operate. The importance of developing "Guanxi," or goodwill, with individuals responsible for production and export is paramount in developing long-term, stable trade relationships . . .

The first phase of CITA's corporate strategy will entail working with Chinese contacts to develop a line of products that would be suitable for sale in Western markets, consistent with the Chinese central guidelines for developing exports. CITA will avoid those few markets where China already has a strong presence: silk textiles, silk apparel, and hand-made household goods such as wicker furniture and vases. It is also important to work in industries where the Chinese have considerable know-how and there are significant cost advantages due to labor savings and/or raw materials sources. This is consistent with the directive from the central planning authorities to stress exports of "native" products which do not require special skills or investment in capital equipment that deplete China's closely guarded foreign currency reserves. On the demand side, it is important to work in a growing market that is not resistant to imports, and where there is an active sales market for small suppliers.

CITA chose ceramic tiles. The Chinese have—literally—centuries of experience in working with ceramics, and indeed produce some of the finest ceramic products in the world. The raw material used in production, kaolin clay, is excellent, plentiful, and extremely inexpensive in the PRC. The labor savings, especially in the areas of quality control and packaging, are significant. There are numerous factories in coastal areas, making shipping and domestic logistics easier. These factories, which appear somewhat primitive by western standards, are capable of producing excellent tiles.

The Chinese are aware that they are unable to market their own products for sale in the United States, and will welcome CITA to their factories to work with them. China's tile exports to the United States have been negligible . . .

CITA intends to use the ceramic tile sales as a profit base which will provide the company with the funds required to expand into other markets and trading activities, thus capitalizing on the firm's unique ability to work within the Chinese system to bring low cost, quality products to Western markets and provide real assistance to firms which produce products that are appropriate for sale to the Chinese.

Source: CITA's Business Plan, 1987.

Richard and Lisa's decision to carry ceramic tile was central to their plan. In addition to China's strengths in producing ceramics, as explained in the plan, CITA was also encouraged by the growing demand for tile in the United States. As Exhibit 3 suggests, imported tile was readily accepted in the United States and the domestic market was growing. In addition, the U.S. market was fragmented with no companies dominating.

In August of 1986, with their strategy better defined, Lisa and a long-time family friend, Dr. Robert Stockwell,* began their attempts to raise $250,000. Dr. Stockwell was a professor of management at Southern University* and had, since the company's inception, been promising to help raise money. Over the next six months, Lisa and Dr. Stockwell contacted everyone they knew who might be interested in investing in the young company and began to present their vision of CITA.

By February of 1987, five different investors had committed $110,000. The five investors also made verbal agreements to provide more funds after CITA was better defined. The investors included Dr. Stockwell, Dr. Stockwell's brother-in-law, Richard's father, a distant cousin of the professor, and an old golf buddy of Lisa's father. Lisa and Richard retained 25 percent ownership in the company, while the six other investors received between 6 percent and 20 percent, depending on the

**EXHIBIT 3   Historical Analysis of Tile, 1975 through 1986
(measured in thousands of square feet)**

Period	Domestic Shipments*	U.S. Imports[†]	U.S. Exports	Total Consumption[‡]	Import Penetration[§]
1975	256,116	91,752	2,009	345,859	26.5%
1976	277,210	136,072	3,199	410,083	33.2%
1977	264,992	217,898	5,548	477,342	45.6%
1978	301,710	253,897	5,802	549,805	46.2%
1979	312,795	291,577	6,688	597,684	48.8%
1980	297,635	255,412	7,942	545,105	46.9%
1981	287,509	254,658	11,151	531,016	48.0%
1982	295,693	225,780	11,829	509,644	44.3%
1983	334,335	297,498	10,008	621,825	47.8%
1984	337,047	448,405	8,337	777,115	57.7%
1985	369,975	507,429	6,126	871,278	58.2%
1986	440,130	485,877	6,055	919,952	52.8%

* Due to discrepancies in Commerce Department data, the all tile domestic shipments for 1975 do not equal the sum of all mosaic, glazed, and unglazed ceramic tile.

[†] Represents imports, as measured by consumption.

[‡] Calculated by subtracting exports from the sum of domestic shipments and imports.

[§] Represents import's share of consumption.

Source: U.S. Department of Commerce, Series M 32D, IM 145X, IM 145, EM 546, EM 522, and FT-410.

amount they invested. In February of 1987, with some funding in place, CITA was legally incorporated as a Subchapter S corporation.[1]

Granite Pavers.   Much of the remaining part of 1987 was spent getting tile samples from dozens of Chinese factories and showing them at trade shows and to various individuals in the tile industry. Although CITA made an occasional sale, the company's primary accomplishment was learning the ins and outs of the tile business. The CITA staff were encouraged when in March of 1988 a well-respected Florida tile distributor thought one of CITA's products, Granite Pavers (GP), could really take off. CITA began to show the tiles to other distributors throughout the nation and received positive feedback from all. The distributors were especially impressed by the tiles' unique yet attractive appearance and felt that the price CITA was tentatively suggesting, $2.50 per square foot, was quite reasonable.

Granite Pavers were 6-inch square porcelain floor tiles resembling granite. Only one company carried a tile, the Ryowa tile, that had a similar appearance. The Ryowa tile was approximately $5.00 per square foot wholesale, about double CITA's proposed price.

As explained in Exhibit 4, the tile industry was comprised of several different levels of distribution and CITA was not sure whether to sell their tile at the manufacturer or the distributor level. They were most interested in supplying tile to two or three manufacturers, thus limiting CITA's role to sourcing the product from China. However, Lisa and Richard questioned whether they could convince manufacturers to carry their line.

After many calls to manufacturers, CITA personnel were unable to arrange a single meeting to show the Granite Pavers. The manufacturers were concerned that the PRC was not a reliable source of supply of tile. This concern was exacerbated by CITA's lack of a track record. The young couple, therefore, decided to sell downstream to distributors and Lisa began her efforts to find distributors willing to carry Granite Pavers. CITA hoped to build a national network of roughly 20 distributors, each of whom would receive an exclusive sales territory (about two states), in-exchange for adding the tile to their preexisting product lines and ordering one container of Granite Pavers (7,500 square feet) at a cost of approximately $18,000. By August of 1988, five distributors agreed they would purchase the tile if CITA could make some minor changes in the products.

CONDUCTING BUSINESS IN THE PRC

Factory Search.   After their discussions with these distributors and others, Lisa and Richard concluded Chinese factories needed to modify GPs for the U.S. market. These

---

[1]A Subchapter S corporation retains the limited liability features of regular C corporations while being taxed as a partnership. This avoids double taxation; i.e., taxation of both company profits and dividends to owners. Also, shareholders can deduct from their personal income annual company losses or writeoffs should the company fail. The amount deducted is in direct proportion to the investors' ownership and cannot exceed the total amount they invested. Should the company begin to become profitable investors can, on a one-time basis, change the company status to a regular C corporation. This avoids taxing company profits as personal income. To obtain Subchapter S status, the company must be domestic and have fewer than 35 shareholders.

EXHIBIT 4   **The Tile Industry**

There are basically three levels of distribution within the U.S. tile and floor covering industry. Furthest upstream are the manufacturers who actually produce the tile. Distributors then purchase the tile to sell it to contractors or builders who use the tile in residential or commercial construction. In addition to the distribution chain described above, do-it-yourselfers, who purchase the product from retail outlets, comprise a small segment of the market.

The industry in the 1980s was composed of small- to medium-size firms with no one firm dominating. Since the industry was fragmented, the role of a given company within the industry might be manyfold. For example, there were carpet distributors that also sold tile and companies claiming to be wholesalers that were actually primarily retailers.

Manufacturers and Importers: In the late 1980s there were approximately 14 tile manufacturers in the United States, each having annual sales of hundreds of millions of dollars. These manufacturers would take responsibility for producing and marketing the tile, often investing millions of dollars in promoting product lines that were new to the marketplace. It was essential for manufacturers to maintain a comprehensive inventory of colors for any given product line.

In addition to producing tile domestically, manufacturers also purchased tiles from importers or acted as importers themselves. In either case, they would private label the tile (sell it under their own brand name). In private labeling the product, manufacturers assume all marketing expenses for the line. They sign long-term contracts (a year or more), guaranteeing minimum purchases at regular intervals, usually totaling hundreds of thousands of dollars. The importer would guarantee exclusive national rights to sell a specific line of tile (i.e., particular styles, colors, and sizes). Although granting a national exclusive, the importer could approach other manufacturers with different styles, colors, or sizes.

Typically, letters of credit are used to make overseas payments. For example, when a manufacturer acts as an importer, the manufacturer's bank automatically pays the supplier's bank in the currency agreed upon when the shipment arrives into the States. When a manufacturer utilizes a separate importer, back-to-back letters are often used to finance the transaction. Upon arrival of the documents to the States, the manufacturer's bank pays the importer's bank in the currency specified. Simultaneously, the importer's bank pays the supplier's bank. In the late 1980s, over 50 percent of domestic consumption was comprised of imported products from Europe, South America, and the Far East.

Distributors: Distributors carried a variety of tile and floor covering products from different manufacturers and importers. Although company size varied greatly, the average distributor grossed about three million dollars annually and represented about twenty separate product lines. Generally they would have the exclusive rights to sell a product line in their territory of one to five states. Invariably distributors would be given credit terms of at least net 30.

Above and beyond any other function, distributors primarily facilitate the distribution process by storing inventory and shipping the quantities needed by builders. Due to high shipping costs, distributors had to order a full container of any given color or style (e.g., CITA's containers held 7,500 square feet of Granite Pavers) and would then ship the amount actually required when an end user placed an order. Depending on the nature of the application, end users' orders generally were for a few thousand square feet but could occasionally be as high as tens of thousands of square feet. In order to decrease their inventory storage requirements, distributors often bought smaller quantities from each other at 15 percent above cost.

Source: Interviews with distributors, importers, and manufacturers, as well as assorted materials provided by the National Association of Tile Distributors.

modifications included rounded corners, beveled edges, and customized colors. Very few of the tile factories in China were modern or sophisticated enough to make the type of changes needed. So as Lisa was convincing distributors to carry CITA's Granite Pavers, Richard searched for an appropriate source of supply for the tile.

Generally, a company wishing to import goods from China needed to contact a Chinese export authority. The authorities then selected a factory to fulfill the requirements of the trading company. More often than not, however, the factory was chosen because the factory manager had connections with the trade authorities and because the factory needed to sell products abroad since it couldn't compete effectively in the PRC. Often these factories had more limited capabilities than other factories, and thus were unable to produce the higher quality goods required for overseas markets.

The recent decentralization of economic authority allowed CITA to avoid this agency problem by concentrating in and around the provinces designated as Special Economic Zones. In these areas, foreign companies were permitted to source products directly from factories of their choosing. Because Richard was fluent in several Chinese dialects, he was able to "beat the bushes" in search of qualified producers who were interested in international trade. Richard would only contact the export authority after reaching a tentative agreement with the manager of a suitable factory.

Richard ended up narrowing his search to the village of Shiwan in the Guangdong province. With a one-thousand-year history in ceramics, the village contained over 100 ceramic factories employing over 100,000 people and produced about 20 percent of the nation's ceramic products. Richard was especially excited about this village because it was in the Guangdong Province which was the major provincial beneficiary of the new openness of China. By 1986, Guangdong had surpassed Shanghai as the largest exporter in China.

Richard asked for prototypes from the only three factories in the village that manufactured Granite Pavers. One of the factories proved completely incapable of making the shades and hues that CITA required. The best prototypes were produced by the Shiwan Porcelain Company (SPC), despite the fact that the factory's 1940s equipment produced under a million square feet of tile annually. The SPC's factory manager was very interested in exporting tile to the West because it would increase his prestige among his peers, provide foreign currency for capital expansion, and justify possible travel overseas. Also, China's domestic demand for tile was unusually slow in 1987 and 1988.

In August of 1988, CITA reached an informal understanding with the SPC. CITA agreed to buy the factory $10,000 worth of equipment needed to mass produce the Granite Pavers to specifications and in return, the factory would give CITA $10,000 worth of free tile on the first order. As a permanent arrangement, the factory would be paid through a letter of credit as soon as CITA received title to the goods.

Factory Problems.   Almost immediately after reaching the agreement, problems began to arise at the factory and it appeared that CITA's first order would be late. Richard learned that it was far easier to get good prototypes of Granite Pavers than to get the Granite Pavers mass-produced. Producing prototypes was primarily an art involving formulating colors and preparing raw materials. However, managing mass production introduced a new set of problems, including equipment failures, large communication gaps, scheduling problems, and equipment changes on the assembly line.

Richard decided to take matters into his own hands. However, given the complexity of the power structure within an industry in China (as described in Exhibit 5), he was uncertain who would be best to approach. Initially, Richard tried talking to the factory manager directly with little result. Although the manager's signature was required on any document regarding production, scheduling, or purchasing, he had no interest in dealing with the day-to-day problems that arose. Frustrated, Richard went to the holding company (as described in Exhibit 5) to see if they could remedy the problems. The holding company was comprised of the managers of local ceramic factories and included the SPC manager. Officials in the holding company gave polite responses and promises about talking to the factory manager, but produced no action.

EXHIBIT 5   Industry Structure and Culture in the PRC

Understanding the role of the province and the role of the holding company creates a greater understanding of industry in the PRC. With economic reform and the decentralization of economic power, it became more necessary for local governments to raise their own tax revenues. This transformed local government officials from mere caretakers and administrators into bureaucratic entrepreneurs who took the lead in developing township and village industrial enterprises. They involved themselves in every aspect of local industry operations, from the appointment of managers to determining the number of workers to be hired. Many of these townships were growing at a dramatic rate and becoming increasingly important to the national economy.

In addition to local authorities, holding companies might also make decisions for the firm. These holding companies were comprised of a collection of individual firm managers whose factories produced similar products (an example is the holding company mentioned in the case, which was comprised of tile factory managers in the Shiwan township). Most of these corporations had been formed to help attain economies of scale, or to upgrade technology by linking with more progressive enterprises. Thus firms could have been under central government administration, under provincial control, under township control, under holding company control, or any combination of the above. This dual or multiple leadership situation led to difficulty, but was still the most common arrangement.

Despite the complex relationship between factory manager, holding company board of directors, and provincial staff, some factory managers achieved quite a bit of autonomy. Who made what decision was situation specific and often depended on the connections of the factory manager, the size of the factory, and the factory's track record. The complex and amorphous power structure often frustrated Westerners who sought to deal with Chinese managers.

Westerners were also frustrated by the different culture they encountered in the PRC. For example, rather than relying on written contracts, the Chinese depended more upon developing long-term personal relationships (*guanxi*) with members of different organizations. In fact, the strong extended family relationships that existed in China often evolved into business relationships. Short-term gain would have been foregone if it were to jeopardize the relationship. Because the Chinese focused on friendships, they recognized the interests, constraints, and risks of "partners" rather than viewing the world in win/lose scenarios. It has been difficult for Westerners to establish friendship relationships with citizens of the PRC.

Relationships within factories were also quite different in the East. Communications through a traditional Western concept of chain of command were less familiar to the Chinese, and worker compliance with instructions was based upon respect, not organizational position. It was common for strife, discord, and conflict to reign between workers and between workers and managers. However, in their dealing with foreigners, the Chinese were generally harmonious and extremely courteous. These factors, however, led to a confusing situation for an American doing business in the PRC.

Sources: J. K. Fairbanks, *China: A New History* (Cambridge, MA: Harvard University Press, 1992); R. Terrill, *China in Our Time: The Epic Saga of the People's Republic from the Communist Victory to Tiananmen Square and Beyond* (New York: Simon & Schuster, 1992).

Finally, at his wit's end, Richard approached the assistant factory manager, a 28-year-old college graduate of the Shanghai Ceramics Institute. It became rapidly apparent that the number two man had no real power and was ridiculed by the factory workers, who called him "the little student" when he tried to implement what he had learned in college.

Richard soon discovered that the only way to get the second in command to assert his authority and "have it out with the people on the line" was to be a constant thorn in his side. It was not uncommon for Richard to sit in the assistant factory manager's office and refuse to leave until told the specific cause of a delay. Finally, after many excuses, Richard would find out what needed to be done. Then, either with or without the assistant manager, Richard would go to the factory floor and engage individual workers. Richard found himself yelling, arguing, cajoling, demanding, and demonstrating in order to correct the problem. Richard explained his assertiveness in the following manner:

> We had to do whatever it took to make sure that the order was shipped within a reasonable amount of time. I knew it was unusual for a Westerner to conduct business with the Chinese in this manner, even though they frequently interacted this way among themselves, but I was convinced that I could pull it off. Besides, I never had much patience for people's irrationality or incompetence, although at least in a Third World country I could understand it better.

Although highly unorthodox, Richard's methods decreased the time it took to process CITA's orders and the five distributors who ordered from CITA received the product close to the date promised. Richard returned to the States after the order for the first five distributors was completed.

Du Wei Ping.   Given the difficulty Richard had getting the order filled on time, CITA decided to hire Du Wei Ping, a Chinese national. Richard first met Du Wei Ping in 1986 at a dinner in Mainland China where Du Wei Ping spoke of his interest in participating in the ongoing opening up of China to the rest of the world and told Richard that if he ever needed a favor to let him know. After extensive correspondence by mail, Du began to handle many miscellaneous tasks for CITA and to explore products and factories with Richard during his trips to China.

As time progressed, a strong friendship developed between Du and the young couple, and Du increased the amount of time he spent on CITA-related activities. If needed, Du left his job as an electrical engineer at Electronics Testing Factory Number Five for periods ranging from a couple of days to several weeks. Richard and Lisa also helped Du out whenever possible. They even sponsored Du's sister and brother-in-law, thus allowing Du's relatives to stay in the States for an extended period of time and eventually become U.S. citizens. Sponsoring an alien required vouching for their character and agreeing to be legally responsible for any debts incurred, laws broken, or problems with the Immigration and Naturalization Service.

With some reservations, late in 1988, Du left his job at the electronics testing factory to work for CITA full-time. Leaving his state job complicated Du's life because he no longer belonged to a work group. This, in essence, changed his citizenship status, forcing Du to live with his parents because he had lost his individual housing rights which were determined by employment. Additionally, he could only receive health care through Du's father's connections in the medical community.

Despite the complications, Du enjoyed the freedom and independence CITA provided including staying at hotels, flying to different parts of China, eating at fancy restaurants, and using CITA's credit cards to access foreign currency. Du's parents were split on the wisdom of Du's decision. His mother felt that someone of Du's background should have the security of a government "recognized" position and that, at a future date, the government might even view Du's role in CITA as protesting communism. In contrast, his father, a former military leader and a risk-taker himself, was very supportive of Du's choice.

Du's job included arranging traveling logistics, translating materials, finding sources of materials, and troubleshooting at the factory. He also had to deal with many issues that are not encountered in the United States. For example, if an individual did not have the right contacts they would be told that hotels, planes, taxis, or trains were booked solid. Also, operating within the PRC was complicated by the feuds that took place between different townships. Once, when driving to the factory site, Du had to stop because the road was blocked by large boulders. A peasant who lived in a hut by the road explained the barrier separated two towns engaged in a feud. Before Du could continue, the peasant forced him to spend two hours tearing down the boulders to proceed and then another four hours reconstructing the barrier!

DOMESTIC GROWTH

With Du and Richard attempting to smooth the relationship with the factory in China, Kathy Tosi, Lisa's sister, handled much of the complexity that was developing domestically. Upon completion of her M.B.A. at the University of Florida in 1987, Kathy began doing odd jobs for CITA. Within a few months she proved indispensable and began working for CITA full time. She was responsible for general administrative functions including accounting, taxes, shipping, and documentation. However, she also became involved in many aspects of running CITA, including all decision making. For her efforts, Kathy received a small salary and equity in the company. Only 14 months apart, Lisa and Kathy had been playing or working together since Kathy was two. Lisa relates:

> Although we are close, we are different in many ways. Kathy has a lot of skills Richard and I don't have. She's super organized. What we didn't need was another free spirit like Richard or me.

Attempts to Broaden the Distribution Network.   As 1988 came to a close, Lisa was still trying to develop a nationwide network of distributors. Finding the best party to approach proved to be of major importance. While each major market (usually comprising one or two states) had about ten distributors, CITA decided there were only two or three in each market that could adequately handle Granite Pavers.

Initial comments by distributors caused CITA to feel even more positive about Granite Pavers. Architects, contractors, and distributors were all impressed by the look and quality of the product. Its price was also a distinct advantage because distributors could buy the product for about $2.50 per square foot and charge $4 per square foot. Also, no products were similar to Granite Pavers in terms of appearance. The Japanese firm that produced Ryowa had stopped selling in the U.S. market. Emphasizing these advantages, Lisa was able to sign up three more distributors, generating more than $200,000 by the end of 1988, as shown in Exhibit 6.

However, it was proving difficult to close additional sales. Distributors considering carrying the product had major concerns. They were unsure of future product quality and the reliability of delivery due to past negative experiences with products from Third World nations. They also had marketing concerns: While they knew the product was up-scale they were unsure of exactly where it would be used. Additionally, since Granite Pavers would probably be specified in plans by architects, it could be one to two years between the initial decision to use the product and the final purchase by a builder or contractor. Finally, distributors wanted to receive credit terms and purchase quantities smaller than a container load.

In the meantime CITA was running short of cash—among other things, their minimal salaries, unavoidable office expenses, and the cost of traveling within the states and the PRC were eating up the initial investment of $110,000. As the year was coming to a close, Richard, Lisa, and Kathy knew that getting a distribution network up and running would be crucial to getting more funds from investors. However, getting additional distributors to sign on the dotted line was proving to be no simple matter.

Faced with disappearing funds and reluctant distributors, Lisa, Richard, and Kathy knew they had to act. On the one hand they could change their strategy, but this might entail starting from scratch, something they were reluctant to do. Alternatively, they felt they might be able to "tweak" things a bit, possibly offering additional incentives to distributors. They were, however, uncertain which incentives would be effective and what they could afford. The one thing they knew was that they were running short of time.

EXHIBIT 6

CHINA INTERNATIONAL TRADE ASSOCIATES, LTD.
STATEMENT OF INCOME
YEAR ENDING DECEMBER 31, 1988

		Percentage
Gross Revenue		
Sales—tile	$222,606.55	98.36%
Sales—other	3,703.93	1.64
Total gross revenue	$226,310.48	100.00
Cost of Sales		
COGS—tile	$ 77,358.80	34.18
COGS—shipping	65,462.40	28.93
COGS—duties	5,005.17	2.21
Total cost of sales	$147,826.37	65.32
Gross profit	$ 78,484.11	34.68
Selling, General, and Administrative		
Advertising—General	$ 5,014.57	2.22
Advertising—Promotion items	10,782.98	4.76
Commissions	10,725.34	4.74
Dues and subscriptions	101.59	0.04
Insurance—group medical	1,617.38	0.71
Insurance—other	1,596.83	0.71
Legal and accounting	4,185.06	1.85
Miscellaneous	9,029.58	3.99
Office	2,854.46	1.26
Payroll taxes	6,009.17	2.66
Postage	7,110.90	3.14
Rent—office	9,863.40	4.36
Salaries—officers	65,999.88	29.16
Selling	8,028.03	3.55
Taxes and licenses	214.04	−0.09
Telephone and telex	17,332.61	7.66
T&E, airline tickets	7,750.56	3.42
T&E, auto rentals	482.26	0.21
T&E, hotel expense	3,598.00	1.59
T&E, meal expense	3,878.66	1.71
T&E, mileage reimbursement	50.00	0.02
T&E, other	5,488.10	2.43
Total selling, general, and administrative	$181,713.40	80.29
Net operating income (loss)	($103,229.29)	45.61
Income before taxes	($103,229.29)	45.61%

EXHIBIT 7

CHINA INTERNATIONAL TRADE ASSOCIATES, LTD.
BALANCE SHEET DECEMBER 31, 1988

		Percentage
Assets		
Current Assets		
Cash in bank	($ 13,307.67)*	−9.96%
Accounts receivable	85,352.05	63.89
Inventory	33,259.00	24.89
Total current assets	$105,303.38	78.82
Fixed Assets		
Computer hardware	2,653.71	1.97
Furniture and fixtures	1,417.10	1.06
Leasehold improvements	372.31	0.28
Less: Accumulated depreciation	(4,229.67)	−3.17
Total fixed assets	$ 213.45	0.16
Intangible Assets		
Organization costs	32,836.06	24.58
Accumulative amortized organization costs	5,472.68	4.10
Total intangible assets	$ 27,363.38	20.48
Other Assets		
Deposit—Rent security	720.00	0.54
Total Other Assets	$ 720.00	0.54
Total assets	$133,600.21	100.00%
Liabilities and Equity		
Accounts payable	$ 71,322.40	53.38
Commission payable	7,684.10	5.75
Taxes payable		
Federal withholding tax	1,387.89	1.04
State withholding tax	985.39	0.74
FICA	1,684.13	1.26
Total taxes payable	$ 4,057.41	3.04
Accrued interest	1,773.09	1.33
Due to officer	1,394.77	1.04
Total notes payable	$ 39,587.36	29.63
Total liabilities	$125,819.13	94.18
Stockholder's Equity		
Capital stock	$ 8,462.00	6.33
Paid-in capital	234,070.25	175.20
Retained earnings	(131,521.88)	−98.44
Current year's net income	(103,229.29)	−77.27
Retained earnings, YTD	(234,751.17)	−175.71
Total Stockholder's Equity	$ 7,781.08	5.82
Total Liabilities and Stockholder's equity	$133,600.21	100.00%

*CITA has a negative bank balance because the account is tied to a revolving line of credit.

Case 2

Heartware International Corporation

A Medical Equipment Company "Born International" (A)

In May 1990, Mr. Gerald Seery, chief executive and founder of Heartware International Corporation (Heartware), a two-year-old multinational venture headquartered in Atlanta, was looking toward the future. He had recently sent a fax that captured his thoughts to Dr. Pedro Cortez,* in Aagst, Belgium. Dr. Cortez was one of the two developers of the medical equipment that inspired Heartware's formation. That fax read:

> Date: May 30, 1990
> To: Pedro Cortez
> From: Gerald Seery
>
> Without repeating myself too much, this past year has been both challenging and greatly frustrating. I believe we all anticipated making further advances than we have.
>
> Certainly, I am able to report several positive developments . . . FDA approval, some early sales, and establishing Heartware as an organization. But as every businessman knows, every business needs cash, cash, cash. For Heartware, that cash has been tough to come by.
>
> I remain a believer, however. I have spoken with my wife, Tricia, and our investors about refocusing the attention of Heartware onto the European market. They have a number of questions. In general, they feel that we should capitalize on the opportunity where it makes the most sense. Obviously, the United States offers a very large market for our products. However, we should exploit the position of leadership we currently enjoy in the international markets.
>
> The key to building upon our early success will be the availability of money. Having expended all that I can afford (and then some), Heartware will be able to expand quickly only with additional capital infusion. This can come from several sources: sales, private investors, venture capital, and a partner. Pedro, I am committed to making this happen. If we can get through these early months, I know we can build Heartware into a company with great products and a sound future.

Heartware entered into the international arena at start-up. Its headquarters and investors were located in the United States. Human resources were in the United States and The Netherlands. Product development and technical support

---

*Names that are disguised are marked with an asterisk the first time they appear.

Source: This case was written by Benjamin M. Oviatt, Associate Professor of Management, Georgia State University (USA); Patricia Phillips McDougall, Associate Professor of Strategic Management, Georgia Institute of Technology (USA); Mark Simon, Oakland University (USA); and Rodney C. Shrader (University of Alberta, Canada). Copyright 1994 by authors.

This case is intended as a basis for class discussion rather than to illustrate either effective or ineffective handling of an administrative situation.

originated in The Netherlands. Early sales came from the U.S., U.K., Italy, Spain, and Brazil. The company set up distributorships in the U.S., U.K., Saudi Arabia, South Africa, and Turkey. Multinational start-ups headquartered in the United States (sometimes called "global start-ups") are unusual. However, Mr. Seery's dedication to international business was evident when in the summer of 1990 he said:

> If all of a sudden someone said, "Here's a chunk of money for your company and for all you've done," and asked, "Now what will you do?" I would definitely do something international. It's in my blood. Atlanta has the Olympics coming up in 1996; so I'd get involved in that. I would love to help smaller and mid-size companies expand overseas, because I think it's a great opportunity and because I could help them overcome that fear factor. It opens up a world that they don't know about.

THE FOUNDER'S BACKGROUND

Acquaintances described Heartware's founder as a friendly, humorous, and personable man. He was born in 1956, raised in Long Island, New York, and traced his international interest to childhood. He had been fascinated by stories about the uncle he was named after who worked overseas. During the summer between his junior and senior years in high school, Mr. Seery traveled to Spain on a student exchange program and studied Spanish with students from England, France, Ireland, and Italy. His international interests were expanded at the Catholic University of America in Washington, D.C., where he earned a B.A. in International Economics. He went on in 1980 to earn an M.B.A. with a specialty in marketing from Columbia University.

Mr. Seery's international exposure continued after graduation. Six months after taking his first job, he completed the management development program in a large chemical company in Philadelphia and was transferred to the international sales department. There he learned the nuts and bolts of international business, including letters of credit, financing, and shipping. In just one and a half years with the chemical company, Mr. Seery generated sales of $7 million.

In 1982, Mr. Seery changed jobs but continued in international sales as product manager for a New Jersey medical supply company. In this job he gained familiarity with medical devices through managing a product line which produced $5 million in revenue annually, Mr. Seery also developed a program to bring doctors from other nations to the United States to introduce them to the company and its products. In 1984, he assumed a position as senior product manager for a dental supply company in New York. For the next two years he managed the worldwide marketing of a dental product line which produced $10 million in revenue annually.

For the five years prior to founding his own company in 1988. Mr. Seery was director of international marketing and sales for Hospicath* corporation, a small medical device company in New Jersey. Under his leadership, annual domestic sales increased from $5,600,000 in 1986 to $9,300,000 in 1988, and international sales increased by more than 40 percent. Mr. Seery managed a network of exclusive distributors in Europe, Canada, and Japan, and during his tenure with

Hospicath, he traveled to Western Europe five or six times a year for two to three weeks at a time. On these trips he met with salespeople and distributors, called on hospitals, and met cardiologists in several European countries. On one of these trips Mr. Seery was introduced to the technology on which he founded Heartware.

ELECTROPHYSIOLOGY LAB AND MAPPING SYSTEM

During a September 1987 trip to Europe, Hospicath's Dutch distributor introduced Mr. Seery to Dr. Pedro Cortez. Dr. Cortez was a Spanish cardiologist who held both an M.D. and a Ph.D. He was employed as a director of the Hospital of Maastricht, located in Maastricht, The Netherlands. The Netherlands was well regarded in the medical community for its pioneering role in cardiology. At the time of Mr. Seery's trip, Dr. Cortez and Mr. Jan van der Swoort,* Chairman of the Engineering Department at the University of Limburg in Maastricht, were actively seeking a commercial outlet for the electrophysiology lab and mapping system they had jointly developed.

Electrophysiology (EP) is the study of the electrical signals of the heart, and Dr. Cortez's equipment was used for the diagnosis and treatment of irregular heartbeats (i.e., cardiac arrhythmias). General[1] EP studies were used to diagnose the type of arrhythmia. The standard approach utilized a catheter, a thin plastic tube, inserted into the blood vessel at the groin and fed into the heart. Wires were fed through the catheter so that twelve electrode leads at the end of the wires touched the heart. A cardiologist then used a cardiac stimulator to deliver a series of electrical signals to the heart. This procedure was known as pacing the heart. The cardiologist studied the resulting pattern of the heartbeat in order to better understand the nature of the arrhythmia.

Mapping studies were special EP procedures performed in a hospital operating room because the studies required that the chest cavity be surgically opened so electrodes could be moved to various positions on the heart's surface. This procedure generated a detailed map of the electrical activity on the heart's surface and inner wall. A general EP study often preceded mapping.

Growing use of EP led Dr. Cortez and Mr. van der Swoort to invest roughly four years in the mid–1980s in the development of their EP system. By 1987, when Mr. Seery was introduced to the system, it was already in use at the Hospital of Maastricht. The system was the only computerized system in the world and was owned and managed by the University of Limburg's Instrumentation and Engineering Department. The full $125,000 EP lab and mapping system (i.e., EP system) is described in Exhibit 1. It could be sold in its entirety to perform both types of studies or it could be sold in subsystems—the EP lab subsystem to perform general EP studies and the mapping subsystem to perform mapping studies. Separate components could be sold for incorporation into a hospital's existing system.

---

[1]Often the prefix "general" is dropped.

EXHIBIT 1   Components of the EP Lab and Mapping System

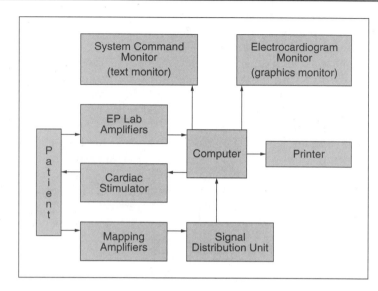

Computer: All the modular parts of the EP lab and mapping system were connected to the personal computer, which served as the heart of the system.

Cardiac Stimulator: The programmable cardiac stimulator (price: $25,000) delivered electrical signals to the heart.

Amplifiers and Signal Distribution Unit: The amplifiers and the signal distribution unit transformed electrical signals received from the heart into a form that could be interpreted by the computer and output to the printer or monitor. Although other components were used for both EP studies and mapping studies, the amplifiers were specially designed for one or the other type study. Each amplifier was priced at $25,000.

Output Devices: One color monitor displayed a menu of command options for running the system, while the other displayed output about the patient's heart. The printer produced hard copy of this output.

EP Lab Subsystem and Mapping Subsystem: The EP lab subsystem (price: $100,000) contained all system components except the mapping amplifiers (EP lab amplifiers were included) and was only used to perform general EP studies. Similarly, the mapping subsystem (price: $100,000), contained all components except the EP lab amplifiers (mapping amplifiers were included).

Supplementary Products Developed by Dr. Cortez.

Belt Electrode: The belt electrode (price: $2,500) used for the mapping procedure contained 21 electrodes and was wrapped around the surface of the heart, enabling information from 21 locations on the heart to be simultaneously relayed to the mapping system.

Cardiac Catheter: The cardiac catheter (price: $100) could be used with the EP lab in general EP studies or in conjunction with other cardiac care products on the market.

HEARTWARE FOUNDED

Mr. Seery was especially interested in the University's EP products because he had already directed the launch of an EP product line for Hospicath. That product line produced $1,100,000 in sales over a two-year period. Upon returning from Europe to the United States, Mr. Seery proposed that Hospicath acquire all of the University's products. Hospicath's president began immediately to work with Dr. Cortez and Mr. van der Swoort to further develop the catheter and to incorporate it into Hospicath's product line. The president decided to further investigate the University's EP system.

In February 1988, Hospicath sent an engineer to Maastricht with Mr. Seery to examine the EP system. Seery and the engineer recommended acquisition and further development of the system. However, the president decided not to pursue capital equipment product lines and to concentrate instead on disposable products like the cardiac catheter.

Frustrated by the president's response. Mr. Seery began to explore the possibility of forming his own company to acquire and market the EP system. During 1988, while still working at Hospicath, Mr. Seery took steps to form Heartware. He solicited funds, prepared a submission for the Food and Drug Administration (FDA), and negotiated with the University.

Because FDA approval was of such vital importance in the U.S. medical products market, Mr. Seery began to seek approval in April 1988, several months before he acquired the product rights. Medical products without FDA approval could not be marketed in the United States, and investors and potential partners usually were not interested in a company whose product was months or even years away from market. The FDA required that medical devices be proven safe and effective. If the product was comparable to others already on the market, it had to be proven equivalent to or better than the others. On September 10, 1988, Heartware contracted the services of Medsys, Inc., a consulting firm that specialized in submitting medical equipment proposals to the FDA. For a fee of $5,000, over the next seven months Medsys prepared Heartware's submission with help from Mr. Seery. This submission included a product instruction book, sample advertisements, quality control procedures, results from general EP, and mapping studies, manufacturing procedures, and charts comparing Heartware's product to similar products already being sold in United States.

Heartware International Corporation was incorporated in the state of New Jersey on October 28, 1988. The following week, the founder opened a corporate suite for the new company in New York City. Six months later Mr. Seery resigned from Hospicath to devote his full attention to Heartware.

During the spring of 1989, Mr. Seery's wife, Ms. Patricia Browne, developed Heartware's business plan as an M.B.A. class assignment. By mid-summer, Ms. Browne became Heartware's chief financial officer. The position was a part-time one with a deferred salary. Before joining Heartware, Ms. Brown ran her own financial consulting firm for three years. Altogether she had nearly 10 years' experience as corporate controller and accountant. Ms. Browne held a B.A. in Economics/Accounting from Catholic University and an M.B.A. in Finance from New York University.

Initial funding for Heartware came from Mr. Seery and his wife. They provided $185,000 from savings, personal debt, and loans against their home equity. In May of 1989, Heartware's founder sent a summary of the company's five-year plan to more than a dozen private individuals. Within five weeks, four close relatives invested a total of $85,000.

HEARTWARE'S CONTRACT WITH THE UNIVERSITY

Heartware acquired exclusive worldwide rights to market the EP system and belt electrodes on May 4, 1989. Under the agreement with the University, Heartware would be credited with all sales of the EP system regardless of whether Heartware or the University generated the sales lead. All price quotations outstanding at the time of the agreement were included. The University would provide assembly, inspection, and testing of all systems ordered for about 50 percent of the list price of the system. Mr. Seery expected that this percentage would decrease dramatically when the sales level made mass production possible.

In exchange for the above services, Heartware was to make an initial payment of 50,000 Dutch guilders[2] (DGfl) followed by ten quarterly payments of 50,000 Dfl. Rights to the product would revert to the University if Heartware failed to meet its obligations.

Mr. van der Swoort was to be Mr. Seery's point of contact at the University. Separate agreements were drawn up for Mr. van der Swoort and Dr. Cortez. They would receive royalties from Heartware on units sold in exchange for providing assistance with sales demonstrations, installations and service calls. Heartware's founder counted on Mr. van der Swoort to service and support all European customers. In addition to the royalties received, Mr. van der Swoort received about $400 a month for providing general support, such as answering inquiries. To Mr. Seery, the spirit of the contract implied that the University would provide technical support to further the development and sales of the EP system to the mutual benefit of both Heartware and the University.

Mr. Seery counted on Dr. Cortez's international reputation as a leader in the field of electrophysiology to help sell the system. Because product and company credibility were crucial in the medical equipment industry, Dr. Cortez was retained in a consultant capacity as medical advisor to the company.

PRODUCTS LAUNCHED

On May 4–6, 1989, Mr. Seery set up a display in Toronto, Canada, at the annual meeting of the North American Society of Pacing and Electrophysiology (NASPE), the professional association of almost all electrophysiologists. Approximately 1,500 doctors, nurses, technicians, and engineers attended the meeting that year, and nearly 75 percent of the 800 cardiologists in attendance had a specialty in electrophysiology. Heartware's products generated significant interest among NASPE members, and Mr. Seery made several important contacts at the meeting.

---

[2]On May 4, 1989, the date the contract was signed, 2.132 Dfl were the equivalent of $1 U.S.

Heartware's founder felt that launching the company at this NASPE meeting was crucial due to the very broad exposure the meeting would bring. Mr. Seery acknowledged that the product needed aesthetic improvements, design alterations to facilitate mass production, and FDA approval for the U.S. market. However, he did not want to wait a full year for the 1990 NASPE meeting.

THE EP MARKET

In the late 1980s, EP was still a relatively new field. EP techniques were used in clinical diagnosis beginning about 1980. However, EP was not widely used in the medical community until about 1986. In 1989, there were 1,300 U.S. coronary care units. These units treated 390,000 patients. Approximately 10 percent of those patients required pacing to return the heart to a normal rhythm. Use of EP was closely tied to the amount of government reimbursement for EP procedures. On October 1, 1989, the reimbursement rate to coronary care units rose from $2,700 to $8,100.

Mr. Seery anticipated that Heatware could take advantage of expansion in the EP market.[3] Growth in the market was expected to come from several sources. An EP study was the preferred diagnostic test in candidates for sudden cardiac death. However, in the late 1980s less than 10 percent of patients who were at significant risk actually underwent the test. One of the major reasons for this low usage was a shortage of cardiologists trained in EP. However, EP represented an attractive specialty and the number of physicians in this area was growing rapidly.

The EP market was segmented into two primary areas: systems designed to perform general EP studies in EP laboratories within hospitals, and systems for performing mapping studies in operating rooms. EP labs offered the best growth potential. The bulk of this growth was expected to be generated by the expansion of cardiology departments into EP technology. By year-end 1989, 400 U.S. EP labs had an installed base of EP equipment. These labs were not expected to purchase replacement systems in the near future. However, these labs were potential customers for add-on components such as Heartware's cardiac stimulator. It was expected that 400 additional hospitals would add EP programs to their cardiology departments between 1990 and 1994. Equipment sales during that time period were expected to be about $45 million.

Heartware's mapping system would be sold in the surgical market. By year-end 1989, eighty U.S. hospitals performed arrhythmia surgery and another eighty were expected to expand into such surgery by 1994.

Heartware's initial product line consisted of the EP lab and mapping system and belt electrodes. Mr. Seery planned to add cardiac catheters later. The company expected to subcontract catheter production until 1992 or 1993. At that point Heartware would build its own production facilities. The market for cardiac catheters was growing. Hospitals were expected to purchase new catheters at an increasing rate because the resterilization and reuse of catheters increased infection-control

---

[3]The statistics and market estimates in this section are from Heartware's business plan.

problems and hospital liability for malfunctioning products. In 1989, EP catheters sales totaled about $6.5 million. Had hospitals used new catheters for each procedure rather than sterilizing and reusing some, the 1989 market would have been about $15 million. The expected market in 1994 was $35 million.

The number of hospitals using EP was expected to increase most quickly in the United States, as health care delivery abroad had greater financial limitations. In the international market, about 80 hospitals in Western Europe, South America, Canada, and Japan used EP. Although smaller, the international market presented several advantages over the U.S. market. First, with the notable exception of Japan, governmental regulations abroad tended to be less stringent than FDA regulations in the United States. Second, the smaller market size and slower growth resulted in less competition. Third, appearance and design features that did not enhance the performance of medical products were not as important outside the United States.

HEARTWARE'S MARKET POSITION

In 1989, several companies competed in the EP market. Exhibit 2 profiles Heartware's major competitors. Heartware's EP system offered several advantages over the noncomputerized systems that dominated the market in the late 1980s. These advantages are summarized in Exhibit 3.

EXPLORING STRATEGIC PARTNERSHIPS

Mr. Seery spent much of his time seeking strategic partnerships with established medical device companies that might want to add Heartware's products to their current product lines. He envisioned an agreement in which another company would receive an equity interest in Heartware in return for that company's financial, marketing, and technical support. Mr. Seery hoped such an agreement might later lead the partner to buy Heartware and provide Heartware's investors a significant return on their investment. With basically only one product, he expected that Heartware would exhaust its market in five years. Thus, his goal was to ally with a company that offered multiple products.

Heartware's CEO contacted dozens of companies of all sizes throughout the United States, Australia, and Japan, sent them a condensed version of Heartware's business plan, and followed up by phone. The contacts led to extensive dialogue in some cases. However, most companies were only casually interested in Heartware's products.

Negotiations progressed furthest with Electrophysiology Company (EPCO),* a U.S. company that specialized in equipment associated with arrhythmia detection and treatment. At the 1989 NASPE meeting, Mr. Seery had discussed Heartware and its products with a cardiologist who recommended he contact EPCO. That cardiologist also told EPCO's officers about Heartware. The day after Mr. Seery returned to New York from Toronto, EPCO's president called Mr. Seery to express interest in Heartware.

Over the next several months, Heartware's founder and EPCO representatives met three times and communicated frequently via telephone and fax. They

Exhibit 2   Heartware's Major Competitors

Most competitors were headquartered in the United States, and less than 20 percent of their sales were generated overseas.

Bard Electrophysiology

Parent:	C. R. Bard, Inc. (a medical supply company with $100 M annual revenue).
Annual sales:	Approximately $11 M.
Main product:	Cardiac catheters.
EP product:	$100,000 cardiac mapping system.
Product advantages:	Bard's system excelled Heartware's in graphics capability by producing a picture of the heart with shading to indicate the intensity of electrical activity.
Product drawbacks:	Bard's system was not portable and its components could not be used for general EP studies. Foreign doctors were unwilling to pay for added graphics capability.
Competitive advantages:	Bard dominated the catheter market, offered a full product line and extensive service, and had a large distribution system and established training programs. Bard derived a significant competitive advantage from the fact that many cardiologists received their initial EP training on Bard equipment. Later, when these cardiologists were in the position of ordering equipment for their own practices or of giving advice about such a purchase, they were inclined to order the familiar brand.
Research and development:	Developing a general EP lab system.

Biomedical Business Instrumentation (BBI)

EP product:	EP system that needed FDA approval.
Drawbacks:	Product had not been commercially marketed or produced.
Other:	Founded in 1986 by two Canadian engineers. In 1989, BBI was considering signing a joint venture agreement with another more-established Canadian medical firm.

Bloom Associates

Annual sales:	Approximately $3 M.
EP product:	Noncomputerized general EP system and mapping system.
Product advantages:	Lower cost than Heartware's systems.
Product drawbacks:	Bloom's systems were slower and stored information on paper rather than disk.
Other:	The firm was for sale for $10 million.

Digital Cardiovascular Incorporated (DCI)

EP product:	$20,000 computer-controlled stimulator for use in EP studies.
Product drawbacks:	Stimulator could not store or record output. DCI marketed its stimulator through Medtronic Inc., the leading manufacturer of cardiac pacemakers. As of 1989, Medtronic was emphasizing pacemaker products, not DCI's stimulator.

(continued)

(*continued*)

Electrophysiology Company (EPCO)	
Annual sales:	Approximately $5 M.
Research and development:	EPCO's mapping system prototype needed FDA approval, and the firm was developing a general EP system.

EXHIBIT 3   Heartware's Product Advantages

- Computerization of the EP system allowed electrical signals from the heart to be displayed or saved in a variety of ways. Certain time segments (e.g., critical episodes) could be marked for later analysis, the scale of output could be changed, or readings from different parts of the heart could be emphasized or deemphasized. This clarified relevant information, led to easier analysis, decreased the chance of error, and decreased the amount of time needed after the study to diagnose the arrhythmia.
- Heartware's computerized cardiac stimulator was the only one that could constantly monitor the patient's condition by measuring and reporting beat-to-beat time intervals.
- Computerization allowed preprogrammed pacing protocols (ordered series of electrical signals sent to the heart by the stimulator) to be used instead of manually delivering individual signals. Pacing protocols could be stored on disk for quick retrieval, thus drastically reducing the time required to deliver protocols and potential errors.
- Computerization allowed the hospital to permanently store output on disk instead of paper, significantly simplifying storage. A single general EP study could last up to four hours, generating a stack of printed output between four and six inches tall.
- Heartware's mapping system could simultaneously obtain and display information about a heart's electrical patterns, reducing the time required in surgery by approximately 30 to 40 minutes.
- In about 60% of the mapping studies, even more time could be saved when the belt electrodes were used. The conventional method of obtaining signals to map the heart involved the use of only two to four electrodes which were moved from one small area of the heart to another taking between 20 to 30 minutes to locate the problem site. Because the belt electrode contained 21 leads that were in direct contact with the heart, the time needed to locate a problem site could be reduced to under a minute.

---

discussed the possibility of EPCO investing in Heartware in return for equity in the company. Mr. Seery anticipated EPCO would eventually buy out Heartware and hire him as a consultant or manager. Negotiations with EPCO, consultations with lawyers, flights to EPCO's home office, and product demonstrations for EPCO consumed much of Mr. Seery's time and resources. During this period he concentrated on these negotiations and greatly curtailed efforts with other companies.

In July 1989, Mr. Seery sent EPCO a two-page summary of the general terms which they had agreed upon to date. A few days later, EPCO sent Mr. Seery a letter of intent, but did not mention his letter regarding terms of agreement. On July

20, 1989, Mr. Seery sent a letter to Heartware's stockholders with the following details:

> We have negotiated with several firms over the past several months. Our efforts have focused most recently on concluding an agreement with EPCO. EPCO has a proven technology in the field of electrophysiology. They are seeking to expand their product line. Heartware's EP System is an attractive opportunity for EPCO.
>
> Consequently, we have concluded an agreement under which EPCO would invest up to $350,000 in Heartware, in exchange for an equity position of up to 35 percent. At the thirty-month point, EPCO could exercise its option to purchase the remaining equity of Heartware for $750,000.
>
> While a final agreement has not been concluded, we are confident of the respective commitment each party has to closing the deal. We believe that the current shareholders of Heartware are well served by this agreement.

In addition to the compensation described above, Mr. Seery also negotiated with EPCO to receive an "earnout"[4] over four years.

FDA ASKS FOR CLARIFICATION

Mr. Seery's negotiations to obtain strategic partners, investments, and sales continued to be blocked by the EP system's lack of FDA approval. After having reviewed Heartware's submission, the FDA responded on July 8, 1989 by asking for further clarification of a few issues. With the help of Medsys's consulting services, Mr. Seery responded to these questions. The issues that needed to be clarified were all relatively minor, and all indications were that FDA approval would be forthcoming. However, the FDA would have another 90 days before it was required to respond to Heartware's clarifications.

FURTHER NEGOTIATIONS WITH EPCO

In August 1989, negotiations with EPCO intensified. Mr. Seery shipped equipment from The Netherlands at Heartware's expense to conduct a demonstration in Atlanta for EPCO's chairman. An engineer from the University of Limburg flew to Atlanta to conduct the demonstration. Mr. Seery flew in from New York.

During the demonstration, Mr. Seery stood in the hallway of the hospital. On one pay phone he spoke to his attorney in Boston; on another he spoke simultaneously to EPCO's president. Mr. Seery recalled the incident as follows:

> The president of EPCO said that the final hitch was FDA approval. I said, "We agreed to this back in June. This agreement is not subject to FDA approval." He agreed. Right then and there he agreed with me that the deal was not subject to FDA approval. I said, "Do we have a deal?" He said, "Yes, we have a deal." I hung up the phones and walked back into the clinical lab where the chairman was. I said, "I just got off the phone and we've got a deal." He shook my hand and said, "Ah, that's great. And of course it's subject to FDA approval." I said, "No. We just agreed that it's not." He said, "Yes it is." I blew up.

---

[4]An earnout is a series of payments, usually made over several years, based upon some measure of the company's performance such as profits or sales.

Because the chairman knew cash was tight, he said, "I'll tell you what we'll do. We'll give you a working capital loan for $50,000 to carry you until the FDA approval." We expected FDA approval to come in September or October, so we weren't that far away, and I had every expectation we would get it. With $50,000 working capital, that could work. He told me to call him later to solidify this $50,000 commitment. By then of course the deal was subject to this and that and some other things. A few days later the $50,000 working capital loan was for one year at some percent interest rate, and the collateral was the technology, and they weren't required to sign the deal even if the FDA approved. They had about ten days after approval to decide whether they wanted it or not.

After consulting with his attorney about the deal, Mr. Seery decided not to go through with it.

ANOTHER MAJOR PUSH FOR FUNDING

When negotiations with EPCO broke down, Mr. Seery responded with what he called "a frantic effort to make new contacts."

I probably sent out letters to and called everybody who was anybody who knew somebody who may have once invested, and I wrote off letters and made phone calls to just about every major medical company who might have an interest. I felt that it was only a matter of time before competitors would develop EP technology as sophisticated as the EP lab.

In addition to reinitiating contacts with possible strategic partners and private investors, Mr. Seery began to actively pursue the venture capital market.

FDA APPROVAL

On October 2, 1989, less than six months after Heartware's initial submission, Mr. Seery received a letter from the FDA stating that Heatware's EP system was approved for the U.S. market. Within days of receiving the FDA's letter, Mr. Seery called EPCO once again to tell them Heartware had received FDA approval and to ask if a new deal was possible. He recalled that phone conversation as follows:

They said, "Same terms?" And I said, "No, we now have FDA approval." That was the last I talked to them for a while. They had no interest in revisiting it because they were now advancing their own system. Not that they didn't have it to start with. I don't want you to think they just took what we had, but they saw our technology and possibly benefited from it. In my heart of hearts, I don't think they wanted to deal. They wanted the information.

SALES

Just as Mr. Seery's efforts to strike an agreement with EPCO seemed to come to a dead end, Heartware began to generate orders. When Mr. Seery acquired rights to the EP system, he also acquired rights to all outstanding quotations made by the University. One quote was to Dr. Jacob Atie, a Brazilian doctor, who had worked on the EP system as a graduate student at the University of Maastricht.

Dr. Atie later decided to buy amplifiers for a mapping system. On October 30, 1989, Heartware's CEP received the following fax from Jan van der Swoort in Holland.

Date: 30 October 1989
To: Gerry Seery
From: Jan van der Swoort
Subject: Orders and safety regulations

Congratulations! You got your first order. Today I got a visit from Dr. Atie and Dr. Cruz. They will finance the system with their personal means. They asked me to inform you about the order. I put it on the fax. I informed them that I needed a deposit of 25 percent for the University in order to start working on the system. Then I have to ask the Financial Department to send them an invoice for this deposit. Now in order not to confuse the Financial Department it makes sense that you order the University to prepare this system and that the invoice should be sent directly to these doctors. The difference between the invoice and the agreed compensation for the University will be credited to the installments or otherwise.

Heartware's second sale occurred the following day and also stemmed from an outstanding quotation to a former Brazilian graduate student at the University. During 1989, three hospitals, the two in Brazil and one in Spain, ordered amplifiers to add to existing EP systems. The sales totaled $66,000. Because these orders were not shipped until May 1990, however, Heartware received no cash in 1989 and the sales appeared on the 1990 income statement. Heartware's only revenue in 1989 was $6,900 from the sale of three belt electrodes. In most cases, customers paid the University directly in Dutch guilders and the University credited the amount Heartware owed for the technology.

MOVE TO ATLANTA, GEORGIA

In December 1989, Mr. Seery relocated Heartware's headquarters to Atlanta, Georgia. He knew that Heartware would be operating on a tight budget and felt that Atlanta's lower cost of living would increase the business's chance for success. Atlanta offered several additional advantages. Mr. Seery had already established a relationship with a cardiology group there. He also planned to apply for entry into the Advanced Technology Development Center (ATDC) headquartered at and administered by the Georgia Institute of Technology.

The ATDC was an incubator, a technology business development center that acted to promote high-technology start-ups. The center was created in 1980 by the state of Georgia to help high-technology entrepreneurs by providing technical and business assistance. The Technology Business Center, an arm of ATDC, offered office space, shared secretarial service, and shared office equipment to its tenants. The sharing of services and assets gave young firms access to resources that might otherwise have been prohibitively expensive.

The technological benefits were as important to Mr. Seery as the other services provided because Heartware had not yet been able to employ an in-house engineering staff. ATDC members had access to the resources of all public universities within Georgia. Most important, Heartware also benefited from its proximity to other high-tech firms. For example, a firm located at ATDC which specialized in engineering development work was helpful to Heartware by suggesting minor product improvements on a limited, informal basis at no charge.

After arrival in Atlanta, Patricia Browne accepted the position of controller at Turner Broadcasting System. She continued to serve as Heartware's CFO.

HEARTWARE'S RELATIONSHIP WITH THE UNIVERSITY OF LIMBURG

Although ATDC offered some technical assistance, most technological support and product improvement came from the University of Limburg. The system was sound in terms of performance. However, it was not particularly attractive in terms of design and aesthetics. Further product design work was also needed before the system could be manufactured efficiently.

Demonstrations for potential customers and distributors were often held at the University of Limburg. Mr. van der Swoort attended shows like NASPE with Mr. Seery. Mr. Seery, customers, and potential customers contacted Mr. van der Swoort when they had questions about the system's capabilities, service, or installation.

Heartware's founder felt his relationship with the two codevelopers was quite favorable, although not problem free. In addition to contractual issues that needed clarifying, confusion about sales or payments often arose. The following fax sent by Mr. Seery to Mr. van der Swoort is an example of some of the confusion that arose as a result of what Heartware's CEO called a "3,000-mile umbilical cord":

> Based upon your first phone call, I thought the doctors were ready to place an immediate order during their visit to you. Now it appears that a great deal of time will go by either before they place an order or accept delivery of the systems.
>
> Because of my initial impression, I compromised significantly on the price, recognizing the potential value of an immediate order and the fact that the University had already provided quotations to these doctors. Now the quotations from Heartware are being interpreted by others as applying to their situation.
>
> I am in a very difficult situation. We cannot increase the quotations that are outstanding despite the longer delivery date. And how am I to modify the quotation to the new doctor to more accurately reflect the value of the product? Heartware cannot survive unless we price our products at a rate which yields a reasonable return.

Mr. Seery also felt that differences in cultural perceptions may have caused difficulty. Mr. van der Swoort seemed to believe that Americans and their firms were wealthy and could therefore afford to pay higher fees and royalties to him. Mr. Seery tried to correct that impression, especially as it pertained to start-up ventures, but the issue was a constant thorn in their relationship. According to the founder,

> When Heartware *could not* afford to do something, the developer interpreted this to mean that we *did not want* to do something.

Nevertheless, Mr. van der Swoort continually upgraded the software for the EP system. Even though Heartware had the most technologically advanced system on the market, Mr. Seery feared that competitors could easily catch up. No other company had FDA approval on a computer-based EP system, but both Bard and EPCO had functioning prototypes. For competitors, the stimulator represented the primary hurdle in obtaining FDA approval. Mr. Seery felt that "If you're a decent engineer, you can put a simulator together." Time was the main issue. He anticipated that a competitor would need six months to develop a stimulator compatible with a computerized EP system and another year or more to obtain FDA approval.

To lessen dependence on the University, Heartware's founder wanted in-house ability to continuously improve products. He felt confident, given his contacts in the industry, that he would have no difficulty finding qualified candidates to fill the position of technical director. However, poor cash flow delayed his plans.

In February 1990, another problem developed, and Heartware's relationship with the University and the hospital changed. Dr. Cortez announced his intention to leave the hospital in May and to move into private practice in Belgium. His future role in Heartware was unclear.

EXPANDING SALES

Heartware's ability to hire additional staff depended heavily on securing more capital and increasing sales. In total, during Heartware's first 19 months of business, the company had sold $83,000 worth of products and had another $60,000 in orders. Exhibits 4 and 5 provide the financial statements as of June 1990.

All sales had been a function of Mr. Seery's personal efforts or contact made by the University. While no one pattern was evident in the way sales evolved, many of the orders came through the University from former students. To prepare for the future, Heartware's founder also began to develop a network of distributors. Most of these distributorships arose from contacts Mr. Seery had made in previous business deals. To date all associations with distributors were informal.

CONTINUED PURSUIT OF FUNDING AND PARTNERSHIPS

During the spring of 1990, fund raising proceeded much slower than Heartware's founder anticipated. He was unable to raise funds beyond the $270,000 invested by family members. Most of those funds had been spent to acquire the technology, travel to Europe, display and demonstrate the product, and seek FDA approval. Mr. Seery anticipated that further development and sales of the EP system would require an additional $1 million.

When Mr. Seery contacted venture capitalists, some told him their companies did not invest in ventures that required less than about $3 million. Others expressed reluctance because Heartware had no track record, was too dependent on one product, was too high-tech, or did not have a well-rounded management team.

EXHIBIT 4   Heartware International Income Statement for Period Ended 6/30/90

	6 Months	Ratio
Sales Revenue		
Amplifiers and signal distribution unit	$ 53,263.30	69.9%
Electrodes	21,919.05	28.8
Miscellaneous income	1,000.00	1.3
Total sales revenue	$ 76,182.35	100.00
Distribution Commissions		
Distributor commissions	405.00	.5
Royalties	2,889.50	3.8
Net sales-revenue	$ 72,887.85	95.7
Cost of Sales		
Amplifiers and signal distribution unit	39,728.80	52.1
Electrodes	12,030.75	15.8
Other cost of sales	5.00	0.0
Gross profit	$ 21,123.30	27.7
Operating Expenses		
Employment	2,617.12	3.4
Marketing and sales	3,955.12	5.2
Travel and entertainment	5,490.35	7.2
Professional fees	2,045.00	2.7
General and administrative	6,032.97	7.9
Depreciation	802.26	1.1
Amortization expense	15,000.00	19.7
Total operating expenses	$ 35,942.82	47.2
Income before interest and tax	(14,819.52)	(19.5)
Interest	8,521.41)	11.2
Net income before tax	(23,340.93)	(30.6)
Income tax	25.00	0.0
Income after tax	$(23,365.93)	(30.7)%

Negotiations with potential strategic partners progressed further than negotiations with venture capitalists. However, none had yet come to fruition. Companies approached about partnerships gave various reasons for not forming an alliance. Some were not interested because the EP system required too large a capital investment for too small a market niche. Others indicated that the EP system was not a good fit with their current product lines. Negotiations with several companies continued.

EXHIBIT 5   Heartware International, General Ledger, Balance Sheet as of 6/30/90

Assets

Current Assets		
Cash and marketable securities	$ 2,919.41	
Accounts receivable	5,025.00	
Total current assets		$7,944.41
Fixed Assets		
Furniture and equipment	8,022.66	
Accumulated depreciation	(1,604.53)	
Total fixed assets		6,418.13
Noncurrent Assets		
System license	150,000.00	
Accumulated amortization	(30,000.00)	
System license, net	120,000.00	
Deposits	604.45	
Total noncurrent assets		120,604.45
Total assets		$134,966.99

Liabilities and Shareholder's Equity Liabilities

Current Liabilities		
Accounts payable	$ 1,758.84	
Payable to officers	33,364.20	
Interest payable	4,529.05	
Total current liabilities		$39,652.09
Long-Term Liabilities		
License payable	88,042.69	
Total long-term liabilities		88,042.69
Total liabilities		$ 127,694.78

Shareholder's Equity

Common stock	2,000.00	
Paid-in capital	$103,000.00	
Retained earnings	(74,361.86)	
Current earnings	(23,365.93)	
Total shareholder's equity		7,272.21
Total liability and shareholder's equity		$134,966.99

ESOPHAGEAL EP TECHNOLOGY

During this period, Mr. Seery also began to explore an opportunity to extend Heartware's product line into esophageal EP technology. This technology took advantage of the fact that the heart and part of the esophagus are very close together. Thus, a specially designed catheter could be placed down the esophagus along with leads from a cardiac stimulator for sending electrical signals to the atria of the heart. The distance from the esophagus to the ventricles was significantly greater; therefore, such a system could only be used to diagnose and treat atrial arrhythmias.

Atrial arrhythmias were relatively less life-threatening than ventricular arrhythmias and could be treated fairly quickly without a hospital stay. Once an atrial arrhythmia was diagnosed, an esophageal EP system could often by used to pace the heart out of the arrhythmia. Thus, esophageal pacing was less invasive to the body and could be performed in an increased number of locations, without a cardiologist, and in a decreased amount of time.

The procedure's speed and mobility often made esophageal treatment an ideal method for stimulating the heart in emergency situations, such as in coronary care units. In contrast to a general EP study, a patient did not need to be disconnected from all other support systems and moved to another location.

Before 1988, esophageal diagnosis and treatment had primarily been used on a clinical basis with the results recorded in scientific journals. Medical equipment could be sold on a "clinical-use basis" prior to FDA approval. Clinical-use sales allowed for a system to be evaluated to obtain FDA acceptance. However, no marketing was allowed, only a limited quantity could be sold, and the product could only be sold at or below cost. Although esophageal technology became more routinely used in coronary care units and emergency rooms after 1988, it was still considered a fairly recent development in 1990.

While Mr. Seery had been employed by Hospicath, the company had been approached about the possibility of acquiring an esophageal EP product developed at an American university. But Hospicath deferred its decision, never telling the developer yes or no. Mr. Seery's interest in the technology had been keen, however, and his interest continues after he founded Heartware.

Mr. Seery projected that each of the 1,300 U.S. coronary care units would install a minimum of two esophageal systems between 1990 and 1995, generating a market of $10 million for the period. In 1990, over 5,300 emergency rooms were providing care in the United States. Mr. Seery estimated this segment of the market would generate sales of $35 million in esophageal products between 1990 and 1995. Other possible market segments included field response teams (ambulances and paramedics) and general practitioners. Hospitals with EP systems could also use an esophageal system to screen a patient. If the arrhythmia was located in the atria, a general EP study might not be needed.

Acquisition of the esophageal stimulator would also potentially lead to the sale of esophageal catheters. Each stimulator sold would generate sales of 15 to 20 catheters per year. The esophageal catheter market was expected to total $40 million between 1990 and 2000. Few companies marketed esophageal products, however. Mr. Serry only knew of one Italian company marketing an esophageal system in Europe and one small U.S.-based medical device company marketing a system in the United States.

HEARTWARE ACQUIRES ESOPHAGEAL TECHNOLOGY

In March 1990, knowing that negotiations were not progressing between Hospicath and the developer of the esophageal stimulator, Mr. Seery decided to approach the developer about acquiring the rights for Heartware. The two agreed that Heartware would make no fixed payments. Rather, Heartware would pay 10–15 percent in royalties to the developer on any units sold in exchange for the product rights. The company gave the schematics to Mr. Seery. However, no formal agreement was signed because Heartware did not have funding available to develop and promote the product.

Prior to this agreement, the developer had already sold two dozen stimulators on a clinical-use basis. However, Mr. Seery realized that he would need assistance to further develop the product. He believed that until he could hire in-house technical expertise, the system's developer would provide support. The system still required FDA approval, clinical evaluations, and a new casing. Additionally, the system had to be redesigned to simplify manufacture. The founder estimated that $250,000 would be needed to complete the development process and to cover management expenses. Another year and a half would be needed before the product was ready to be marketed commercially in the United States. Initially, to limit expenses, Mr. Seery planned to concentrate sales efforts for the esophageal product in the U.S. market. He felt that was feasible because the United States contained many outlets and almost no competition.

Heartware's CEO planned to target the domestic distributors of cardiology products as sources of capital. Ideally, he hoped to raise the needed $250,000 in lots of $25,000. Mr. Seery believed that if distributors invested in the product they would also actively promote it. Distributors would be offered 15–20 percent commissions to generate sales, collect receivables, and maintain inventory. The product was expected to sell for about $7,000. Mr. Seery anticipated exhibiting the esophageal system at the next NASPE meeting in 1990.

Mr. Seery also planned to sell esophageal catheters and started to investigate manufacturers who would make catheters under Heartware's label. He anticipated that the selling price per esophageal catheter would be $100. Hospicath was one of the only companies selling esophageal catheters.

NEWS FROM THE UNIVERSITY OF LIMBURG

On Mr. Seery's way to work on May 1, 1990, he contemplated the strategic direction his company should take. When he arrived at the office, the following fax from an attorney at the University of Limburg awaited him:

From: Ben van Werscht
To: Mr. Gerry Seery

Dear Mr. Seery,

I have a painful message for you. The Head of the Instrumental Department, Mr. Jan van der Swoort, has been suspended from duty. I will take duty from him and in this capacity I would like to settle some things with you.

As we both know there is a contract between Heartware Corporation and the University of Limburg for the Cortez Electrophysiology System. So far Mr. van der Swoort settled this business, but I have no sound judgment on the administration yet.

It is important for me to get answers on the following questions: What is the general rule of conduct when a new system is ordered? Who fixes the price? Who is taking care of product liability, etc.?

News of Mr. van der Swoort's suspension from the University, coming from an attorney and accompanied by a question about product liability, led Mr. Seery to wonder if the system had failed and a patient had died. However, a letter soon arrived from Mr. van der Swoort explaining that his suspension was due to budget problems and internal politics. Mr. Seery promptly arranged a trip to Holland to meet Mr. van Werscht, get an explanation of events, and reevaluate Heartware's relationship with the University of Limburg.

Mr. van Werscht became the main contact between Heartware and the University, but Mr. Seery felt the attorney was more concerned with enforcing the strict letter of their contract than abiding by the spirit of the agreement worked out between Mr. Seery and the product's developers. University support and interest in further development of the EP system's hardware and software waned.

HEARTWARE'S OPTIONS

With technical support no longer coming from the University, Mr. Seery began to explore alternatives. He continued to contact U.S. companies with technical infrastructures already in place who might be interested in a partnership. Mr. Seery identified several small U.S. firms that had the ability to upgrade the technology and the willingness to do so on a contract basis, but Heartware lacked the operating cash to pay for their services. Another alternative was to add a full-time technical expert to Heartware's payroll, but Mr. Seery did not feel comfortable bringing someone on board until Heartware had a solid capital base.

On several occasions the founder had examined the possibility of moving his home and Heartware's headquarters to Europe. From there he could better manage relations with the University, Dr. Cortez, and Mr. van der Swoort. Both The Netherlands and Belgium were considered as possible locations. Heartware's products were receiving recognition and sales in Europe, and competition was hardly an issue there. Investors in Europe consistently presented the warmest responses to Heartware's business plan. By spring 1990, Mr. Seery was spending approximately one-fourth of his time overseas. The main obstacle to making the move was the need for a steady cash flow for personal support while the company got off the ground. A major disadvantage to a European headquarters would be that less attention would be given to the larger U.S. market, where Heartware had the most advanced system with FDA approval.

If the company did not move to Europe, another option Heartware's CEO considered was to begin concentrating exclusively on marketing the esophageal technology in the United States. If Mr. Seery focused on the esophageal technology, he would have to essentially abandon Heartware's relationship with the University of Limburg, since the start-up did not have enough resources to invest in both directions.

A final alternative was simply to go out of business. Resources were already stretched, and the other options would risk additional capital. To Mr. Seery, no option was clearly superior.

CASE 3
PROFESSIONAL STAFF LIMITED

Taking a Venture Abroad

I can still see my hand reaching out to the telephone for the first time to call a potential client. I just picked a name off the list.

Ben Blackden, CEO, Professional Staff Ltd.

In September 1994, Professional Staff Ltd. (PSL) was holding its quarterly board of directors meeting at its headquarters in Slough, U.K. Ben Blackden, the CEO of PSL, was reflecting on the humble beginning of the company as a two-person venture in London. There had often been moments in the first year when it seemed as if the concept were doomed to fail in the United Kingdom. However, the business had grown remarkably since that time, and PSL had expanded into France by acquiring a small company there in 1992. The French acquisition had been fraught with problems from the outset. Chief among them was the unsuccessful search for a qualified président directeur général (PDG).[1] After two years and two failed searches, Ben believed they had identified a winner in Ivan Mentré.

The other principal issue on the agenda was future direction. The management difficulties in France were forcing Ben to reevaluate the business strategy and ask a lot of questions. Why had they been so successful in the United Kingdom but not in France? How should PSL evaluate expansions into other markets in Western Europe? Also, would their recent decision to start Executives on Assignment prove to be a success? Did PSL have the capabilities to successfully provide temporary services in other industries?

BACKGROUND

PSL is the holding company for a group of businesses operating in the professional niche of the temporary services industry (Exhibit 1). The company was founded in April 1990 by Bruce Culver and Ben Blackden with the backing of venture capitalists, Advent International and Security Pacific Bank. The primary operating entity is Lab Staff Ltd. (LSL) which supplies laboratory scientists and technicians on temporary assignments to scientific employers throughout the United Kingdom. The original business plan envisioned developing scientific temporary personnel businesses throughout Europe. The founders had planned to rapidly grow the company to the point where it could be listed on the London Stock Exchange within five years. Bruce

---

[1] A PDG in France is the equivalent of a CEO in the United States.

Source: Prepared by Kimberly Abell and Aditya Dehejia, M.B.A. 1996, under the direction of Assistant Professor Thomas Hellmann at the Stanford University Graduate School of Business. Reprinted with permission of Stanford University, Graduate School of Business. Copyright © 1995 by the Board of Trustees of the Leland Stanford Junior University.

This is intended as a basis for class discussion rather than to illustrate either effective or ineffective handling of an administrative situation.

EXHIBIT 1   **Organization Chart**

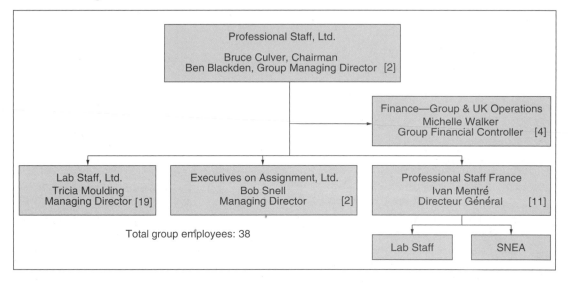

Culver had developed the model for PSL, which he based on a successful venture he had started in the United States in 1985.

BRUCE CULVER'S EXPERIENCE IN THE UNITED STATES

By 1985, Bruce had accumulated more than 13 years' experience as an executive in the scientific instrumentation sector, management consultant, and small business owner (Exhibit 2). In 1985, Bruce embarked on his most ambitious venture to date—he founded his own company, Lab Support, Inc. Over the course of his search for financing, Bruce modified the business plan on the basis of suggestions from the venture capital community. The business mission was "to be the largest employment organization providing scientific personnel (predominantly temporaries and specialists but also permanent staff) and related support services to industrial and government clients." Bruce planned to grow the firm from its California base to a nationwide company. As the first temporary scientific services company in the United States, the firm's success was predicated on creating a new market niche. The company was funded by Sierra Ventures.

Market research revealed that there were 65,000 laboratories employing approximately 700,000 scientists in the United States in 1986. Of the 700,000 scientists, approximately 0.3 percent were working on a temporary basis, a level well below the national average of approximately 1 percent. Bruce calculated that the available market for supplying temporary scientists was $380 million. As a pioneer, Lab Support faced no competitors within its niche.

EXHIBIT 2   Professional Staff Limited

Bruce R. Culver, Chairman   **Professional Staff**

Bruce Culver (48) has more than 20 years' experience as an executive, manager, management consultant, and small business owner. He is CEO of Business Partnerships, Inc., a company specialising in helping retiring small business owners with their succession plans as well as finding buyers for them. He helped form the original concept for Business Partnerships, Inc., and spearheaded the concept's implementation. In 1985, he founded and served as CEO and Chairman of the first scientific personnel company in the United States (Lab Support, Inc.), and he successfully raised the venture capital to fund and develop the business which is now publicly traded on the NASDAQ exchange as "On Assignment, Inc." (ASGN).

He is also a small business owner. He purchased California Distribution, a public warehouse distribution and transportation business located in La Miranda, through the Business Partnership program.

Bruce cofounded and is currently Chairman of Professional Staff Ltd., a highly successfully group of employment businesses located in the U.K. and France. Founded in 1990, Lab Staff Ltd. (the original company) was recently acknowledged as one of the fastest growing companies in the U.K. with revenues in FY94 exceeding £9M.

Bruce has held management and executive positions with public and private companies (Bausch & Lomb, Varian and Hach), in the scientific instrument industry. In addition, he has a number of years' experience as a business management consultant where he assisted small business owners developing and implementing their marketing, finance, and strategic business plans.

Bruce holds B.S. and M.S. degrees in Chemistry from the University of South Dakota and Montana State University, respectively. He lives in Agoura Hills, California, with his wife, Donna.

Ben Blackden, Group Managing Director

Ben Blackden (49) is a graduate in Economics and History from Durham University. His early career was spent in personnel and human resources management with the General Electric Company (ventilation equipment and then gas turbine engineering), followed by further appointments as Head of Personnel in both light engineering and capital goods industries.

He was appointed Personnel Director of Fisons PLC, Scientific Equipment Division, in 1982. This was an international role with an organisation operating in both the scientific instrument and laboratory supply sectors. He moved into general management when, in 1985, he became President of a Fisons Instruments subsidiary in New Jersey, U.S.A.

On returning to the U.K. in 1988 he became involved for the first time in the temporary help industry as Director of P-E International's Temporary Executive Service, the original provider of "interim management" in the U.K.

In 1990 he cofounded Lab Staff Ltd. (Professional Staff Ltd.) in partnership with Bruce Culver.

Ben lives in Gerrards Cross, Buckinghamshire, with his wife and four children; the eldest two are at University. Still an active squash player, he also plays golf and enjoys gardening and bridge.

Lab Staff

Tricia Moulding, Managing Director

Following an Honours degree in Food Science, Tricia (35) gained a Ph.D. in Food Biochemistry at Leeds University.

Her post-doctoral research was undertaken at the Procter Department of Food Science at Leeds and was sponsored by the Ministry of Agriculture Fisheries and Food.

(continued)

(continued)

In 1987 she joined Oros Instruments as a Development Scientist. Oros is an instrument company specialising in automation for bioseparation and innovative sensor technology equipment. She quickly progressed to project management and then Product Manager for Oros's International Marketing Group.

Tricia joined Lab Staff Ltd. at its start-up as Branch Manager at Langley. As the company grew she assumed progressive responsibility for the other branches after these were established and was appointed General Manager in 1993. She successfully took responsibility for all marketing operations and opened the company's newest office in Glasgow. She was appointed Managing Director in 1994.

Tricia lives in Cookham, Berkshire, and likes climbing and trekking (she has visited Nepal and the Himalayas on two occasions). She enjoys swimming, squash, and golf.

Ivan Mentré, Directeur Général

Ivan Mentré (51) followed a degree in Chemical Engineering with a Masters in Organic Chemistry and a Ph.D. in Physical Sciences.

He began his career with Procter & Gamble where he was head of R&D for a number of well-known products. Subsequently, with the Gamma Hay Group and ECM-Bernard Julhiet Group (both marketing services and consulting companies), he was Operations Manager and General Manager, respectively.

For the past ten years he has enjoyed a very successful career at Socotec, France's leading organisation for the inspection of buildings, construction, and civil engineering projects. He was initially Director of Development and latterly Commercial and Marketing Director.

He lives with his wife and two daughters at Orgeval, on the outskirts of Paris.

Executives on Assignment

Bob Snell, Managing Director

Qualified as an accountant, Bob (52) spent his early career with Ford Motor Co. and British Leyland Motors. Initially involved in project accounting, he then moved into marketing with the parts division of British Leyland.

Following a period with Warner Lambert he joined BoozAllen & Hamilton, the management consultants, and worked in Turin, Paris, as well as London. He left as Vice President (a partner of the firm). This period has left him with a good working knowledge of Italian and he is fluent in French.

In 1985 he joined Saatchi & Saatchi PLC as General Manager of the Consulting Division and operated in both London and Washington, D.C. While with Saatchi he was appointed Director of Corporate Business Administration and company Secretary.

In more recent times he has been a self-employed management consultant including a two-year interim management role at Nuclear Electric PLC and Director of International Operations for a partnership based in Boulder, Colorado, U.S.A.

Bob lives with his partner in Chesham, Buckinghamshire; he has 2 children at University.

THE TEMPORARY SERVICES MARKET IN THE UNITED STATES

Both demographic and employment trends favored the use of temporary workers. Payrolls in the temporary employment industry had grow rapidly from $0.9 billion in 1975 to $5.3 billion in 1986.[2] Temporary employment was growing much more rapidly than overall employment. Between 1982 and 1986 temporary employment had grown by 19.1 percent annually, while nonfarm payrolls had grown

---

[2]Information from the National Association of Temporary and Staffing Services, Alexandria, VA.

2.7 percent annually. In 1986, temporary employment accounted for 0.84 percent of the total workforce, up from 0.46 percent in 1982.[3] The high growth rate in the temporary market was expected to continue over the next decade.

There are two broad segments within the temporary employment industry—low-skilled workers and professionals. Low-skilled workers account for 75–80 percent of all temporary employees and typically serve needs in office/clerical positions as well as light and heavy industrial positions. The other 20–25 percent of the temporary market is higher skilled professional or white-collar workers employed as scientists, data processors, accountants, computer programmers, and health care providers. Firms in the professional segment have focused on particular niche markets, supplying workers with industry specific or functionally specific skills.

The professional segment was growing much more rapidly than the overall temporary services market registering mid-20 percent growth rates. This niche was in the early part of its life cycle much like the general temporary market two decades earlier. Strong double digit growth was expected to continue for the next five years. Growth was driven by both demand and supply side factors.

Demand-Side Factors.   Historically, temporary workers have been principally used to fill in for employees who are either sick, on vacation, or on maternity leave. Through the 1980s, the use of temporary workers proliferated to a number of professional, value-added positions. Temporary professionals became an essential element of an integrated, flexible workforce strategy. As companies downsized, hiring temporary workers allowed firms to manage personnel costs more carefully by converting some fixed costs to variable costs. Companies were able to respond more quickly to changing business conditions by hiring temporary employees to meet surges in demand. On a fully loaded basis, temporary employees were no more expensive than permanent employees.

Hiring on a permanent basis could be a time-consuming endeavor. Temporary employees acted as a just-in-time supply of personnel. Another critical reason for hiring temps was to use the temporary employment period as a screening process. The rationale was to lower recruiting, training, and turnover costs by finding potential permanent employees who demonstrated a strong fit with the company. By the end of the 1980s, an increasing number of temporary professionals were being offered permanent positions following an assignment. The increasing trend of "temp-to-perm" assignments was viewed positively by both employers and employees.

Employers felt the use of temporary workers was not completely riskless. The largest problem was the fear of breaches in confidentiality and industrial espionage. It was not easy to assimilate temporary employees into the culture of a firm. Many employers doubted the level of commitment of temporary employees and were concerned about failing to align the interests of the employee with the firm. Sometimes the rest of the workforce could be unsettled by the use of

---

[3]Bureau of Labor Statistics.

temporary employees, viewing it as a signal of a downturn in the economic fortunes of a firm.[4]

Supply-Side Factors.   Changes in demographics, life style preferences, and the employment relationship were also responsible for the increased popularity of temporary work. Cost-of-living increases which outstripped wage growth increased the number of two-income households. Additionally, people were placing increased value on flexibility in the workplace and variety in job content. Unlike earlier economic downturns, during the recession in the early 1980s a large number of white-collar workers were laid off. Many professionals who were laid off (particularly those who were older) entered the temporary employment pool.

The Economic Model.   The economics of a professional temporary employment services firm were compelling. Supplying professionals workers was more financially rewarding that placing lower-skilled temporary employees for two principal reasons. Professionals typically generated more revenue because the average assignment was significantly longer and the charge rate was higher. In addition, gross margins increased with the skill level of the worker supplied. Firms supplying highly skilled professionals were able to generate 30–31 percent gross margins compared to 24 percent for the industry as a whole. The other primary expenses were branch expenses, corporate expenses, and taxes.

Keys to Competitiveness.   Being successful as a supplier of skilled temporary workers was more complex than simply supplying temporary clerical help. To establish a long-term relationship with an employer and build a recurring revenue stream, a firm had to consistently supply personnel who performed their responsibilities well and had the specific skills requested by the client. Employers evaluated firms supplying professional workers on the basis of quality and availability of personnel, a level of service particularly understanding their specific need, and speed of response. While price certainly mattered, low-quality service would jeopardize any relationship.

To be successful also required attracting high quality scientists and technicians. Such candidates would only be attracted if the potential assignments were high quality, the salaries and benefits offered were attractive, and assignments could be found quickly. Placing candidates rapidly was critical because many scientists were often simultaneously pursuing full-time jobs and also using other temporary service agencies.

EXPORTING THE BUSINESS MODEL TO WESTERN EUROPE

Bruce had always envisioned expanding the Lab Support concept beyond the United States. From his prior work experience, Bruce had contacts within the sci-

---

[4]As human resource management has been recognized as an increasingly important element of a firm's competitive advantage, several academics, including Stanford's Jeffrey Pfeffer, have argued that the use of temporary employees is contrary to the long-term goals of the firm.

entific communities in France, Germany, and the United Kingdom. As chairman of Lab Support, Inc., Bruce took an active role in researching expansion opportunities.

Preliminary research revealed that unlike the United States, many countries in Western Europe strictly regulated or even banned the use of temporary workers. The level of regulation could be divided into three basic tiers: (1) countries with low levels of regulation similar to the United States, including Denmark, Ireland, The Netherlands, and the United Kingdom; (2) countries with stringent regulations, including Belgium, France, Germany, and Portugal; and (3) countries which generally banned temporary employment through agencies, including Greece, Italy, and Spain.

Although temporary workers were fairly common in certain sectors, the growth of temporary employment in the professional segment had been slower in Western Europe for cultural reasons. In Europe, the employment relationship was generally considered to be long term. Many professionals considered temporary work to be an anomaly, reserved for those with seasonal jobs or those in low-wage, low-skilled professions. The cost of temporary employees was substantially increased by onerous regulations. Additionally, the regulations restricted the conditions under which temporaries could be hired.

Ironically, the impact of such regulations was tempered by social legislation. Strong social legislation made it particularly difficult to dismiss employees. To avoid the huge costs associated with layoffs, many firms opted for the flexibility of temporary employees. Moreover, the social legislation contributed to higher levels and longer terms of unemployment in Europe. In a poor job market, many workers sought temporary employment to earn a living.

TARGETING THE UNITED KINGDOM

Bruce chose to target the U.K. as the first potential overseas market, due to the relative similarities in culture and language with the United States, the large scientific base, and the absence of onerous government regulations. In early 1989, Bruce traveled to the U.K. to assess the possibilities of transferring the Lab Support, Inc., business model there. The first step was to conduct market research. Bruce met Dr. Ian McKinley who had been responsible for the membership at the Royal Society of Chemistry. He had extensive resources and established contacts in the laboratory management sector. After 17 years, McKinley was leaving his post and Bruce retained him to research the market.

Market Research.   Market research was compiled over the course of several months. The United Kingdom had the second largest chemical industry in Europe after Germany, and the promise of a single market was expected to benefit British companies (Exhibit 3). There were approximately 250,000 scientists and technicians employed in the United Kingdom. Regional concentrations were high with almost 40 percent working in southeast England, an area about the size of southern California. Unemployment among scientists was equivalent to the national average but trends suggested a tighter market in the future. Demand for scientists was increasing, and was expected to exceed the supply of scientists graduating from British universities.

EXHIBIT 3   **Employment in the European Chemical Industry**

Country	Number of Employees	Percentage
Germany	572,000	28.9%
United Kingdom	337,100	17.0
France	263,900	13.3
Spain	239,000	12.1
Italy	225,000	11.4
The Netherlands	91,000	4.6
Belgium/Luxembourg	90,700	4.6
Switzerland	69,300	3.5
Portugal	50,800	2.6
Denmark	26,200	1.3
Ireland	12,000	0.6
Western Europe	1,977,000	100%
United States	1,024,000	
Japan	391,000	

Note: Of the 15 largest chemical companies in the world, 10 are European companies.
Source: National Chemical Federations (1987).

While there were over 1,000 temporary agencies listed in the London phone book alone, most supplied general office staff. Some firms specialized in supplying professionals in accountancy, computers, and public relations. Very few agencies supplied any scientific personnel at all, and McKinley identified only one potential direct competitor, CPL Scientific, which had been established in 1987.

Dr. McKinley conducted interviews with a number of laboratory managers to get direct feedback on the business concept. In general, laboratory managers expressed "conservative reluctance" in hiring highly skilled temporary scientists on a regular basis through an agency. When questioned, several laboratory managers responded, "We would never use [skilled] temps in the labs" and, "If we did, we would never get them through an agency." Temporary workers suffered from a poor reputation as "low grade, low skilled, and poor quality," and were only used in low-skilled positions in laboratories. Those firms that used temps were typically hiring graduate students to fill the bulk of their needs. In the course of his interviews, it became clear to McKinley that laboratory managers were unconvinced that temporary agencies could supply "good quality staff who knew what they were doing." Some laboratory managers indicated that they might consider temporary scientists to balance staffing needs when there were sudden surges in demand or absences. Many managers, especially those in pharmaceutical R&D departments, were concerned about the problems of confidentiality. Cost, however, was not a primary concern.

The Decision to Leave Lab Support.   When Bruce presented these findings to the board of Lab Support, Inc., he concluded that an opportunity existed to be a pioneer in the U.K., just as the company had been in the United States, by providing a high quality service. He felt strongly that the response from the interviews was not entirely negative. McKinley had never been told by laboratory managers something like "We tried skilled temps once, and it was a disaster." Bruce felt that lab managers in the United Kingdom were being presented with a completely new product and asked whether they would use it. While they theoretically grasped the concept, they didn't understand how to utilize skilled temporary scientists. Bruce was confident he could convince laboratory managers of the value of temporary scientists and build a successful business in the United Kingdom. However, the Board decided that Lab Support, Inc., should focus its expansion within the United States, solidifying its leadership position. In late 1989, Bruce resigned from Lab Support, Inc., and moved ahead independently with plans to build a similar but separate business in the United Kingdom.

NEW VENTURE CREATION IN THE UNITED KINGDOM

Although Bruce was fairly certain he wanted to start his own venture, he arranged to meet the management of CPL Scientific to evaluate whether he ought to acquire or partner with them. Their business strategy was to support the laboratory efforts of R&D managers. After two years they had over 1,000 candidates on their database, sorted by five main skill classifications. Each month they circulated a newsletter to their clients highlighting the available candidates. His initial meeting revealed that the CPL culture was entrenched in a traditional, R&D mind-set. CPL management preferred to grow through existing client relationships and referrals. Bruce concluded that this was not a business environment suited to an entrepreneur who believed an opportunity existed to dramatically grow the market.

Drawing on the market research and his previous experience, Bruce developed a business plan for his new venture, Lab Staff Limited (LSL). Bruce recognized that the two most important steps in starting a new business were finding the right senior management talent and a source of capital.

A Managing Director.   From the outset, Bruce intended to attract and hire a local managing director (the equivalent of a CEO) to lead the U.K. venture. He actively sought an experienced British executive to bring his business plan to life and adapt it to local market conditions. Bruce did not plan to relocate to the U.K. on a permanent basis, preferring instead to commute from Southern California for two or three weeks of every month. In addition, Bruce knew that finding the right person would be instrumental in attracting venture funding. Personally, he desired a business partner, not just a manager—someone who shared his enthusiasm and belief in the business concept.

Bruce recounted his first efforts to find a managing director (MD):[5]

---

[5]A managing director in the United Kingdom is the equivalent of a CEO in the United States

> I first tried an executive search firm to recruit an MD for LSL. Their advice to me was simply to place a classified advertisement in the Sunday *Times*. It wasn't cheap—the going rate was £5,000, about $8,000 at the current exchange rate. The ad generated 40 résumés.

Bruce reviewed the candidates and narrowed the field to five; Ben Blackden was among them (Exhibit 2). His experience included the general management of a scientific instrument company and experience as a personnel director. When he replied to the *Times* ad, Ben had been working for the last year as a manager of a company supplying temporary executives. Bruce remarked:

> Ben's was the only résumé with management experience in both the scientific and temporary services' sectors. And because of his stint at Fisons in the U.S., it turned out that we had some mutual friends back in the States. I checked up on him, and I'm quite sure he did the same.

Simultaneously Bruce was seeking venture capital funding. Pleased by his initial interview with Ben, Bruce invited him for a second meeting. Ben was surprised by the circumstances. That meeting was not just a standard second interview, but a visit to the offices of venture capitalists Advent International, where Bruce introduced Ben as the new managing director of the venture.

Venture Capital Funding.   Finding the right venture capital partner was of great concern to Bruce. He had approached seven or eight top-tier British venture capital partnerships with limited success. Generally, the British venture capital community did not provide seed capital to start-ups, focusing instead on second and third round financing. The only start-ups attracting any attention were biotechnology deals with huge projected payoffs. Venture capitalists were not interested in a service company, especially one with an unproven market.

The first nibble came from the newly formed Security Pacific Bank's European Venture Fund. Fund manager Dmitri Bosky was born in Russia but educated in the States. He had been a star in Security Pacific's U.S. banking operations based in Los Angeles prior to moving to Europe. However, his background was in commercial lending, not science, and his investing experience in Europe was limited. Bruce kept hunting.

On a recommendation from Lab Support, Inc., board member Jim Schlater, Bruce contacted Jerry Benjamin of Advent International in London. Jerry was American and had worked at Monsanto for several years before joining Advent. He had substantial experience in both the scientific and international business arenas. Jerry was intrigued with Bruce's concept.

> I felt that the employment market was moving toward a more flexible paradigm—more responsive to change than the traditional career-oriented hierarchy. Bruce was a proven entrepreneur and he was selling an experienced model that was working well in the U.S. On the other hand the initial market research was discouraging. Labs just didn't use temporary workers and if they did, they didn't trust an agency. LSL would first have to sell the concept if they were to succeed. There was really no competition within their scientific niche so finding the right person to pioneer the idea in the U.K. was the first order of business.

During initial discussions Bruce requested £1.25 million in seed money. Jerry's response was that Bruce needed to find someone to run the venture prior to any negotiation on terms. At the second meeting, Bruce brought along Ben Blackden, whose experience and zeal convinced Jerry that he would be the right person to run the venture. A deal with Advent was in the works. More importantly, Bruce had found his new partner and MD.

Within Advent, Jerry had a tough sell.

> It took a lot of convincing internally. My personal reputation as much as anything helped to overcome the skepticism of other partners. Typical responses were "It's a start-up and start-ups usually fail" or "It's a people business and people businesses are risky ventures."

In the end, Advent International acted as the lead and Security Pacific as the secondary investor. Their investment totaled £300,000 (about US$450,000), roughly one quarter of the original amount requested, for 40 percent of the equity. Professional Staff Ltd. was formed in April 1990. Jerry Benjamin was named to the board, along with Bruce, Ben, and one outsider, Rick Baldwin, an experienced manager in the temporary employment industry. Ironically, PSL needed only £270,000 (about US$350,000) before turning a profit in the seventh month of operations. Ben later commented, "Bruce and I could have mortgaged our own homes for that amount."

BUILDING THE U.K. BUSINESS

Putting companies and candidates in touch with one another was the primary role of LSL. The priority for employers was to receive quality candidates, accurately matched to their needs. The immediate challenge was to build a sales team to recruit candidates as well as identify potential assignments and develop long-term relationships with clients.

Recruitment: Sales Consultants, Branch Managers, Candidates, and Clients.   Ben and Bruce sought to hire sales consultants and branch managers who were themselves qualified scientists and understood the importance of "doing it right the first time, every time." Consultants and branch managers needed to be both commercial-minded salespeople and skilled interpreters of clients' needs. They also had to be nurturing and attentive job counselors for candidates. Their first-hand knowledge of the available candidate pool augmented the database's job-matching capabilities.

LSL's first hire as a sales consultant was a familiar face, Dr. Ian McKinley. Already acquainted with the business plan, Ian fit easily with the organization. The first hire as a branch manager, an outsider, was not suited to a start-up and had to be let go. As Ben reflected on that episode, he thought, "It's amazing that we rode through that. Hiring mistakes in the early stages could have been fatal." Future hires required a much more intensive search and screening process. Previous scientific training and work experience were a must—most had a B.S. or Ph.D. in science and prior experience as a sales or marketing representative for a scientific instruments company. Experience in personnel services was nearly impossible to find, however. During the interview process, Ben favored charismatic, service-oriented personality traits that would lend themselves to the softer side of the job.

LSL actively pursued potential placement candidates through a variety of different media including advertisements in trade magazines and less frequently in local newspapers, as well as by attending trade shows. They set a company policy of not actively recruiting candidates who were already employed and had not approached the company seeking an employment opportunity. LSL viewed this policy as essential for developing long-lasting customer relationships.

In addition to temporary placement services, candidates were given career counseling. Most candidates had little experience in temporary work. Despite their qualifications, their résumés and interviewing skills were often lackluster. Recruitment consultants assisted candidates with polishing their résumés before entering them into the candidate database system. In addition, LSL produced a training video that addressed many of the issues candidates would face in their interviews. General business etiquette and a friendly, flexible demeanor were stressed. Candidates were reminded, "For all the experience and qualifications you may have, you are there to sell yourself as a person."

LSL clients were the laboratory or personnel managers within companies that employed scientists or lab technicians. LSL knew that attracting clients would be a far more difficult task than identifying prospects. Building Lab Staff's profile in the scientific industry was an important aspect of the recruitment strategy. Ben assumed the role of public relations specialist, writing press releases and authoring articles for scientific publications such as *Food Manufacturing, Chemistry in Britain*, and *Nature*.

Prospective clients had expressed a number of concerns during initial market research interviews about the quality and commitment of temporary scientists. It was clear that the company had to establish credible references to ameliorate such skepticism among the scientific community. More importantly, they would need to educate laboratory managers about the benefits that could be provided by a firm dedicated to laboratory employment.

Marketing and Promotion.   In April 1990, Bruce and Ben rented lists of names of personnel directors and laboratory managers to target through a direct mail campaign. PSL conducted three separate mailings each targeted at 200 individuals. They got no responses from either of the first two mailings and in mid-June they received their first and only reply from the third mailing. Neither founder had anticipated such a low response rate, and both spent a lot of time between April and June following up with potential clients by telephone. By August, PSL had only nine temporary employees on assignment; it was clear that a revised marketing approach was necessary to build the business more rapidly.

In the first few months, the founders realized that just about every employer had a hang-up with temporary workers. Employers were worried about quality, commitment, confidentiality and costs. To overcome the reputational problem, Ben and Bruce decided to tackle these notions head-on and rely on educational marketing. Ben produced a series of brochures to address issues raised by lab managers such as "Why use temps?" "When would one use a temp?" and "What benefits do temps provide?" High quality, professional marketing material was instrumental in attracting the attention of busy laboratory managers. An introductory brochure highlighting "Six very good reasons for needing to know more about Lab Staff Ltd." provided a means for interested recipients to request additional information (Exhibit 4).

Exhibit 4   Temporary Laboratory Workers: What Are the Benefits?
Lab Staff Introductory Brochure

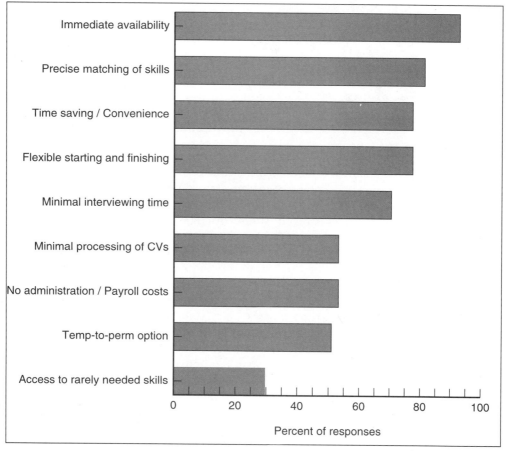

Source: Client surveys in 1991 and 1993. Clients were asked to EVAL-U-RATE all the factors in the table above. These show the extent to which the factors were rated as "important" or very "important."

Benefits Summary

- **Immediate availability:** We respond promptly to your needs and our extensive nationwide database allows us to provide candidates who are immediately available.
- **Precise matching:** With a Lab Staff Ltd. recruitment consultant you will find you are dealing with a qualified scientist, experienced in laboratory work, who understands your needs.
- **Time saving:** The rapid appointment of a skilled temporary laboratory worker means maintained laboratory productivity. Instrument downtime or project interruption is minimized.
- **Flexible starting and finishing:** A quick start and flexible assignment duration are key benefits. No-fuss finishing means you can use a skilled temporary worker for just as long as needed.
- **Minimal interviewing:** We interview candidates for every assignment. You only see the best—the ones we have matched carefully to your needs.

(continued)

(concluded)

- **Minimal CV processing:** We advertise weekly and process CVs continuously. We select for *your* assignment and send you just a small number of candidates.
- **No administrative/payroll costs:** We pay the temporary worker and employer's national insurance. We handle all PAYE and statutory returns, as well as providing employment insurance.
- **Temp-to-perm option:** The ideal method of avoiding mistakes and of hiring the right people. We make no charge for the conversion after a month (or more) temporary assignment.
- **Access to rarely needed skills:** You may need specific skills for just one project or for part of a development program. Using a Lab Staff Ltd. temporary keeps you in control and avoids today's recruitment becoming tomorrow's redundancy.

In early 1991, PSL expanded its educational marketing to include seminars. Ben recalled: "We had no intention of doing seminars at the beginning. We learned the art of the possible as we went on." The Lab Staff seminar program was geographically focused. It targeted laboratory managers and personnel professionals with responsibility for scientists in all industries. The program emphasized the quality and careful matching of temporary workers to client needs, the flexibility and short-term availability, as well as the cost and time savings in recruiting including the temp-to-perm option. For Ben, the seminar program, entitled "The Changing Trend in Laboratory Staffing," was an opportunity to listen and respond to clients' needs. For participants, it delivered information rather than a sales pitch, and offered a free lunch. The lunchtime briefings helped established credibility among the scientific community. Ben attributed the marketing success of PSL to the staff's intuitive skill at cultivating and nurturing client relationships. Ben noted, "we were not very pushy or overly aggressive in our marketing."

The seminar program served as a ongoing market research tool as well. Surveys were regularly administered to seminar participants to evaluate questions such as under what circumstances temporary laboratory workers were used and in which scientific industry sectors, lab functions, and scientific disciplines were they assigned. From the survey results, Ben created the most widely distributed collateral piece, "How to Avoid Excessive Staffing Costs in the Laboratory." Complementing the seminars, this booklet explained the relationship between permanent staff costs and the costs of a LSL temporary scientific worker. The widely held myth that temporaries were more expensive than equivalent permanent staff was discredited with statistics and colorful graphs.

Operations.   In pioneering Lab Support, Inc., in the United States, Bruce had identified a wide range of scientific skills and techniques employed in laboratories. His experience had shown that employers placed demanding selection criteria on temporary scientists and were very specific when describing the scientific workers they needed. Bruce had developed a candidate database system that covered all levels of educational and experience requirements. For instance, a client that requested an analytical chemist would be asked to specify the tasks that needed to be done. The final request might be for someone with experience in "graphite furnace, atomic absorption spectroscopy," a specialty many levels below the general description of "analytical chemist." At LSL in the U.K., Bruce implemented a database similar in design but with some significant improvements, including streamlined data entry screens and a more user-friendly interface. Total development time was three months. The new database covered every category of educational qualification, separated into 40 different physical and biological sciences. It recognized some 55 industrial sectors and included over 80 primary laboratory techniques, subdivided into 400 discrete laboratory skills. This degree of sophistication and flexibility was a strategic tool in guaranteeing a precise match to a client's most detailed specifications. Ben believed that the LSL database was "the heart of the operation."

In the first few months, Ben and Bruce both served multiple functions; at times they were executives, branch managers, sales consultants, or even secretaries. Bruce demanded modern office systems from day one. "A PC on every desk and no secretaries," was the prevailing culture. Because money was tight in the early days, LSL placed a priority on timely invoicing to optimize its cash flow position. As a start-up with limited funding, the founders were dedicated to operating the company efficiently. As the company grew that frugal mind-set remained a hallmark of PSL.

THE DECISION TO EXPAND TO FRANCE

The board of PSL firmly believed that success in the United Kingdom was necessary prior to undertaking geographic expansion. Jerry Benjamin noted, "If management is always running after a grand scheme, they will never make the core scheme work." By mid-1992 LSL had 150 temporary employees on assignment, and both revenues and profits were entering a rapid growth stage. Expansion into France was the first step in a long-term plan to expand the geographic scope of PSL.

Regulatory Environment in France.   Extensive government regulation affected the temporary employment business in France. Regulation was intended to encourage the hiring of permanent rather than temporary workers, and the Labor Department strongly recommended that temporaries comprise no more than 10 percent of a firm's workforce. Specific regulations prohibited temporary agencies from offering services such as headhunting or from earning a fee for temporaries who followed the temp-to-perm track. Agencies were required to advertise that all jobs were only temporary. Temporary services agencies were required to produce a financial guarantee as a condition of receiving a business license. The contract for a temporary employee had to be for a fixed period not to exceed 18 months and could only be renewed once. Temporary workers could only be used in three basic situations: (1) to replace an employee who was ill, on vacation or leave; (2) to complete specific projects; or (3) to assist in exceptional increases in workload. Use was also allowed in industries which were seasonal such as tourism and construction. However, temporary workers could not be hired to replace striking workers or in companies which were petitioning the government to downsize.

Employers were required to provide temporary workers with the same employment conditions (salary level and benefits) as the person replaced. By law, temporary workers also received a 10 percent insecurity allowance at the end of their employment period to compensate them for the risky nature of their job. Therefore, temporary workers typically cost at least 25 percent more than permanent workers, an amount equivalent to the gross margin of the temporary agency.

Market Research.   In January 1992, LSL conducted a market research study of the French temporary services market focusing on the professional segment. Although heavily regulated, the temporary employment business was large in France, estimated to be $8.5 billion in 1992. Over 5,000 temporary services agencies were active in France, although most operated out of single offices or on a regional basis. It was estimated that one million individuals were employed on a temporary basis. Most temporary workers were in low-skilled jobs and professionals represented only 4.5 percent of the temporary workforce. The protracted economic weakness in France was hurting the temporary services industry. France was in the midst of a recession, causing volume and revenues from temporary employment to fall in 1991. Unfavorable economic conditions were expected to persist in 1992 and beyond.

France offered a large scientific base; it had the third largest chemical industry in Europe. Large private sector and government laboratories were concentrated in three primary regions: Greater Paris 30–50 percent, Lyon 20–30 percent, and Marseilles 10–15 percent. The market research identified three potential competitors serving the temporary scientist niche including two of the larger agencies, ECCO-Chimie and Manpower Pharmacie-Chimie, as well as a smaller company SNEA-Chimie. In addition to direct competition, fixed-term contracts were popular in France. Fixed-term contracts, negotiated directly between the employer and employee for a prescribed period of time, were a rapidly growing recruiting tool and had doubled in number between 1985 and 1989.

Unlike in the United Kingdom, in large French companies the primary decision maker in the hiring of temporary scientists was an administrator in the human resources department rather than the laboratory manager. PSL conducted only a limited number of interviews in France, and those were generally with personnel managers. These individuals reported that they were spontaneously receiving a large number of résumés from people soliciting employment and were able to hire people on a fixed-term basis. In addition, the perception was that the three agencies in this niche were often unable to supply adequately trained personnel.

The Acquisition of SNEA and Subsequent Problems.   While France placed significant restrictions on temporary employment, PSL management felt that they could operate successfully within the rules. Ben Blackden and Bruce Culver both felt that PSL would enter the French market through a start-up operation, as they had done successfully in the United Kingdom. They knew that Société Nouvelle Engineering Assistance (SNEA), a small business based in Paris, was already supplying scientific workers on a temporary basis to private laboratories. SNEA had been founded by M. Weinmann, a scientist of Swiss heritage, and was being run by his widow as a family business out of a single office in Paris. Further investigation revealed that the business was fairly well respected and that the widow was looking to sell and retire. An acquisition would allow more rapid entry into the French market. Given the positive feedback from their due diligence, PSL decided to purchase the business in July 1992. SNEA became the first operating entity of Professional Staff France.

However, imposing the successful business model developed by LSL on SNEA proved more difficult than anticipated. Madame Weinmann's retirement left a void in the principal leadership position and recruiting a qualified PDG was difficult. LSL management knew the major challenge was to professionalize the culture of SNEA, which had been operated as a lifestyle business since its founding 17 years earlier. The office closed daily at noon to allow two-hour lunch breaks, and the entire month of November was dedicated to purchasing holidays gifts for clients. A strong PDG was necessary to spearhead the effort to change the culture, as well as coordinate the successful transfer and customization of the systems and marketing programs from England. A candidate identified by a headhunter was hired, but had to be let go after eight months when it was clear that the person was not capable of running the business and extremely poor at developing working relationships with the employees. In April 1993, Ben Blackden had to serve as the CEO until a second person was hired to be PDG in September 1993; it was soon evident that another mistake had been made and that person was let go after seven months, to be replaced by another interim manager.

The problem with Professional Staff France went beyond the lack of a quality manager. PSL had not performed sufficient due diligence prior to the acquisition. Bruce Culver and Ben Blackden soon discovered that the business had been neglected. Bruce recalled, "The vacuum cleaner didn't even work. Their software was eight years old and they didn't own a copy or fax machine— it probably would have cost less money to start a business from scratch." Two years following the acquisition, a computer system similar to that being used in the United Kingdom finally replaced the antiquated filing system.

In September 1994, Ben had identified Ivan Mentré as a candidate for the PDG position. Ben hoped Ivan would be the right person for the job. Ivan had a Ph.D. in the physical sciences and a proven track record in general management (see Exhibit 2). Following two years of poor results, the primary goal for the new PDG was to break even in fiscal 1995. Additional challenges would include reducing the larger than necessary corporate staff, and growing the client base by increasing the emphasis on marketing. The initial response to the marketing efforts, however, and in particular the seminars, showed little sign of success. Ivan Mentré was wondering whether the French market would respond favorably to their marketing efforts, or whether there needed to be a greater emphasis on sales itself. There thus remained some open questions about the appropriate mix of the commercialization technologies.

PERFORMANCE TO DATE

The performance of PSL, particularly in the United Kingdom, exceeded the expectations of both its founders and Jerry Benjamin (Exhibit 5). The average number of temporary workers supplied had grown steadily to 548 by the end of 1994. In the first six months of fiscal 1995, revenues and profits grew 41.9 percent and 69.4 per-

EXHIBIT 5   Group Business Development

£000s	Actual FY91	Actual FY92	Actual FY93	Actual FY94	Actual FY95	Forecast FY96
Revenue	**597**	**1,1963**	**6,124**	**9,990**	**14,279**	**19,333**
Cost of services	356	1,263	4,233	6,973	9,988	13,580
Gross profit	241	700	1,891	3,017	4,291	5,753
Expenses	504	600	1,600	1,984	2,615	2,910
Operating income	(263)	100	291	1,033	1,676	2,843
Other income/(expenses)	33	8	29	(39)	80	22
Earnings before tax	**(230)**	**108**	**320**	**994**	**1,756**	**2,865**

cent, respectively, compared with the same period in fiscal 1994, capping off 15 consecutive quarters of pre-tax profit growth (Exhibit 6). PSL had successfully held over 30 educational seminars since early 1991.

For every temporary appointment arranged by LSL, their clients:

- Received an average of only 2.4 résumés.
- Interviewed an average of 1.2 candidates.
- Waited an average of only 7 days from their first call to the employee starting work.

The average temporary employment period through LSL was four to five months and over 50 percent of assignments were extended beyond the period initially planned. These figures demonstrated LSL's emphasis on quality, service, and speed of response. In September 1994, the candidate database had topped 18,850 and the prospect database, 22,000. LSL reported 33 percent market penetration but noted that their original estimate of market size had increased significantly since their marketing effort stimulated primary demand. The visible success of Lab Staff, publicly recognized as one of the fastest growing companies in the United Kingdom, had prompted the entrance of two new regional competitors, who had operated in others niches of the temporary services industry.

FUTURE DIRECTION

In 1994, PSL decided to expand vertically in the United Kingdom into a related niche in the temporary employment business. Executives on Assignment Ltd. (EOA) was founded with the mission of being the only employment business exclusively dedicated to providing top quality temporary managers and executives. Management sought to develop a candidate database using promotion techniques that had been successful in the growth of LSL. The current EOA database boasted 2,210 candidates, 36 percent of whom were chief executives, and another 38 percent of whom were functional heads in their former posts. Executives on Assignment would face competition from established accounting firms as well as other agencies, all of whom dabbled in the business of supplying temporary executives.

EXHIBIT 6   **Consolidated Balance Sheet, 31 March 1995**

	Note	1995 *English Pound*	1994 *English Pound*
Fixed Assets			
Tangible assets	10	249,719	181,159
Investments	11	2,796	2,599
		252,515	183,758
Current Assets			
Debtors	12	2,718,736	1,898,090
Cash at bank and in hand		1,317,294	764,889
		4,036,030	2,662,979
Creditors: amounts falling due within one year	13	(3,022,235)	(2,194,332)
Net Current Assets		1,013,795	468,647
Total Assets Less Current Liabilities		1,226,310	652,405
Creditors: amounts falling due after more than one year	14	(61,081)	(47,402)
		1,205,229	605,003
Capital and Reserves			
Called up share capital	15	410,164	407,464
Share premium		37,924	40,924
Capital redemption reserve		300	-
Other reserves		(134,148)	(61,505)
Profit and Loss Account		890,989	218,120
		1,205,229	605,003
Attributable to equity shareholders		830,229	230,003
Attributable to nonequity shareholders		375,000	375,000

The market for temporary executives was relatively older than the scientists' market, and hard sales had to be made to CEOs.

Bruce Culver and Ben Blackden believed that there were a number of other opportunities to grow PSL. First, there was the opportunity to expand the core business through organic growth in the U.K. and France. In France, the challenges were greater—including widening the client base by targeting new sectors, transferring the successful marketing techniques from the U.K., and expanding the regional presence beyond Paris. Second, there were numerous opportunities for geographic expansion in other parts of Europe for both Lab Staff Ltd. and possibly Executives on Assignment. Additionally, management felt that PSL might expand into other niches.

In deciding on growth strategies the founders were faced with a number of significant personal questions. The company was preparing for a public offering in

---

Exhibit 7   Quality Statement

"Lab Staff Ltd. operations, and the attitude and commitment of its staff, are based firmly upon the principles of scientific understanding, professionalism, and customer care."

Our operations and business procedures have been carefully developed over many years to ensure that our Clients and our Candidates consistently receive a service of the highest quality.

Lab Staff Ltd.'s imperatives for ensuring service and quality in our dealings with Clients and Candidates are as follows:

For Clients

Every Client will receive a prompt written acknowledgment of its "Request," together with copies our Terms of Business and other documents.

For each request, the full extent and nature of the Client's scientific and technical requirements will be researched and understood by Lab Staff Ltd. so that only Candidates actually possessing the relevant skills and experience will be submitted to the Client.

Every Candidate interviewed by a Client will first have been interviewed by Lab Staff Ltd. (in the very exceptional case where this cannot apply, the client will be informed in advance).

Lab Staff Ltd. will in its Candidate interviews, verify and validate Candidate's actual laboratory skills and experience and will also appraise the Candidate's suitability for the Client's specific requirements.

In the case of temporary assignments Lab Staff Ltd. will ensure its employee (the Candidate) has full understanding of the assignment, has a written statement of terms, and has agreed to the assignment duration. Lab Staff Ltd. will also ensure the employee receives a good and appropriate rate of pay and is paid regularly and promptly; Lab Staff Ltd. will meet all PAYE, National Insurance, and other statutory employer obligations.

For Candidates

All applicant Candidates will receive prompt written acknowledgement of their letters and CVs.

Every letter and CV will be carefully keyworded by qualified staff and all technical information entered onto the Lab Staff Ltd. Candidate database, within 7 working days of receipt.

All candidates for permanent appointments or temporary assignments will be interviewed by Lab Staff Ltd. At that time each will receive, free of charge, information and guidance on interview and presentation skills as well as a copy (if required) of the Lab Staff Ltd. booklet "How to write a CV."

Each Candidate selected for a temporary assignment will receive from Lab Staff Ltd. a written offer stating terms, duration, rate and frequency of pay, and any other special or relevant conditions.

Audit

During each assignment Lab Staff Ltd. seeks, from its Clients, an assessment of the quality, skills, and overall performance of its employee and also the service from and responsiveness of the Lab Staff Ltd. branch office.

1996 and that would be a large step. There were plans to expand the board and add personnel to the senior management team, including an experienced Finance Director. Undoubtedly, the culture of the organization would change. Ben and Bruce also needed to evaluate what their future goals would be. Would each be happier as entrepreneurs focused on building new businesses or were they excited by the challenge of managing an established, growing business for the long term?

II MARKET ENTRY— EXPORTING, LICENSING, DIRECT INVESTMENT

CASE SUMMARIES

CASE 4: AIRVIEW MAPPING INC.

By Kris Opalinski and Walter S. Good (both of University of Manitoba, Canada)

Airview Mapping is an aerial surveying and mapping company that is considering entry into international markets. At the time of the case, it operates in Canada and its sales are $1.1 million. However, sales growth has stalled as a result of a recession, a decrease in demand in the Canadian market, and increased competition. The company has recently assumed significant debt to finance the acquisition of state-of-the-art photographic and computer equipment. Although Airview Mapping is a profitable operation, the company is having difficulty servicing its debt because of negative cash flow. An analysis of the company's cost structure indicates that a 10 percent increase in sales could produce an incremental cash flow more than sufficient to service existing debt. Therefore, management is considering international market entry and identifies the United States, Mexico, Latin America, and the Arab World as possible target markets for growth. Management's analysis of each of these markets is presented in the case, and readers are asked for their advice.

CASE 5: GRAPHISOFT: THE ENTRY OF A HUNGARIAN SOFTWARE VENTURE INTO THE U.S. MARKET

By Robert D. Hisrich (Case Western Reserve University, USA)
and Janos Vecsenyi (International Management Center, Hungary)

This is a case about a technology-sophisticated Hungarian software company's efforts to penetrate the U. S. market. The case describes the company's problems and opportunities in their effort, with the reader needing to develop a business strategy for this effort.

CASE 6: POWER BEAT INTERNATIONAL LIMITED

By Rajib N. Sanyal (Trenton State College, USA)

Power Beat International is a New Zealand emerging technologies company. The company was formed to commercialize an important breakthrough in lead-acid battery technology. The battery lasts much longer than conventional batteries and enables a motor vehicle to start even if lights, radios, and other electrical accessories have been left on for long periods of time. After developing a prototype, obtaining American patents, and successfully market testing the product in New Zealand, the company is looking to commercialize the technology. The company is examining licensing its technology for commercial manufacture and sale in North America, western Europe, and east Asia. The company is also considering the possibility of manufacturing the batteries itself.

CASE 7: SYTKO INTERNATIONAL LIMITED

By Walter S. Good and Kris Opalinski (both of University of Manitoba, Canada)

The founder, Les Sytkowski, of Sytko Custom Homes Inc. is considering expanding his home building business into his native country of Poland. All sales are currently in Canada. The case is set in 1990. Mr. Sytkowski earlier attended a Conference on New Opportunities for Canadian Businesses organized in Canada by the Polish Trade Mission. Subsequently, he visited Poland and identified several business opportunities which he is evaluating. ∎

CASE 4
AIRVIEW MAPPING INC.

In early March 1994, Rick Tanner, the principal of Airview Mapping Inc., started drafting plans for the upcoming summer season. For him, late winter typically involved making sales calls on the company's established and potential clients for the purpose of determining the expected demand for his services and then drafting his sales forecasts for the upcoming year.

Airview, which had traditionally dominated the aerial surveying markets of Central and Eastern Canada, had recently been faced with increasing competition in its traditional territories from other air surveyors from across Canada. The protracted recession of the early 1990s, combined with the anti-deficit measures introduced by all levels of government, had reduced the overall demand for geomatic services in Canada, producing significant overcapacity in the industry, including the particular markets in which Airview was involved.

This situation had already reduced the company's profits, but the real threat lay in the fact that the new competitors, once established in Airview's region, would stay there, permanently capturing a significant share of the Central Canadian market. These competitors, typically larger than Airview, could expand their market coverage, even if it meant creating a temporary operating base in a distant location. At the same time, their home markets were extremely difficult for small companies from other regions to penetrate due to their fierce price competition.

Rick realized that his company might face difficult times if he could not redirect his attention to some new areas of opportunity. His view was that these opportunities had to be found in international markets. He had already gathered some information on several foreign markets which looked promising from the company's perspective. It was now time to review the overall situation and decide whether to attempt penetrating any of the identified foreign markets, and, if so, what entry strategy to choose.

THE COMPANY

Airview Mapping Inc. was incorporated in November 1979 by a group of former employees of Aerosurvey Corporation Ltd., with Tom Denning and Rick Tanner as the principal shareholders of the new entity. For the first two years, the company operated without an aircraft, providing mapping services based on externally developed photogrammetric images to clients in Central Canada. Airview's early success provided

Source: Prepared by Kris Opalinski and Walter S. Good of the University of Manitoba, Canada as a basis for classroom discussion rather than to illustrate either effective or ineffective handling of an administrative situation.

The name of the company and its officers have been disguised. Support for the development of this case was provided by the Centre for International Business Studies, University of Manitoba, Canada.

sufficient capital to acquire an aircraft and a photographic processing laboratory, which in 1981 was initially placed under the company's subsidiary, Airtech Services Ltd. The two operations were amalgamated in November 1983 under the parent company's name.

When Tom Bruise retired in 1990, Rick took over his duties as president. He acquired Tom's shares in the company and offered 40 percent of them to his employees.

Airview's sales grew steadily throughout the 1980s, from an annual level of $500,000 in 1981 to $1.2 million in 1989. Sales stabilized during the 1990s at a level of just over $1.1 million.

Airview had traditionally maintained an advanced level of technical capabilities, investing in the most up-to-date photographic, film processing, data analysis, and plotting equipment. This, combined with the technical expertise of the company's staff, had enabled them to built an excellent reputation for the quality, reliability, and professionalism of its services.

PRODUCT LINE

With its extensive technological capabilities, Airview provided a range of services associated with the development of spatial images of terrain, referred to (in Canada) as geomatics. The company's primary specialization was to make, process, and analyze airborne photographs of the earth's surface.

The major groups of services provided by Airview included:

Aerial Photography and Photogrammetry.   Aerial photography occupied a pivotal place in Airview's business. The majority of the complex services provided by Airview were initiated by taking photographs from the air. However, aerial photography was also a separate product, that, depending on the light spectrum applied in taking the photograph, could provide information on forest growth and diseases, quality of water resources, wildlife migration, land erosion, and other physical features.

Photogrammetry involved a number of image processing techniques using aerial photographs as a basis for the development of maps, composite views, or spatially referenced databases. Photogrammetry was distinguished from aerial photography by its capability to identify three-dimensional coordinates for each point on the captured image.

Aerial photography/photogrammetry was very capital intensive, requiring a specially prepared aircraft with specialized cameras and sophisticated photo-laboratory equipment. Airview was considered one of the best equipped aerial photography companies in Canada. Its Cessna 310 L aircraft with 25,000 feet photo ceiling was capable of producing photographs at scales of up to 1:10,000. A recently (1992) acquired Leica camera represented the latest in optical technology, meeting all calibration and accuracy requirements set by North American mapping agencies, and accommodating a wide variety of specialized aerial film. Finally, Airview's photo laboratory, which was certified by the National Research Council, processed all types of aerial film used by the company.

Aerial Surveying.   Aerial surveying involved taking photographs with the purpose of defining and measuring boundaries and the configuration of particular areas on the earth's surface for a variety of uses, such as establishing ownership rights (cadastre), triangulation,[1] locating and appraising mineral resources, forests, and wild habitat, and detecting earth and water movements.

Mapping.   This service group comprised the development of maps from either internally or externally acquired photographic images. Before the 1980s, map making had largely been a manual process of drawing the terrain's contours and elevations, and then inserting the accompanying descriptive information. From the early 1980s, however, the process had been increasingly computer-driven. This resulted in a reduction in the manual labor required and increased accuracy of the images produced. The new technology also permitted the storage of maps in an easily accessible, digital format, which created demand for converting maps from the traditional, analog format into a computer-based one.

CADD.   This area also dealt with map making, but was based on computer-operated scanners supported by CADD/CAM (Computer-Aided-Design and Drafting/ Computer- Aided-Mapping) software. With this technology, the digitizing of analog images, such as existing maps or photographs, was fully automated. The scanners interpreted the subject image as a series of dots identified by their coordinates, colours, and illuminance, and then produced their digital presentation. The computer-stored images could then be enhanced by adding descriptive information, using a process still performed manually by the CADD operators.

Consulting.   Over its 15-year history, Airview had developed a multidisciplinary team of specialists, whose expertise was also employed in providing consulting services associated with the planning and execution of comprehensive mapping projects. Consulting involved advising clients on the optimal method of gathering spatial information, the interpretation of client-provided data, and supervising data gathering projects conducted by the client or his or her subcontractors.

Data capture (aerial photography/photogrammetry) and data processing (mapping and CADD) projects had traditionally generated (in equal proportions) around 90 percent of Airview's sales. The remainder had come from consulting projects (9 percent) and surveying (1 percent).

By 1994, this sales distribution of sales did not reflect the changing structure of the marketplace where data capture had become a relatively small part of the overall scope of geomatic activities.

---

[1]A specialized technique for defining an accurate three-dimensional coordinate system for determining the location and dimensions of objects on the earth's surface.

CUSTOMER BASE

Airview Mapping Inc. provided services to a variety of clients locally and nationally. The majority of the company's sales had traditionally come from the public sector. Over the period of 1991–93, government agencies (both federal and provincial), local municipalities, and regional utilities in Ontario, Manitoba, and Saskatchewan had accounted for between 65 percent and 75 percent of the company's total dollar sales.

Energy, Mines, and Resources Canada; Transport Canada; the Department of Indian Affairs; Manitoba Hydro; and Manitoba Telephone System were Airvew's most significant clients. Procurement by public tender, the significant size of individual contracts (from $50,000 to $100,000+), and clear specifications of requirements characterized these clients' approach to project management.

The private sector, accounting for the remaining 25 percent to 35 percent of sales, was represented predominantly by clients from the mining sector (such as Hudson Bay Mining and Smelting Company; Inco; Delcan; Noranda; and Placer Dome), whose contracts were typically in the range of $20,000–40,000. Companies representing such diverse areas as construction, recreation, and environmental protection provided projects valued at up to $20,000 each. Companies from the private sector did not apply a rigorous procurement procedure, and frequently needed guidance in defining (or redefining) project requirements.

GEOGRAPHIC COVERAGE

Airview concentrated its activities within a 1,200 mile radius of its Brandon, Manitoba, headquarters. This was the area where the company was able to deal directly with its clients and had a cost advantage over its competitors from other provinces. It included northwestern Ontario, Manitoba, Saskatchewan, and Alberta, each contributing equally to the company's revenues.

The company had never attempted to expand beyond the national market, even though the sizable market south of the U.S.–Canada border was well within its defined geographic radius. In the past, this was justified by the abundance of opportunities available in Canada and restrictions on foreign access to the U.S. market. However, this situation had recently changed on both counts, which caused Rick to consider changing his company's geographic orientation.

ORGANIZATION AND STAFF

The production process associated with the services provided by Airview involved grouping activities into three functional areas: airplane operation and maintenance (two staff members), film development (two), and image processing/output (ten). Managerial, marketing, and administrative activities required four additional staff members.

Each production area (aircraft operations, photo lab, data capture, and data conversion) was assigned a coordinator, responsible for quality assurance and overall coordination of the work load. These coordinators also provided expert advice to their staff and were responsible for individual projects within their respective production areas.

Airview's production activities were characterized by the relatively small number of concurrent projects (4–6) and their modest size. This, combined with the well-trained staff (13 out of 18 had completed post-secondary education in geomatics-related fields), enabled the company to apply a skeleton project management structure.

Coordination of project work among different production areas was the responsibility of the production coordinator, Sean Coleman. Garry Howell was in charge of marketing. Tim Connors, who occupied the position of vice president, also acted as the general manager responsible for all projects. Rick, who was the company's president, oversaw general administration and communication with customers.

PRICING

Each price quotation was based on Garry Howell's assessment of the scope of work required to complete it. This was broken down by category of activity (aircraft operation, film processing, digitization of images, or image analysis). For each of these activity categories a budget hourly rate was developed, based on historical cost figures (both direct and fixed), the budgeted number of hours for a given planning period, and the company's profit targets. Recently, rates had ranged from $25 for digitization of images to over $900 for aircraft flying time, with an overall average of $70.

The initial price was determined by multiplying the estimated number of hours required in each category by its budgeted rate, and than adding these figures for all activity categories involved in the project. This price was later adjusted by Rick's assessment of the competitive situation (in the case of a tendered bid) or his negotiations with the customer.

Generally, Airview's budgeted rates, and—consequently—prices, were within average values prevailing in Canada. This situation reflected their general knowledge of the cost structure of the industry. Any undercutting of price tended to raise suspicions of lower standards. This being the case, the competition between bidders had severely squeezed profit margins, with many firms trying to survive by quoting their services on a break-even basis.

FINANCIAL RESULTS

In the late 1980s and early 1990s, Airview had acquired advanced photographic and mapping equipment, and computer hardware and software with a total value of close to $900,000. Financing for these acquisitions had been provided by bank loans and capital leases at interest rates ranging from 12.25 percent to 17.25 percent.

During the past two years, the cost of servicing this debt load had created a real strain on the company's cash flow, requiring an annual outlay of $200,000, split evenly between interest expenses and repayment of the principal. This was extremely difficult for a company traditionally only generating a free annual cash flow in the range of $100,000 to $150,000.

Airview's operating cost structure was characterized by a high proportion of fixed costs. Currently, some 75 percent of direct costs and 83 percent of total costs did not vary with changes in their sales level. This cost structure might seem surprising for a business with some 60 percent of its direct expenses associated with wages and salaries. However, considering the unique nature of the professional qualifications of the company's staff, it was extremely difficult, if not impossible, to vary the number of staff in line with fluctuations in sales levels.

This situation reduced the company's profitability at their current sales level, but, at the same time, created significant profit potential with the possibility of a sales increase. It was estimated that the company, barely breaking even at its current sales of $1.1 million, could make over $200,000 in profits by increasing sales to $1.4 million.

OVERALL STRATEGIC PROFILE

Viewed from a strategic perspective, Airview could be characterized as a locally based company with strong technical capabilities, but limited expertise in marketing, particularly outside its traditional markets. Rick recognized the importance of having a clear view of his company's current position, as well as its goals for the next few years.

Analysis of Airview's structure and performance led him to develop the corporate profile presented in Exhibit 1.

INDUSTRY TRENDS

The term "geomatics" was widely used in Canada to describe a variety of fields which acquired, managed, and distributed spatially referenced data. The term was applied to generally refer to several disciplines, including the following:

- Aerial photography.
- Ground-based (geodetic) and aerial surveying, i.e., assessing and delimiting boundaries of land.
- Mapping, i.e., cartography (map making based on ground measurements) and photogrammetry (converting photographic images and measurements into maps).
- Geographic Information Systems (GIS), i.e., computer-based systems for the storage and processing of spatial information.
- Remote sensing, i.e., satellite-borne images and measurements; quite often, airborne images were included in the remote sensing category.

The use of this general term, however, was limited to Canada. In other countries these disciplines were referred to by their individual names. On the other hand, the term ``remote sensing'' was frequently used to describe all satellite and airborne observations of the earth's surface, regardless of their purpose and the techniques applied.

EXHIBIT 1   **Airview's Corporate Profile**
Current versus Target (5-year perspective)

	Current	*Target*
Rank and size	$1,100,000 sales $0–$25,000 profits 18 employees Medium-sized aerial surveying company No export sales	$2,000,000+ sales $300,000+ profits 30+ employees Medium-sized GIS company $700,000+ export sales
Product line	Aerial photography—40% Mapping—30% Surveying—1% CADD—20% Commercial—9% 5–10 concurrent projects	Aerial photography—30% GIS—40% Mapping—20% Commercial/Consulting—10% 3–5 concurrent projects
Geographic coverage	Canada—100%	Canada—60% International—40%
Performance goals	Maintenance of cash flow Profit margin Protecting market share	Sales/Profit growth Market penetration Technology adoption New product development Productivity
Strengths	Customer goodwill Technological expertise – aerial photography – digital imaging	Customer goodwill Active marketing Geographical diversification Flexible offer Technological expertise • Digital imaging • Aerial photography • System development
Weaknesses	Marketing Narrow product line Balance sheet	International exposure
Strategy	Passive	Active

Although traditionally distinct, these disciplines were becoming increasingly integrated due to the commonality of the computer tools employed to acquire and process spatial information, and generate the final product.

The emergence of satellite-based remote sensing had also affected the geomatics industry worldwide. Its impact on air-based services had been largely positive, despite the fact that both technologies served the same user segments. Advances in satellite technology had received a lot of publicity, which sensitized users of geomatic services to the cost advantages of remote sensing in general, and aerial photography/photogrammetry in particular. Consequently, those users who could not use satellite-based services turned to airborne imagery. In many cases, satellite trajectories limited the frequency at which information on a particular earth location could be gathered. This problem was further exacerbated by the prevalence of cloud cover over certain territories. It was expected that, despite recent plans to increase the overall number of remote sensing satellites, aerial photography/photogrammetry would maintain its advantage in applications requiring high resolution capabilities (aerial images could produce resolutions in a 2–3 inch range versus a 10 meter range available from most satellites) and full color capabilities.

AIRVIEW'S MARKETS

In the first half of the 1990s, the Canadian geomatics industry was comprised of over 1,300 firms from all geomatic disciplines employing some 12,000 people. The largest number of firms were located in Quebec and Ontario, followed by British Columbia. The distribution of primary activities within the industry was as follows:

Major Line of Business	*Percent of Establishments*	*Percent of Billing*
Geodetic (ground) surveying	65%	53%
Mapping	9	16
Remote sensing	5	11
Consulting	10	4.5
GIS	7	12
Other	4	3.5

The vast majority (86 percent) of geomatic firms were small establishments generating sales of less than $1 million. However, the remaining, small number of larger firms generated the majority (68 percent) of the industry's revenues. Airview belonged to the growing category of medium-sized businesses (10 percent of all establishments) with sales of between $1 million and $2 million.

The overall market size in Canada was estimated at $630–650 million, and was dominated by local companies. The industry also generated some $120 million in foreign billings (mainly GIS hardware and software). Interestingly, export of services had traditionally been directed outside of North America and Europe, and concentrated in Africa, Asia, and the Middle East.

COMPETITION

Competition in the Canadian geomatics industry was on the increase. The overall economic climate, characterized by fiscal restraint in both the private and government sectors, had reduced the growth rate of the demand for services provided by the industry. As a result, geomatic companies, with their increased production capacities and reduced costs, had become more active in competing for the constant volume of business. This had resulted in a decrease in profitability. Overall industry profit levels were the same as in the early 1980s despite a doubling of overall industry demand.

GLOBAL OPPORTUNITIES OVERVIEW

By March 1994, Rick had spent considerable time reviewing global market opportunities for his company. He had taken a general look at several foreign markets, identifying such major factors as their overall size and growth prospects, political stability and entry barriers, competition, and the availability of funding for geomatic projects.

This step had resulted in rejecting the possibility of entering Western European markets, which—despite their size—were characterized by ferocious competition and limited growth prospects. Eastern Europe was felt to be too unstable politically (the countries of the former USSR), lacked funding, and was fragmented along national borders.

Rick also felt that the distances associated with dealing with markets in Southeast Asia and Oceania would put a significant strain on the company's financial and human resources, particularly in view of increasing competition from locally based companies. On the other hand, other Asian markets either lacked the size or financing required to support Airview's long-term involvement.

Finally, he decided that Sub-Saharan Africa, although in dire need of the services offered by Airview, was either dominated by companies from their former colonial powers, or could not afford any significant level of geomatics-related development, particularly in view of the declining level of support received from international financial institutions like the World Bank.

On the other hand, Rick found the characteristics of some of the remaining regions quite interesting. Consequently, he decided to concentrate his deliberations on these markets, which included North America (the United States and Mexico), Latin America, and the Arab World (North Africa and the Middle East).

AMERICAN MARKET

The U.S. market was somewhat different from its Canadian counterpart in that it had a larger proportion of geodetic and GIS firms among the 6,300 businesses in its geomatic industry. The larger proportion of geodetic firms in the United States was due to its higher population density, which increased the need for cadastral surveying. At the same time, faster adaptation of computers in a variety of industrial applications in the United States had stimulated demand for GIS applications and related services.

On the other hand, in view of the relative size of the U.S. and Canadian economies, the Canadian market was disproportionately large. The American market was estimated at $3 billion in 1994, only five times the size of its Canadian counterpart, or only half the relative difference in the size of the economies between the two countries. This disparity could be largely attributed to structural differences between the economies of the two countries. Canada's economy was largely dependent on the mineral and forestry sectors; both industries supported a high level of geomatic activity.

The demand for geomatics services in the U.S. market was growing at a 15 percent annual rate, and was particularly dynamic in the areas of airborne photography and (satellite) remote sensing, digital conversion of existing data, and consulting.

Access to U.S. Markets.   In 1994, there were few tariff obstacles when entering the U.S. market. Previously existing barriers related to licensing and local presence requirements were being removed as a result of the passage of the North American Free Trade Agreement. In some cases, Canadian companies who had succeeded in penetrating the U.S. market indicated that it had been easier for them to cross the national border than to overcome provincial barriers within their home country.

Although there had been some opportunities in the U.S. geomatics market during the 1980s, Canadian firms had traditionally been reluctant to pursue them. For aerial surveying companies like Airview, one of the reasons was the fact that aircraft maintenance and licensing requirements were much more lenient in the United States than they were in Canada. As a result, a company operating an aircraft out of Canada was not able to compete with American firms on price if there was any significant amount of flying time involved. Although these differences still remained, the recently falling value of the Canadian dollar had all but nullified the cost advantage previously enjoyed by U.S. companies.

In general, the level of competition in the United States was not much different from that in Canada except that the American firms, particularly the larger ones, marketed their services much more aggressively than their Canadian counterparts.

User Segments.   It was estimated that local and state governments accounted for some 25 percent of the total U.S. market for geomatics products and services, and that close to half of all local/state budgets allocated to the acquisition of geomatic services was allocated for data capture purposes.

The greatest potential lay with the 39,000 municipal/county governments. A trend to modernize land records and registration systems which document the 118 million land parcels in the United States was the most significant factor in stimulating the demand for data capture, their conversion into a digital format, their subsequent analysis, and graphical presentation.

The average contract performed for local/state governments ranged from $60,000 to $190,000 for aerial photography/photogrammetry services. Although the Northeast, Southeast, Southwest, and states bordering the Pacific Ocean accounted for the greatest demand, there was also an abundance of opportunities in the states closer to Airview's base, such as Minnesota (3,529 local government units), North Dakota (2,795), and South Dakota (1,767).

Federal government agencies represented the second largest user group, accounting for slightly less than 25 percent of the total U.S. geomatic market. Digital mapping was the major area of demand within this segment. This corresponded closely to Airview's principal area of expertise.

Contracts with the federal government ranged from $30,000 for surveying projects to $1.5 million for data digitizing projects. On average, they tended to be larger in size than those with state and local governments and were typically awarded to larger firms. As a result of the U.S. federal government policy of de-centralizing contracting for services, the demand from this user sector was spread across the country.

The third largest segment in the U.S. geomatic market was the demand from regulated industries, such as communication firms and gas and electric utility companies which traditionally generated between 20 percent and 25 percent of the overall U.S. demand for geomatic services. Customers from this category were in-terested in more cost-efficient management of the large infrastructures under their administration. Consequently, they had been among the early adopters of GIS technology, and their major thrust was in implementing AM/FM (Automated Mapping and Facilities Management) systems, which combined digital maps with information on the operation of their facilities.

The utilities market for geomatic services was spread across the United States, with the size closely related to the population density of individual regions. These regional markets were dominated by large companies, such as Baymont Engineer-ing and AT&T, which—due to economies of scale—became very price competitive in catering to the utility sector.

Finally, the rest of the demand for geomatic services came from the private sec-tor, with the most significant segments being the resource industries, mining and forestry. The rate of adoption of GIS technology in this sector was rather slow, and remote sensing of data and basic mapping were the primary services contracted out by resource companies.

THE MEXICAN GEOMATICS MARKET

Overview.   By the early 1990s, Mexico had developed significant capabilities in geomatics. Between 40,000 and 50,000 people were employed in all surveying and mapping related disciplines. Yet, in view of the country's problems with rapid urbanization, deforestation, and land use change, local demand for geomatics products and services in the early 1990s exceeded the available supply in some product and service categories.

The primary demand for geomatics services in Mexico was created by carto-graphic agencies of the federal and state governments. The National Institute of Statistics, Geography, and Informatics (INEGI) had the primary responsibility for integrating the country's geographical data, carrying out the national mapping project, and developing the National Geographic Information System.

Each state in Mexico was responsible for undertaking and maintaining a land survey of its territory and maintaining land cadastre. Therefore state markets were the second largest in volume after the federal market.

Several large municipalities also purchased geomatics products and services. In 1993–94, they were in the process of establishing databases of property boundaries, partly in cooperation with SEDESOL (Directorate of Cartography and Photogrammetry) under the One Hundred Cities Program.

The private sector was also a significant user of spatially referenced information. PEMEX, the state oil monopoly, was by far the largest of those users. It was also in the strongest position to acquire the most technologically advanced products and services in this area.

The total size of the Mexican market for geomatics services in 1993 was estimated at between $160 million and $200 million.

There were two cycles which affected the volume of geomatics work available in Mexico. First, there was the annual rainy season (June to September) during which the inclement weather had a negative impact on aerial surveying. Second, there was the change in Mexico's presidency every six years. As government agencies were the main purchasers of geomatic services, the political environment had a profound effect on business. In general, the first three years of any presidency resulted in minor projects, while the final three years were noted for major works.

The demand for geomatics services in Mexico was increasing. In addition, most Mexican companies competing for this business were interested in foreign participation, particularly if these relationships carried with them better technology and more modern equipment.

Mexico offered a significant operating benefit to Canadian aerial photography firms in that its weather patterns (the rainy season between May and September) counterbalanced those in Canada. This could enable Canadian exporters to utilize their aircraft and photographic equipment during the slow season in Canada (December–March).

Competition.   The Mexican geomatics industry was well developed in the traditional areas of ground surveying and cartography. However, its technological and human resource capabilities in the more technical areas, such as digital mapping and GIS, were generally limited.

In the area of aerial mapping and surveying, there were about 20 companies, located principally in Mexico City. Six of these companies owned their own aircraft, and dominated the national market. The remaining 14 were quite small, did not have their own aircraft, and were fairly new to the industry.

Market Access.   Public tender was the normal method for obtaining projects in Mexico. Most tenders were open to all companies, but some were by invitation only. The tendency was for contracts to go to those companies that had their own aircraft and the proper equipment. Subcontracting was a popular way for smaller companies to obtain a portion of larger projects.

If a foreign company was awarded a contract, it had to obtain permission from the state geography department and from the Mexican Defense Department. In addition, until 1996, foreign companies were not allowed to operate aircraft over Mexican territory without local participation.

THE LATIN AMERICAN GEOMATICS MARKET

In the early 1990s, the geomatics market in Latin America was at an early stage of transition from traditional to digital technologies for data capture, analysis, and storage. Although general awareness of GIS and remote sensing was widespread, their adoption was largely limited to international resource exploration companies and some public institutions.

The market for geomatics products and services was dominated by the public sector on both the supply and demand sides. However, the private sector was becoming the primary growth area, particularly in the resource sector (agriculture, forestry, mining, and energy), where significant investment programs created demand for cadastral surveying, mapping, and GIS. This demand potential, in turn, was providing a growth opportunity for the local surveying and mapping industry. This industry had traditionally been dominated by government organizations (mostly military-controlled), that over the previous few years had gained a significant degree of business autonomy and were actively competing in both local and international markets.

International Financial Institutions (IFIs), such as the World Bank and the Inter-American Development Bank, were very active in Latin America. Their major concern was economic development of the region, thus they concentrated on the less-developed nations of the region. The IFIs recognized the importance of infrastructure projects and their geomatics components and provided financial support for such basic services as topographic and property mapping and cadastral information systems. As a result of this fundamental focus, the geomatics contract activity was not confined to the more economically advanced countries of the region. From the point of view of foreign-based geomatics companies attempting to enter the Latin American market, the IFI-sponsored contracts provided a very attractive opportunity since they were open for public tender.

It was anticipated that the Latin American market for geomatics products and services would grow significantly in the near term. Over the 1993–98 period, the total demand for geomatics products and services in the region was anticipated in the range of US$650 million and US$1,500 million (the low and high estimates).

The provision of spatial information and its conversion to a digital format, as well as the delivery of GIS applications and the provision of training to local staffs, constituted the major demand area, expected to comprise three-quarters of the region's market.

Geographic Distribution.   Brazil was by far the largest market for geomatics products and services, with an estimated 50 percent of the total demand in the region.

Argentina, with the second largest territory and population in the region, was also the second largest market for geomatics products and services, accounting for 20 percent of Latin American demand.

Chile, with its significant resource sector, was the third significant geomatics market in the region with a 5 percent share of total demand.

Interestingly, Bolivia, with its relatively small population and economy, had a disproportionately large market for geomatics products and services (4 percent of the overall demand).

The other 13 countries of the region shared the remaining 21 percent of the Latin American market, with Venezuela and Colombia leading the group.

Competition.   By the 1990s, Latin American companies had developed substantial capabilities in the areas of surveying and mapping. The mapping sector in the region had originated from the military and until recent years had been protected from foreign competition by trade barriers. Consequently, the capabilities of local firms were significant, particularly in larger countries such as Brazil and Argentina. More significantly, larger surveying and mapping companies had already invested in digital mapping technology and remote sensing. With their developed expertise and low labour and overhead costs, these firms had a significant advantage over their competitors from North America, Europe, and Australia. Their knowledge of the local market was an additional factor placing them ahead of competitors from other continents.

Larger Brazilian and Argentinean firms had used this advantage to penetrate the markets of the smaller countries of the region. Since each national market was characterized by wide fluctuations in demand, the markets in other countries provided them with an opportunity to stabilize and, possibly, expand their sales.

In view of this situation, service firms from outside the region had to compete on the basis of their technological and managerial advantage. Large-scale projects, possibly involving digital imaging, provided the best opportunity to compete with local companies.

Despite all these impediments to foreign participation in the Latin American market, European companies had succeeded in capturing a significant share of the region's business. Their success was built on the strong business network established in the region by their home countries. Their penetration strategy was to establish their presence initially (through international assistance programs and the provision of training and education), and then to develop ties with local government agencies and companies from the private sector. European firms were also characterized by their ability to form consortia to pursue larger contracts. These consortia combined European technology and equipment with local labour and market experience.

American firms had obtained a significant degree of penetration of these markets for GIS hardware and software. However, their presence in the other sectors was less pronounced, probably due to their uncompetitive cost structure.

Australian geomatics firms involved in Latin America were typically affiliated with Australia's mining and forestry companies active in resource exploration activities in the region.

THE ARAB WORLD (NORTH AFRICA AND THE MIDDLE EAST)

Countries of the Arab World were characterized by the dominance of their oil and gas industries as the market for geomatics-related projects. Their economies and political systems were relatively stable and provided a good foundation for establishing long-term penetration plans by a foreign geomatics company. In terms of economic development, countries in this region were less dependent on international aid than was the case of the countries of Latin America. Consequently, their approach to the development of topographic, cadastral, and administrative mapping was based more on long-term planning.

With generally higher levels of resource allocation, countries of this region had developed their own companies, typically originating from the national cartographic agencies. In the early 1990s, these agencies still dominated the industry in the region, employing from 30 percent to 60 percent of the total number of personnel working in the geomatics field. However, their role had been steadily declining over the past few years.

At the same time, the level of saturation of the industry with locally-based manpower differed significantly among individual countries. Egypt, Iran, Jordan, Kuwait, Lebanon, Qatar, Syria, and Tunisia each had a substantial number of local specialists in the field (relative to their populations and territory), whereas Algeria, Libya, Iraq, Saudi Arabia, and Yemen had rather limited geomatics capability. Even more significantly, this latter group also had a relatively low proportion of geomatics specialists with a university education.

The combined market size for geomatics services in the region was estimated at between $400 million and $600 million in the commercial sector. Some of the markets restricted foreign access. Libya and Iraq, for example, were not open to Canadian companies. Also Syria, with its militarized economy, was of limited attractiveness to Canadian companies.

Iran was the country with the best opportunity for geomatics firms. The climate for Canadian firms was favourable due to Canada's position as a politically noninvolved country and the technological advancement of the Canadian geomatics industry.

Major opportunities in Iran were associated with several national development programs in the areas of energy production (construction of hydroelectric and nuclear power stations and upgrading the country's power distribution system); expansion of the mining industry (production of iron ore, copper, aluminum, lead/zinc, and coal); the oil and gas sectors; and construction of the country's railway system.

Kuwait and Saudi Arabia had traditionally been the target markets for several Canadian geomatics firms. The expansion of the two countries' oil production and refining capacity had triggered major investment outlays in both countries (for a total of over $20 billion between 1992 and 1994) and would continue (albeit at a slower rate) for a number of years. These two national markets were dominated by American companies and any penetration effort there would require cooperation with Canadian firms from the construction, mining, or oil and gas sectors.

Tunisia represented an example of a country which had developed its own expertise in the area of cartography, which in turn had created demand for external assistance in the provision of more sophisticated products and services, such as digital mapping and GIS applications.

Egypt represented yet another type of geomatics market in the region. Its major thrust was now on environmental concerns. The country had developed an environmental action plan which addressed problems with water and land resources management, air pollution, marine and coastal resources, and global heritage preservation, all of which had a significant geomatic component. The cost of implementing phase 1 of the plan was estimated at some $300 million over the period of 1993–1995.

Egypt also provided opportunities created by a $3 billion power generation and distribution project, and some $2 billion in construction projects associated with the expansion of the country's gas production and oil processing capacity. Although the majority of work in the geomatics-related field was conducted by local companies, subcontracting opportunities were significant.

Egypt was also a significant market from another perspective. Historically, Egypt had exported its geomatics expertise to other Arab states. Consequently, penetration of this market could be used to leverage access to other markets in the region, particularly in conjunction with Egyptian partners.

Market Evaluation.   In order to evaluate each of the four geographic regions from Airview's perspective, Rick developed a summary of the primary characteristics of each market under consideration. This summary is presented in Exhibit 2.

He also reviewed several ways of establishing Airview's presence in the regional/national markets, as indicated in Exhibit 3.

Discussion.   Regarding the choice of Airview's optimum target area, Rick assumed that once he had arrived at a sensible, coherent marketing plan, Airview could apply for financial support from the government. In fact, he had already discussed this possibility with Western Economic Diversification (WED) and the Federal Business Development Bank (FBDB). In addition, he could expect some assistance from the Program for Export Market Development if he chose to establish an office or participate in bidding for projects in a selected market. This assistance could cover 50 percent of the cost of travel and setting up a permanent foreign office.

His overall concerns included not only the immediate costs of implementing his marketing plan but also the process he should use to select the best market in view of its salient characteristics and the company's goals.

Rick's view of the American market was generally positive. His major concern was with price competition from local firms and possible fluctuations in the exchange rate, which over a short period of time might undermine Airview's cost structure. At the same time, he felt that Airview's technological advantage in the United States was less significant than in other markets. Finally, he assumed that his best opportunity south of the border would be in GIS–related areas, which would require either a substantial investment in obtaining greater expertise in this area or a joint effort with a GIS company.

The Mexican market was also viewed positively, particularly after the lifting of restrictions in 1996. However, Rick felt that due to the high cost of his staff, Airview would probably be competitive only in complex projects involving both data capture and their conversion into a computer format. At the same time, he was attracted by the operating advantages of having the company's flying season extended beyond the current few summer months.

EXHIBIT 2   **Market Review**

Characteristics	Market			
	United States	*Mexico*	*Latin America*	*North Africa and the Middle East*
Economic and political environment	Stable	Stabilizing	Stabilizing	Fluctuating
Access restrictions	None	Local agent required, no flying in Mexico	All mapping on-site in Brazil	Language, culture
Market size	Large	Small	Medium	Medium-large
Entry and operating costs	Low	Medium	Medium	Medium-high
Growth	Slow, stable	High	High	High
Financing	Cash, immediate	Transfer, delays	Transfer problems, IFI	Ranging from cash to IFI's financing
Contract procurement	Transparent, fair	Ambiguous, improving	Frequently ambiguous	Ambiguous
Major products	Digital mapping, GIS	Cadastral mapping, GIS	Topographic and cadastral mapping	Topographic mapping, surveying
Long-term advantage (technology, expertise)	Limited advantage	Diminishing, but not disappearing	Slowly diminishing	Sustainable
Primary customers	State and municipal governments	Federal and state governments	Federal governments, resource sector	Central cartographic agencies, resource sector
Pricing	Competitive, but based on high local costs	Competitive, based on low local costs	Extremely competitive, based on low local costs	Relatively high
Competition	Local, very high	Local, U.S high	Local, international, extremely high	Local, international, moderate
Entry strategies	Direct bidding, local partner	Local partner or subsidiary	Network of agents or local partner, IFI's projects	Local partner or agent, IFI's projects
Strategic advantages	Close, similar to the Canadian market	Entry to South America, technological advantage, active during Canadian slack	Technological fit, active during Canadian slack	Technological advantage, growing, less competition, long-term prospects
Expansion opportunities	GIS consulting systems, integration	Acquisition of local subsidiary	Training	CIDA project, Libya (with restrictions)

EXHIBIT 3   Airview Entry Strategies

Project Oriented Penetration

This is a strategy suitable for small, niche-oriented firms. The company would have to target a specific area and seek a specific contract. Involvement would be limited to the scope of the specific contract. The main barrier to this approach could be associated with local presence requirements.

Establishing a network of local agents in the countries of interest in the region may provide access to information on upcoming tenders and allow for participation in the binding process. Bidding for local contracts may serve as a foundation for establishing the company's presence in the region and could be treated as part of an entry strategy.

Subcontracting to Local Firms

This strategy offered the advantage of overcoming local presence restrictions.

Strategic Alliances

An alliance with a Canadian or foreign partner can work quite effectively provided the firms complement one another in resources and business philosophies.

Establishment of a Branch Office

This could be an effective way of overcoming local presence restrictions provided the firm was sufficiently financed to undertake the costs of setting up such an operation. The choice of location would also be crucial in determining the success of such a venture.

A Corporate Buyout

This seemed a somewhat risky proposition, requiring both adequate financing, business acumen to succeed, and lack of restrictions on foreign ownership of local companies. If successful, however, the result would be an immediate presence in the selected market.

Establishment of Head Office Outside of Canada

Although this could enable a company to access the selected market, this possibility could only be considered for large and stable markets, such as the United States.

Foreign Ownership

Like the strategic alliance option, this could offer opportunities, particularly with U.S. firms, provided this route is in keeping with the long-term goals of the firm and the two firms are compatible.

Alliances with Local Geomatics Firms

An alliance with a local partner could be beneficial if based on the combination of local experience and inexpensive labour with Airview's equipment and data processing and mapping capabilities.

Joint ownership of a Local Company

Acquiring a local company in partnership with another Canadian company may provide some advantages if the partners' product lines complement each other. A provider of GIS software or system integrator may be a good candidate for joint ownership with Airview.

Latin America seemed to be too competitive to support Airview's solo entry. On the other hand, the region's fragmentation into many small national markets could prove challenging from an operating point of view. Rick felt that seeking an alliance with Canadian mining and resource companies, thereby successfully establishing their operations, might prove to be attractive, particularly if Airview's entry could be supported by the provision of some elements of GIS. As in Mexico's case, the countries of Latin America provided the possibility of operating the company's aircraft during the Canadian off-season.

Finally, Rick regarded the markets of the Arab World with particular interest. Airview would definitely have a technical advantage over its local competitors in these markets. At the same time, pricing in this region seemed to be generally less competitive than in the other areas, whereas the similarity of the individual national markets, in most cases based on the demand created by the resource sector, would allow for gradual penetration of the region. At the same time, Rick realized that Airview's lack of experience in international markets in general, and in the Arab World in particular, would create a very challenging situation for the company's staff.

CASE 5
GRAPHISOFT: THE ENTRY OF A HUNGARIAN SOFTWARE VENTURE INTO THE U.S. MARKET

In Budapest on a sunny summer day in 1990, Gabor Bojar reflected on the history of his ten-year-old company, Graphisoft. His feet on the desk, the entrepreneur pondered his most critical decision—how to successfully penetrate the Western market, especially the United States.

COMPANY HISTORY

Graphisoft dates from 1980, when a group of enterprising mathematicians in Budapest established one of the first private ventures in Hungary. They were collectively disenchanted with the inefficient, bureaucratic operation of the country's large corporations. Most distressing to them was the widespread practice of employing and advancing the incompetent, because as skilled technicians this practice significantly diminished their prospects.

As did other Hungarian private partnerships, the firm suffered from a lack of both capital and credit, but certainly not from a lack of enthusiasm and endurance. Unlike most of their enterprising compatriots, these partners completely eschewed state support, opting instead to work longer and harder for themselves. This may have been the defining difference between Graphisoft and the few other Hungarian entrepreneurial ventures.

Due to the oversupply of good engineers and mathematicians at that time in Hungary it was frequently more difficult to get a good housekeeper than a good software specialist. Nonetheless, in the early 1980s, software development was among the most fashionable of private business ventures. The fashionability resulted from respect for entrepreneurial innovation and creativity rather than respect for access to infrastructure or depth of capital.

The company's first stroke of good luck came at the end of 1982 when the Hungarian Ministry of Industry approached Graphisoft seeking an advanced computer-aided design model for the Paks Nuclear Power Plant. Its construction having already been delayed for three years, the ministry was anxious to see some progress. However, no Hungarian company could hope to win such a bid because the necessary design products were high on the COCOM list.

Taking on the project would constitute a significant change of direction for the young Graphisoft. This was the first "handicap" the company turned to its benefit. Defying the odds, Graphisoft (a partnership of only two at the time) bet

Source: This case was prepared by Professor Robert D. Hisrich, Case Western Reserve University, U.S.A. and Professor Janos Vecsenyi, International Management Center, Hungary, to form the basis for class discussion rather than to illustrate either effective or ineffective handling of a business situation. The case was sponsored by the European Foundation for Enterpreneurial Research (EFER). Copyright © 1991, EFER. Not to be altered or reproduced without permission.

it all on their ability to generate a workable design model and the fact that the Ministry of Industry would take a long time to process all the bids. They hoped to develop a completed program in the interim while the other, much larger firms would still be struggling with prices and uncertain deadlines. What ended up being a tremendous development effort was initially self-financed by Graphisoft only through credit from friends and the pawnshop.

The result was a new program called RADAR. It was worth the risk. Big money flowed to Graphisoft right away, and it was able to pay its debts, pay the "wages" of the principals, and still have enough left over to reinvest in the RADAR program itself.

Most of Graphisoft's success can be attributed to Mr. Bojar's outlook. He reflects, "To leave the domestic market and start to compete on the Western market was a hard but challenging decision at the time. But I have considered myself always a sportsman who wanted to compete at the tennis tournament in Wimbledon or in Flushing Meadows rather than for the Budapest championship." In 1982, the future of the company seemed more secure if it could find a way to successfully export and bring necessary hard currency into Hungary. At that time, of course, it was impossible to foresee the major economic and political changes that were waiting just beyond the horizon.

ENTERING THE WEST EUROPEAN MARKET

Graphisoft invested its little remaining capital in marketing to the West. In the fall of 1983 the company displayed its three dimensional (3D) modeling program at a software exhibition in Munich, Germany. Mr. Bojar maintains that there was no intention to offer the program for sale; instead it was hoped that the program would demonstrate Graphisoft expertise and that as a result similar Western companies would offer them opportunities as "contributors." Mr. Bojar recalls that the Graphisoft program was running on a seven-year-old museum piece and "We saw much better programs than ours on the latest machines at the Munich exhibitions."

However, as luck would have it, Graphisoft's use of comparatively small-capacity computers turned out to be a blessing in disguise. The company was able to capitalize on the subsequent explosion in the professional use of personal computers. Western companies were offering similar systems on a more expensive basis, because they did not think the segment was promising. None of the Western companies foresaw the dramatic transformation, and consequently Graphisoft was ready and able to fill an unanticipated need. Demand was driven by hardware manufacturers looking for software capable of yielding spectacular and professional results running on small, inexpensive machines. According to Mr. Bojar, the president of Graphisoft, "This was no exceptional marketing foresight on Graphisoft's part that made the company choose an inexpensive machine; simply, the company did not possess a better alternative."

Since Apple II had been a major worldwide success, a more professional machine, Apple's Lisa, looked to be an excellent platform machine for 3D modeling. In spite of its power plant experience, Graphisoft thought that targeting the architects of smaller projects with its program, ArchiCAD, plus working in conjunction with Apple's proposed marketing of Lisa was the most promising marketing scheme. They felt this strategy was more beneficial for a small ambitious company going up against larger ones because the architectural marketplace was smaller, usually composed of only one or two purchasing decision makers. Large power plants, on the other hand, tended to be hierarchical with top management more readily influenced by name and reputation rather than by demonstration and application. The larger companies were not inclined to choose Graphisoft, nor were they initially prepared to choose Apple.

In an immense undertaking, Graphisoft debuted its first true personal computer 3D designing software at the 1984 Hannover Fair in Germany. The debut did not enjoy immediate success because Apple's Lisa was considered too expensive. However, Graphisoft gained a more successful entree in the Apple world through Lisa's successor, the Macintosh. Although the Macintosh was initially offered for nonengineering purposes, some Graphisoft applications were purchased with the new Apple machines. This inauspicious beginning spawned a network of business and trading partners all over Europe.

The coming years were lean, however. Many Western companies, impatient with Apple's long incubation period, changed over to the IBM platform. The disparity in living standards between Eastern and Western Europe exacerbated the difficulties. However, Graphisoft continued to expand its market due to the lower overhead costs and moderate living standards in Eastern Europe. The expansion was not reflected in sales, which remained low at only 50 to 100 packages annually and generated only a few hundred thousand deutsche marks. During this period ArchiCAD was refined and several other versions were developed, including TopCAD for engineering plant and pipework network design.

In order to market in Europe, Graphisoft found republishers in each country who developed the Graphisoft image, and organized a marketing and sales network partly at their own risk. The republishers, as distributors, collected and coordinated the dealers. George Kafka, vice president for marketing, explains, "In Switzerland we have an agent who knew almost all of the architects in the country and saw an opportunity to establish his own business for marketing and distributing ArchiCAD." However, it sometimes took years to find the right people in each country.

At the end of 1987, a new Apple high-performance engineering-capable machine, Macintosh II, finally came to the market. By this time, with 20 highly skilled and capable software specialists ready to work, Graphisoft was ideally situated to take advantage of the opportunity. ArchiCAD was the first program to rely on the enhanced capacity of Macintosh II, making full use of its inherent advantages.

With the advent of the Macintosh II, Graphisoft blossomed. In 1988 about 1,000 ArchiCAD programs were sold and that figure was nearly doubled in 1989 with the sale of almost 2,000 programs worldwide. Most of the sales were in France,

Germany, Switzerland, Italy, and other European countries. Additional sales were made in Australia, Korea, Taiwan, Malaysia, Indonesia, Hong Kong, the United Arab Emirates, Israel, Canada, and the United States.

In 1989 Graphisoft had become the market leader in Apple architectural design systems in Western Europe with some 40 percent of the market. This success came despite ArchiCAD's higher price and relative obscurity with respect to other brands like AutoCAD, VersaCAD, or Integraph.

In Italy, ArchiCAD became (and still remains) the leading software running on the Macintosh. Similar success occurred in France, in the Benelux, in Switzerland, and in Germany. In 1988 Graphisoft announced TopCAD, a program aimed at the high-end in two dimensional (2D) design. TopCAD features a vast array of tools and functions that is paralleled only in programs running on much larger workstations and mainframes. Initial reception and sales promised that TopCAD would achieve the same popularity among engineers and tool designers as ArchiCAD had achieved with architects.

ENTERING THE U.S. MARKET

Entry into the U.S. market became Graphisoft's most significant milestone. By this time Mr. Bojar wanted it all: "We wanted to be closer to the fire, no matter how much it would cost. We recognized that a software company which wants to be a global competitor should gain a foothold in the Silicon Valley. When our previous partners threw in the towel we decided to enter the ring." As an exercise in the marketing process, he compiled the following list of positive and negative aspects of tackling the U.S. market.

The positive aspects include:

- The United States currently comprises one-half to two-thirds of the world market; therefore, Graphisoft cannot be first in the world without a U.S. presence.
- The overwhelming majority of similar firms operate in the Silicon Valley. Proactive networking requires a physical presence.
- Emphasis should continue on developing the special relationship with Apple, both with technical/developer support and with marketing.
- The U.S. computer market has the longest history and the deepest culture. As a result, it provides prime market feedback.
- The United States has the most advanced marketing techniques, thereby providing the best training and proving ground.
- Following the U.S. example will lead to progressive structural and operational changes for Graphisoft.

The negative aspects include:

- The European and Far-Eastern markets are growing more rapidly.
- The U.S. market has the most competition, and Graphisoft's lack of local knowledge puts it at a significant disadvantage.

- The physical distance makes it difficult to maintain an intensive connection.
- Marketing in the United States is expensive. It requires more investment capital since the desired profit/undertaken risk ratio is worse than it would be elsewhere. The usual share of income for the "developer firm" is less than the share for the "manufacturer firm."
- Success is doubtful. Most hi-tech European firms entering the United States have come out croppers.
- Graphisoft has twice underestimated its requisite investment and realistic profitability horizons. There is no objective guarantee the U.S. estimates will be more accurate (even when accounting for lessons learned).
- As is typical in Europe, Graphisoft's financial stability is ensured by a lack of substantial human capital investment. As the foregoing list makes clear, marketing in the United States requires a substantial human capital investment.

Tackling the U.S. project proved to be less than smooth. Emulating the successful European pattern, the company enlisted the service of an Israeli firm, and then a French firm to handle the republishing work. Neither firm could make a go of it. Nonetheless, they did establish Graphisoft and its products with the professional journals. Messrs. Bojar and Kafka soon realized the U.S. market posed a different problem requiring a new solution. They decided Graphisoft needed to act independently and to begin selling in its own name.

Messrs. Bojar and Kafka landed in San Francisco on January 18, 1989, for the Macworld trade show at the end of the month. They jumped right in, renting a car, an office, and an apartment, and then printing brochures and business cards. By May they had $52,000 in sales. Most of the sales came after their showing at the American Institute of Architects trade show and a favorable review of their product, ArchiCAD. In the review, Don Pecham, an engineer, and Martin Ramsey, an architectural consultant, gushed over it: "ArchiCAD from Graphisoft is like an architect's dream come true. Far and away, first place would have to be ArchiCAD." The rest, as they say, is history.

Today, Graphisoft has over 60 full-time employees and some 40 consulting or development engineers. The Graphisoft team has branched to include marketing experts, salespeople, and office managers. In addition to engineers, the company employs several architects and mechanical designers to ensure the highest levels of functionality and competence. Although most of the research and development occurs in Budapest, personnel constantly rotate to offices abroad to customize products to fit local rules and to tailor marketing efforts.

The company is headquartered in Budapest. Its equity remains split among the still-working principals. It is also the exclusive Hungarian Apple representative. The international office, Graphisoft GmbH Germany, is located in Munich. The Munich office supports satellite offices in San Francisco and Toronto which in turn spearhead the North American marketing efforts. Graphisoft also has a worldwide network of financially independent professional dealers and local distributors.

Products.   The company presently sells two packages, ArchiCAD and TopCAD. While both are high-priced products due to their quality, they are much cheaper than comparable workstation products. Sales have doubled every year since 1984, reaching 3,000 units in 1990. However, since the company is European, most of these sales come in Europe. Nevertheless, it has continued to devote considerable effort to increasing U.S. market presence and sales.

Over six years in production and development, ArchiCAD is a high-end and comprehensive architectural solution designed to think and work like an architect. It integrates 3D modeling and parametric techniques rendering with 2D drafting and flexible quantity take-offs to generate accurate cost estimates.

TopCAD is a high-end 2D CAD solution running on Macintosh for those users who need precision, advanced editing, associative dimensioning, 2D parametric, and other features normally found in workstation or mainframe programs.

THE CURRENT CONDITION OF GRAPHISOFT USA

From the start, the activity of the company has been characterized by uncertainty due to a lack of experience. It is clear the company, despite its best efforts, underestimated the cost and time requirements of entering the American market. The initial cost projection for the first year was $200,000 which was raised to $400,000. The American division was scheduled to become self-supporting by the end of 1990. (See Exhibit 1, where the present situation of Graphisoft USA is most clearly shown by the dollar costs and income figures.)

During its 19 months of operation, Graphisoft USA's total sales were $476,519, while total expenses were $864,644. Not reflected are travel and per diem expenses and Munich packing costs. Nor do they reflect the as yet unpaid developers' license fees. Graphisoft USA's total loss as of the end of July 1990 was about $550,000.

By the end of July 1990, the company had sold 150 programs to 101 clients. Additionally, 45 discounted dealer copies and 100 free copies were distributed. Nearly half (23) of the registered American dealers (45) did not sell programs. The remainder (22) had only seven or fewer sales each, spaced at regular monthly intervals.

Graphisoft USA's history has had four stages: the start-up period (from January to August 1989), the growth period (September to October 1989), a continued sales period (November 1989 to July 1990), and a final period (August 1990 to the present).

One by one Graphisoft USA missed those periods with the highest potential for growth. The company admits that its allocation of resource decisions were flawed. In retrospect, hiring a secretary, telemarketing teams to "work on" and follow up with interested parties, and a sales network was necessary from the start. Additionally, it would have been desirable to have Americanized the company at that time.

Some objective critiques of Graphisoft's American venture follow.

EXHIBIT 1   **Sales and Cost Data**

	Sales	Costs
January 1989	—	13,404
February 1989	2,765	12,850
March 1989	1,681	26,598
April 1989	—	29,410
May 1989	3,140	45,116
June 1989	16,057	13,057
July 1989	18,642	28,503
August 1989	10,085	51,085
September 1989	52,385	33,990
October 1989	32,995	24,993
November 1989	31,467	35,701
December 1989	34,308	75,514
January 1990	31,300	38,329
February 1990	47,960	41,907
March 1990	34,021	45,907
April 1990	38,390	87,345
May 1990	31,986	45,907
June 1990	44,090	87,345
July 1990	45,247	71,414

Positive Features.   The products have a good reputation and are known all over the United States. The professional level of technical support is outstanding in comparison to that of its competitors.

Graphisoft USA's employees are favorably judged. (Tom Harris addressed the company stating, "You have a sincere, dedicated, and intelligent group of employees.")

Negative Features.   The sales channel is weak. The publicity campaign was overdone considering the capacity of the sales channel. Client follow-up and the dealer networks are inadequate. The shabby appearance of the office, stand, and brochures give the impression of an underfinanced company. Language problems, concerns about alien status, and some behaviors have created some barriers to success.

The company's neglect of regular telemarketing follow-up, lack of an intensive exchange of views with dealers, lack of review of their control and reporting obligations, and not maintaining daily contacts with Apple are the most troubling shortcomings. Similarly, unwise staff and organizational expenditures demonstrate other notable deficiencies in the project's implementation. Technical support people and sales representatives still work 11–12 hours per day despite the team's expansion to seven members. At present, technical background and office problems are only moderately solved. Graphisoft USA is understaffed—a conclusion supported by comparing the output generated by similarly sized staffs supporting company operations in France and Italy. Staff expenditures in Germany are lower still.

The foregoing litany of shortcomings would apply for the final period, but for the establishment of the first ArchiCAD User Club. Rose N. Williams, the club's general manager, brought considerable experience in sales organization as did other professionals employed by the club.

The Size of the American Market.   The size of the American market is defined by its overall customer base, the market for Macintosh CAD, and marketplace trends. The U.S. ArchiCAD customer base is composed of small architect design companies, builders, and interior designers. Some general figures on this group are listed below:

Number of architects, interior designers, and builders	300,000
Approximate number of firms	100,000
Percent of computer users	75%
Percent of Macintosh users	14%
Percent of CAD users (on any computer)	22%

The figures are collective averages only. Within the first group of architects, designers, and builders, more than three times as many architects use Macintosh (28 percent) and CAD (49 percent) than do builders. Homebuilders, the clients whose professional demands are best met by ArchiCAD, barely use Macintosh (8 percent) or CAD (13 percent).

The Macintosh CAD Market.   In 1989, a total of 35,000 Macintosh CAD programs were sold in North America. This figure accounts for roughly 65 percent of CAD programs sold worldwide (Europe accounts for 29 percent while the Pacific Rim and elsewhere account for 6 percent).[1] Of the Macintosh CAD market, the architect segment represents about 40–45 percent of the total. The following table lists the number of programs sold worldwide, broken out by lines:

---

[1] Sales of MacDraw and MacDraft, the simplest drawing programs, were not taken into account, neither were visualizing programs (Zoom, Dynaperspective, Modelshop, Swivel 3D, or Stratavision). The estimates do not consider the former to be CAD products because of their simplicity and the latter because they cannot produce documentation that meets the demands of industrial design (permit, construction, composition, or other production designs). Visualizing programs are widely used in the Macintosh architect market. In 1988, 1,000 units were sold, while in 1989, 600 were sold, roughly equaling the unit sales of CAD programs priced over $2,000. The sources for the data are: *CAD-CAM, CAE Users 1990: Current Applications and Future Directions* (CAD-CAM Publishing Inc., 1990).

	1986	1987	1988	1989
Architecture	2,200	4,800	13,500	22,000
Mechanical engineering	1,800	3,200	9,800	17,000
Electronics	2,370	2,900	3,100	7,700
Others	355	907	2,200	8,300

Since 65 percent of worldwide sales were made in North America, it follows that about 14,300 Macintosh architect CAD programs were sold in 1989. Market division is normally done on the basis of price categories. The best differentiation divides programs into three groups: those costing less than $1,000, those costing between $1,000 and $2,000, and those costing over $2,000. Based on the number of sales, architect Macintosh CAD programs costing more than $2,000 account for 22 percent of the total market, while income bases to 56 percent of it. According to assessments of the American market, 3,150 Macintosh architect CAD programs priced over $2,000 were sold in 1989.

Trends.   The American architecture industry has been in recession, and as a result many firms have been reluctant to make purchases. However, 31 percent of architects and 21 percent of builders intend to purchase CAD programs in the next two years. Projecting this figure to the ratio of those already using CAD translates to a 66 percent increase in the number of architects and a 160 percent increase in the number of builders using CAD in the next two years.

The Macintosh architect CAD market has increased threefold after the introduction of programs designed for Macintosh II in 1987. It has been growing ever since, albeit at a decreasing rate, exceeding the 10–20 percent annual increase of the CAD market as a whole. The approximate growth rates are listed below:

Year-over-Year Period	Percentage of Macintosh Architect CAD	Percentage Priced over $2,000
1987	100%	—
1987–88	190	75%
1988–89	65	57
1989–90	54	51
1990–91	41	38
1991–92	28	21

Apparently growth is slower for those programs priced over $2,000, probably due to competition from visualizing programs. Although it is one of the most essential services of the expensive CAD programs, photorealistic visualization can be inexpensively achieved. The data displayed above and below indicate the market for these products is less than halfway saturated.

Year Period	Number of Macintosh Architect CAD Units Sold	Number of Units Sold That Were Priced over $2,000
1986	1,480	—
1987	2,990	1,140
1988	8,700	2,000
1989	14,300	3,146
1990	22,100	4,750
1991	31,200	6,000
1992	40,000	8,000

Using an average price of $3,500 per unit, Macintosh architect CAD programs similar to ArchiCAD had a U.S. market capitalization of about $70 million between 1990 and 1991.

THE ArchiCAD MARKET SITUATION

The European Market.   As a benchmark for Graphisoft USA it is important to examine Graphisoft's 1989 European results. The company sold a total of 1,200 ArchiCADs in Europe that year. Europe accounted for 29 percent, about 6,400 units, of the 22,000 Macintosh architect programs sold the world over in 1989. Worldwide, some 22 percent of the market consisted of programs priced over $2,000. Therefore, it seems that the total European market universe for ArchiCAD would be around 1,400 units (22 percent of 6,400). This figure seems impossible since Graphisoft's European market share would then be some 85 percent of the Macintosh architect CAD programs priced over $2,000 (1,200 as 85 percent of 1,400).

Inexpensive and medium-priced American programs (such as VersaCAD, Mini-CAD, Claris, VELLUM, Dreams, DesignCAD, PowerDraw) also have a share of the European market. CAD is a more exclusive tool in Europe than it is in the United States, and its price range is higher, so products priced over $2,000 still have the major share of the European market. It is known from the statements of Apple and Gimeor that about 800 Macintosh architect programs were sold in Europe that year by Gimeor, a French company started in 1987, and that about the same amount were sold by AutoCAD and MicroStation.

Despite the ambiguous statistics it is reasonable to assume that half of the 6,400 units sold were priced over $2,000. In light of this assumption, ArchiCAD captured about 40 percent of the 1989 European market.

The American Market.   In the United States, ArchiCAD has two main competitors, AutoCAD and Architron. The following is a brief comparative listing of the two competitors.

AutoCAD.   Technically, the Macintosh version of AutoCAD differs in five main respects from ArchiCAD:

1. The degree of integration.
2. Degree of tailoring to the user.
3. Adjustment to Macintosh standards.
4. Mode of 3D modeling.
5. The connection of design and construction.

The first three directly affect the simplicity of product use. ArchiCAD is a "Macintosh-like" architect target program which integrates plan drawing, 3D modeling, and materials listing. However, from a marketing perspective, Auto-CAD has considerable advantages:

1. AutoCAD is the CAD standard in the IBM milieu.
2. AutoCAD is strong in "third-party" connections. In other words, the standard symbol libraries of the electronics, mechanical engineering, and architectural design industry segments have been made primarily for AutoCAD. DXF is the most widely used CAD design communication standard.
3. Autodesk has been the most rapidly growing U.S. software producer for five years and therefore is a recent big entrepreneurial success story.
4. As a result of this success, AutoCAD is popularized by the media and by word-of-mouth of professionals.

Despite all this, Graphisoft dealers also handling AutoCAD report that Archi-CAD has greater sales worldwide. Other evidence of AutoCAD's apparent recession is given by Autodesk's absence at the two recent Macworld Expos. Data shows that many people marginally sophisticated in designing choose to use CAD programs. As a result, many of these programs cannot be functionally refined.

MacArchitron.   There are several major differences between MacArchitron and ArchiCAD:

1. Degree of integration.
2. Basic mode of design (in plan drawing or 3D modeling).
3. Process of user interface and design.
4. Quality of rendering.

Contrary to ArchiCAD, MacArchitron is modular, with listing, 3D rendering, and plan drawing occurring in three separate modules. One marketing problem stems from the ease with which impressions can be created in 2D rendering suggesting that MacArchitron is a superior product. Although MacArchitron is a function-rich 2D model, Graphisoft steadfastly maintains that ArchiCAD is superior in both 2D and 3D rendering.

Although Gimeor has outsold Graphisoft in the United States, selling about 500–600 units, it has only covered between three and five percent of the total Macintosh architect market (or about 15–20 percent of the priced-over-$2,000 market). Both products seem to enjoy a simultaneous market dominance, as almost all publications discuss them both ("What is worth buying now"), with equal emphasis.

However, last fall MacArchitron created its own network of full-time sales representatives, sparing no expense. As a result the company estimates that it is selling 100 units per month. As compared to Graphisoft it seems they are better organized, are more "American," and have a more attractive market presence. Their technical support is capable of loading whole designs, convincing to some important buyers. As a general rule buyers are reluctant to go with smaller European firms because they fear the companies will go out of business. This tendency also gives Gimeor an edge.

A conclusion by MacWEEK is illustrative: "Leading players have failed to convince users of the benefits of using a dedicated CAD program. . . . Among companies that produce final drawing on Mac, 40 percent are using MacDraw II, followed by Claris CAD (28 percent) and AutoCAD (25 percent)." Although Graphisoft's present market share is minimal, some moderate estimates suggest its sales could top $70 million over the next three years, within its limited market segment. Although its marketing has been weaker than that of its competitors, ArchiCAD is a technically superior product. There is sufficient room in the market to beat rivals with greater sales since less than half the market has been saturated and none of the competitors has acquired oppressive dominance.

GRAPHISOFT USA'S GOALS FOR THE NEXT THREE YEARS

Based on its attained European position, Graphisoft should have 35 percent of the U.S. market share by the end of 1993. The following projected sales figures show the interim progress to that goal.

	1991	1992	1993
Market share	15%	25%	35%
Units (to be) sold	770	1,579	2,653
Monthly average	64	132	221
Turnover (sales)	$1,617,525	$3,315,900	$5,571,300

It is also advisable to convert Graphisoft USA's income data to a fiscal year (FY) basis. Their fiscal year runs from June 1 to May 31.

	Fiscal Year 1990–91	Fiscal Year 1991–92	Fiscal Year 1992–93
Turnover	$840,000	$2,400,000	$4,500,000

Economic Efficiency Calculations.   The cost projections listed on the next page are based on the experience from the past one and a half years. More detailed figures are presented in Exhibit 1.

	Fiscal Year 1990–91	*Fiscal Year 1991–92*	*Fiscal Year 1992–93*
Marketing	$348,000	$420,000	$ 901,000
Personal incomes	930,000	874,000	1,109,000
Overhead	406,000	697,000	1,101,000
Production	132,000	420,000	480,000

Comparing these costs with the projected income yields the following results:

	Fiscal Year 1989–90	*Fiscal Year 1990–91*	*Fiscal Year 1991–92*	*Fiscal Year 1992–93*
Turnover	$380,000	$840,000	$2,400,000	$4,500,000
Expenses	880,000	1,450,000	2,560,000	3,500,000
Profit (loss)	(500,000)	(610,000)	(160,000)	1,000,000

The break-even point for regular monthly investments occurs at the beginning of 1992. Prior to this time a total capital investment of $1,400,000 is required. Half will be spent from January 1989 to September 1990, and the remainder is to be spent to the end of 1992. The total investment cannot be expected to be recouped prior to May 31, 1993, since the accumulated financial statement for the period running from January 1, 1989 to May 31, 1993, still shows a loss of $300,000. Only the remaining investment of $700,000 will break even by May 31, 1993. From a purely financial perspective the American venture is not a good investment—other aspects of the business would have to justify the existence of Graphisoft USA.

FINANCIAL SITUATION

The company as a whole is in an excellent financial position, with strong liquidity. This position and its future direction reflects the customer base of Graphisoft in Europe as well as the United States. Exhibits 2 and 3 show the nonconsolidated income statements and balance sheets for year-end 1989 and 1990.

THE ORGANIZATION

Right from Graphisoft's inception, Mr. Bojar has worn several hats. He was the entrepreneur initiating the venture and putting up his personal financial resources to overcome some of the early cash flow difficulties. He was the software programmer, and he also had to assume the role of salesperson and manager. In subsequent years, as he hired professional programmers, he became the company's managing director. At that point he gave up programming and devoted

EXHIBIT 2   Graphisoft Hungary Income Statements

	Year Ended Dec. 31, 1989 in HUF (000)	Year Ended Dec. 31, 1990 in HUF (000)
Revenues		
License	59,874	149,912
Other	531	1,077
Total revenues	60,405	150,989
Expenses		
Materials	(534)	(389)
Wages	(5,717)	(8,551)
Social security costs	(1,162)	(2,948)
Depreciation	(1,101)	(1,378)
Other expenses	(49,823)	(99,343)
Other taxes	(663)	(15,136)
Profit	895	23,244
Profit brought forward	16,996	2,462
Total profit	17,891	25,706

EXHIBIT 3   Graphisoft Hungary Balance Sheets

	Year Ended Dec. 31, 1989 in HUF (000)	Year Ended Dec. 31, 1990 in HUF (000)
Assets		
Cash and bank account	7,918	25,199
Financial securities	—	1,175
Accounts receivables	6,974	17,268
Other receivables	—	2,132
Inventories	225	3,837
Total current assets	15,117	49,611
Fixed assets	6,576	3,375
Total assets	21,693	52,986
Liabilities		
Accounts payable to creditors	1,363	7,407
Accounts payable to others (tax, etc.)	754	873
Total liabilities	2,117	8,280
Equity		
Paid-in-capital	1,685	19,000
EBIT	17,891	25,706
Total equity	19,576	44,706
Total liabilities and equities	21,693	52,986

his attention to the overall control of the whole operation and to Graphisoft's marketing functions. Esther Dyson, in the *Harvard Business Review*[2] praised his acumen noting that, "Gabor Bojar is one of the more business-savvy people I encountered on my travels."

As the company's operations grew more complex several programmers became managers. George Kafka was one those programmers who was promoted as Graphisoft's marketing manager. Mr. Bojar recalls, "He was the best salesman of the programmers with an easygoing nature and good command of English and French. It was difficult for me to give him the span of control in one of my favorite fields. We together started the U.S. operation. And I have to admit that George did a great job." Imre Pakozdi, another programmer, became the all-round manager responsible for human resource management and internal coordination. However, he also prepared the first business plan for the U.S. penetration, and he bought and managed the reconstruction of the new office building in Budapest. He summarizes the Graphisoft philosophy as follows:

- Close connections with the products and with the customers.
- Employees dedicated to the products and to the company.
- Enthusiastic managers, dedicated to people and the products.
- Informal structure and personal relations.

Mr. Pakozdi credits Mr. Bojar with much of the success saying, "Everybody accepts the leadership of Gabor Bojar, who created a good, open atmosphere, excellent jobs, and good money for and with us."

Peter Hornung, a born engineer, was the only senior programmer willing to tackle the financing and accounting responsibilities. Mr. Hornung's comment is illustrative of the challenges he faces: "I learned a lot but I would appreciate a professional in the international financing." Istvan Tari, an outstanding software developer, was a partner from the very beginning. He advanced as the R&D director for ArchiCAD and TopCAD. Rose N. Williams advanced from the User Club to general manager of the Graphisoft USA office after Messrs. Bojar and Kafka left the San Francisco office. With so many people fulfilling so many roles, it was common for the employees to wonder about just who was in charge. Eva Bisztricsany, the office manager in Budapest, sums it up: "No one really knows who is competent in which decision; everybody is doing everything." Exhibit 4 illustrates the formal organizational structure.

THE FUTURE

Graphisoft is currently developing some exciting new products that should integrate well with both existing and future applications. The long range plans are to develop a family of high-end products bringing innovative solutions to existing

---

[2] Esther Dyson, "Micro Capitalism: Eastern Europe's Computer Future," *Harvard Business Review,* January–February (1991).

EXHIBIT 4   **Organization Chart of Graphisoft**

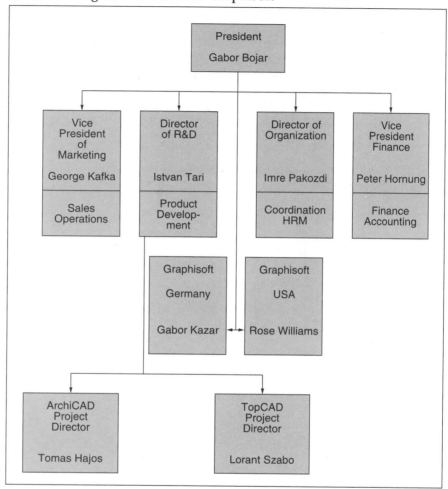

and potential CAD applications. The family of applications will address not only specific fields, but will also open doors to other applications produced by Graphisoft or by other producers. The strength of the personal computer resides in its ability to enable single users to work more productively: one machine, one user. However, the next challenge for developers will be to network these individual users. Developers at Graphisoft hope to integrate a number of networking and communications solutions that will allow the individual user to participate efficiently in networked group efforts. While the company sees development of future Apple products, they also plan to expand the number of potential users by broadening their base to incorporate non-Apple users. Some of these developments include the further development of ArchiCAD and TopCAD, adapting the software for other platforms, and producing software for similar computers and laptops.

The company's principal clients are small companies in America, France, Italy, and Switzerland. The three latter countries are also the best markets for Apple products. European automobile makers like Renault of France or Alfa Romeo of Italy; aircraft companies like Air France or Lockheed Aircraft; and entertainment companies like Disneyland are typical of the large company clients Graphisoft seeks.

With his feet still on the desk, Mr. Bojar thought about all of the foregoing as he contemplated the problems associated with entering the U.S. market. Mr. Kafka, vice president of marketing, interrupted Mr. Bojar's reverie, calling him to start the meeting on problems in marketing to America.

CASE 6
POWER BEAT INTERNATIONAL LIMITED

With the failure to consummate a successful licensing agreement for the manufacture and sale of its new invention—an innovative automobile battery—Mr Peter Witehira, the chief executive officer of Power Beat International, was faced with finding a way to commercialize the new technology. Apart from finding a new licensee or even building a factory to manufacture the battery on his own, he wondered what other options he could pursue.

THE AUTOMOBILE BATTERY

As late as 1987, the technology incorporated in the standard car battery had been virtually unchanged for 70 years. The standard automobile battery could well be the only item that could be taken out of a sixty-year-old car and placed into a new vehicle (though voltages had changed). By contrast, automobiles in the 1990s bore no resemblance to vehicles manufactured in those early years. No one had thought of producing a standard car battery that didn't go dead if the electrical components were left on for an extended period of time. Meanwhile, sophisticated automobile design and the demand for more accessories (such as radio, compact disk player, cell phone, power windows) were multiplying the electric load placed on batteries.

A lead-acid starter battery, referred to as Starting, Lighting, and Ignition, or SLI, battery, must provide electric power for starting in all conditions. Once the engine starts, the vehicle's alternator will recharge the battery, thus replacing the power used to start the engine. Two to three years was the average life for conventional SLI batteries—less if the unit was subjected to overcharging and/or repeated deep discharges because auxiliaries (such as the headlights) had been left on.

THE POWER BEAT BATTERY

The Power Beat battery was an alternative to the existing automotive batteries. All vehicles require at least two levels of power. High current is needed, temporarily, for starting a vehicle. Lower current is required for auxiliaries such as lights and radios, for extended periods of time. Recognizing this, the Power Beat battery used advanced lead-acid battery cells in an ingenious configuration. This battery supplied different current to match a vehicle's two different power needs. Thus, if lights, radio, ignition, or accessories were left on, only separate, heavy duty,

Source: This case was prepared by Rajib K. Sanyal, Trenton State College, Trenton, New Jersey, USA, as a basis for classroom discussion rather than to illustrate either effective or ineffective handling of an administrative situation. The author would like to thank Dr. Verl Anderson for introducing him to Mr. Peter Witehira.

rechargeable auxiliary cells were discharged that did not affect the starter portion of the battery. Therefore, the likelihood of the battery dying due to the lights or other accessories being left on was greatly reduced, if not eliminated.

Instead of the conventional six-cell design, this 12-volt battery used a 12-cell configuration split into two groups. One six-cell group, constructed from low-density, thin electrode plates, produced the fast, high-discharge current needed for engine cranking. The other six cells contained specially designed, double grid, high-density plates capable of withstanding repeated slow, deep discharge cycling, and thus provided needed power to the vehicle's accessories and electrical auxiliaries for much longer.

Controlling the operation of these two different six-cell groups was an integrated electronic control unit called the Discharge Management System (DMS). Through an electronic sensor, the DMS unit determined whether or not the vehicle was in use. If the vehicle was not in use, the sensor isolated the starting plates so they could not be discharged. The sensor reconnected the starting and auxiliary plates when the driver started the vehicle.

The lead-acid battery was now a standardized, mass produced, commodity-like product for the automobile industry. It was cheap to produce relative to its output of energy. The Power Beat battery, on the other hand, was a premium quality battery which cost more to produce and more to install than standard batteries. The new battery was assumed to last between 7 and 10 years, much longer than the common lead-acid battery.

PETER WITEHIRA, THE ENTREPRENEUR

There is probably a bit of Gyro Gearloose, a slightly bewildered eccentric inventor whose constant companion was a flying, talking light bulb and Donald Duck's mate, in every New Zealander. Given its remote geographical location and the pioneering spirit of its original settlers, New Zealanders developed a reputation as a nation of fixers, adapters, tinkerers, fiddlers, and modifiers. Peter Witehira belonged to that tradition and drew on a family heritage which was part Maori and part Scottish.

In school he was an average student. In 1966 at age 15, he left school and became an apprentice in the aluminium joinery industry. There he met Harry Dean, a tradesman who became not only his workmate but also his "buddy and mentor." Harry Dean taught the young Witehira the principles of pride in the job and of doing things properly.

Like most kids growing up in New Zealand in the 1960s, motor cars had a huge influence on Peter. As he said, "I loved cars. My first car was a one-owner, Ford Popular. I was just 15 and found it wasn't fast enough." The Popular was followed by a Humber 80 and then a Wolseley 6/90. "Cars really were a major factor in my life. I helped build hot rods. I got to know the local racing drivers and would traipse off to Pukekohe for all of the major race meetings."

In 1974, Peter became a police officer. Ten years later he quit at a time when the most radical economic and social changes in New Zealand were being ushered in.

After years of protectionism, the government opened up the economy. The country embarked on a roller coaster ride that saw fortunes made. Peter went into construction. "I was not only building houses but also designing them and about as busy as I could be. But there wasn't a lot of money in it. Because of the extreme competition, you had to keep profit levels low to get the work." In 1987, the stock market crashed. "The building boom was over. I wanted something new to do and decided to invent something. I didn't really know what it was that I wanted to invent, but I knew I had some potential in that area. I had earlier invented a scrambling device to stop people from copying videos."

The disciplines instilled in him by Harry Dean and as a police officer had played a strong part in developing his work ethic and now they really came to the fore. Always a keen reader, he now started reading anything and everything. "One book changed everything for me. It was called *Inventions That Changed the World.* There was a section that listed the ten inventions that the world still needed the most. The first four were medical inventions—cures for arthritis, for cancer, and so on. It was number five that interested me—the world needed a better battery. I thought that was something I could handle."

Witehira found that there were very few books about the principles of a battery. After reading all that he could, he decided to go about learning in the most direct way. He bought a brand new battery, took his hacksaw and cut the top off it and started prodding and poking and learning. "The principles were reasonably complex but I bought more batteries and cut them up and gradually got to the stage where I began to understand how they were constructed."

In his mind he had visualized the car battery as a "refrigerator—instead of storing food and milk, the battery was storing electric power. But to me it seemed car batteries were a refrigerator without a deep freeze unit. I began to think of ways to include the battery equivalent of a deep freeze unit—and that's where the concept of the Power Beat battery came from."

The Power Beat battery was invented by Peter Witehira, who obtained a U.S. patent for his invention in 1987. With that initial patent, he developed a crude prototype battery and had it approved by a government scientist in Auckland who gave a written letter confirming the system would work. Armed with that confirmation, and little else, Witehira approached friends and relatives who put up NZ$40,000 toward development costs. He now needed the support of a scientific body to test his prototypes. The positive attitude of the Hamilton-based University of Waikato's physics department so impressed him he moved his family—his wife and their six children—to Hamilton.

POWER BEAT INTERNATIONAL LIMITED

Witehira formed a company to exploit the binary battery technology. He named his new company Power Beat International Limited (PBIL). Beat was an acronym for Binary Electric Automotive Technology, which was the technical description of the electric system. But the word needed some marketing clout and Witehira added "Power" to the name so it could be used in future marketing. It was registered as a

New Zealand company in September 1989 with paid-up capital of NZ$10,000 and with Witehira as the majority shareholder.

With no source of venture capital for budding entrepreneurs in New Zealand, PBIL was launched as a nonlisted public company. A float was made of 2,600 new NZ$1 shares at a price of NZ$1,000 each. Nearly NZ$1.4 million was immediately raised. To obtain extra funds, shares worth NZ$180,000 were sold to the Maori Development Corporation—a majority-owned New Zealand government agency for promoting economic activity among the country's leading ethnic minority—and to Australian and Canadian interests.

In October 1993, PBIL was listed as a public company on the New Zealand Stock Exchange. On the first day of trading, the shares were sold for NZ$18. The company had more than 900 shareholders who had invested NZ$4.8 million. Among the shareholders was Witehira's local paperboy. Brendan Mitchell, age 10 at the time, had heard about the company. He told his sister, Desiree, age 16. Together they bought one NZ$1,000 share, he with savings from his paper route, she with baby-sitting money.

The firm was now focusing on commercializing its battery, convinced that the technology had been suitably demonstrated as practically feasible. Technical praise for the battery had come from many sources. In 1994, it won the prestigious RD100 Award—the so-called Nobel Prize for technology innovation—which in the past had been given to the development of products such as desktop computers and photocopying machines.

The company's approach was to take an idea from invention through the prototype and the evaluation stage to establish a proven, test-manufactured product. When a satisfactory consumer market had been demonstrated, the resultant business opportunity would be ready for transfer to outside interests for mass manufacture and marketing.

PRODUCT DEVELOPMENT

PBIL did not have the financial resources, technical ability, or managerial skills to mass-produce its battery. To determine the reliability and functional characteristics of the battery, it was necessary to carry out a limited volume test production run. This would give the company valuable technical information about the product and the manufacturing process.

A family-owned independent battery company, Amplex Consolidated Private Limited, in Sydney, Australia, agreed to make Power Beat batteries under contract. Amplex was one of only three automotive SLI battery manufacturers operating in Australia and New Zealand. The first batteries were produced in February 1990. This was not an ideal situation though, as PBIL needed to exercise control over the product quality and manufacturing procedures, deeming them critical for any new product. So, PBIL purchased a majority shareholding in Amplex, changed the name to Power Beat Australasia Limited, and for a short period operated the business. Capital had to be injected and production facilities improved. Once safe and reliable production was underway, PBIL sold the company back to the previous owners in 1993, retaining only a 19 percent shareholding to protect its interests. Nearly two years were spent fine-tuning the battery, developing various versions for specific applications, and establishing marketing contacts for the company. The company had deliberately avoided the giants of the worldwide battery manufacturing industry in the belief that they would have quietly killed the design because of the threat it presented to their own technology. Witehira felt his new battery would not be attractive to any of the established producers.

MARKETING

The battery as was configured was designed as an aftermarket, drop-in replacement for (but not limited to) most modern cars made after 1976. A heavier version was planned for trucks and a different-dimensioned battery for European cars. Installation was straightforward on many modern vehicles that divided the starter motor cable from the auxiliary power harness at the battery's terminals. Where this was not the case, the auxiliary and alternator wires had to be separated from the starter motor cable for connection to the smaller positive terminal. The battery was therefore being promoted to automobile dealers, not manufacturers. To be sold as original equipment by manufacturers of motor cars, the battery required certain modifications. Although priced higher than the conventional battery—the recommended retail price was NZ$146 compared with between NZ$80–110 for a conventional battery—PBIL touted the advantages of the product in terms of security, convenience, safety, and longer life. However, because of the product's youth, it was not yet known for certain how long the average Power Beat battery would last. Some had been in use since 1988. The company claimed that the binary battery's life expectancy was expected to be more than double that of conventional batteries.

Power Beat Australasia sold batteries under the Power Beat name in Australia and since the middle of 1993 had been shipping less than 1,000 units a week to New Zealand. Production costs in Australia were high and the small size of the output militated against scale economies.

Very few retail outlets in New Zealand carried the Power Beat battery. Some new car dealerships acted as marketing agents for the product. Among them were Jaguar and Nissan dealerships. When the first batteries were produced in Sydney, Witehira went to Nissan New Zealand with some samples in the hope that they would appreciate the new product. This tactic was successful and Nissan New Zealand offered the battery as optional equipment to new-car buyers. It also offered the Power Beat battery as a replacement for all vehicles checked in for battery replacement at Nissan service centres in the country. In Australia, Power Beat batteries began to be fitted to all Toyota Previa ambulances manufactured in Australia, and the technology was also in use in some four-wheel-drive vehicles used by the Australian government, in particular the defense department.

An advanced industrial economy, New Zealand has a small population of 3.5 million with a gross domestic product of about NZ$75 billion. The total stock of all motor vehicles in 1992 was 2,352,000 of which two-thirds were motor cars. The relatively small size of the domestic market was indicated by the number of cars sold annually. In 1993, less than 53,000 cars were sold. This was equal to a single day's sales in Japan and half a day's sales in the United States. About 600,000 batteries were being made in New Zealand annually at two relatively old plants. As a consequence, automotive battery sales in New Zealand were quite small and any plans to either manufacture the product or license it necessarily involved international markets.

Various efforts had been made to enter into arrangements with overseas firms to produce, market, or license Power Beat batteries. Mitsubishi, a giant Japanese conglomerate, signed a cooperative marketing agreement in 1990 that covered Japan, Europe, and the United States. Mitsubishi acquired a 6 percent shareholding in PBIL. After three years, the agreement was ended with no sales developing. Mitsubishi sold its stake. According to PBIL, Mitsubishi wanted to cash in a lot quicker than was appropriate for this sort of project. With the termination of the Mitsubishi connection, PBIL turned to U.S.-based Standard Communications, a subsidiary of electronics giant Philips, and signed a licensing deal in late 1993. It was envisaged that Standard Communications would introduce a special version of the power distribution system developed by PBIL together with the binary batteries for use in boats in the U.S. marine market. That agreement had been put on hold, however, following the collapse of a technology transfer agreement with a Canadian firm, Trend Vision Technologies, since Standard Communications wanted to see the outcome of the dispute before proceeding. In early 1994, Hyundai, the Korean carmaker, signed an agreement to test Power Beat batteries in its cars. In the United States, New Zealand racing driver, Steve Millen, was test marketing the Power Beat battery and its related vehicle power management system on a selection of Nissan luxury and high-performance vehicles.

By the time PBIL went public with its share offering, its battery was available on the market, the manufactured versions having been tried and tested. The yearly advertising budget had been less than NZ$50,000 per year, with some television and print—both newspapers and magazines—advertisements. Brochures and other printed material had also been produced. PBIL planned a major advertising launch during 1994 with a budget of NZ$150,000. Typical copies are provided as Exhibits 6 and 7 at end of the case.

PBIL was competing against conventional battery manufacturers. As yet though, these competitors had not reacted to PBIL's efforts to produce and sell its binary batteries. However, there were no real incentives for the battery industry to become enthusiastic, as the expected extended life of the Power Beat battery could reduce industry volume.

OTHER PRODUCT LINES

PBIL's expertise lay in the design of energy management systems. The company's main income was drawn from the sale of licenses, technology transfer fees, and royalties. Apart from the binary battery, the company also held patents for advanced electrode plates for use in various battery applications; a new low-cost technology for power distribution and multiplexing; a load leveling system that could allow homes to be powered from a trickle-fed storage battery system; and a variable stroke internal combustion engine.

One of Witehira's new projects was to build a house next to the PBIL offices, equipped with what was in effect a *house battery*, or "individual house electricity storage unit" that used PBIL's electrode technology. The household's electricity would be supplied from the storage unit which would in turn be continuously trickle-charged by the present power stations operating at their optimum economic loadings.

Yet another project was a semiconductor device that allowed multiple instructions to be planted within a wiring system. In practical terms that could mean just one single wire would suffice for an entire house. At the throw of a switch, the device would *know* whether the power was intended for a light, television, iron, or whatever. Witehira also foresaw a potentially global application for airplanes and automobiles and any machine requiring expensive and complex wiring. Wiring harnesses would be replaced with a single wire, saving weight, expense, and space.

Although the firm was developing new technologies, much of Witehira's energy and efforts were directed toward obtaining a partner who would take the Power Beat battery technology and use it to mass-produce the product for the world market. Nearly all of the company's revenues derived from royalties and technical fees related to the battery.

FACILITIES AND ADMINISTRATION

The company's modern offices and research center were located on a five hectare (15 acre) site just south of Hamilton in the North Island of New Zealand. Within easy reach of Auckland 75 miles away, Hamilton was itself the country's fourth largest city. The firm employed a total of 14 workers. A team of three scientists worked on developing and improving the various technologies. With Witehira as the managing director, the members of the board of directors included a prominent Maori businessman as chairman, a University of Waikato electronics professor, an owner of a plastics company, and a representative of minority shareholders. Witehira and his wife held a 51 percent controlling interest in the company.

Witehira was the brain and driving force behind the company. He was the inventor of the Power Beat battery and other technologies. He served as the firm's spokesperson, giving press interviews and explaining the technology to curious audiences at home and abroad. He negotiated with potential partners and clients and supervised the research and development work. The workload, by any measure, was very heavy and his daily schedule, hectic.

THE WORLD AUTO BATTERY INDUSTRY

The total market for automobile batteries was about 240 million units annually. The market size was determined by the number of motor vehicles produced; the total car population, as it influenced replacement sales; and the average battery life measured from the date of installation in the vehicle. Worldwide demand for car batteries was expected to grow at an annual rate of about 2.5 percent until the year 2000 but the growth was expected to be lower in Japan, the United States, and Europe. The car battery industry in Europe and the United States already had excess production capacity. Japanese battery makers were increasingly catering to the country's electronics industry.

Original Equipment and Replacement Markets.   Out of the 240 million automotive batteries shipped in 1991, 24 percent or almost 57 million units were to meet original equipment manufacturer (OEM) needs. The demand for OEM batteries was highest in those countries that were major automobile producers—the United States, Japan, and Western Europe. Demand for replacement batteries was particularly high in Latin America, Africa, and the Middle East as these regions had little motor vehicle production. However, because of stagnating car production and sales in the developed world, the sale of OEM batteries had correspondingly slowed. Demand for batteries for replacements was estimated at about 20 percent of the registered vehicles in a country. In Japan for instance, where there were 56 million registered automobiles, the annual size of the replacement battery market would be over 11 million units.

The proportion of OEM batteries ran from a high of 40 percent of total automotive battery sales in the Asia/Pacific region to about a third in western Europe, to 15 percent in North America, 12 percent in Latin America, and less than 5 percent in Africa/Middle East.

The regions of North America, Western Europe, and Asia/Pacific made up almost 80 percent of the market for automotive batteries. North America (United States and Canada) was the largest market, almost one-third of the world. However, the growth rate in this market was only about 2 $1/2$ percent annually. The end of the recession in the early 1990s and the reduction in imports from Japan could

EXHIBIT 1   **1991 Automotive Battery Shipments**

Region	Units (in million)	Percent
North America	81.4	34.2%
Canada	4.6	2.0
Asia/Pacific	58.8	24.6
Western Europe	47.9	20.1
Eastern Europe	21.7	9.1
Latin America	18.9	7.9
Africa/Middle East	9.6	4.0
Total Volume	238.2	100.0%

Source: George Kellinghusen, "Five Year Forecast Report," *Proceedings of the 104th Convention of Battery Council International*, May 17–20, Monte Carlo, Monaco, 1992, pp. 44–47.

mean increased sales of OEM batteries. The size of the Canadian automotive market was about 5 million units and sales of OEM units are expected to rise at a faster rate than replacement units.

Of Japan's production of 28 million units of automotive batteries, more than half (51 percent) were installed as OEM, another 42 percent were sold as replacements, and the rest exported. As Japanese automobile makers expanded production overseas, (particularly in the United States), and the yen appreciated in value, Japanese battery companies too established facilities abroad. Overall, the Asia/Pacific region had generated high growth rates.

Most east European countries were more or less self-sufficient as far as production was concerned. Improvements in productivity and quality depended mostly on the decisions made by major motor vehicle manufacturers such as General Motors, Fiat, Volkswagen, Iveco, and Suzuki, who had invested in these countries. As far as the Russian Commonwealth of Independent States was concerned, demand for car batteries exceeded supply by at least 20 to 30 percent. However, given the political uncertainties and funding shortages, it was unclear that this gap could be bridged.

In western Europe, with over 375 million people, there were about 150 million vehicles on the roads, whereas, in eastern Europe, there were only 30 million vehicles on the roads for 400 million people. The rate of car ownership was more than eight to one in western Europe as compared with the Commonwealth of Independent States, and about three to one if western Europe was compared with Poland, Hungary, and the former Czechoslovakia. The growth rates for the next few years in western Europe, eastern Europe, and the Commonwealth of Independent States were likely to be on average 2, 6, and 3 percent, respectively.

The elimination of trade barriers among the European Community (EC) members had created fierce competition among the various battery manufacturers. In 1993, about 35 percent of the batteries of various types sold in one country were manufactured in another EC country, compared with a figure of about just 10 percent in 1980. Following the internationalization of the automobile market, the battery industry too was undergoing restructuring.

In 1990, out of some 40 battery manufacturers, 18 controlled more than one percent of the European market and accounted for 92 percent of the total. The four leaders—Varta, CEAC, Chloride, and Tudor Spain—alone controlled 41 percent of the market. In two years, these 18 manufacturers had been reduced to only ten and accounted for almost 95 percent of the market. Among them, the four leaders— CEAC, Varta, Tudor Spain, and Hawker-Siddeley—controlled 75 percent of the total. A number of firms were acquired by others. For instance, Hawker-Siddeley acquired Chloride; CEAC acquired Sonnenschein; Deta bought Sonnenschein Portoguesa; Varta merged with Bosch; and Tudor Spain bought Neste Batteries.

The worldwide auto battery market (except in China and the former communist countries) was about US$12 billion in 1992. The ten largest car battery companies (see Exhibit 2) accounted for 68 percent of the market.

Technical Developments.   Intensive competition among battery makers had made the products very reliable. Historically, technical changes in batteries had

---

Exhibit 2   Major Car Battery Producers in the World, 1992 (in sales)

1. CEAC (Italy–France)
2. Varta Batterie (Germany)
3. Pacific Dunlop (United States–Australia)
4. Yuasa (Japan)
5. Johnson Controls (United States)
6. Tudor Spain (Spain)
7. Delco Remy (United States)
8. Japan Storage Battery (Japan)
9. Exide (United States)
10. Matsushita (Japan)

Source: George Kellinghusen, "Five Year Forecast Report," *Proceedings of the 104th Convention of Battery Council International*, May 17–20, Monte Carlo, Monaco, 1992, pp. 44–47.

taken place under the influence of the car manufacturers. With changes in the design of the vehicles themselves, batteries too were changing. For instance, the reduction in space under the streamlined hoods, the increase in temperatures around the engine, and the increase in electricity consumption due to the greater number of accessories all placed additional demands on the battery's design and power. There had been a continued movement away from the traditional battery toward reduced maintenance units (topping-up of water levels once every six months or once a year) or sealed units (maintenance free).

Among the electrochemical cells, lead held the strongest position by far both in terms of its price/performance ratio and recycling potential when compared with the other cells currently available. The superior physical characteristics of other cells such as, for example, nickel-cadmium or nickel-hydride, sodium sulphur, and the different lithium-based systems suggested opportunities for additional research by battery manufacturers.

Environmental Issues.   Scrapped automotive batteries constituted one of the more visible sources of lead contamination. Although battery recycling was close to 97 percent, concern over environmental pollution remained high. For example, in the United States, as of 1992, over 35 states had laws banning the disposal of wet cell lead-acid car batteries; 15 of these states had mandatory takeback laws. Congress was formulating a plan to tax all lead at the smelter, with a view to discourage lead usage. The tax on both new and reclaimed lead at the rate of U.S. 45 cents a pound—a pound of lead is about 2 $1/2$ cubic inches—would increase the price of lead by 200 percent, and add US$7.38 to an average 12 volt automotive battery and about 16 percent to the cost of industrial truck batteries. Imported batteries would be taxed on their lead content.

Severe air pollution in many urban areas had forced public opinion and regulatory authorities to mandate strict emission rules. The electric vehicle concept was being advanced as a potential solution. Two main factors restricted the use of the electric vehicle—the recharging ability of batteries and the purchase price of such vehicles. However, from 1996 on, 10 percent of U.S. cars would be required by law to run on alternative power. Thus, there was a demand by American car and component manufacturers for a battery to meet alternative power requirements.

LICENSING ARRANGEMENT WITH TREND VISION TECHNOLOGIES

As part of its efforts to commercialize the battery technology, PBIL was always on the lookout for overseas partners. In March 1993, Trend Vision Technologies Inc. or TVT, a public company registered in Vancouver, Canada, but operating from offices in Arizona, the United States, approached PBIL to obtain manufacturing and marketing rights for the Power Beat battery in North America, Europe, and Asia. TVT was listed on two stock exchanges—the Vancouver stock exchange in Canada and NASDAQ in the United States. PBIL understood these listings to mean that TVT had financial credibility and the ability to raise funds. In May 1993, an agreement was signed between TVT and PBIL by which TVT would pay a minimum license fee of US$9 million over three years for the rights to Power Beat's technology. In addition, royalties of 4 percent on sales of batteries and power management technology would be payable as well as a separate royalty payment of US 1 cent per plate (an average automobile battery requires between 50 and 84 plates) to cover the new electrode plate technology designed by the company. The agreement also required TVT to have manufacturing facilities in place within three years capable of producing a minimum of 3 million Power Beat batteries annually. An escape clause in the agreement said that should there be any problem with the payment of the license fee, TVT would forfeit all monies paid and would have no further rights on Power Beat's battery.

Initially, there was no cash payment. Instead, based on business trust between Peter Witehira and Massimo Fuchs, chairman and CEO of TVT, PBIL agreed to a series of payments for the first US$750,000 deposit. TVT advised PBIL that raising cash for future payments would present no problem. TVT even provided a letter stating their shareholders included a number of Swiss, Canadian, and American banks. Soon after the agreement was signed, Fuchs issued a statement saying that TVT's capital structure would be increased to allow them to fund commercial manufacture of Power Beat batteries.

Under the schedule of installments included in the agreement, TVT was to make the first payment of US$100,000 to PBIL on the 12th of May 1993. That payment was late in arriving. The second payment of US$150,000 was also late. In mid-June, Fuchs tried to persuade Witehira and the directors of PBIL to take US$150,000 worth of shares in TVT in lieu of the cash. "At first, we said, no thank you," said Witehira. "But, finally, we agreed on a specific one off departure to facilitate the completion of the already overdue second payment, and accepted US$100,000 cash and US$50,000 in TVT shares." Fuchs insisted that it was simply taking longer than TVT had anticipated to raise the cash to complete the purchase of the battery technology. "The next payment was for half a million dollars (US) due on the 15th of July 1993," says Witehira. "We had some thoughts that were beginning to nag us a little." The payment of US$500,000 was to signal the point at which PBIL would officially hand over the technology in the form of technical specifications and a Nissan Infiniti Q45 sedan that was fitted with a Power Beat battery.

The payment was late again. However, Fuchs made a dramatic appearance at the annual general meeting of PBIL shareholders in New Zealand in July. He gave a rousing speech at the meeting outlining TVT's payment commitments to PBIL. After the meeting, Fuchs handed a check for US$500,000 to Witehira. The check, though, was postdated to September 29, 1993. PBIL declined to accept it and was already thinking of terminating the agreement with TVT. When PBIL threatened to do so, Fuchs offered to immediately arrange for a bank check to be sent via overnight mail from the United States. A check drawn on an Arizona bank did come, and was deposited by PBIL. It finally appeared that the contract was on track. The information on the battery technology was transferred to TVT and so was the Nissan demonstration car.

On receipt of the technology and the car, Fuchs issued media releases stating that TVT had now made all required payments to PBIL and that a technology license for North America and Asia would be issued in addition to forming an Asian joint venture. In October, PBIL's bank informed it that there were problems in negotiating the bank check issued on behalf of TVT—in fact, the check had effectively been dishonored. While TVT continued the appearance of business as usual, maintaining consistently that all they needed was more time and issuing media statements about the technology, PBIL was both frustrated and concerned as it had listed itself on October 12, 1993 on the New Zealand stock exchange. It was now becoming clear to PBIL that TVT was using the agreement to promote their own stock. After deciding on legal advice, the relationship with TVT was formally terminated in mid-December.

Since PBIL was a minority shareholder in TVT and in view of the misleading statements and claims Fuchs was making to the American media, PBIL informed the U.S. Securities and Exchange Commission about TVT's failure to meet its contractual obligations. TVT shares were suspended from trading for a few days in mid-January 1994. It was forced to make announcements to NAS-DAQ and the Vancouver stock exchange where TVT finally admitted that they had failed to make all payments, and as a direct result of this had been denied the licensing rights for the Power Beat technology. However, no mention was made of the fact that TVT had issued a bounced check for half a million dollars. Instead, it stated its intention to initiate legal action against PBIL for withholding its technology from them. Although trading in TVT shares recommenced following the issue of this statement, it was suspended again when the company failed to file their annual financial statement or annual return, a requirement for all publicly listed companies. In early January 1994, PBIL issued a press release announcing the termination of the agreement with TVT. TVT's threat of a lawsuit against PBIL did not materialize. Subsequently, TVT was delisted from NASDAQ.

The continuing controversy was reported in the New Zealand media, but in a one-sided way, according to Witehira. Newspapers presented TVT's press releases without referring to PBIL for comment. PBIL's share prices dropped and were trading for NZ$6.

The failure of the TVT licensing agreement was most disappointing for PBIL as until now, it had appeared to be the most lucrative and successful effort to commercialize the Power Beat battery technology. The media publicity, though, brought renewed attention and interest in the company, both domestically and overseas. It forced Peter Witehira and his senior managers to consider other options (such as domestic manufacturing) to commercialize the battery technology. He was, however, reluctant to sell the technology outright to another firm.

FINANCES

Although total revenue in 1993 was lower, the company's net profits continued to grow. It had been able to fund its development costs at a satisfactory rate and had adequate cash resources. In addition, the company had no long-term debt and all property was freehold. The collapse of share prices led Witehira to apprehend a takeover attempt of the company. The 1994 results would certainly be disappointing.

Exhibits 3 and 4 provide financial results of the firm for the past four years.

FUTURE DEVELOPMENTS

While Peter Witehira traveled around the world presenting details of his inventions to highly appreciative technical audiences around the world, the head office in Hamilton continued to receive eager enquiries from firms seeking licensing or production rights. One of the proposals being considered was to build a plant to produce its batteries at an industrial town, Huntly, twenty-five miles from Hamilton. The factory would cost NZ$10 million and would require joint venture partners. Potential partner companies, several of them foreign, had already expressed interest. Cautious after the TVT setback, Witehira said, "We need to pick the right partner, somebody who can do it right. It'll crack the battery industry worldwide because we will be able to produce a very high quality battery at a relatively low price." Given the small size of the domestic market, the plant would certainly export the bulk of its output, most likely to New Zealand's major and growing trading partners—Australia, Southeast Asia, and southern California. Producing batteries would also mean a major departure for the company which had seen itself only as a technology development outfit. Also, it was not apparent that the firm had the resources and competency to engage in manufacturing and sales.

Saddled with a proven technology that he was finding difficult to commercialize, Witehira might have to consider selling the technology of the Power Beat battery. This might mean the end of all prospects of the battery being available on the

EXHIBIT 3   **Balance Sheet, 1990–1993: Power Beat International Ltd.
(in New Zealand dollars)**

	1993	1992	1991	1990
Shareholders' Funds				
Share capital	$2,520,000	$2,520,000	$ 12,600	$ 11,338
Share premium account	92,620	92,620	2,600,020	1,336,662
Foreign currency translation				
reserve	—	101,096	92,259	—
Retained earnings	409,521	70,633	(165,925)	(233,364)
Total shareholders' funds	$3,022,141	$2,784,349	$2,538,954	$1,114,636
Current assets				
Cash	$623,034	$161,314	$ 756,877	$619,812
Receivables	149,070	42,032	281,384	25,926
Stock of finished goods	17,624	30,600	—	—
Amount due by Witehira	—	322,500	—	—
Deposits and prepayments	81,430	—	—	102,867
	$871,158	$556,446	$1,038,261	$748,605
Current Liabilities				
Payables	$(135,063)	$(102,788)	$ (101,484)	$(113,328)
Provisions for deferred				
taxation	(205,219)	(48,280)	—	—
Working capital	530,876	405,378	936,777	861,933
Investments	1,863,413	2,003,042	1,361,222	—
Fixed assets	274,483	108,670	90,092	432,145
Intangible assets				
Patents	353,369	267,259	150,863	47,214
Net Assets	$3,022,141	$2,784,349	$2,538,954	$1,114,636

Source: Annual reports.

market. On the other hand, it would provide funds to PBIL to continue its research and development on new technologies.

With all the difficulties that PBIL had encountered and the various options he had, Witehira may have felt disappointed. However, he needed only to look out of his office to see an example of Kiwi ingenuity that had succeeded. PBIL's office complex was directly opposite Hamilton airport where a New Zealand–built Fletcher crop-dusting aircraft was mounted on a podium.

EXHIBIT 4   Income Statement, 1990–1993: Power Beat International Ltd. (in New Zealand dollars)

	1993	1992	1991	1990
Income				
Sale of licenses	$1,100,000	$1,527,093	$751,221	—
Interest received	7,751	36,971	31,237	$39,373
Sale of prototype samples	5,628	47,211	—	—
Consultancy and engineering	74,520	—	—	—
Total income	$1,187,899	$1,611,275	$782,458	$39,373
Expenses				
Administration	$195,426	$254,416	$252,741	$123,625
Audit fees	8,000	15,000	6,000	6,000
Depreciation	37,658	17,990	18,186	3,426
Foreign exchange gain (loss)	(35,712)	2,676	—	—
Operating expenses	185,121	136,304	270,347	67,904
Rental and lease costs	18,827	7,703	—	—
Research and development	105,432	99,194	154,331	—
Promotion and marketing	166,554	182,051	—	—
Purchase of NZ license	—	645,070	—	—
Interest	667	7,647	13,129	928
Loss on sale of fixed assets	10,099	936	285	916
Other	—	7,798	—	69,938
Total expenses	$692,072	$1,376,785	$715,019	272,737
Net Operating				
Profit (loss)	$495,827	$234,490	$67,439	$(233,364)
Taxation	(156,939)	(48,280)	—	—
Net profit after taxation	338,888	186,210	67,439	(233,364)
Extraordinary item Gain on sale of subsidiary	—	50,348	—	—
Net profit attributable to shareholders	338,888	236,558	67,439	(233,364)
Retained earnings brought forward	70,633	(165,925)	(233,364)	—
Retained earnings carried forward	$409,521	$70,633	$(165,925)	$(233,364)

Source: Annual reports.

EXHIBIT 5   Time Line

1987   Patent for Power Beat battery obtained.

1989   Power Beat International Limited established.

1990   First Power Beat batteries produced by Amplex Consolidated.

1990   Marketing agreement signed with Mitsubishi.

1993   Power Beat International Limited listed as a public company.

Agreement with Mitsubishi canceled.

Technology transfer and licensing agreement signed with Trend Vision Technologies.

Licensing deal signed with Standard Communications.

1994   Power Beat International Limited announces cancellation of agreement with Trend Vision Technologies.

Agreement with Standard Communications put on hold.

EXHIBIT 6   Note on Licensing

Licensing is an agreement under which the licensor (selling firm) allows its technology, patents, trademarks, or other proprietary advantages to be used by another firm (the licensee) for a fee, called royalty. Licensing is a well-established market entry strategy. It allows the licensor to exploit its technology quickly and cheaply; enables access to markets that are too small to justify larger investments or too big for the resources it has; and permits relatively easy entry into international business compared to exporting, joint ventures, or foreign direct investment. To the licensee, licensing permits the acquisition of new technology cheaper and quicker than developing them on its own.

A major risk of licensing is that the licensor may lose its proprietary advantage to the licensee. Thus, the licensor must try to ensure that its licensee will not be a future competitor. Also, the licensor has to beware that its reputation worldwide may be hurt if the licensee produces a shoddy product or otherwise engages in questionable practices.

The licensing agreement is a commercial contract between the licensee and the licensor and consequently it has to be drawn up carefully especially since rights to the use of technology, patents, trademarks, copyrights, and such other intellectual property are involved. A typical license agreement would include the following:

- Clear and correct description of the parties to the agreement, identifying the names of each party, where registered, and their main place of business.
- An introduction that describes the reasons for the parties entering into the arrangement and their respective roles.
- Definition of all terms that are ambiguous or vague.
- Explicit definition of the nature of the rights that are being given to the licensee.
- Definition of the geographical limits imposed on the licensee's manufacturing, selling, or sublicensing activities.
- Duration of validity of the agreement and the manner of its renewal or termination.
- Statement of whether the licensee would receive rights to improvements to the process/product made by the licensor.
- Provisions for "technological flowback" clauses where improvements made by the licensee revert to the licensor.
- Details regarding royalties—amounts, manner of calculation, method and time of payment, and currency and exchange rates to be used.
- Specification of minimum performance requirements such as minimum royalty payments, production and sales volumes and other evidence to ensure that the licensee is making the best efforts to fully utilize the license potential.
- Clauses dealing with protection of confidentiality of know-how, quality control, the applicable language of the contract, method of settling disputes, and assignability by either party of rights to third parties.

EXHIBIT 7

EXHIBIT 8

No more DEAD batteries from leaving...

* headlights on

* doors open (interior lights on)

* boot lid open (boot light on)

* radio or stereo on

* ignition on

* even added accessories left on

No more Jumper Leads!

No more Push Starts!

No switches to turn!

For example, leave your lights on overnight, get in your vehicle, shut the door, turn on the key and the *POWER BEAT* SP55 **battery Can Come Alive!**

POWER BEAT
The Smart Battery

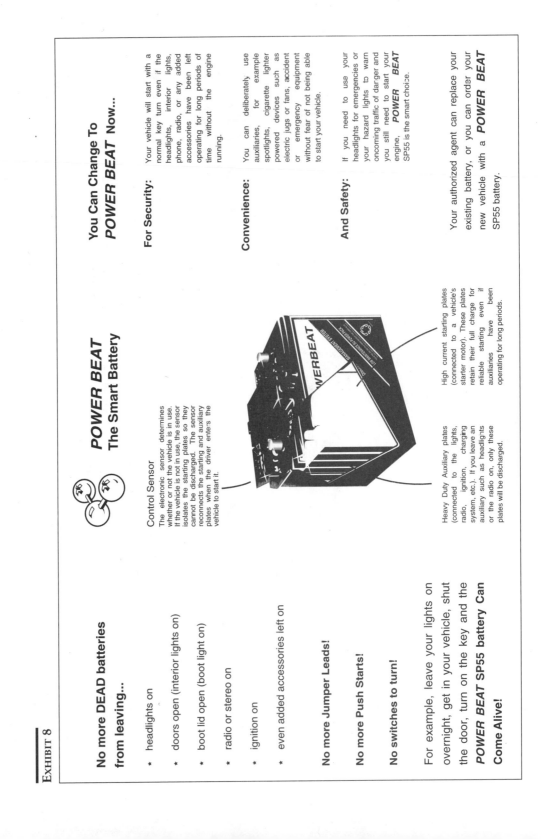

Control Sensor
The electronic sensor determines whether or not the vehicle is in use. If the vehicle is not in use, the sensor isolates the starting plates so they cannot be discharged. The sensor reconnects the starting and auxiliary plates when the driver enters the vehicle to start it.

Heavy Duty Auxiliary plates (connected to the lights, radio, ignition, charging system, etc.). If you leave an auxiliary such as headlights or the radio on, only these plates will be discharged.

High current starting plates (connected to a vehicle's starter motor). These plates retain their full charge for reliable starting even if auxiliaries have been operating for long periods.

You Can Change To *POWER BEAT* Now...

For Security: Your vehicle will start with a normal key turn even if the headlights, interior lights, phone, radio, or any added accessories have been left operating for long periods of time without the engine running.

Convenience: You can deliberately use auxiliaries, for example spotlights, cigarette lighter powered devices such as electric jugs or fans, accident or emergency equipment without fear of not being able to start your vehicle.

And Safety: If you need to use your headlights for emergencies or your hazard lights to warn oncoming traffic of danger and you still need to start your engine, *POWER BEAT* SP55 is the smart choice.

Your authorized agent can replace your existing battery, or you can order your new vehicle with a *POWER BEAT* SP55 battery.

CASE 7
SYTKO INTERNATIONAL LIMITED

In early November 1990, Les Sytkowski, the founder of Sytko Custom Homes Inc., was reviewing his plans to do business in his native country in anticipation of his December visit to Poland. Sytko, a Winnipeg-based home building business, was not performing particularly well. Local demand had declined and although there was no immediate threat to the survival of his company, its profits had also declined substantially and little improvement was expected over the next couple of years. The company needed a change in focus. This was not easy to find in the saturated Canadian housing market.

Les, who had strong feelings toward his native Poland, had first considered a business venture in this formerly communist country in early 1990. In January he had participated in "The Conference on New Opportunities for Canadian Business" organized in Toronto by the Polish Trade Mission. As a result, he believed he could join the wave of some 1,700 new, foreign-owned businesses launched in this East European country within the last year. He felt that with his expertise in the home construction industry he would have a substantial advantage over local competitors. His subsequent visit to Poland in early June confirmed these feelings and allowed him to establish some important business contacts. His upcoming visit was expected to lead to a final decision on going abroad and the scope and focus of his Polish venture.

COMPANY BACKGROUND

Sytko Custom Homes Inc. was founded by Les in 1985. He had originally come to Canada in 1960 with his parents. Although only six years old at the time, over the next 30 years Les still managed to maintain his national ties. He participated in activities of the Winnipeg Polish community and was fluent in both Polish and English. Les also completed university degrees in Political Science and Economics. He spent a year in Poland during 1978–79 working on a research project that was part of his graduate thesis.

In 1982 Les started his own business. As a student, he had once built a house during the summer and sold it at a profit. Therefore, he had some experience in home building and starting as an independent home builder seemed to be a natural choice for him. His first year in business resulted in the construction and sale of five houses. During the Winnipeg housing boom of the mid-1980s Les managed to sell an average of 25 houses annually. His brother Jack joined him in 1985 and

Source: Prepared by Walter S. Good and Kris Opalinski of the University of Manitoba Canada as a basis for classroom discussion rather than to illustrate either effective or ineffective handling of an administrative situation. Copyright by the Case Development Program, Faculty of Management, University of Manitoba. Support for the development of this case was provided by the Centre for International Business Studies, University of Manitoba, and the Canadian Consortium of Management Schools. A follow-up case entitled "Sytko International Inc. 1994" is available from the authors at the University of Manitoba.

the business was incorporated. Les and his wife held a 55 percent share in the business, with Jack having the remaining 45 percent. This capital structure has been maintained.

Sytko custom homes were built exclusively for customers who wanted to have some input into all stages of the design and construction of their single-detached houses and were also willing and able to finance construction through all its stages. The company's sales averaged $2 million between 1985-1989. Sytko was considered small relative to other home builders in Winnipeg, but would be considered as medium-sized in the custom-built segment of the market.

THE RESIDENTIAL CONSTRUCTION INDUSTRY IN CANADA

Residential properties were purchased for the purpose of individual use, renting-out, or speculation. The number of apartments built in a given year depended on demographic and economic trends. In 1989 the total value of new residential construction in Canada was estimated at $35 billion. Approximately $21 billion could be attributed to construction of new residential buildings, with the remainder to renovations, alterations, and conversions. In Manitoba these figures were over $1 billion and $400 million, respectively. These dollar sales translated into 216,000 housing units across the country and over 4,000 in Manitoba. However, 1990 brought a drastic decline both in the number of new houses and their dollar value. In Manitoba, it was estimated that the number of units built would be reduced to 2,500 with a proportional decline in their dollar value. A further 20 percent decline in national demand was anticipated in 1991 due to the economic downturn, high interest rates, and introduction of the Goods and Services Tax. Subsequent years were expected to turn around with projections for 20 percent annual growth (till 1995) due to the economic recovery and an influx of almost 1.5 million new immigrants to Canada. However, Manitoba—being less attractive to newcomers—was not expected to benefit substantially from this influx. It was anticipated that the local demand for new housing would be maintained at a stable level of 2,200 units per year throughout the period of 1992–1995.

Residential buildings were classified into four major categories: single detached, semi-detached (including duplexes), apartments (including row housing), and other residential construction (recreational, etc.). Typically, 70 percent of the number of dwellings built in a given year fell into the single-detached category.

COMPETITION

The building industry in Canada was very competitive in nature with over 19,000 companies specializing in residential construction. Of these almost 800 were in Manitoba. The majority of these companies were subcontractors providing specialized services to home builders, companies, or individuals who were direct suppliers of residential buildings to the final customer.

To become a home builder specializing in single-detached houses required little initial capital. All construction work could be subcontracted to specialized companies, leaving the home builder with the task of coordination and supervision of construction work. According to industry sources, all that was initially required to get into the business was a telephone and a half-ton truck.

The primary bases for competition among firms were price and location. Houses in popular areas provided a higher return, even after accounting for differences in the cost of land and its development. The ability to follow existing trends in design and finishing were unquantifiable factors, but according to some analysts, had some significance in the overcrowded market.

In 1990 there were 196 home builders in Manitoba, 150 in the small (fewer than 10 employees), 40 in the medium (10 to 35), and six in the large (over 35) size categories. Most of the small companies were local operations with only five of the biggest firms having a national focus. The majority of houses were developed by "tract builders," that is, those who had only a few standard models to choose from. In many cases, companies from this group would start construction without a firm contract from a purchaser. This group of home builders was particularly vulnerable to changes in the economy. An error in evaluating current economic conditions and any consequent delay in the sale of finished houses could result in bankruptcy.

Sytko Custom Homes Inc. was among some 20 "custom-builders" in Manitoba. It was estimated that this segment built approximately 200 units in Manitoba in 1990. The competitive factors in this segment were pricing, customer relations, flexibility in adjusting to customer requirements, and quality of work. The fact that a lot of new business resulted from referrals highlights the importance of customer satisfaction.

The risk for these companies came from fluctuations in demand and competition rather than as a result of holding excess inventory because virtually all financing was arranged by the customer. Overall, it was estimated that 50 percent of new small companies and 25 percent of medium-sized companies did not survive their first five years of operations.

BUYER BEHAVIOUR

At the beginning of their working life, young people typically satisfied their need for shelter by renting an apartment. A decision to raise a family was usually followed by the commitment to invest in a house. The increased participation of women in the workforce helped the average family to carry the associated costs. As the family grew, so did its housing needs which could result in subsequent adjustments to their house size and quality. In addition, variations in employment opportunities across the country resulted in the high mobility of Canadians, which further boosted real estate sales. As a result, frequent moves became a landmark of the Canadian lifestyle.

Single-family houses were generally affordable by the majority of Canadian households in the early 1990s. A well-established market system facilitated exchange and allowed families to change their houses as their needs changed.

SYTKO CUSTOM HOMES INC.

Over its five-year history Sytko built more than 100 single-detached houses. The company applied simple, wooden-frame technology that did not require a lot of specialized equipment in the construction of its houses. During the good times company employees were engaged in framing, insulating, and finishing single-family homes under the close supervision of Les or Jack. All specialized work was subcontracted to other companies. The brothers found that only their direct involvement could assure efficiency and the quality of the work. They did not shy away from working on some of the finishing jobs themselves if their schedules permitted. Their business did not follow any kind of strong seasonal pattern since winter construction became feasible during the 1980s.

A typical contract to construct a custom house would require some preliminary discussions with the customer ranging from a couple of days up to several months before signing a formal agreement. After two weeks or so to finalize financing, construction could begin. Construction work took approximately two months. During good times the company would have up to 10 houses under construction at the same time.

Over time, the division of responsibilities between the partners gradually changed. Les was primarily involved with customer relations, whereas Jack worked as the direct supervisor of Sytko's employees and dealt with subcontractors. Sytko did not employ any administrative staff. Their office was located at Les's house and was run by himself and his wife.

The unit price of their homes ranged from $75,000 to $300,000. A typical unit (a 3-bedroom, 1,800–2,000 sq. ft. house) was priced between $80,000 and $90,000. Sytko Custom Homes Inc. required the customer to provide a 10 percent down payment, allowing the company to subcontract the initial stages of construction. Additional partial payments upon completion of subsequent stages allowed the company to reduce its requirement for working capital.

Sytko Custom Homes Inc. established its reputation based on reasonable price, quality of work, flexibility in adjusting to individual requirements, reliability, and excellent customer service. Les attributed 30–40 percent of their new business to referrals from his former customers. The rest came from advertising in newspapers and running show homes.

In Les's opinion it was too risky for the company to pursue other segments of the home building market. "Tract building" was subject to high risks. Construction of apartment buildings required the application of different technology and equipment, neither of which was within the firm's reach. Construction of cottages, farm buildings, and log houses did not seem attractive because of the established competition and the large geographic dispersion of construction sites.

The company managed to make substantial profit throughout the 1980s. Their 10 percent average profit margin on a typical home resulted in a $200,000 average annual net profit before taxes over the previous five years. These profits were primarily used for land speculation in the local real estate market.

Their good performance resulted from carefully scrutinizing all expenses and their experience in determining appropriate prices acquired after a few initial miscalculations. Their basic pricing method was "cost plus margin" applied against the market.

Their 1990 fiscal year was not as strong as the previous five years. Average prices of houses declined to their 1988 level whereas the cost of materials kept increasing, which led to the reduction of profit margins to 2–3 percent. With contracts to build only 10 houses during 1990, the company's expected profit shrank to $20,000–30,000.

The only factor which could brighten this picture for Les and Jack personally (although not for the company) was that with the decrease in the number of orders they were able to increase their own labour input by laying off several employees.

THE FUTURE

The only positive element Les saw in the housing environment for the near future was that more baby boomers would probably want to move up to their second and third houses and this category of buyers was his target group. He expected some improvement in his business to 15 houses per year when interest rates decreased and the economy recovered. However, this level of sales was not sufficient to satisfy Les's personal objectives. Seeing no other immediate, attractive business prospects in Canada, Les focused his attention on opportunities in Poland. He had conducted extensive research on that country's market before his June trip. The visit identified some new factors which indicated that Sytko International, his newly established venture, could be successful.

POLAND—GENERAL PERSPECTIVE

The legacy of communism heavily influenced the way business was conducted in Poland in 1990. The one-year-old noncommunist government, the first in the 45 years of Soviet-dominated Eastern Europe, inherited an economy that was in shambles (see Exhibit 1 for comparative statistics on Canada and Poland). A widespread program of reforms attempting to gear the economy to the free market model had been undertaken. Austerity measures, including slashing the money supply to reduce a 1,000 percent annual inflation rate were introduced, with surprisingly high support from the population. As a result, unemployment, which had been practically unknown, reached over 1 million in the summer of 1990. In addition, production output dropped by 20 percent and real incomes shrank by 30 percent.

Most businesses in Poland were still state-owned and run by old cadres of communist party members, accustomed to following orders from the top. Most manufacturing sectors were dominated by large, inefficient plants able to control their profits by raising the prices they charged for their products.

Some changes in ownership had already been initiated but many experienced a number of problems. These resulted from the lack of investment capacity by individuals and financial institutions. A "socialist mentality," characterized by passive participation in economic and political activities and the expectation of government's active role in providing free basic services, was still the prevailing attitude. However, there were some positive signs of economic recovery. The exchange rate stabilized at a level of zl 9,500/US $ throughout most of 1990, despite the continuing high inflation rate. Inflation was curbed from a rate of 40 percent monthly at the beginning of the year to a moderate (by local standards) 1–2 percent monthly throughout the third quarter and 3–4 percent at the end of the year. Previously, real interest rates had traditionally been negative. The recent central bank rate, however, was 43 percent annually, which was 5–6 points above the annual inflation rate. Regional commodity exchanges were being inaugurated almost daily.

EXHIBIT 1   Canada and Poland—Comparative Statistics

	Canada	Poland
Size (sq. kms.)	9,558,160	312,677
Population	26.5 million	38.0 million
Population growth (percent per year)	1.1%	0.7%
Structure of population by age		
Below 20 years of age	35%	32%
20–35 years	25%	
35–46 years	13%	
46–64 years	21%	
Above 64 years of age	4%	9%
Life expectancy at birth	76.6	71.9
Labour force	10.38 million	17.5 million
Women as percent of labour force	39.8%	45.5%
Unemployment rate (1990)	8%	7%
Employment by sector (1988)		
Agriculture and forestry	5%	29%
Mining	2%	3%
Manufacturing	19%	25%
Construction	7%	8%
Trade	19%	9%
Transport, communications, and utilities	8%	8%
Finance, insurance, and real estate	6%	2%
Public administration and other services	35%	16%
GDP (1987)	US$405 billion	US$74 billion
GDP per capita (1987)	US$15,640	US $1,950
Foreign debt (1990)	—	US$40 billion
Exchange rate per unit US$ (Nov. 1990)	Can. $1.16	zloty 9,500
Number of cars per 1,000 population	435	105
Percent of population above 25 years of age with secondary education and above	33%	40%
Exports (1987)	US$97 billion	US$13 billion
Imports	US$88 billion	US$15 billion
Average monthly earnings	US$1,770	US$115

Source: All statistical data on Canada is based on *Canadian Statistical Review*, years 1987–1990. Most data on Poland is based on the 1987–1990 issues of *Rocznik Statystyczny*.

New regulations recently introduced by the government were directed toward attracting foreign investment. Although the transfer of profits out of the country was limited to 15 percent of annual volume, this limit was to be waived by the end of 1995. A three-year tax holiday, followed by a 40 percent income tax and

15 percent withholding tax, a state guarantee for foreign-owned assets, and a provision in the law permitting foreign ownership of real estate were recent amendments that made Poland's business environment similar to that of many Western economies.

The general advantages of entering the Polish market included: low labour costs; a highly educated and skilled labour force; and (potentially) high domestic demand for a wide range of consumer goods, services, and industrial technology, materials, and equipment. A willingness to participate in the expected rapid development expressed by private entrepreneurs and a new wave of managers, hastily trained in the market economy, contributed to the newborn feeling of business excitement. Generally, no recurrence of the old, centrally controlled system was anticipated.

However, there were some impediments to foreign-owned business operations in Poland. Red tape affected almost all areas of business activity. Virtually dozens of permits were required from state and local agencies for almost any business and it took months to obtain them. In many cases the local municipal administration had too much discretion in deciding on vital aspects of business activities, which resulted in corruption. Information on market demand and supply situations was typically not available and the accuracy of available economic data were poorer than in North America. Telecommunications were underdeveloped; it was difficult to have a telephone installed and, once installed, obtaining a connection was also a problem. Quality of products and, frequently, subassemblies, as well as raw materials, was low and prices high. Business practices in Poland were ineffective, emphasizing protocol and formal position rather than level of competency. Lack of knowledge about the market economy (particularly in finance and marketing) made it difficult for Westerners to communicate investment objectives to their local counterparts. In addition, despite Poland's relatively large population, the internal market for many goods and services was very small. Considering average income levels, it was estimated that the aggregate consumer demand for goods and services was no more than US$30 billion annually. Finally, a significant number of people maintained an unrealistic view of the Polish economy, expecting it to miraculously recover from the deep recession of 1990. This could potentially bring political instability and a demand for populist changes in economic reforms.

THE HOUSING MARKET IN POLAND

The housing problem in Poland had always been acute. Several factors from the past contributed to the situation. World War II destruction had required a substantial effort to reconstruct most major cities. The state's emphasis on the development of heavy industry also shifted resources away from housing construction. It was estimated that Poland's total needs for housing units due to population growth between 1991 and 2000 would be close to 2.9 million units. Additional needs due to deterioration of existing housing stocks were estimated at a further 1.8 million units.

However, real demand was expected to be much lower due to generally low income levels and declining state subsidies to the housing sector. The situation was further exacerbated by very high interest rates (over 40 percent annually) making mortgage financing virtually unattainable even for high-income earners. As a result, most housing construction was financed on a cash basis.

Until the recent economic and political changes, housing had been subject to allocation rather than free market forces. Severe limitations had been placed on ownership (only one house or apartment could be owned by a family), trade (revenue from the sale of real estate was treated as income for the year without allowing for purchase costs), and private rental (permitted only when the apartment owner was out of the country). The average size of a typical apartment unit was just over 50 square meters at a prevailing price for new units of $300/square meter.

In 1990 there were several distinct housing systems in Poland.

- *Communal housing* consisted of the stock of houses taken over by the state or built by municipal authorities after World War II. The quality of communal housing was rather low, which was reflected in the rent charged to the tenants.

- *Cooperative housing* was built by cooperatives controlled and subsidized by the state. This was the predominant type of new housing in Poland, accounting for some 70 percent of new apartment units. Although the most popular way of obtaining homes in Poland, cooperative housing was far from easy to obtain. The procedure leading to obtaining the right to rent a cooperative apartment could take anywhere from 10 to 25 years to complete.

- *Employer housing* was provided by some large state enterprises to their employees. This enabled them to attract young employees who often joined the company only to obtain an apartment. Even if they later quit their jobs, they were allowed to stay in their units because Polish law did not allow for eviction if tenants had no place to go. The number of units in this category was not expected to grow significantly.

- *Private apartments* could be located within communal and cooperative apartment buildings. Owners of many of these units were provided with the opportunity to acquire their units under a number of home ownership incentive plans offered by the state in the 1970s and 1980s. Some inhabitants of cooperative housing also became owners of their apartments under an apartment acquisition program where payments were spread over 20–30 years.

- *Single-family houses* were typically solid brick houses built by their owners at considerable expense in terms of time, money, and personal labour. Much larger than an average apartment, these homes were also much better equipped.

MARKET SEGMENTATION

In comparison with the situation in Canada, the following groups of prospective customers could be identified in Poland (see Exhibits 2 and 3 for information on family incomes, purchasing power, and breakdown of expenditures):

Low- and Middle-Income Individuals.   For all practical purposes, customers from this segment were forced out of the market in 1990. Even members of large cooperatives, despite receiving credit subsidies, could not afford to make mortgage

EXHIBIT 2   Structure of Family Expenditures—
Canada versus Poland (excluding taxes)

	Canada (%)	Poland* (%)
Food	17.5%	52.6%
Housing, household furnishings, and equipment	24.2	9.6
Household operation	4.3	2.9
Clothing	5.3	11.2
Transportation	16.2	6.1
Personal and health care	4.5	3.3
Education, recreation, and culture	7.9	8.4
Miscellaneous	16.6	5.9
Total family expenditures	US$29,900	US$2,500†

* The 3rd quarter of 1990 statistics. Annual average would be different due to the rapid decline of real incomes throughout the year.

† The total family expenditure for Poland is based on zloty incomes from the third quarter of 1990, translated into dollar figures at an exchange rate of zl 9,500/US $. This dollar figure does not represent the purchasing power parity between average incomes of the two countries because of different price structures.

payments amounting to more than a typical salary. The only exception within this category were those who received new apartments from local governments under the state subsidy program. There were some additional changes in the subsidy programs expected in 1991, but their effect on housing demand by this group was not clear. Some analysts predicted that, within the next 5 years, 4–6 million average income earners would create a new middle class that would generate demand for the bulk of goods and services in the country, including housing.

High-Income Individuals.   This group included those capable of making mortgage payments at a level substantially above the typical average monthly salary. Private entrepreneurs, some professionals (such as dentists, lawyers, and physicians in certain specializations) and local employees of foreign companies were in this category. Statistics on the number of individuals in this group and their actual income levels were unavailable, but it was known that they were principally concentrated in urban areas (notably the cities of Warsaw, Poznan, Katowice, and Krakow). The number of private entrepreneurs was growing rapidly due to the liberalization of the economy. It was estimated that there were at least 500,000 private enterprises in the country. Depending on their individual incomes, customers from the high income category might be able to purchase houses within any building category.

Hard-Currency Earners.   This segment was specific to Eastern Europe, where even low (by Western standards) incomes in hard currency were multiplied to very high values in local currencies by notoriously inflated exchange rates. The

---

EXHIBIT 3   Poland—Selected Housing Market-Related Statistics

Income Statistics, October 1990:

Average monthly income per person	zl 483,000
Average monthly earnings	zl 1,083,000
Social minimum per person	zl 400,000

Distribution of monthly incomes per
family member (workers' families):

zloty income	Percent of families
zl 0–200,000	5%
zl 200,001–400,000	39%
zl 400,001–600,000	33%
zl 600,001–800,000	13%
above 800,000	10%

Land Utilization, 1987*

Agriculture	61.0%
Forests	28.5%
Waters	3.0%
Roads and railways	3.5%
Industry and housing	3.0%
Nonutilized	1.5%

Rocznik Statystyczny, 1987.
Source: Current announcements of Glowny Urzad Statystyczny published in the October
issues of *Rzeczpospolita*.

high end of this segment would be expatriate workers of foreign businesses, diplomats, and Polish emigrants deciding to resettle in their native country. They were generally expected to be able to pay the full transaction price for single detached houses, amounting to up to several hundred thousands of dollars. Quality and the size of houses were their primary considerations, since they were accustomed to price levels well beyond those in even the hottest local markets (such as Warsaw). According to official sources there was the equivalent of some U.S. $5 billion in 5 million private, foreign currency bank accounts within the country. In addition, another $2 to $3 billion was held outside of the banking system. Another indicator of the size of this market was the fact that at least 50,000 Poles were earning hard currency working on construction and service projects abroad. There were no estimates available as to the size of this market; however, the number of people in this category was growing.

COMPETITION

Until recently, competition in housing construction was virtually nonexistent. Production was concentrated in the hands of some 1,500 state enterprises and over 300 cooperatives which employed over 900,000 workers and accounted for over 70 percent of the total number of apartments built in the late 1980s. Their productivity was low due to a shortage of materials, the lack of appropriate equipment, and obsolete technology. Virtually all apartment buildings were erected with the use of large, prefabricated-panel technology. Recently, however, some of these companies had started using different, more effective technologies and had undergone some management changes that could improve their competitiveness.

Single detached houses were typically built using traditional heavy materials, such as bricks and concrete blocks. This was due, in part, to the perception that these were durable houses ("If I am spending all my money on my own house, it should be good for my grandchildren"). Traditionally, most houses in this category were built by their owners with the use of the services of over 100,000 small artisan-type private enterprises. Productivity in the single-family housing sector was particularly low. Completion of a single-detached house required six years on average—nine times the average time for other countries in Western Europe where similar technology was employed. The lack of financial resources and shortages of materials and equipment were the primary factors contributing to this problem.

Literally thousands of new private enterprises, foreign joint ventures, and co-operatives emerged as a result of the introduction of the new housing regulations. In addition, as a result of a decline in demand, building materials became more readily available (although expensive). New-construction cooperatives were mostly engaged in the construction of multiple-family apartment houses. Since they were started principally for the purpose of providing housing for their members, they did not bid for general construction contracts.

Recently, there had been an increase in the number of private companies penetrating the single-family housing market segment. Some of them were using more effective technologies, similar to those applied in Canada. The most advanced of these firms was Drewbud, a joint venture involving domestic companies in the wood-processing industry with some foreign capital. The company offered catalog houses provided in single-detached, duplex, and row categories in several locations across the country at an average price of $250/sq. m. The distinctive feature of Drewbud's program was that the company provided its customers with a 30-year, 15 percent mortgage[1] for the amount of the purchase price above a 20 percent down payment. This down payment was required as part of the contract to initiate construction of an individual unit. The company seemed to have been overoptimistic in its initial hope of attracting thousands of customers and was in financial trouble by the second half of 1990.

There were several foreign-based home builders in the single-family housing market as well, virtually all offering similar, wooden-frame homes. However, the nature of their experience differed widely, depending on the customer segment targeted. For example, Curtis Construction Ltd., a U.S.-based company, confined its activities to metropolitan Warsaw. It offered six types of single-detached houses built from materials imported from the United States. The company required a financial commitment for the full price of the home from the customer (US$350 per sq. m.) before signing the contract. Curtis ordered all materials from the United States, allowed up to two months for their delivery and then completed construction

---

[1]The mortgage value was to be adjusted to the exchange rate of the zloty to the Swiss franc. This would mean an increase in the mortgage value every time the zloty was devalued.

within six weeks. No data on the number of units sold by the company was available. However, indications were that the company was contemplating raising prices in the near future, which would indicate that its customer base was more than adequate. There were at least three other companies providing similar services in the Warsaw area.

Similar developments in other regions of the country stimulated a lot of initial interest from potential customers, but were beyond their financial capabilities. Labo-Lang, another foreign company, attempted to sell up to 1,000 houses per year at an average price of $250 per sq. m. Over 4,000 individuals initially expressed interest in purchasing these houses, but fewer than 100 were able to finance the purchase.

BUYER BEHAVIOUR

The housing problem was a basic fact of life for people in Poland. Most young families could not afford to either purchase or rent a separate dwelling. A married couple typically spent some 10 years living with one set of their parents in substandard conditions before receiving an apartment in cooperative housing. This resulted in a desperate search by many people for some solution to the problem. They were ready to make substantial sacrifices in order to achieve their goals of living independently and having a home of their own.

On the other hand, the ingrained tradition of low-cost, subsidized housing provided by local administrations made people reluctant to get involved in trying to solve their housing problem by themselves, even if they could potentially combine the resources of their families and build or purchase their own homes. There was no tradition of real estate ownership in Poland and housing was not treated as an opportunity to build one's equity base. Consequently, the real estate market was in a primordial stage of development.

In addition, cost and the problems associated with acquiring a home resulted in very low mobility of the Polish population. It could be assumed that even the best job opportunities created by local markets would not attract people with appropriate qualifications either due to the lack of housing in the area or the reluctance of those who had homes to move from their established location to a new one, even if housing was provided. However, those who did not have a home of their own (mostly young, married couples) could be easily attracted to a new location by the availability of housing there.

SYTKO INTERNATIONAL LIMITED

Contacts with private entrepreneurs from Poland established by Les at the Toronto conference in January allowed him to set up an itinerary for his June visit to the country. The most important piece of information he received during the conference was the name of an aspiring consultant from Torun, Mr. Perzuch, who was ready to act on his behalf in Poland. Thanks to him, Les was able to make contact with municipal leaders in the cities of Torun (150 kms north of Warsaw), Wloclawek (200 kms northwest of Warsaw) and Poznan (150 kms west of Warsaw).

Through Porzuch, Les also made contact with other businesses who were eager to cooperate with him. In addition, his new partner provided Les with some information on the housing market in Poland, especially on competition from other North American companies trying to establish themselves in the country.

Meetings with local businesspeople provided him with an abundance of infomation on opportunities in Poland. Contrary to his expectations, he found a newly developed spirit of entrepreneurship among all the people he met. He had originally been skeptical about the ability of members of municipal governments to act in a businesslike manner, remembering his experiences with the red tape in Poland from his previous visit. Actually, he found them eager to cooperate and flexible in adjusting their policies to the requirements of business.

Les's visit convinced him that his involvement in Poland could be possible and profitable. Promptly after returning to Canada, he began developing the organizational and legal framework for his Polish venture. He approached several people in Canada, mostly of Polish descent, who would potentially participate in his venture. His idea was that this group of 10–15 individuals would initially raise up to a total of US$50,000 in equity and some of them, such as Les himself, having experience in home building, would go to Poland to run the business. He was particularly interested in the participation of a group of owners of other construction companies in Toronto, who could provide expertise to train Polish workers in the wooden-frame technology used in Canada.

Having received some preliminary commitments from a number of these people, Les registered Sytko International Inc., a new private company, to provide an organizational framework for his venture. Les became president of the company and it was planned that all the original shareholders would form the company's board of directors. He thought that the diverse skills of his partners would be beneficial to the company and was still looking for some shareholders who could bring other valuable experience in addition to capital to the venture.

During a recent meeting of the participants in Sytko International, the following ventures in Poland were considered as the initial business opportunities for the company. All of these possible projects emerged from Les's June visit to the country:

Housing Development in Torun.   His meeting with the city mayor gave him the impression that the local government was genuinely concerned about solving the problem of acute housing shortages in the municipality. He liked the business attitude of Mr. Jaszczynski. It was clear that the possibility of quickly constructing several hundred houses, even though not for the average wage earner, had some benefits for him as well. First, local pressures for new housing would be somewhat eased. Second, the possible creation of up to 150 jobs was an important consideration during the period of rising unemployment. Third, the availability of high-quality housing was expected to attract new private entrepreneurs who could increase the number of jobs available under his jurisdiction.

The most important feature of the mayor's proposal for cooperation was that the municipality would develop land for the purpose of building 300-largely single-detached homes. A joint venture between the municipality and Sytko International Ltd. would be the legal framework for the deal. Logistic, legal, and technical support were additional features of Mr. Jaszczynski's proposal. As a result of a series of meetings, a letter of intent was agreed upon and signed.

Sytko International would import most of the materials. To Les's surprise, it was cheaper to import almost all materials from Canada than to get supplies from local distributors. Besides, the quality and reliability of supplies purchased in Poland was questionable. Sytko would also provide the necessary equipment and independently contract for the construction of the homes with interested customers.

It was tentatively agreed that the land would be put at Sytko's disposal in the spring of 1991. Les estimated that he would be able to complete 25–50 houses in the first year. He did not consider a more extensive commitment in the first year due to his lack of experience in the Polish business environment and his uncertainty about the capabilities of the local labour force.

Initial calculations indicated that, thanks to the lower costs of labour in Poland (he assumed US$3.00/hr. as an average, including fringe benefits; this was generous compensation by Polish standards) and almost negligible (relative to the price of the house) costs of land development, he would be able to sell houses at US$300 per square meters, the market average. His total costs of constructing a single detached house of 100 sq. m. in size would be no more than US$24,000. This consisted of US$14,000 in costs for imported materials and equipment, and $10,000 for local labour, materials, and subcontracted services. He estimated that Sytko International would have to put up US$50,000 (the equivalent of almost half a billion zlotys) to start the business. The $50,000 was required to cover the cost of establishing an office and the purchase of basic equipment such as a truck and hand tools. It was assumed that the subsequent financing of construction work would be from customers' down payments and the proceeds of completed sales.

Overall, the picture seemed to look almost too good to be true. However, Les realized that there were some risks involved. First, some of the construction work had to be subcontracted. Laying foundations required heavy equipment that was beyond the immediate capacity of Sytko International. Electrical wiring required knowledge of local standards (Poland, as the rest of Europe, used 220 V A.C. current). Les did not have experience in these areas and did not know whether these differences would result in increased cost. If these tasks were to be subcontracted, he was concerned about the reliability of local firms as they could affect his credibility as a contractor.

Second, gas or oil heating in Poland was not widespread and Les was not sure whether coal furnaces were acceptable within the fire protection regulations in Poland. Electric heating seemed to be an option, but the cost implications for home owners needed to be investigated before deciding on this issue.

Finally, there was the question of marketing the product. He thought that, after the next five years, Sytko might approach any of the basic customer segments except low-income individuals. However, he wanted to concentrate on the highest income groups with emphasis on hard-currency earners in the short term.

Hotel Construction in Torun and Poznan.   The municipalities of Torun and Poznan were interested in a proposal to form a joint venture company to construct hotels in their cities. Construction of these hotels had originally been started back during the investment boom of the 1970s but was soon abandoned due to a lack of funds. Sytko International would be expected to arrange the necessary financing and the municipalities of both cities were ready to form companies to run the hotels.

The proposal by the municipality of Poznan seemed to promise a substantial return on investment. Poznan was the site of a number of international and national fairs and all hotels in the city operated at virtually 100 percent occupancy all year round. The financing required to complete each of the two projects was in the range of US$1 million. The joint venture company could negotiate a loan of an undetermined amount from the local bank, as well as apply for credits from international development agencies. It was estimated that construction could be completed within one year. Potential profits were difficult to estimate at this point, but Les was aware that similar projects undertaken in Poland had provided investors with at least a 40 percent return on investment and he might expect even more due to the high financial leverage.

Les felt, however, that the required initial capital outlay required estimated at more than US$200,000 was too high for the company without outside additional equity financing. Sytko's shareholders were mostly small entrepreneurs. In order to increase the company's equity base, Les would have to either attract a relatively large number of small, or one or two larger, investors. Either of these alternatives would diminish the role of Les's current partners. He was apprehensive about this since the more elaborate organizational structure required for a larger company would take away from his venture some of the entrepreneurial aspects that he personally enjoyed. However, at the same time, the hotel market in Poland was virtually untapped and a good location would guarantee the company steady, high income for at least a decade. Finally, under the current legislation, foreign investments in the hotel industry could qualify for income tax exemption for up to six years, compared to three years applied to foreign investments in other industries, such as the construction of single-detached homes.

Housing Construction in Warsaw.   Based on his research and the information provided by Mr. Porzuch, Les felt there might also be an immediate opportunity to establish his company as a custom-home builder in Warsaw, the capital of Poland. There was no commitment from the municipality of metro Warsaw to cooperate, partly due to the fact that land was scarce within the immediate proximity of the city. However, the shortage of housing in the Polish capital was the most severe in the country. This shortage extended across all types of apartments and had increased prices to astronomic levels.

The influx of foreign businesses establishing branches in Poland was concentrated in the capital as the standard services they required, such as office space, translation services, and telecommunications facilities were more readily available here than anywhere else in Poland.

In Warsaw, Les would have to start slowly by promoting his company to prospective customers and the company's growth would be limited because of competition from other builders. In addition, due to the wide dispersion of building locations, the initial training of employees would be erratic and costly. But continued demand in and around Warsaw was guaranteed for the foreseeable future. Les did not consider moving into land development and tract-housing as a real alternative at the start, but that could be a good way to reinvest any initial profits.

Export Markets.   With the cheap labour available in Poland, Les felt it might be possible to export these skills to the rest of the European market. Under this alternative, Sytko International would provide initial training for workers in Poland and then, using this cheaper labour, market its products outside of the country. There were opportunities in both Western and Eastern Europe that could be captured by the company.

Poland had just applied for association with the EEC and, although not finally approved, it received a guarantee of automatic acceptance after free parliamentary elections had been held (scheduled for next year). This would mean lower custom duties on material components exported from Poland to other countries in this region. In addition, some current restrictions on the movement of labour between Eastern and Western Europe would be waived, giving Poland's construction industry a competitive edge over its Western counterparts.

Les did not have much opportunity to evaluate the financial feasibility of such an option, but there were substantial arguments to support this idea. First, profits made from export activities could be immediately transferred out of Poland, as opposed to those made in Poland. Prices of houses in Western Europe were higher than those in Poland, which could provide him with an even higher return on his investment. And, finally, there were tax incentives for exports from Poland, which would make such a venture highly profitable even after the initial, 3-year tax holiday. Les was particularly interested in investigating opportunities in what had formerly been East Germany. Housing shortages were not as severe there as in Poland, but with the economic recovery of the region, a substantial demand for higher quality housing could be anticipated. Other countries in Eastern Europe could also be considered, but Les was not sure whether his prices could be attractive there. However, Les was aware that Canadian-style housing was not all that well accepted in contrast with the more traditional housing construction in Europe, and that his homes could be unattractive without discount pricing.

CRITICAL QUESTIONS

As Les contemplated his forthcoming trip overseas, he reflected on a number of issues. Perhaps forming Sytko International was a mistake. Maybe he should concentrate on developing his business in Canada rather than investigating opportunities in Poland. Did he really have any competitive advantage relative to other construction companies active in the country? What criteria should he use to evaluate the range of alternatives facing Sytko? And should he decide to actually make the move, which of these alternatives would appear to be the best fit for the company?

However, the financial risks associated with Sytko entering the construction market in Poland seemed to be low and, in Les's view, there were indications that the potential payoff could be high. If he went ahead, Les was inclined to go after the deal with Torun,

---

EXHIBIT 4   Housing Statistics—Canada and Poland

	Canada	Poland
Number of households (1986)	9 million	12.1 million
Average number of households per dwelling*	0.99	1.18
Percent of households with		
Running water	99.8%	80%
Telephone	98.4%	25%
Age structure of housing (1986)		
Apartments/houses built:		
Before 1946	20%	36%
1946–70	39%	34%
1971–80	30%	19%
1981–86	11%	11%
Number of dwellings completed per year (1983–1988):		
1983	163,000	196,000
1984	153,000	196,000
1985	139,000	190,000
1986	184,000	185,000
1987	218,000	191,000
1988	216,500	177,000
Housing standard (1987):		
Average number of rooms per apartment	5.7	3.3
Average number of persons per room	.5	1.1
Structure of ownership:		
Percent of dwellings owned	62%	46%
Percent of dwellings rented	37.5%	54%
Percent of dwellings on reserve	.5%	—

*Serves as an indicator of nominal demand for housing. Numbers lower than 1.00 indicate that the total number of dwellings available on the market exceeds the number of families.

but he was afraid that Sytko's involvement with this project would tie all its resources to this local market. There was a danger this market segment could be easily saturated at the price level the company was contemplating.

The Warsaw market seemed to be more immune to such risks. Knowing that virtually all competitors in this area charged prices higher than those being considered by Sytko, he was confident he could gain access to that market. Moreover, Les had not investigated the possibility of approaching the governments of small municipalities within driving distance from Warsaw and offering a joint venture, similar to that negotiated in Torun. This could give him an additional competitive edge. However, in this, as well as in the Torun case, he was afraid of being dependent on a single contract with a public agency for the success of his business. There had

EXHIBIT 5

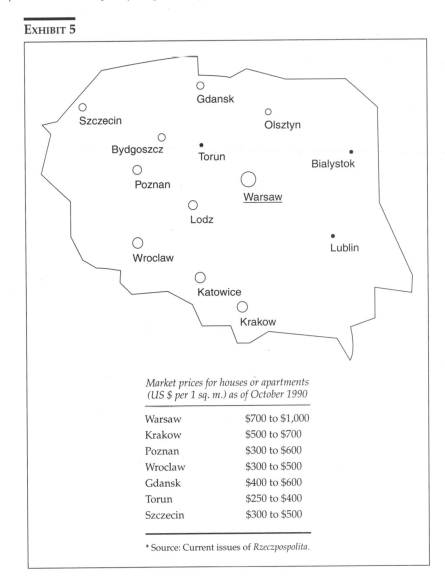

*Market prices for houses or apartments
(US $ per 1 sq. m.) as of October 1990*

Warsaw	$700 to $1,000
Krakow	$500 to $700
Poznan	$300 to $600
Wroclaw	$300 to $500
Gdansk	$400 to $600
Torun	$250 to $400
Szczecin	$300 to $500

* Source: Current issues of *Rzeczpospolita.*

been some cases he was aware of where business deals struck with local governments were subsequently canceled under the mounting populist pressure from
their constituencies.

Yes, his visit to Poland promised a lot of excitement. As the founder of Sytko
International, Les still had a good deal of freedom in deciding on the company's
strategy and shaping its corporate profile. At the same time, he felt a burden of
responsibility to the company's other shareholders who, having committed their
capital and time, were relying on his judgment. This feeling made his decisions
far more difficult.

III Cross-Border Alliances

CASE SUMMARIES

Case 8: Foreign Market Entry and Internationalization: The Case of Datacom Software Research

By Nicole Coviello (University of Auckland, New Zealand)

Datacom Software Research (DSR), headquartered in Christchurch, New Zealand, was formed in 1982 as an independent subsidiary of Datacom Group and produces software for land and seabed surveying. The case focuses on the formation of the business and the development of its extensive network of licensees, distributors, and other partners marketing DSR's products around the world. These relationships have been essential to DSR's start-up, survival, and internationalization. However, in late 1990 Alan Townsend, DSR's general manager, is concerned that these relationships, especially one with Sokkisha (a Japanese firm), are limiting DSR's growth potential because its partners are of uneven quality and because their loyalties are divided between DSR's products and the products of other companies. DSR employs 40 people, and the case provides details about products, partners, managers, organizational structure, and some financial information about markets and finances. Readers are asked to decide what DSR should do.

Case 9: Lobatse Clay Works

By David Osgood (George Washington University, USA) and edited by Richard G. Linowes (American University, USA)

Lobatse Clay Works manufactures clay products for the construction industry in Botswana. The company is a joint venture between the Botswana Development Corporation and an American brickmaking company, Interkiln. The path from feasibility study to start of the operation is filled with unexpected difficulties. Shortly after starting production, the local partner and major customer is beset with corruption charges for offering kickbacks in the construction bidding process, and all further procurement ceases. The resulting fall-off of orders now throws into question the economic viability of the entire joint venture.

CASE 10: INTERNATIONALIZATION AND THE ENTREPRENEURIAL HIGH TECHNOLOGY FIRM: THE CASE OF MANA SYSTEMS, LTD.

By Nicole Coviello (University of Auckland, New Zealand)

MANA Systems Ltd (MSL) is a privately held company and was founded in Auckland, New Zealand, in 1979 by Mr. Robert Barnes to design and market system software. It began by direct selling in New Zealand and Australia and by attempting to ally with a distributor in the United States. However, the New Zealand market was too small, the Australian market was too untrusting of a small start-up, and the failed U.S. effort nearly bankrupted MSL. In 1984, MSL entered into an agreement with Fujitsu in which the Japanese firm funded product development at MSL in return for worldwide marketing rights under Fujitsu's name. Since that time, MSL has been a successful development laboratory for Fujitsu, and MSL's markets have expanded in New Zealand, Australia, and Japan. By 1991, MSL employed 25 people and is completely dependent on Fujitsu for marketing and customer intelligence. However, Mr. Barnes wants to introduce new products and is ambivalent about his relationship with Fujitsu because of MSL's dependence and disappointing level of growth. Readers are asked to suggest an appropriate strategy. ∎

CASE 8
FOREIGN MARKET ENTRY AND INTERNATIONALIZATION: THE CASE OF DATACOM SOFTWARE RESEARCH

In December 1990, Alan Townsend, General Manager of Datacom Software Research (DSR), was considering the future of his organization.

DSR is a wholly owned subsidiary of the Datacom Group (an unlisted public company), and is headquartered in Christchurch, New Zealand. It competes in the international Geographic Information Systems (GIS) market for land and hydrographic survey software. Since being founded in 1982, DSR has grown to 40 employees.

As stated in the 1988 plan for DSR, the company's mission is:

> To become a major supplier of quality product, service, and support to the international land surveying market, and to provide additional growth by product diversification into other international niche markets, not necessarily related to land surveying.

Land surveying products are marketed worldwide through the Sokkisha Company Limited (headquartered in Japan) and The Lietz Company (the U.S. subsidiary of Sokkisha).[1] Hydrographic surveying products are marketed through a different set of relationships, including a DSR-controlled distribution network, and a joint marketing agreement with two European companies—Simrad A/S (Norway) and Geotronics AB (Sweden). A new product designed for the utility mapping market will be distributed exclusively in the U.K. by a small British firm, Subtronic. All international operations are overseen by DSR Christchurch and DSR support staff located in the U.K., Holland, and France.

Currently, the Sokkisha relationship is of primary interest to Townsend. He believes that "How we work our relationship with Sokkisha from now on is crucial to our future." Townsend's priority as of December 1990 is resolution of this issue, and he is actively examining all potential options. Also of interest to Townsend is how to develop stronger end-user support in DSR's international markets.

A BRIEF HISTORY OF DSR

In the early 1980s, Alan Townsend was involved with project management for the Datacom Group, and had the responsibility of assisting a subsidiary company, Datacomm Equipment, adapt a land survey data collection product for the New Zealand market. This also involved Townsend identifying opportunities for product and market development. In his search for narrow vertical markets he made contact with the manager of the Australian subsidiary of Sokkisha, "By accident . . . but it wasn't an accident that I saw the opportunity for a vertical market in Sokkisha Australia."

To manage the potential product development relationship with Sokkisha Australia, a two-person department within the Datacom Group was formed in 1982,

Source: This case was written by Nicole Coviello of the University of Auckland, New Zealand. The author is indebted to TRADENZ for financial support for this research. This case is intended as a basis for class discussion rather than to illustrate either effective or ineffective handling of an administrative situation.

---

[1]Please see Appendix A for all partner details.

with Townsend as its head. The relationship was soon formalized, and by 1986 the small team had grown to six full-time employees. At that time, the department was established as a separate and independent organization, known as Datacom Software Research. By then, DSR's data collection software had already entered the U.S. market through Sokkisha distributors (1984) and Japan (1986). Preliminary contacts (through Sokkisha Australia) had also been made in the U.K. and Europe. In 1987, two products accounted for all of the company's business: the SDR2 Electronic Field Book (a data collector) and SURVIS (an office computer system for surveying and engineering). In 1988, a hydrographic survey software product was introduced (HYDRO). In early 1990, a new product was being championed within DSR: Manholes (system software for the utility mapping market).

As of 1990, the company consists of 40 employees operating in three general product areas: land survey and engineering software, hydrographic survey software, and utility mapping system software. These products are sold in New Zealand, Australia, the United States, Japan, Europe, the U.K., Canada, and Asia/Africa.

PRODUCTS AND MARKETS

Products.   All products serve the land and hydrographic survey market, and have been developed to minimize the time and effort needed to produce finished plans and designs in survey work. The Data Collection software was developed for land surveyors using handheld computers connected to survey equipment on the field. The PC Software product provides contour mapping and design functions for surveyors and engineers (e.g., Union Pacific Railroad in the United States used it to survey railroad curves, while the British Army has used it to locate and plot minefields in the Falkland Islands). HYDRO is used to precisely position and map seabeds in harbour and coastal survey work. It is also used in the oil and gas industry to position ocean rigs and undersea pipelines. The development of HYDRO, and more recently the Manholes product, capitalizes on highly accurate positioning ability, available through satellite global positioning technology (i.e., Global Positioning Systems).

All DSR software products are standardized, and customization is done by varying modules and software parameters. All products have a similar obsolescence factor, and releases are planned every 6–12 months. They run on IBM and IBM-compatibles, although the UNIX platform is being planned for. Also, as computer technology evolves, products such as the handheld data collection software require a major platform change every three years. DSR reinvests approximately 33 percent of annual revenues into product development (programming and software generation).

Markets.   For planning purposes, Alan Townsend defines the company's market as ". . . the international land and hydrographic surveying market."

Land surveying encompasses both the land survey market and the civil engineering market. It is seen by Townsend to be very price competitive and with static sales, although no industry shakeout has yet occurred. Clients in this niche market include consulting engineers, architects, surveyors, mining and quarrying firms, and utility companies. Strong geographic markets include the United States, Europe, and some Asian countries.

The hydrographic survey market consists of customers in ports and harbours, as well as the oil industry (primarily offshore oil operations). Criteria for product selection are technically complex, with price low on the list. Product competition is increasing in the market, and strong geographic areas include New Zealand and Australia (ports and harbours), and the Middle East (oil industry).

In addition to the two primary markets, utility mapping is developing into a new customer base for DSR. This will involve software development for foul sewer and storm water system management. Geographic markets for the Manholes product are worldwide.

Overall, Townsend believes DSR's markets are changing rapidly, with customer needs changing as users become increasingly sophisticated. A major influence in 1990/91 is that all major product markets for the company are in simultaneous recession due to a construction recession in the United States and U.K., and political turmoil in the Middle East.

DSR'S CURRENT ORGANIZATION AND PERFORMANCE

The Founder/Manager.   Alan Townsend has been general manager of DSR since 1982. He is on both the DSR board and the board of directors for the Datacom Group. His current responsibility is to manage and build DSR, maintain profitability levels, and provide a 20 percent return on revenues to the Datacom Group.

Age 42, Townsend has worked within the Datacom Group for 19 years. He joined the company as a trainee programmer after graduating with a B.Sc. in Economics, and then moved into systems analysis and design work. This led to becoming assistant manager of the Group's Christchurch operation, where he was responsible for operations, systems, and programming. In 1979 Townsend moved to a broader staff role for project work. One project involved exporting a legal computing system to Australia, providing Townsend with experience in a new market. In the early 1980s Townsend received increased responsibility for handheld data collection products, and in 1982 initiated the relationship with Sokkisha Australia.

Currently, Townsend is responsible for all general planning and strategic marketing decisions at DSR. While individual product responsibilities are delegated to product managers, he remains involved with key areas and retains final review of all decisions. Townsend is also responsible for maintaining and negotiating the Sokkisha relationship.

Company Structure.   DSR is organized in four departments, based on identified product-markets (see Exhibit 1). Refer to Appendix B for biographical notes of key managers reporting to Townsend.

Exhibit 1   **DSR Organizational Structure**

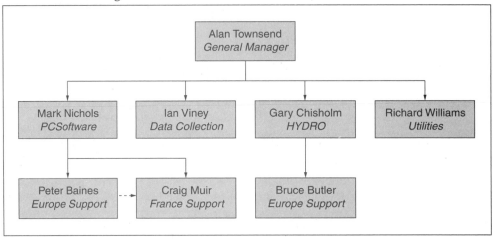

The largest department, referred to as PC Software, focuses on land survey products, particularly PC engineering and surveying software. It consists of 24 employees including Alan Townsend, and is managed by Mark Nichols (Product Manager—Surveying and Engineering Products). A second department, responsible for data collection products, is titled Data Collection. This group is managed by Ian Viney, and includes six employees.

The complete PC Software product is shipped from Christchurch, and is sold through the majority of Sokkisha's international subsidiaries, distributors, and agents. The data collection software is licensed to Lietz, who then sells to Sokkisha's distributors worldwide. For these products, the DSR department supports Sokkisha sales in Europe with staffs in Holland and France. They provide a technical support liaison between major clients and DSR, and have a marketing role in terms of providing feedback on market requirements, introducing new products, and performing sales calls with the Sokkisha distributor. Peter Baines is based in Amsterdam, and is responsible for all of Europe including the U.K. and Eastern Europe. Craig Muir is in France for one year on a specific "one market" market development exercise.

The third department, named HYDRO, focuses on hydrographic survey products, and is managed by Gary Chisholm. It consists of nine employees, including Bruce Butler (European Support, based in the U.K.). HYDRO is sold through international distributors established by DSR, and a joint marketing agreement with Geotronics and Simrad (based in Sweden and Norway, respectively). Please see Appendix A for partner details.

The fourth and newest department, referred to as Utilities, consists of one employee, Richard Williams. Williams focuses on the development and growth of the Manholes product, and will support Subtronic sales to the U.K. market.

Trend in Sales and Financial Performance.   1989/90 gross income for DSR (12 months ended 31 March 1990) was approximately $NZ 3.2 million (see Exhibit 2). This represents a 45 percent increase on 1988 figures.

Of the total 1989/90 sales, 48.7 percent were accounted for by data collection products, followed by 43.5 percent from PC Software, and 7.8 percent from HYDRO (see Exhibit 3). Sales reflect growth in PC Software sales (in the fourth quarter) and HYDRO (through expansion into the United States, Canada, and Europe). No growth in data collection products occurred, and in fact, sales of this product line decreased in Asia/Africa, Australia, and Canada.

By geographic market, sales growth is concentrated in Europe (see Exhibit 4 for a 3-year sales comparison by market, 1987–1989/90) and the United States accounts for 32 percent of company sales. By product in geographic market, there are clear variations in sales performance (see Exhibit 5) with data collection products strongest in the United States, PC Software in Europe and the United States, and HYDRO strongest in Australia. Of note, as of late 1990, no sales had been made for the utility mapping software (Manholes).

For the 1990/91 fiscal year, sales are expected to reach nearly $4 million. Townsend expects, however, that in spite of the launch of the Manholes product, and receiving a major contract for HYDRO, actual performance could be less than budgeted. This is due to a recession in all major markets, as well as a delayed market introduction of the new version of the PC Software product.

INTERNATIONALIZING DSR

As of 1990, DSR serves a number of product-markets. The internationalization process for DSR will be described chronologically, beginning in 1982.

DSR's Original Product—Data Collectors.   In 1982, Townsend was identifying vertical market and product application opportunities for the Datacom Group. During this process, he met Mike Beckingham, a New Zealander managing the Australian subsidiary of Sokkisha. Beckingham was interested in the growth potential for handheld electronic devices, and with Townsend, developed a new product specification for data collection software. The SDR1 was then developed by Sokkisha under the agreement that DSR would carry all development costs, and be paid as each product sold. In 1984, the product was launched into Australia, and then the United States. Sokkisha Australia undertook all marketing efforts and feedback of market information to DSR.

The Second Product Area to be Developed.   In 1984, DSR entered a licensing agreement with an Australian firm to sell PC Software for the land survey and engineering market into New Zealand. Although DSR was in fact focusing its resources on developing the data collection product, the chance to expand its product range presented itself and was felt to be opportune. DSR had no internal development capabilities for PC engineering software at the time, however,

EXHIBIT 2   Trend in Gross Income (NZ$), 1982 to 1989/90 (Year ended March 31, 1990)

Year	Gross Income
1982	$74,457
1983	$577,875
1984	$226,418
1985	$1,266,000
1986	$2,141,800
1987	$1,501,583*
1988	$2,193,845
1989/90	$3,181,801

* The 1987 decrease in gross income is a result of DSR transferring the assembly of hardware and software back to the United States. From that point on, revenues accrued from licensing fees, and not the product which included sale of hardware.

Source: Adapted from DSR Position Statement, February 1987, and DSR May 1990 Annual Plan, p. 25.

EXHIBIT 3   Product by Market Gross Revenues (12 months ending March 31, 1990)

	Data Collection	HYDRO	PC Software	Totals
Asia/Africa	137,872	52,990	177,122	367,984
Australia	87,994	117,863	119,175	325,032
Canada	101,168	12,765	81,801	195,734
Europe	341,309	6,875	409,893	758,077
Japan	149,947	0	0	149,947
New Zealand	3,695	42,613	105,057	151,365
United Kingdom	57,717	0	157,099	214,816
United States	669,554	16,422	322,870	1,018,801
Totals	$1,549,256	$249,528	$1,383,017	$3,181,846
Percent	48.7%	7.8%	43.5%	100%

Source: DSR May 1990 Annual Plan, p. 16.

it quickly moved to increase staff numbers to support this area (with the intent to replace all Australian product with software developed in New Zealand).

Entering the U.S. Market.   In 1985, Townsend made the decision to base himself in the United States, and for 12 months joined The Lietz Company in Kansas

EXHIBIT 4   Three-Year Sales Comparison by Market (percentage figures only)*

Market	1987	1988	1989
Asia/Africa	13.6%	10.8%	11.6%
Australia	15.5	9.2	10.2
Canada	3.1	5.0	6.2
Europe	3.4	13.7	23.8
Japan	12.5	8.4	4.7
New Zealand	7.6	8.5	4.8
United Kingdom	8.5	14.4	6.8
United States	35.5	29.8	32

* Percentage of total DSR products sold into each geographic market.

Source: Adapted from DSR May 1990 Annual Plan, p. 25.

EXHIBIT 5   Percentage of Products into Markets (1990 YTD)

Market	Data Collection	PC Software	HYDRO	Total
Asia/Africa	8.9%	12.8%	21.2%	11.6%
Australia	5.7	8.6	47.2	10.2
Canada	6.5	5.9	5.1	6.2
Europe	22.0	29.6	2.8	23.8
Japan	9.7	0.0	0.0	4.7
New Zealand	0.2	7.6	17.1	4.8
United Kingdom	3.7	11.4	0.0	6.8
United States	43.2	24.1	6.6	32.0

Source: Adapted from DSR May 1990 Annual Plan, p. 16.

(Sokkisha's U.S. subsidiary). The choice to manage DSR from a distance was governed by his belief that to develop key markets, firms have to:

> Put the best person they possibly can in the target market. The person they can least afford to send to Australia or send to the States, that is the person who should go.

During his time with Lietz, Townsend focused on developing the U.S. market for DSR, and launched an upgraded version of the SDR1 data collector. In 1986 Townsend signed a three-way licensing agreement with Sokkisha Japan and The

Lietz Company for the exclusive sale of DSR software coupled with Lietz hardware. All products were to be sold through Lietz in the United States, and through Sokkisha subsidiaries worldwide.

According to Townsend, the Lietz relationship offered good coverage of the U.S. market given the company's strong sales force and large retail network. Lietz is over one hundred years old, with a reputation of being a stable Midwest company able to provide strong support. This piggy-backing relationship meant that DSR products were used to enhance Lietz's core products and provide added-value to both the distributor (through increased sales) and end user. The relationship was seen by Townsend to allow early penetration of the U.S. market for DSR; however, Townsend also felt the relationship presented a potential disadvantage to DSR. That is, if the DSR software was not perceived to add value to the core hardware product, sales of the software might not be supported.

A Third Product Area Emerges.   In 1987, DSR made the decision to diversify, ". . . because if we stuck to the data collection business, we would have been sold to Sokkisha." As a result, HYDRO was developed for the hydrographic survey market, using Trimble Navigation position equipment (see Appendix A for information on Trimble).

HYDRO was identified as a niche market product with limited potential in New Zealand, therefore Townsend planned early for expansion into foreign markets. Also, Townsend notes that in order to justify HYDRO product development expenses, international expansion was required.

Australia was entered in late 1987, through direct sales made by Gary Chisholm (the HYDRO product manager). These sales resulted from a direct-mail campaign to Australia's ports and harbours which yielded an unexpectedly high response rate of 80–90 percent. The high level of interest encouraged DSR to serve the market without distributors, and Chisholm approached interested buyers himself. HYDRO is now in most major Australian ports, including Perth, home of the product's major competitor, Qubit.

According to Townsend, no consideration was given to any other form of business relationship to serve Australia (e.g., a joint venture or merger with an Australian company). Cubit was the only other competitor in the market, and he preferred to compete directly against it. Also, the use of a distributor network was believed inappropriate as the Australian market was estimated to be small (a total of 15–20 systems), and the costs of establishing and training distributors were felt to be prohibitive.

Further Market Entry for PC Software and HYDRO.   In January 1988, DSR entered a formal licensing agreement with The Lietz Company to distribute its New Zealand–developed PC Software products in the United States. Lietz would generate the software and pay DSR a licensing fee. The relationship is fairly informal in comparison to the agreement structured for the handheld data collection products.

Also in 1988, DSR established a HYDRO distributor in Asia through a contact of Chisholm's, and it was decided that DSR would explore distributors for the United States and Europe. The possibility of distributing HYDRO through the Sokkisha network was considered, but discarded as the product offered Sokkisha no added value.

Further market entry for HYDRO was planned at two levels. First, DSR wanted to identify global partners for the product. Ideally, these partners were to be hardware manufacturers that could benefit from the product enhancements' added value offered by HYDRO. This approach was based on the company's earlier successful experience with Sokkisha in the land survey market. Second, DSR wanted local/regional distributors handling a range of products DSR could sell. DSR wanted no exclusive deals, but wanted the regional and international distributors (the manufacturers) to overlap in their marketing and sales efforts.

To accomplish the first objective, trade shows and word-of-mouth contacts were used to identify a number of manufacturing companies in the echo-sounding and positioning industries. Specific partner attributes were identified, with the most critical being that the firm(s) were to be international in their operations (regardless of head office location) and well-respected. Through this process, two Scandinavian companies were evaluated: Geotronics (producing vessel positioning equipment) and Simrad (producing echo sounders and depth finders).

A Fourth Product Opportunity Identified.   The opportunity for software development for the U.K. utilities market (underground drainage and sewage systems in particular) was identified by Mark Nichols in 1988. He met with Subtronic managers, and learned that the U.K. government had legislated records for water authorities. Nichols saw an opportunity to produce a computing product for these authorities, and championed a marketing relationship with Subtronic. However, DSR's efforts were largely focused on market development for HYDRO, and the Manholes project was temporarily placed on hold.

HYDRO Expands Further.   In 1989, a joint marketing agreement was signed involving formal distributor relationships between DSR and each of Geotronics and Simrad, and an informal relationship between Geotronics and Simrad. As a result, HYDRO is sold through Simrad and Geotronics' distributors (supported by Bruce Butler in the U.K.) and the three companies together market HYDISP, a joint product. Townsend notes that the joint marketing agreement "seemed to fit the business at the time." Both companies were active and well established in their markets, with extensive contacts and an interest in joint arrangements.

The second stage of market entry planning for HYDRO then proceeded with the identification and selection of regional distributors to sell the product. Contacts were identified by trade shows, word-of-mouth, international trade journals, and industry magazines. Townsend and Chisholm developed a list of formal selection criteria, and informally, evaluated a number of distributors worldwide. Mike Beckingham provided assistance to Chisholm in working through distribution options for the United States. Relationships have now been established in Singapore, Hong Kong, Canada, and the United States.

As of 1990, DSR's expectations for initial market success have not been met. Townsend notes that in the "equal" relationship with Simrad and Geotronic, the former has benefited most in the year since the relationship was formed, and sales have been slow. This is seen as a disadvantage by Townsend; however, he expects the balance to even out in the future. In addition, although no formal product development partnership is in place with these companies, he believes the potential is there. Finally, Townsend believes that further time is required for the international distributor network to mature with the new product. Townsend anticipates continued growth for HYDRO, and an improvement in returns from the Simrad-Geotronics relationship. Interestingly, the relationship with Geotronics is perceived by Sokkisha to be unsatisfactory in that the two are direct competitors in the instrument industry. However, Townsend notes that in the hydrographic area, Sokkisha does not have a competing product.

Further New Product Development and a New Relationship.   In 1990, DSR introduced their global positioning systems software (GPSmap). Like HYDRO, this product interfaces DSR software with positioning equipment developed by Trimble Navigation in the United States. No formal development relationship was established with Trimble, however, and the product is distributed through Sokkisha.

Also in 1990, attention was redirected to the Manholes project when Richard Williams reidentified the product's potential. This led to Manholes product development being financially supported by DSR, as from 1990. Manholes development is driven by market need in the U.K., and as a result, initial sales will be made there. The market is a very specialized and narrow niche, and the product has not been fully adapted for use outside the U.K. Subtronic acts as distributor for the product, and is supported by Williams in Christchurch. Townsend notes that Subtronic is not technically advanced, but he believes this weakness will change, and is more than balanced by their market knowledge and strong geographic focus.

Although another U.K. company (Key Systems) approached DSR to sell Manholes, DSR decided the nature of the market prohibited two companies competing with the same product. Thus, Key Systems was encouraged to work with Subtronic to support the U.K. market. Manholes is on a two-year plan, currently being examined for adaptation to the New Zealand, Australian, and U.S. markets. It is anticipated that Subtronic will be unable to develop markets beyond the U.K. and potential distributors for New Zealand and Australia are currently being identified.

The Evolving DSR–Sokkisha Relationship.   According to Townsend, DSR's alliance with Sokkisha is fairly informal and "person-to-person" rather than "company-to-company." As a result, negotiations were begun in 1989 to increase the formality of the relationship, and in fact, form a joint venture. This continued into 1990 with DSR seeking a 50/50 partnership for onward development of the data collection business. To support the planned joint venture, Ian Viney was named JV Manager Designate. In December 1990, Sokkisha advised Townsend they wished to renegotiate some points on the proposed agreement, and invited DSR to Tokyo to undertake negotiations.

TOWNSEND'S ROLE IN THE INTERNATIONALIZATION PROCESS

In terms of managing the internationalization process, Townsend established the original Sokkisha relationship, and negotiated the licensing agreement with Lietz. To date, he has done all the negotiation and contractual work with DSR distributors, and manages general communication with them. For HYDRO and Manholes, he was involved with identifying partner and distributor attributes, targeting and evaluating potential partners and distributors, and choosing them. This, however, also involved Gary Chisholm (Product Manager of HYDRO) and Mark Nichols (who identified the opportunity with Subtronic).

Although Townsend is still responsible for all legal work in relationship management, the day-to-day management of relationships now rests with the three product managers. Townsend believes this is necessary in order for these managers to develop a strong personal rapport with the partners. Therefore, Townsend acts as a facilitator for the product managers. He believes that the rate of DSR's growth is controlled by the growth in people (both in volume and skills) and believes his managers have reached a level where they are able to control their own destiny.

PLANNING PROCESSES AT DSR

The formality of the DSR planning process has varied over time. Initially, DSR followed a formal, documented planning system, and between 1985 and 1988, the company had a formal plan with mission and objectives. According to Townsend, having a formal plan gave DSR a focus for the first few years of operations. He states further that if a major change in markets or strategic relationships were to develop, a formal planning process would reappear to help focus the company's direction.

Currently, however, DSR's planning approach is less formal, with "general" planning documents contained in the annual report. Although goals are set by product and for the company as a whole, strategy development occurs fairly informally among DSR management. According to Townsend:

> Market information which can alter our strategic direction comes up all the time. Strategy can change radically . . . it is important that you grab hold of the opportunities as they come through. The rate of change is rapid and we have to react quickly to those changes. Consequently, our market strategy can also change rapidly.

At the same time, Townsend believes that while planning is quite informal, management of the company and its internationalization process has evolved to a more mature level. Chance plays less of a role than it did at the initiation of the early relationship with Sokkisha. He notes, however, that there is always an element of chance, and each company has to be "in the game" to take advantage of it.

MARKETING AT DSR

No one person is defined to be the Marketing Manager at DSR. Townsend makes the company's strategic marketing decisions (e.g., regarding market development), but not in isolation of his product manager's day-to-day market involvement. He reviews all marketing decisions, and is responsible for all legal aspects of these decisions, particularly when negotiating relationships. Each product manager sets goals and strategies for product development, and is responsible for pricing decisions, promotional material, and channel management.

In terms of marketing activities, DSR tries to understand international market growth rates and forecast sales in order to plan more accurately (for budgeting and reinvestment). The depth of competitive analysis varies, ranging from a database of information for HYDRO (including demographic information on 17 international competitors, markets sold to, number installed, and so on) to informal information for land survey products, based on industry magazine analyses and market experience. DSR management has no formal system for evaluating competitor moves or potential market entry, and most market intelligence and customer education/service activities are outsourced to partners. However, based on DSR's recent experience of underestimating the time required to introduce HYDRO and the new PC Software product, it now recognizes the importance of fully understanding the customer's buying process.

DSR RELATIONSHIPS: TOWNSEND'S CONCERNS

According to Townsend, initial options for internationalization (e.g., joint ventures and joint marketing agreements) were limited by the original arrangement established with Sokkisha Australia. While this agreement enabled DSR to readily access international markets through a well-established, successful, and well-managed distribution network, it now provides certain limitations to future growth. For example, DSR's ties to Sokkisha restrict its ability to establish a secondary distribution network for its products in the land-survey market. Also, DSR must use Sokkisha's distributors, good or bad. Should DSR establish a competitive distributor in a geographic area poorly served by Sokkisha, they run the risk of upsetting the entire network.

Although the DSR–Sokkisha relationship is perceived by Townsend to be successful, there is a growing battle for power between the two companies, and recently, Sokkisha introduced a product in competition with DSR's handheld data collection product. As a result, Townsend questions the degree of Sokkisha's loyalty to DSR.

Townsend is also concerned about managing partner quality, given that many marketing activities are outsourced. Across all DSR products, he estimates there are approximately 1,000 distributors and subdistributors. Of these, approximately 20 are "first tier," 10 of which are active HYDRO distributors, and 10 are Sokkisha subsidiaries (including Lietz). These 20 are actively communicated with; however the remainder are less tightly managed. They vary in technical and market skills and are concerned with losing control of their market to DSR. Business philosophies and practices vary by country, increasing the complexity of international relationships. Establishing these relationships is difficult and time-consuming, and once operational, may require further time to generate sales (based on DSR's experience with HYDRO). Also, Townsend notes that language and cultural differences have posed difficulties outside the Australian and U.K. markets.

Overall, however, Townsend is generally pleased with his strategic relationships with Sokkisha, Lietz, Geotronics, Simrad, Subtronic, and DSR's many distributors, but he recognizes problems in dealing with them. He states:

> I work on the basis that you go carefully into these linkages because there is a fair cost in getting out of them. We haven't identified each cost, we just know we have to be pretty sure of the relationship before we get into it.

THE FUTURE OF DSR

The overall strategy of DSR is to be international; therefore, any product considered must have overseas potential. As stated by Alan Townsend:

> We are continually looking for new product opportunities. These are evaluated in the context of addressing a narrow vertical niche . . . a market that we are, or can become experts in.

In terms of the future, the Sokkisha relationship is of primary concern to Townsend. Of critical importance are DSR's negotiations to establish a joint venture with Sokkisha for the land survey data collection products. With Sokkisha particularly interested in this area of DSR, Townsend is concerned about protecting the interests of his firm and staff. For example, at the outset of negotiations in November 1989, Sokkisha initially wanted to acquire a percentage of the entire company. Townsend felt this could potentially engulf DSR, and over the course of a year, agreed on a form of joint venture to be located in Christchurch. The joint venture will include only that product Sokkisha is strategically interested in, thus protecting other product lines.

Regarding the Sokkisha distribution channel that is used worldwide, Townsend believes DSR will outgrow it. In fact, a sales barrier in all Sokkisha markets is expected over the next two years, and the exclusive relationship with Lietz is now perceived to be a potential weakness (given DSR sales levels are restricted to the market share achieved by Lietz). Currently, Townsend is starting negotiations with Sokkisha regarding the establishment of a U.K.–based support group to take responsibility for some of Sokkisha's current support roles. He notes that, in terms of the company's relationships with Sokkisha, "How we work our relationship with Sokkisha from now on is crucial to our future."

For the future, Townsend believes there are at least three options:

1. To develop the joint venture with Sokkisha for data collection products, with the remainder of DSR operating independently.
2. Discontinue the relationship with Sokkisha, and have DSR operating *without* a strategic partner.
3. And/or have DSR operate with a multitude of strategic partners, and no one dominant relationship.

Townsend's priority as of December 1990 is resolution of this issue, and he is actively examining all potential options.

Townsend also wants to develop stronger support in DSR's international markets. He notes:

> We plan to have our overseas support bases staffed by nationals of that market. This should improve our knowledge of those markets and lead to a better long-term commitment.

Issues related to managing the DSR position in Europe are being considered very carefully. For example, Townsend would like to aggressively develop the German market in the same way as the French market. If DSR were to establish a U.K.–based support group to assume some of Sokkisha's responsibilities for Europe, it could improve sales to the existing marketplace, and change the DSR–Sokkisha relationship in an evolutionary process. DSR doesn't have the resources to do it all at once, however, and would consider acquiring, merging, or developing a joint venture with a European company (in a similar but noncompetitive product line) to establish a European marketing base. Ultimately, Townsend would like a DSR European marketing manager based in Europe and managed by DSR in Christchurch. This manager would likely be a national, and be responsible for the promotion of a product range (with DSR products as its core) into his or her markets.

As 1990 draws to a close, Townsend is looking forward to the new year and the critical decisions he will have to make regarding DSR.

APPENDIX A: BRIEF DESCRIPTION OF DSR PARTNERS (IN ALPHABETICAL ORDER)

Geotronics AB

- Founded 1947, based in Sweden (with offices in 11 countries serving a total of 25 markets).
- Manufactures precision distance measurement and positioning equipment.
- Ranked no. 4 behind Sokkisha in world survey instrument sales (10.31 percent).

The Lietz Company

- Founded in late 1880s.
- Sokkisha's U.S. distribution subsidiary, based in Kansas City.

- Includes network of six district offices and over 600 independent retailers.

SIMRAD A/S

- Founded pre–1960, based in Norway.
- Produces advanced marine electronic equipment (e.g., echo sounders, depth finders).

Sokkisha Co. Ltd.

- Founded 1920.
- Head office, Tokyo, with wholly owned subsidiaries in 16 countries throughout North America, Europe, Asia, and Oceania, and represented in 16 other European countries.
- World leader in surveying instrument sales (1989 global sales of $US178 million).
- Manufactures and supplies over 30 percent of the world's surveying instruments.

Subtronic

- Based in the U.K., employing 30–40 staff members.
- Subcontractor in the underground services business (foul sewer and storm drains).

Trimble Navigation

- Founded in 1978, based in California.
- Pioneer and world sales leader in commercial markets for satellite-based navigation and positioning data products using Global Positioning Systems (GPS) technology.
- 1989 net sales of $US32 million, with 550 staff members.

APPENDIX B: BIOGRAPHICAL NOTES

Outlined in this appendix are brief biographical notes of DSR's product managers and key overseas personnel.

Ian Viney—Joint Venture Manager Designate (age 30). Viney is currently responsible for developing a business plan for the proposed joint venture with Sokkisha, organizing the joint venture, and working on the new data collection product. His appointment as JV Manager Designate was strongly influenced by his technical abilities and the respect held for him by Sokkisha.

Viney has been with the company for 10 years, and has a B.Sc. (Honours) in Computer Science. He joined the Datacom Group as a systems programmer, and after working with Alan Townsend on the legal accounting systems project, moved to handheld data collection. His experience with DSR since then has been focused on the land survey products, involving programming, systems design, writing standards, and some product management.

Mark Nichols—Product Manager, Surveying and Engineering Products (age 34). Nichols is currently responsible for the development and management of PC Software products, and control of DSR Land Survey support staff in Europe. He also manages the Sokkisha and Lietz relationships for these products.

Nichols joined DSR in 1984 with a degree in land surveying. He had held technical positions in land surveying, spent three months in the Air Force, and had experience in sales. Since joining DSR, Nichols has spent two years in Europe, developing the U.K. market and identifying market opportunities in Spain and France. He also identified the utility mapping product opportunity, and was instrumental in developing the PC Software line to its current position.

Gary Chisholm—Product Manager, HYDRO (age 33). Chisholm has championed the growth of HYDRO, and is responsible for its continued development and management. He also manages the distribution network for HYDRO, including the Simrad and Geotronics relationships.

He officially joined the company in early 1987, although prior to then, he had consulted with DSR on the land survey. Chisholm has a B.Sc. in Land Surveying, and a Masters degree in Global Positioning Systems (GPS). He also has technical and management experience in the oil industry.

Richard Williams—Product Manager, Manholes (age 32). Williams followed up on the utility mapping opportunity identified by Mark Nichols in 1987, and is responsible for championing the Manholes product. He has developed the product and handles DSR relationships with its U.K. distributor, Subtronic. Currently, he is adapting Manholes to meet market requirements outside the U.K.

Williams joined DSR in 1989, and has a Ph.D. in Parallel Processing. Highly technical, his experience is in programming.

Peter Baines—Europe Support (age 31). Baines provides technical and marketing support to Sokkisha Europe BV, and is based in Amsterdam. He reports to Mark Nichols. Baines works out of Sokkisha's European headquarters, dealing with their distributors and the joint end users.

Baines joined DSR in 1987, and prior to moving to Amsterdam in early 1990, Baines had been a programmer and project leader for the company. Baines has a Ph.D. in Physics, and prior to leaving for Europe, he was sent by DSR on various "fast-track" management courses.

Craig Muir—Product Support, France (age 30). Muir is based in Paris and provides software support and direct technical and marketing support to Sokkisha France for PC Software products. He is on-site at the Sokkisha office, and reports to Mark Nichols. He communicates regularly, however, with Peter Baines.

Muir joined the company in 1988. He has a B.Sc. in Land Surveying, and experience working in engineering surveying and planning.

Bruce Butler—HYDRO Support, Europe (age 35).   Butler provides technical and marketing support for HYDRO in Europe. He has been in the U.K. since 1989, and supports all European distributors, including Simrad and Geotronics.

Butler has a technical degree in Applied Science and a Graduate Diploma in Land Surveying. The only non–New Zealander, Butler is Australian, and joined DSR in 1989.

Case 9
Lobatse Clay Works

Peter Williamson, the newly appointed general manager of Lobatse Clay Works (LCW), looked out of his office window at the tangible evidence of his frustration. There, laying on the factory grounds, were over three million stockpiled bricks, and there were no reasonable prospects they would be sold anytime soon. The situation had grown so bad in recent months that the previous week he had felt compelled to shut down the entire production line and lay off all 100 factory workers indefinitely. If these firings were not bad enough, he now faced the very real possibility of defaulting on the company's bank loans, due the upcoming week. With no revenues coming in from the company's principal buyer—now embroiled in a corruption scandal that had forced it to halt all purchases six months ago—the company's prospects looked very dim, quite different from the way things had seemed just nine months before when the company first began production.

Peter once thought he would be happy with a promotion to the role of General Manager. For over 25 years he had worked as a Production Manager for Interkiln Corporation of America (ICA), a parent company of the joint venture, Lobatse Clay Works, which over the years had posted him to various production assignments throughout the developing world. In the past year, he had decided to leave ICA to work directly for its newly formed Botswana joint venture, Lobatse Clay Works, so that he could stay in one place and lead a "normal" life with his wife. After 20 years of infrequent visits to his family, Peter looked forward to being a full-time husband and father. He envisioned this production job as being his last overseas assignment before taking early retirement and moving back to England. To his surprise, however, within a few months on the job he was thrust into the General Manager role and asked to manage a crisis situation, clearly the biggest challenge of his professional career. Reflecting on his experience at LCW, he smiled ironically: Everything was supposed to be relatively easy to manage; it looked good for the company, good for the country, and good for himself. Recent events, however, now made it seem that the entire joint venture was in question. The bank called him every day asking when they could expect their current loan repayment.

THE INTERKILN CORPORATION OF AMERICA

The Interkiln Corporation of America (ICA) was a privately held U.S.–based company headquartered in Houston, Texas. They constructed and managed ceramic manufacturing facilities around the world. The company was wholly owned by

Source: This case was written by David Osgood of George Washington University and edited by Richard G. Linowes of American University, and is intended as a basis for class discussion rather than to illustrate either effective or ineffective handling of an administrative situation. This case originally appeared in a casebook published by the Free Market Development Advisors Program, which is sponsored by the United States Agency for International Development (USAID) and administered by the Institute of International Education (IIE). The case was written by an advisor based on experience within a host company in a developing country.

Elmer Salgo, its president of the past 45 years, and under his leadership it had found a niche for itself building "turnkey" brick-making facilities for governments throughout the developing world. Beyond building and managing production facilities, the company provided technical and management support to train local personnel to take over management responsibility. By providing economically and politically viable industry to developing countries, ICA had become one of the premier construction companies in the world. ICA had built factories in China, Nigeria, Libya, Eastern Europe, and elsewhere.

ICA revenues were primarily generated from two sources. First, it earned fees for its management work, conducting feasibility studies for proposed new production facilities and providing technical assistance and on-site supervision before, during, and after the construction itself. Second, it earned a profit from the sale of equipment installed in these facilities, purchased from wholesalers or on the open market. While these business activities had been quite lucrative in years past, the company's cash flows from these agreements were always short-lived. Once the factory was complete and the new management trained, the turnkey agreement ended and the company had to search for new opportunities. During times of worldwide recession, few countries showed much interest in the company's services. Recognizing its vulnerability to such unmanageable factors, the company for many years had been seeking a "good" longer-term investment opportunity: A deal that promised a steady cash flow over a longer period of time with a reasonable return on investment. Such deals were difficult to find given the firm's specialty in building facilities for developing countries. These environments were often politically volatile and economically unstable, so positive cash flows were not readily assured. At long last, however, ICA management thought they had found what they were looking for. A potential joint venture with the Botswana Development Corporation, a state-owned company of the newly prosperous country of Botswana, seemed like the perfect business opportunity.

HISTORY OF BOTSWANA

Botswana is located in southern Africa, surrounded by Namibia, Zambia, Zimbabwe, and the Republic of South Africa. It is approximately the size of the state of Texas, but with a population of only 1.3 million people. The country is situated primarily in the Kalahari Desert, giving it an arid landscape similar to northern Arizona or New Mexico. The temperature routinely reaches 120° during the summer months (December–February), and below freezing during the winter months. This harsh climate makes it close to impossible to obtain consistent agricultural crop yields. Historically, the people of Botswana relied on cattle and goat herding as their source of nutrition and wealth. Their semi-nomadic nature meant few urban centers were established prior to Botswanan independence from Great Britain in 1966. With no industrial base and no business centers, Botswana at the time was the fifth poorest country in the world with gross domestic product (GDP) of $200 per person. The newly independent government made its primary focus the country's industrial development and the increased employment and wealth of its citizens. It aggressively searched for opportunities to exploit what they believed at the time to be the country's very few natural resources.

In 1969, the South African DeBeers Diamond Company discovered a vast diamond supply in the central region of Botswana. The diamond reserves were so large that it was estimated that the proposed mines could operate at full capacity through the year 2020. After negotiating mining rights for the excavation and handling of diamonds, Botswana found itself with vast economic wealth. The 1980s were marked by GDP growth of 12 to 15 percent per year and a general economic "boom" unseen in the area's history and, in fact, rarely seen in the world.

The construction sector could not keep pace with the newfound need for industrial and residential construction. Botswana's lack of natural resources and minimal industrial capabilities allowed foreign construction companies and products to enter the country and dominate the local marketplace. This became a source of concern for the government. They were wary of the country's complete dependence on South Africa. Botswana's landlocked position and lack of natural resources forced it to import 85 percent of all goods and services from South Africa. Even those goods and services originating from outside South Africa entered the country via South African ports and highways. The future political uncertainty in South Africa made it imperative that Botswana, and every other country in southern Africa, lessen its dependence on South Africa for its commercial needs.

Fortunately, Botswana was spared the racial tensions that had long strained social relations in South Africa and Zimbabwe. A unique feature of Botswana was the accepting relationship between the indigenous people, with family roots going back hundreds of years, and the "white" expatriate community that immigrated to the country during the twentieth century. The expatriates came primarily from South Africa and the United Kingdom but also from India, the United States, and Sweden. The mixing of people from different cultures was quite successful and even permeated the highest offices of government. The first freely elected President of Botswana was married to a Caucasian English woman. The appointed Governor of the Bank of Botswana was a Caucasian American. Expatriates dominated management positions in most private companies. The local people, the Batswana, lacked Western-style management experience, and people accepted that the country relied on foreign expertise to create an effective economic environment. Most Batswana wanted more of their own people in positions of power, but local businesspeople lacked the education and experience to manage large operations. Though the government now aggressively sponsored the overseas education and business experience of qualified local people, significant change would take some time. After all, rapid economic growth had transformed the country from a pastoral society to a thriving economy in less than one generation.

THE BOTSWANA DEVELOPMENT CORPORATION

The government of Botswana attempted to use revenues from diamond mining to create indigenous industries. They formed the Botswana Development Corporation (BDC), a parastatal organization funded by the government, to create new business and industry within the country. The BDC had the freedom to search for projects that they believed would enhance the country's economic base. Over the years, they had made investments in a wide range of businesses, including a cement manufacturing plant, hotels, a furniture manufacturing company, and a variety of other businesses, all geared to diversifying the local economy.

Although it was an independent entity and expected to make a profit, the BDC had much latitude on how it conducted its mission. It was allowed to make decisions based on what it perceived to be long-term growth potential and not worry much about short-term financial losses. Though it aspired to live by free market principles, it did not always practice this ideal. The wealth generated from its diamond reserves allowed it to invest in projects that were far more risky than projects normally undertaken by developing countries. Inevitably, political and economic concerns shaped its decision making. It developed a particular interest in challenging the foreign-owned companies that were operating within Botswana's borders.

The BDC felt that the country needed its own clay products facility to give entrenched South African companies some much-needed competition. For decades, foreign brick suppliers had received premium prices for their products, and the BDC was determined to break that monopoly. The housing industry was booming, and BDC officials felt it was time to encourage some domestic producer to supply needed construction materials.

THE BOTSWANA HOUSING CORPORATION

The main engine of growth in the construction industry in the country was the Botswana Housing Corporation (BHC). The BHC, like the BDC, was a government parastatal created to build new residential housing for the rapidly growing population. This housing program consisted of high-cost, medium-cost, and low-cost units. Low-cost housing for poor families was subsidized by high-cost housing sold at a profit to wealthier families. Because of this "mix" of residential building activity all undertaken by the BHC, very little residential construction was done by private firms. The BHC had a virtual monopoly. To compete in the Botswana marketplace, any large construction materials manufacturer had to sell its products to the BHC.

FOREIGN COMPETITION

Once the government decided that a clay building products factory was needed in Botswana, the Botswana Development Corporation had to select a company that could build and manage the project to the satisfaction of both the public and private sectors. The public sector demanded that any new industry create employment for its citizens, introduce new job skills, and lessen dependence on foreign companies for essential building materials. The private sector wanted products that were competitive in quality, quantity, variety, and price compared to those of established foreign clay products suppliers.

There were risks with this plan of action, however. For years the primary supplier of clay building products was the South African company, Corobrik. The BDC was quite concerned as to how Corobrik and other brick manufacturers might react to new competition from a state-supported company. They knew quite well that Corobrik's large size—estimated to produce 150 million bricks per year—could easily overwhelm the much smaller plant planned for Botswana, expected to peak at 25 million bricks per year. The planned capacity for the new plant would supply nearly all the government's requirements for face bricks, eliminating the need for a second major face-brick supplier in the country, and so either the BDC factory or Corobrik would have to abandon the face-brick market in Botswana. The stock brick market, on the other hand, would still require tens of millions of bricks per year, but the lower profit margins of that business made it much less lucrative than the higher-quality, higher-margin face-brick business. Neither company wanted to lose its most profitable market segment. There was fear Corobrik might "dump" its products on the Botswana market, selling at unfairly low prices, forcing the new manufacturer out of business.

THE FEASIBILITY STUDY

The economic growth of the 1980s created demand for all types of construction, and foreign-owned construction companies already dominated the contract-tendering process for new construction. Their projects required extensive import of bricks and other clay products. As part of its ongoing search for new business, Interkiln Corporation of America (ICA) approached the BDC about building a clay products plant in Botswana to respond to the growing demand for bricks. The BDC was delighted by their inquiry. Here was an opportunity to fulfill its goals of creating a new industry while adding employment in the country.

The BDC entered into negotiations with ICA to produce a feasibility study for a new clay products factory in Botswana. The study was extensive, including an analysis of the current market situation, projections of future demand, availability of raw materials, transportation issues, estimates of employment to be created, and assessments of costs for building the plant and supporting facilities. The Executive Summary of the report appears in Exhibit 1.

The feasibility study was conducted by ICA personnel with experience in constructing clay products facilities. It found that:

1. An indigenous plant could compete against foreign suppliers on quality and price. This was due to the quality of the clay and lower transportation costs associated with being situated near the capital city.
2. Future demand would slow but remain strong throughout the decade, due to world demand for diamonds and the resulting increased local wealth and growing demand for housing.
3. There was a large, high quality clay deposit only 50 miles south of the capital city of Gaborone, in the vicinity of the town of Lobatse.
4. The optimal size of the plant would produce 25 million units per year and employ nearly 200 factory workers plus administrative staff. This plant size would force it to utilize nearly 100 percent of its capacity to supply the Botswana Housing Corporation's needs for clay brick materials.
5. The plant could be built for just over US$10 million.

Exhibit 1   Joint Venture Feasibility Study: Executive Summary

---

This revised study appraises the technical and economic viability of the establishment of a high quality facing brick and ceramic tile facility near the town of Lobatse, in Southeast Botswana. The study has been prepared by INTERKILN CORPORATION OF AMERICA, utilizing previous detailed information provided by the BOTSWANA DEVELOPMENT CORPORATION during recent meetings.

Over the last six years, Botswana has had an average annual consumption of building bricks and roofing tile products of 90 million brick equivalent units. Demand is expected to grow by at least 5 percent per year, as Botswana's rapid economic development continues and the drought, which has affected the country since 1982, appears to have come to an end. The Government has introduced special measures to alleviate the shortage of serviced plots for housing and commercial construction. This would stabilize demand, should drought return.

Most of Botswana's building brick and roofing product requirements are being covered by locally made concrete blocks and, in the case of roofing materials, by imports. The market for clay bricks is presently catered for by either imported face bricks or locally produced low-quality stock bricks. A sound market potential is available in the manufacture of split tiles, ceramic pavers, and clay roofing tiles, to displace current imports. The proposed plant has a modest production level of some 25 million units, which the market potential justifies.

The clay deposit near Lobatse is admirably suitable for the production range envisaged, and proven reserves are at least 1.2 million cubic meters, which is sufficient for over 20 years at full plant capacity. The land area and clay deposit are Government property, and a royalty of 3 percent will be paid on the annual turnover for the use of the land and the material.

The plant design is flexible and allows for the production of a wide variety of high-quality products at low cost. The plant will allow the production of the high-quality products with all local materials, thereby having a considerable impact on the economy. The plant will utilize known and proven technology and will be a combination of modern cost-effective equipment linked with labor intensive handling operations.

The project as envisioned is a commercially sound investment, even with the conservative approach regarding revenues and costs. The operation would be profitable from the first year onward and in the fifth year of operation, the return on equity is 40.1 percent. The break-even point is estimated at 54.2 percent in year 5 of operation. The financial projections allow for the payment of corporation tax from year 2 onward. The projected net cash flow calculations show that the total indebtedness of the venture could be returned in 3.8 years with accelerated loan repayments.

The need for competent management for the operation has been recognized and it is envisaged that INTERKILN will provide competent knowledgeable on-site staff in key positions. INTERKILN will also provide an ongoing management service to monitor the technical production and financial aspects of the operation.

Further details of the feasibility study appear in Exhibits 2 through 5. Exhibit 2 describes the technology planned for the facility, highlighting its state-of-the-art features. Exhibit 3 details the capital investment requirements, showing how anticipated costs were to be shared by the joint venture partners. Exhibit 4 shows the anticipated production volumes and operating costs once production began. Finally, Exhibit 5 shows in graph form the impressive cash flows anticipated from the operation in the ensuing years.

The results of the study made the project seem very attractive to the BDC. They were thrilled to learn that the BHC, the largest purchaser of building supplies in the country, would utilize nearly 100 percent of the plant's production output. That meant that BDC's "sister parastatal organization" would utilize almost *all* the production capacity of a proposed indigenous clay production facility. With such promising news, the biggest questions facing BDC management now became: (*a*) how to fund the project, and (*b*) who they should contact to request a bid to build and manage the new factory. There were not many companies in the world that could oversee the construction and management of a clay products factory, much less in a developing country like Botswana. The BDC realized its options for a business partnership were going to be limited.

THE JOINT VENTURE DECISION

The BDC management decided that creating a joint venture with a private company would be the most effective and efficient way to get the new industry started. Although the goal of the BDC was to create employment for its own people, there were no Batswana with the experience or formal training to manage a state-of-the-art clay products factory. In fact, the entire upper management of the new company would have to be brought in from abroad by the joint venture partner. Given the Batswana's positive attitudes toward living and working with expatriates, there was little political concern about utilizing foreign expertise. Although the BDC did not like giving that much control to a joint venture partner, it saw no alternative. Maintaining oversight of the company would depend on the vigilance of the Board of Directors, of which the BDC would have majority representation proportional to its equity investment. The BDC would actively oversee the operation, thus controlling its financial investment in the project. The actual amount of the investment would not be known until a joint venture partner was found to sign an agreement.

The large brick manufacturers located in neighboring South Africa were the easiest to contact as potential partners for the new joint venture. The BDC's main concern about contacting these companies, however, was their inherent conflict of

---

EXHIBIT 2   Description of the Proposed Production System
Tunnel Kiln Firing

The product, after drying on the dryer/kiln cars, will then be fed directly to the INTERKILN tunnel kiln. The kiln will be a continuous operation unit, which will utilize coal as the means of firing. The kiln will be complete with a coal handling system automatically linked to a temperature control system to ensure uniform firing of the product.

The kiln will incorporate the latest construction materials and technology, to ensure that the fuel consumption levels and the thermal gain in this department will be low, providing reasonable working conditions for the operatives.

The heating, firing, and cooling cycles will be automatically controlled by both temperature and internal pressure, to ensure that the critical firing ranges associated with the firing of clay-based products will be accurately maintained.

EXHIBIT 3   **Projected Capital Investment for Plant, Equipment, and Services**

	Investment	
Cost Category	*Foreign (USD)*	*Local (USD)*
Site preparation	$ —	$ 46,000
Site infrastructure	—	196,000
Plant buildings	513,100	200,300
Machinery and equipment	6,931,495	95,375
General plant services	217,680	—
Erection and installation	—	383,600
Marine freight and insurance	578,450	200,000
Design and engineering services	660,000	—
Preproduction services	150,000	72,000
Technology know-how	70,000	—
Construction supervision	288,000	—
Commissioning supervision	138,000	—
Precommissioning interest	1,160,000	—
Foreign supervisor's related costs and contingency	—	60,000
Fixed capital investment	$10,706,725	$1,253,275
Total capital investment	$11,960,000.00	

interest: if anyone became a partner, they would be helping to create a new competitor for their existing factories. The economic recession plaguing South Africa had already forced local brick companies to lay off thousands of workers and to stockpile hundreds of millions of bricks that could not be sold to the stalled South African construction sector. The logical move for the South African manufacturers was to sell their excess capacity to the strong construction sector in Botswana. But the BDC had made a conscious decision to reduce the country's reliance on foreign products. After reviewing the business and political ramifications of entering into an agreement with a South African company, the BDC decided to contact clay manufacturing experts outside the region regarding the possible joint venture agreement.

ICA BECOMES JOINT VENTURE PARTNER

The BDC contacted ICA about submitting a bid for the joint venture. The political and economic stability of Botswana seemed a perfect situation for ICA. They could profit short term from the management fees and sale of equipment, and benefit longer term by owning part of a clay products factory operating in a "booming"

EXHIBIT 4   **Projected Production Volumes and Operating Costs**

A. Design Criteria

I.   Annual Production Capacity

    i.   25.0 million clay brick and tile products or 60,000 metric tons

    ii.   Provision for 2.0 million glazed split tile expansion

II.   Basic Products

    i.   Face brick 222 × 106 × 73 mm @ 2.4 kg. ea.

    ii.   Semi-face brick 222 × 106 × 73mm @ 2.4 kg. ea.

    iii. Split tile 222 × 106 × 10 mm @ 1.2 kg./Pair

    iv. Split paver 222 × 106 × 25 mm @ 2.4 kg./Pair

    v.   Roofing tile 420 × 240 × 15 mm @ 2.6 kg. ea.

    vi. Ridge tile shape 400 × 220 × 15 mm @ 2.2 kg. ea.

III.   Production Plan

		Year of Operation (Pcs. × 1000)		
	Products	*First*	*Third*	*Fifth*
i.	Face brick	4,200	5,400	6,000
ii.	Semi-face brick	7,000	9,000	10,000
iii.	Split tile	1,400	1,800	2,000
iv.	Split paver	3,500	4,500	5,000
v.	Roofing tile	1,260	1,620	1,000
vi.	Ridge tile	140	180	200

IV.   Scheme of Operation

i.	Clay preparation	8 hrs/day, 6 days/wk., 300 days/yr.
ii.	Forming and pressing	8 hrs/day, 6 days/wk., 300 days/yr.
iii.	Drying and firing	24 hrs/day, 7 days/wk., 365 days/yr.
iv.	Sorting, packing, and storage	8 hrs/day, 6 days/wk., 300 days/yr.
v.	Services	8 hrs/day, 6 days/wk., 300 days/yr.

V.   Raw Material Requirement

		Year of Operation (M tons)		
		First	*Third*	*Fifth*
i.	Woodhall clay deposit	42,000	54,000	60,000

VI.   Fuel, Power, and Water Requirements

i.	Bituminous coal	235 kg/1000 pcs. or 5,900 M. tons/yr.
ii.	Diesel fuel oil	10 liters/1000 pcs. or 25,000 liters/yr.
iii.	Electric power	200 KWH/1000 pcs. or 5,000,000 KWH/yr.
iv.	Water	100 liters/1000 pcs. or 2,500,000 liters/yr.

(continued)

VII.   **Manpower Requirements**

		Operating Shifts		
		First	*Second*	*Third*
i.	Management and office	21	0	0
ii.	Production	71	6	6
iii.	Maintenance and laboratory	9	0	0
iv.	Total personnel	101	6	6

VIII.   **Factory Site Area**

    i.   27,000 square meters, approx. land area

B.   **Financial Criteria**

  I.   **Product Sales Price**

i.	Face brick	@ USD 220/1000 pcs. or pula 440 /1000 pcs.
ii.	Semi-face brick	@ USD 125/1000 pcs. or pula 250 /1000 pcs.
iii.	Split tile	@ USD 275/1000 pcs. or pula 560 /1000 pcs.
iv.	Split paver	@ USD 330/1000 pcs. or pula 660 /1000 pcs.
v.	Roofing tile	@ USD 440/1000 pcs. or pula 880 /1000 pcs.
vi.	Ridge tile shape	@ USD 880/1000 pcs. or pula 1760/1000 pcs.

  II.   **Gross Sales Revenues (USD $\times$ 1000)**

		Year of Operation		
		First	*Third*	*Fifth*
i.	All products	4,016.6	5,164.2	5,738.0

III.   **Total Investment**

i.	Total fixed assets	—USD	11,960,000 (Incl. Interim Int.)
ii.	Working capital needs	—USD	500,000 (Overdraft)

IV.   **Share Capitalization and Financing**

i.	Initial paid-in capital		
	—55% Botswana Development Corp.	—	USD 2,375,000
	—25% Interkiln Corp.	—	1,080,000
	—20% Other American investors	—	865,000
ii.	Local project loan, BDC	—	3,575,000
iii.	Local project loan	—	2,905,000
iv.	Local interim interest loan	—	1,160,000
v.	Local overdraft loan	—	500,000

(continued)

(concluded)

V.   Operating Costs (USD × 1000)

		Year of Operation		
		First	*Third*	*Fifth*
i.	Direct operating costs	783.80	989.75	989.75
ii.	Factory overhead costs	175.00	175.00	175.00
iii.	Admin. overhead costs	411.10	411.10	411.10
iv.	Sales and distribution costs	38.37	38.37	38.37
v.	Depreciation	1,185.88	1,185.88	1,185.88
vi.	Finance costs	843.15	592.69	293.47
	Total production costs	3,473.30	3,392.79	3,093.57

VI.   Profitability (USD)

		Year of Operation		
		First	*Third*	*Fifth*
i.	Net sales revenue	3,896,102	5,009,274	5,565,860
ii.	Operational margin	1,301,945	2,209,167	2,765,752
iii.	Cost finance	843,151	592,693	293,468
iv.	Gross profit	458,794	1,616,474	2,472,284
v.	Taxes	—	161,647	741,685
vi.	Net profit	458,794	1,454,827	1,730,599
vii.	Percent return on sales	11.42	28.17	30.16
viii.	Percent return on equity	10.62	33.67	40.06
ix.	IRR on net worth—25.06%			

economy. The lack of prior long-term involvement by ICA in a venture did not affect the BDC's final decision. After all, the BDC and ICA had worked together well during the feasibility study, and both parties would have a financial stake in the project. ICA would supply the management expertise, specialized equipment, and nearly one-third of the total equity in the company—over $3 million. The BDC, utilizing its substantial financial resources, would supply the other two-thirds of equity, and provide the loan guarantees necessary for the project to borrow from private financial institutions. The BDC's political clout might also be important if problems arose jeopardizing the company's attempt to become the major brick supplier in the country.

The arrangement seemed ideal for both parties. The BDC would meet its goals of creating new industry and employment while receiving technical assistance to get the project started. ICA would offer its management assistance, sell specialized equipment, and benefit longer term from its equity infusion and semi-annual management fee. The long-term potential would more than make up for the initial capital expenditure, providing the company at last with an on-going income stream.

EXHIBIT 5   Projected Accumulated Cash Flows from Operations

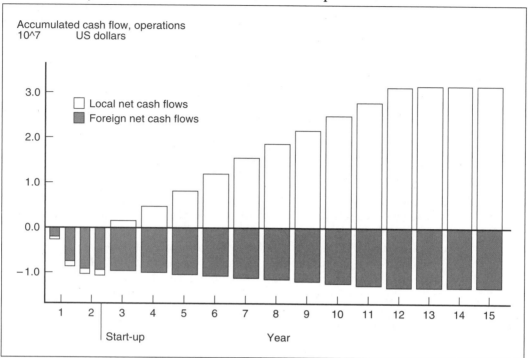

Accumulated cash flow, operations
10^7   US dollars

□ Local net cash flows
■ Foreign net cash flows

Start-up   Year

Both partners thus felt confident that the joint venture would be the ideal way to achieve their individual goals.

FACTORY CONSTRUCTION BEGINS

Peter remembered that his first few weeks on the job as ICA's technical consultant were better than most of his previous assignments. He did not have to deal with the bureaucratic red tape or corruption that plagued other overseas experiences. The national and local officials whom he met seemed thrilled to have a new industry in their country. The town of Lobatse, where the company was to be located because of its ample clay deposits, had a population of 25,000. Its main industry, the national slaughterhouse, employed several thousand people. LCW would bring additional employment and revenue to the local economy. The joint venture partners had little trouble getting the land or improved utilities needed to begin the groundbreaking process.

With BDC and local government support, construction on the factory began in August 1990 and was completed less than 17 months later. The management team was able to get the factory built on schedule despite a 20 percent cost overrun. The majority of these extra costs occurred during the first stages of construction. The concrete foundation for the factory floor was totally completed before it was discovered that the ground underneath the foundation could not support the weight of the factory equipment. The substantial weight of the equipment combined with the numerous bricks expected to be used during production actually cracked the concrete floor. The entire floor had to be broken up, removed, and replaced with reinforced concrete. Two months of work and $2 million of unbudgeted expense were wasted correcting this oversight.

ICA's costly error with the floor did not make management at the BDC happy. Many people within the BDC felt that ICA should have realized that the floor needed reinforcement. After all, ICA's expertise was the main reason it was brought in to the joint venture project to begin with. Peter admitted to the BDC that the problems with the floor had been a major mistake, but he felt confident that ICA would make up for its oversight by producing an excellent quality product.

During the construction process, ICA argued for using coal-fired burners for the heating kiln instead of the more modern gas burners commonly used in other countries. ICA technicians reasoned that coal burners would take advantage of Botswana's plentiful supply of coal, and by utilizing an indigenous resource, they would further avoid importing natural gas from South Africa.

The overriding goal of building the factory, and the dream of locally produced goods dominating the construction materials market in Botswana, kept everyone focused on a common objective. Despite the problems with the floor, the factory was eventually ready for its Grand Opening. Lobatse Clay Works looked like a sure bet to be a good investment for both the country of Botswana and the Interkiln Corporation of America. The joint venture was ready to begin manufacturing its first clay building products to compete directly against the entrenched South African suppliers.

THE GRAND OPENING

The mood was festive throughout the factory grounds. The employees and guests at the Grand Opening of Lobatse Clay Works enjoyed the food and drink that accompanied a big celebration. The guests of honor, especially the Minister of Commerce and Industry, were very proud of Botswana's first state-of-the-art ceramics production facility. The past two years had been filled with intense negotiation over the joint venture agreement, the cost overruns, and the completion of the factory on schedule, but each obstacle along the way had been conquered. The process had, at times, made both parties skeptical about the factory's eventual completion. But, today, they were all smiles and handshakes as the fruits of their labors finally ripened. Full-scale production was to begin the next day. During his speech to the assembled crowd, the Minister remarked:

> This new clay products facility will allow Botswana to manufacture its own clay bricks, roof tiles, floor tiles, and pavers, and not be dependent upon foreign manufactured construction materials to meet the increasing demand for new commercial and residential construction in our country. This is a great moment in the economic development of Botswana.

The board of directors and the management staff of Lobatse Clay Works had also been excited about the beginning of production, but each realized that they would soon be facing a highly competitive marketplace. The previous lack of a modern clay products manufacturing facility meant that foreign competition had been able to control the supply of brick and other clay products used throughout Botswana for the past 15 years. Breaking into the building materials market was not going to be easy for the new company. Many hurdles had to be overcome before the company would begin to show the sales revenues expected by the joint venture partners.

Nonetheless, LCW's prospects seemed bright. The feasibility study showed ample opportunity, and the full knowledge and experience of the expatriate management staff now on-board would likely steer the venture well. The country was experiencing an economic boom from its diamond deposits, with GDP rising over 10 percent a year. The construction craze was forecast to last through the year 2000. If all went according to plan, LCW would be well positioned to take advantage of the demand for construction materials and make a handsome profit for both joint venture partners.

PRODUCTION BEGINS

There were several stages to the production process. Highlights of the work are portrayed in the photographs shown in Exhibit 6.

Once the plant began operation, everyone immediately recognized the unfortunate consequences of installing coal-fired burners in the heating kiln. The low-grade coal used to heat the oven created excess ash when it was burned. The ash literally fell onto the bricks and cooked into their surface, creating ash "lines" and off-color marks on the brick faces. While the ash did not diminish the physical strength of the clay, it did leave a residue that made the bricks look "dirty." Architects and builders refused to use Lobatse Clay Works face bricks for the external walls of buildings because the walls would not have the clean, classic look of red or brown clay. The BDC was upset that the kilns produced "inferior" face bricks. Until the problem could be corrected, material purchasers would continue to buy South African bricks. This made the BDC furious because they did not want to give construction companies any reason to continue purchasing bricks from outside Botswana. It was clear that LCW would not achieve its full sales potential until its face bricks conformed to accepted building standards. The company began assigning crews of workers to scrub the bricks manually to remove as much ash as possible before shipping the bricks to customers.

Another drawback to using coal to fire the kiln was soon discovered. The products coming out of the oven were of inconsistent size. The coal did not burn in the kiln at even temperatures, so there were "hot" and "cold" areas in the kiln. This temperature variation caused the bricks to differ in size from one part of the kiln to another, producing unacceptable results. Current building standards in Botswana specified that face bricks be 222 mm + or −3 mm in length, whereas the LCW coal-fired kiln was creating variations up to + or −10 mm. These extremes in size made the bricks impossible to sell as face bricks. This quality problem also undermined the company's effort to sell its products to public and private construction material buyers. It also reinforced the notion held by many Batswana that products made in Botswana were simply inferior to those from other countries. Until a better heating system could be installed,

Exhibit 6   Photographic Portrait of the Production Process

A slab of clay emerges from the extrusion machine before being sliced into bricks.

General Manager Peter Williamson repairs the brick slicing machine.

New sliced bricks are transported by conveyer belt before drying in the kiln.

Bricks leave the oven with stains from the coal-burning furnace.

A truckload of finished brick leaves for delivery to the customer construction site.

Bricks are scrubbed clean manually to remove the coal ash stains.

LCW would lose market share to companies that supplied "clean" and properly sized bricks.

The inability to produce consistently proper face bricks also made it impossible for LCW to guarantee delivery of bricks to its customers.

As an emergency measure, the company had resorted to sending teams of employees to job sites to hand-sort previously delivered bricks to ensure that only "good" bricks were supplied to the customer. This quality control procedure was extremely expensive and time-consuming. The problem could have been avoided from the beginning if ICA had installed gas-fired burners in the kiln instead of the inconsistent coal-fired burners. The burner problem was the second mistake that ICA admitted to making during the construction phase of the project. The board of directors did not approve the conversion to gas-fired burners until November 1992.

DEPENDENCE ON THE BOTSWANA HOUSING CORPORATION

When conducting the feasibility study, ICA knew full well that the joint venture's survival was dependent on the BHC. Lobatse Clay Works had been created on the assumption that a majority of its overall production capacity would be dedicated to fulfilling the clay product needs of the BHC. Once the venture was under way, LCW management recognized the need to maintain close cooperation with the BHC. LCW could not prosper without the BHC buying up to 70 percent of the company's total production capacity. This reliance on a single entity for such a large percentage of sales had its positive and negative points. The positive side was that LCW did not have to search for market share from other sources; extensive marketing was not required to cultivate private sector sales. The negative side was the dependence on a single source for a majority of its sales; if anything happened to disrupt BHC construction projects, LCW would be very vulnerable in terms of lost demand and lost revenues. The BDC and ICA knew the risks of starting a company dependent upon a single state-owned organization. The feasibility study acknowledged LCW's vulnerability to one main purchaser, but the BDC and ICA decided to proceed nonetheless. The political issues of moving away from dependence on South African companies, of creating a new, indigenous industry, outweighed the strictly business decision that might have been made by a purely private company. ICA took the investment risk because they felt that the BDC would be able to influence the government in its favor if competition became too keen. The BDC and ICA each focused on overall potential for profit, not on the inherent risk of relying on a single buyer for the majority of its production. The management of LCW bet its very existence on the hope that the government of Botswana would provide some sort of assistance if times got really tough.

WORST-CASE SCENARIO: BHC SCANDAL

In April 1992, just three months after LCW began operations, a worst-case scenario happened to the company. A massive scandal was uncovered within the Botswana Housing Corporation. The National Legislature called a halt to every construction project in progress throughout the country. The construction stoppage was to remain in effect throughout the government's investigation of corruption in the upper management of the BHC. The managing director of the BHC, a Batswana, allegedly had taken payoffs from construction companies and material suppliers to award them BHC contracts. The scandal shook the people of Botswana who had prided themselves on the honesty of their government officials and representatives. Botswana had not had the endemic corruption that plagued many developing countries throughout the world. The democratically elected government has been open about its operations, and allowed total freedom to the local press to fully investigate its operations.

The government investigation found several high-ranking managers guilty of taking bribes and vowed to "clean house." The BHC had been one of the few organizations that had a Batswana in a top leadership position, but now he was to be replaced by an expatriate. The National Legislature leaders involved with the investigation were so angered by the fact that one of their countrymen could take bribes that they declared, "There are no Motswana with the experience or education to properly manage the BHC." Until a suitable Batswana could be found to manage the Housing Corporation, a foreigner would be hired to keep the corporation operating. Though it disrupted the housing construction industry, this zeal to maintain a high standard of integrity within the government helped Botswana continue making steps toward becoming a more independent, politically stable nation.

The BHC scandal was uncovered just as LCW was beginning to receive sizable orders from the BHC, other government organizations, and the private sector. The decision by the National Parliament to stop BHC activities was a crippling blow to everyone at Lobatse Clay Works. No one had any idea how long it would be until the investigation was finished and the BHC resumed purchasing materials. Both joint venture partners were at risk of losing all their investment if sales did not materialize soon. The BDC faced the loss of a new industry that was important to the future of the national industrial base. ICA faced the possibility of accepting a devastating financial loss in its very first joint venture investment.

While the investigation was proceeding, the management of LCW was frantically searching for alternate markets. Unfortunately, not many markets were available. Other government organizations could not use more bricks for their buildings, and private builders were too small to make much of a dent in LCW's vast inventory. Even export markets were not promising. Botswana's robust economy, fueled by diamond exports, made its currency, the pula, strong against the other currencies in the area. Trade in the area was coordinated by the Southern Africa Development Commission (SADC) involving the countries of South Africa, Namibia, Zambia, Zimbabwe, Lesotho, and Swaziland, as well as Botswana. The SADC was a regional organization that promoted free trade among member nations. The pula was approximately 30 percent stronger than the South African rand, for example, and twice as strong as the Zimbabwe dollar. The pula's appreciation against these currencies made it more expensive to sell Botswana products in these countries. Without domestic or international buyers, LCW found itself with an increasing stockpile of bricks on its factory grounds, no new prospects for sales, and an inability to pay its increasing debts.

PRESENT SITUATION

As Peter's thoughts came back to the present situation, he could not help but feel nostalgic about the euphoric expectations of the past. The current realities were much different. First, Peter had inherited his new position just three weeks previously because the former general manager of the company, an American, and the financial manager, an Indian, had been fired for attempting to negotiate a deal to sell American cornmeal to the Zambian government. They were conducting personal business on company time and with company money. When their activities were discovered by ICA and the BDC, they were immediately fired, and Peter was asked to step in and fill their shoes.

Peter was eager to demonstrate that he was the best choice for the general manager position, and that the company could rebound from its present dilemma and produce the sales and revenues originally envisioned. The reality, however—almost no sales for the past six months, the loss of two top managers to scandal, the indefinite layoff of every factory worker, the stockpile of millions of bricks, and absence of any sign of future sales—was quite daunting. Peter would certainly be earning his "battle pay" during the current crisis.

Peter knew that ICA had been optimistic with its projected sales. The feasibility study based its conclusions on past economic strength, and Peter felt it had been "slanted" by ICA to make the project look as promising as possible. Peter felt ICA glossed over the fact that any construction materials manufacturer was almost totally dependent on the Botswana Housing Corporation for its revenues. The joint venture partners assumed the BHC would continue to purchase construction materials at historic rates, and no unexpected situation would interrupt its purchasing schedule.

Year-to-date revenues were about 20 percent of what had been forecast in the feasibility study for the first year of operation. Though the company had not been expected to make a profit for the first three years, it was also not expected to face bankruptcy. Peter's immediate problem was how to meet his monthly loan payments. If he could not make the payments, the bank could foreclose on the company, closing the factory permanently. The country of Botswana would lose a new industry and jobs for its citizens, the bank would lose the millions of pula already loaned to the company, and the BDC and ICA would lose their investment in the joint venture. Given the present situation, Peter felt that he had only three workable options from which to choose:

1. Get the joint venture partners to invest more equity to pay the monthly expenses.
2. Ask the bank for an additional loan to keep the company solvent until sales increased.
3. Close the factory permanently.

Peter reached for the telephone. He had three phone calls to make to plan his next steps. He faced a tough decision—with major consequences both here and abroad—and he needed to know the wishes and flexibility of the key parties involved: the Botswana Development Corporation in Gaborone, the Interkiln Corporation of America in Texas, and his wife across town.

CASE 10

INTERNATIONALIZATION AND THE ENTREPRENEURIAL HIGH TECHNOLOGY FIRM: THE CASE OF MANA SYSTEMS LTD.

In March 1991 Robert Barnes, founder and Managing Director of MANA Systems Ltd. (MSL) was pondering the long-term growth opportunities for his organization.

MSL is a privately held firm based in Auckland, New Zealand. It develops system software to suit a variety of programming tasks. The company's core product, MANASYS, is sold in Australia through an agreement with Fujitsu Australia Limited (FAL), and in Japan through Computer Engineering and Consulting Limited (CEC.) MSL has also signed an agreement with Fujitsu Japan (FJ), for the development of system software for the world market. (Refer to Appendix A for notes on Fujitsu and CEC.)

Since being founded in November 1979, MSL has grown from two to twenty-five employees. According to Barnes, the overall aim of MSL is:

> To produce innovative products and services which meet the wide-ranging requirements of the highly competitive world software market.[1]

At the same time, Barnes sees his company as a Fujitsu development laboratory. Direct control of all markets and customers is in the hands of Fujitsu or CEC (which also has a relationship with Fujitsu). While Barnes feels little loss of independence in this situation, he has become concerned about MSL's lack of end-user contact, and a relatively low penetration of the Japanese market. The question now facing Barnes is how to best manage MSL's existing relationships to maximize long-term growth opportunities for the firm. At the same time, he wishes to maintain the perceived strength of his company, that is,

> . . . The ability to produce innovative software, relatively quickly . . . a combination of having technological skills and being able to employ them effectively.

A BRIEF HISTORY OF MSL

In the late 1970s, Robert Barnes was employed at Air New Zealand, with responsibility for evaluating productivity tools. He became convinced that the company needed a system software product different from those already available, and based on his programming experience and the perceived product

---

[1] More specific objectives for MSL can be found in Appendix B.

Source: This case has been prepared by Nicole Coviello of the University of Auckland, New Zealand as a basis for discussion rather than to illustrate effective or ineffective handling of an administrative situation. Case information was obtained through a series of personal interviews with Robert Barnes (managing director), archival data, press releases, and other published information. The author is indebted to TRADENZ for financial support of this research.

need, he designed the initial version of MANASYS for the IBM platform. According to Barnes:

> . . . The whole thing arose the way a product should arise in that someone perceives a market need based on their actual needs themselves, and then they say, gee, you know, has anybody else got this sort of need—how can I broaden it out and make a product?

Following initial success with MANASYS, Barnes left Air New Zealand to found MANA Systems Limited. MSL was incorporated in November 1979, with $2,000 capital and a $10,000 loan obtained through the New Zealand Government's Applied Technology Programme. MSL's first client was the Auckland Regional Authority (responsible for local government and city planning), followed by a sale to the Sydney City Council (Australia). Thus, MSL entered the Australian market almost immediately, and for the early years, served Australia through direct sales efforts and exclusive agents.

In mid-1982, Barnes attempted to establish an agency agreement in the United States. However, the potential agent filed for bankruptcy immediately prior to formalizing the relationship. By late 1982, MSL was technically insolvent.

The company restructured and was returned to solvency in late 1983, and continued to develop MANASYS for the IBM market. In 1984, Barnes saw a product development opportunity in the newly emerging area of relational databases. Although the area was considered to be largely unproven, Barnes's product concept caught the interest of Fujitsu New Zealand, and then, Fujitsu Australia. Within six weeks, an agreement had been reached for MSL to develop the new product, funded by Fujitsu New Zealand. In 1985, an agreement was signed with Fujitsu Australia to market and support the new product in Australia. In April 1986, the new version of MANASYS was released, designed to enhance the productivity of Fujitsu's information systems products.

Following from this, Fujitsu Japan took an interest in MANASYS, and introduced Computer Engineering and Consulting Ltd. (CEC) as a potential agent for Japan. An agreement between MSL and CEC was reached in 1987 for developing and marketing a Japanese version of the software.

In July 1989, Fujitsu Japan's software division agreed to fund MSL's development of further products. In 1990, an additional agreement with Fujitsu Japan was reached to provide direct financial support to MSL. Also in that year, Fujitsu Australia obtained sites for MANASYS in Europe and Asia, thus internationalizing MSL's end-user base.

As of 1991, MSL consists of 25 employees operating in two general product areas: Mainframe Software and UNIX Software. All employees are based in Auckland, while MSL software sites are located in New Zealand, Australia, Spain, Malaysia, and Japan.

PRODUCTS AND MARKETS

The Product.   MANASYS is a fourth generation language (4GL) application development software. It is designed to suit programming tasks ranging from simple system development (e.g., personal record keeping) to those which are more complex (e.g., on-line banking). The product is dictionary-based and interactive, and produces Cobol code. The current version of MANASYS is designed for the Fujitsu platform, and is offered on AIM/ISP (advanced information manager/information systems products). The product is promoted under the Fujitsu name, however, Fujitsu is not required to tender the MANASYS software in its proposals.

MANASYS is a typical mainframe software product in that it is sold in low volume and at a high unit cost (e.g., $50,000–$90,000). It is a standardized product, consisting of five modules. Barnes notes that the product is similar to competitive offerings, in that it is "systems software" and requires little customization. The high degree of standardization means that enhancements are available to all end users.

Direct client contact is mandated by the nature of the product, its long life cycle, and the high investment required. This contact is provided by MSL's marketing partners, and not the company itself. MANASYS is supported with on-line help, documentation, telephone support from Fujitsu System Engineers, contract systems development support, software enhancements, and MANASYS education courses.

The Market.   MSL serves three geographic markets: Australia, New Zealand, and Japan. In both Australia and New Zealand, MANASYS sales are a function of new computer sales. However, Barnes notes the hardware market is flat, and with bleak prospects for the future. Between the two countries, MSL has over 30 customers through the Fujitsu network. Clients are generally large organizations, including the Melbourne and Metropolitan Board of Works in Australia, and Fuji Electrochemical in Japan. When making their buying decision, these organizations place high priority on system and software reliability rather than extra or new features.

IBM is the major competitor for both hardware and software sales. Other competitive systems include Adabas/Natural, IDMS/ADSO and Datacom/Ideal.

The Australian market has historically accounted for nearly half of MSL's sales, although Barnes believes the market is saturated.[2] New Zealand sales of MANASYS account for a much smaller proportion of the company's total revenue. Of note, sales in New Zealand are limited by the small number of Fujitsu sites available. As of 1990, MANASYS is on four of six potential sites. Only one customer exists in Auckland.

The Japanese systems software market is the second largest in the world after the United States. With CEC, MANASYS has 19 sites. The market is dominated by hardware suppliers including Fujitsu, Hitachi, and NEC. For example, Fujitsu has over 30 percent of all mainframe computer sites in Japan, including 2,700 AIM sites. The Japanese market is where Barnes expects growth for MSL to occur.

---

[2] These figures include FAL's overseas operations, including MANASYS sales to Spain and Malaysia.

MSL'S CURRENT ORGANIZATION AND PERFORMANCE

The Founder/Manager.   Robert Barnes (44) is the original designer of MANASYS and founder of MANA Systems Ltd. He is currently responsible for general management of the organization, with particular emphasis on long-term planning and management of the company's relationship with Fujitsu. He has been primarily responsible for the firm's overseas expansion and believes his experiences with MSL's growth provide strength in managing the company.

Prior to founding MSL, Barnes was employed by Air New Zealand for three years, with a major responsibility for merging the Air New Zealand and NAC computer systems. He has also worked as an analyst, programmer, and project leader for Databank (6 years), and in the research laboratory at Auckland's National Women's Hospital. Barnes's computer skills are self-taught, and he graduated with an M.Sc. in Chemistry. He has no formal management education.

Company Structure.   Robert Barnes considers MSL to be a development laboratory for Fujitsu. The company is organized in three departments (Management, Mainframe, and UNIX), and employs a well-educated and young staff.[3] This includes three Japanese hired to provide liaison with Fujitsu and CEC.

The administrative department (*Management*) includes Robert Barnes, James Penfold, customer support personnel, a technical writer, and general administrative staff. This department oversees all MSL operations. Barnes provides long-term direction and management of the Fujitsu and CEC relationships. Penfold is MSL's software development manager. He reports to Barnes, and is responsible for day-to-day operations and management of the *Mainframe* department.

The Mainframe department consists of Penfold and eight analyst programmers. Staff members comprise the "Maintenance Team" (responsible for improving the MANASYS, the existing mainframe product) and the "New Development Team" (working on new products).

The *UNIX* department was established in late 1989, and as of early 1991 has 12 staff members including two managers: Mark Townsend and Paul McGlashan. Townsend moved from Mainframe to UNIX and his role is to provide product direction. He is also responsible for coordinating the market research function across both Mainframe and UNIX. McGlashan is responsible for organizing the UNIX development team.

Trend in Sales and Financial Performance.   Until 1984, MSL's product development was very dependent on short-term sales and advance royalties. However, the various Fujitsu relationships (especially that with Fujitsu Japan), now provide strong growth potential, credibility, and significant financial stability for MSL. In 1990, export income accounted for 98.6 percent of MSL's revenues (up from 88.5 percent in 1988 and 93.2 percent in 1989). Growth in the number of employees is also shown in Exhibit 1.

---

[3] See Appendix C for biographical notes on key managers.

EXHIBIT 1   **MSL Income and Employee Levels, 1979–1991**

Year	Total Income	Employee Level
1979	$ 10,000	2
1980	NA	3
1981	NA	4
1982	67,000	2
1983	69,000	2
1984	103,000	3
1985	141,000	5
1986	291,000	7
1987	515,000	12
1988	738,000	12
1989	1,356,000*	18
1990	2,391,000†	22
1991	TBA	25

* Includes royalty revenue.

† Royalty revenue replaced by development funding from Fujitsu Japan.

Source: MSL Press Release, July 18, 1990, and interview with Robert Barnes, March 1991.

EXHIBIT 2   **Income by Country, 1987–1990 ($NZ)**

Country	1987	1988	1989	1990
New Zealand	$ 69,000	$ 85,000	$ 92,000	$ 33,000
Australia	253,000	363,000	422,000	40,000
Japan	193,000	290,000	842,000	2,318,000
Total	$515,000	$738,000	$1,356,000	$2,391,000

Source: Robert Barnes, March 1991.

The Japanese market is now the company's major source of income (see Exhibit 2). In 1990, approximately $2 million of the Japanese revenue was generated by development funding from Fujitsu Japan, with the remainder accounted for by royalties earned through CEC. Barnes notes, however, that royalty potential in Japan is estimated at $1.1 million. Income generated in New Zealand and Australia is very small in comparison with Japan, particularly in 1990.

INTERNATIONALIZING MSL–PRE-FUJITSU

According to Barnes, it was apparent from the inception of MSL that "We were going to have difficulty selling to a market of this size [New Zealand]." He notes, for example, that the Auckland market consisted of twelve prospects for the original (IBM) version of MANASYS, half of which were not interested in his software. As a result, alternative geographic markets were considered at an early stage of MSL's development, the first of which was Australia, followed by the United States.

Entering Australia.   Barnes's explanation for the company's early expansion to Australia is that "In the days of export incentives, it was cheaper to go to Sydney [Australia] than to Wellington [New Zealand]." In addition, the market potential in Sydney alone was seen to be much greater than in New Zealand as a whole. Therefore, the company's first international sale was to the Sydney County Council (in 1980) and to begin with, the market was served by Barnes acting in a direct sales capacity, "selling out of a suitcase." While Barnes believes his direct sales efforts to be a valuable education, it was also a struggle as the Australian market was uninterested in a company from "nowhere." Further, Barnes experienced a high level of competition and comments:

> I have several cases where we had a better product than some of the American competition at two times our price, but they [potential Australian clients] still bought the competition because it had all the fancies: The nice manuals, the salesman, the suit.

He notes that such competitors relied on a well-established company name and support system, neither of which could be offered by MSL.

At that stage of the company's development, few options other than direct selling were considered for internationalization. Barnes comments that while he was always open to the suggestion that growth and overseas expansion should not be done independently, he never got any support.

> It wasn't so much that we hadn't considered other options than selling on our own; it was just that we had even less chance of bringing them off, than we did at selling our product ourselves . . . because what the IBMs of this world are really interested in is results.

However, direct selling required significant effort and time investment by Barnes. Soon the search began for an Australian agent in order to improve sales efficiency. In 1981, a Sydney-based agent was appointed (Adrian Schmidt). Schmidt was known to Barnes and was experienced as an IBM systems engineer and contract systems engineer. Thus, he was familiar with the technical side of the market and had market contacts. Schmidt's approach was very technical in orientation, and he marketed one other product (noncompetitive and noncomplementary to MANASYS). After one year, Schmidt's performance was not considered successful, as little incremental or new business was generated. Barnes therefore terminated the agreement in 1982, and comments that:

> What we were doing was really just splitting the royalties, and if you are going to give someone 50 percent, you have got to at least double your sales.

After this experience, Barnes focused his efforts and interests on expansion into the United States.

Entering the U.S. Market.   In 1980 the search had already begun for a U.S. agent, and by late 1981, Insac (a potential agent based in Atlanta) was identified and evaluated relative to MSL's needs. The identification process began with Barnes approaching a variety of contacts, and consulting secondary information such as *Data Sources* (an industry publication). Barnes then contacted approximately 180 possible agents that carried complementary products and were active in the IBM software market. He comments:

> With the lack of knowledge I had at that stage, I really wrote to anybody and every-body that looked remotely suitable, which in retrospect wasn't such a bad idea anyway . . . at least you sort out those that were prepared to answer your letters. But the prob-lem is that the approach is bound to look amateurish, and you will not reach the atten-tion of probably the best companies.

Choosing a U.S. Relationship Partner.   Of the companies contacted, approxi-mately ten responded, and a short list of three was made. MSL requested bank re-ports on each, and examined their financial circumstances. All three were visited in 1982. Insac was then selected because its products were oriented toward the same market as MANASYS, and the agent was searching for a new product to complement its existing line.

Refocussing on Australia.   While progressing with the Insac relationship in the United States, Barnes decided to reestablish a focus on Australia by selling directly into that market. To accomplish this, Barnes decided to hire a manager for the Aus-tralia and U.S. markets with a background in both marketing and programming. This was believed necessary in order to bring a stronger marketing/sales balance to what Barnes felt was a technically driven organization. In 1982, Dave Hopkinson was hired.

Problems in the United States.   The Insac agreement was negotiated, letters of intent written, and the contract was ready for signing when Insac experienced fi-nancial difficulties. In mid-1982, Insac filed for bankruptcy. As MSL had already expanded operations in anticipation of U.S. sales growth, it found itself on the verge of insolvency.

Back to Australia.   Hopkinson then focused his efforts solely on Australia, and although sales leads had been established, the financial position of MSL was per-ceived as risky by potential clients. In addition, Hopkinson was based in Auck-land, and the Australian market required a local (Australian-based) contact for MSL. He therefore identified a second Australian agent, and Logica (a U.K. con-sulting company) was signed in 1983 for a 3-month exploratory period. The tenta-tive nature of the agreement was initiated by Logica, who covered all marketing costs and received a percentage of nominated sales. However, Logica had little ex-pertise or success in selling the software, and the agreement was subsequently ter-minated. The agent did, however, assist in finalizing an important sale in

Australia. This, combined with a restructuring of MSL to bring in extra shareholder capital, returned MSL to solvency.

INTERNATIONALIZING MSL—THE FUJITSU RELATIONSHIP

Growth with Fujitsu.   In 1984, Barnes decided to try and develop a relationship with a major hardware manufacturer for development of his new relational database concept. Such a relationship was expected to reduce risk for MSL, develop economies of scale, and provide access to needed technology (as a basis on which MANASYS could provide added-value). It was also expected to provide marketing expertise and access to international distribution channels, thus enhancing MSL's competitive position. Of particular importance to MSL was the access to financial resources, and the need to reestablish credibility in the international software market. Overall, Barnes believed the development of an international relationship was necessary to ensure survival for MSL.

The Fujitsu New Zealand Relationship.   Barnes approached leading New Zealand hardware vendors including IBM, NCR, DEC, and Fujitsu, regarding a marketing/development agreement. Of these, only Fujitsu New Zealand (FNZ) saw potential in the new product concept, and contacted Fujitsu Australia (FAL) with Barnes's idea, as FAL was seeking new product ideas and improvements on behalf of Fujitsu (worldwide).

The Fujitsu Australia Relationship.   In 1984, an initial agreement with FNZ was signed, providing: (1) funding for MSL's development of the new product concept, and (2) advances on royalties. This was followed eight to nine months later by an agreement granting Fujitsu Australia world marketing rights to the new product upon final development. This relationship was ideal for MSL as it provided computer facilities, funding for further development, and marketing arrangements. Also, FAL assumed all marketing, sales and support activities, and client contact for MSL. Importantly, the Fujitsu name was used to promote MANASYS. Benefits also accrued to Fujitsu as the new product was expected to add value to the organization's hardware sales.

Developing Relationships in Japan.   In 1987, FAL approached Fujitsu Japan to sell MANASYS in Japan. Although FJ was interested, it was unable to market the software due to the risk of conflict with its own products. Barnes then asked FJ to identify potential agents for Japan and two were suggested. Both options were contacted by MSL, and one, Computer Engineering Consulting (CEC), responded.

CEC was signed in July 1987, obtaining the sole marketing rights in Japan with support from FAL. Barnes notes the CEC relationship has contributed revenue, insight to the Japanese market, market contacts, and a number of customers. Barnes sees this as an ongoing investment in Japan which helps relations with Fujitsu:

I actually see everything in terms of the benefit, or converse in terms of how it affects our relationship with Fujitsu.

Barnes comments that the approach to establishing a Japanese agent was different from the legwork necessary for the U.S. attempt, largely due to the role played by Fujitsu. No formal evaluation procedure was followed as Fujitsu had recommended the agent; it was therefore believed to be satisfactory. CEC was also interested in marketing MANASYS, and according to Barnes, "looked as though they could do it."

Sales by CEC, however, have been less than anticipated. While the lack of performance in Japan is not due to a lack of effort by CEC, Barnes notes:

I am very frustrated because the potential in the market is huge. Instead of getting one sale every two or three months, they could be getting four or five sales every month.

Also, MSL has experienced cultural differences with CEC, and has found their translation work to be delayed and of poor quality. As a result, MSL employs Japanese staff for all document translation (noting that this also improves the English documentation). Finally, Barnes comments, "If CEC were successful, it would make life a lot easier for us." The issue in this situation is strategic rather than financial, as success in Japan would allow MSL greater independence in negotiation, and control in developing strategies for that market.

The Evolving Relationship with Fujitsu Japan.   In 1988 Barnes was faced with a decision to seek alternative financing or restrict MSL's growth and operations, due to the poor sales in Japan and slow growth in Australasia. Fujitsu Japan then expressed interest in strengthening their existing relationship, and in 1989 Fujitsu Japan initiated an agreement between its software division and MSL for product development. The agreement covers new products for international markets (not Japan), and was established to encourage faster development of MANASYS.

As of 1991, direct control of the Australian and international markets (other than Japan) is completely in the hands of Fujitsu. Indirect control of Japan is also maintained by Fujitsu Japan given its relationship with CEC. No loss of independence is felt by Barnes, however, as he sees strength in the increased resource base for the company, and new market potential for MANASYS. Also, he believes that Fujitsu deliberately allows MSL to grow and learn by making its own assessments and mistakes. He comments that:

We have a very interesting, I think unique, situation in that we are part of a major computer company's vision of what the computer industry will be like in the mid-1990s. I love working with them [Fujitsu], and I think we actually do have a great partnership, but there's no question as to who's the dominant partner. The golden rule: He who has the gold, makes the rules.

For example, Barnes notes that the nature of the relationship precludes MSL entering markets that Fujitsu does not want. While he recognizes that this might result in missed market opportunities, he comments, "The chances are I wouldn't have addressed them anyway because we wouldn't have had the ability to do so."

MARKETING AT MSL

As previously noted, early marketing efforts at MSL consisted of Barnes traveling around Australia with a suitcase of tapes. Currently, all marketing functions are the responsibility of Fujitsu and CEC. Fujitsu monitors international trends and developments, and is responsible for end-user training. MSL's contact with the end user is limited to preparation of training courses and course material. However, MSL communicates daily or weekly with FAL regarding market developments and end-user requirements or problems. As noted by Barnes:

> Do we do any marketing at all? In one sense you could say marketing is vital because what I have to do in my negotiations with Fujitsu is marketing. But in the other sense, we do very little at all, because apart from publishing a newsletter and the odd visit to a few key customers, I don't go near a customer. And that is a real problem.

As a result of this concern, a specific marketing unit was established in late 1990 to improve MSL's marketing and competitive intelligence. The development occurred as Barnes felt MSL relied too much on Fujitsu for market and technical knowledge, and additional resources for investment in research were available through the FJ relationship. In particular, Barnes saw a need for technical feasibility studies and secondary research to identify market opportunities for MANASYS. The unit was disbanded within six months, however, due to personnel conflicts. This left no specific marketing function in MSL to provide market analysis and planning information. Barnes now feels that MSL management has only average market knowledge to facilitate future growth, and stronger market analysis and planning skills are required.

THE FUTURE OF MSL

Product Issues.   The primary goal for MSL is to enter the UNIX market with a July 1992 early release. By 1993 Barnes expects the product to be fully accepted into the marketplace, and pay its way by 1994 (i.e., pay back Fujitsu's investment). By 1995, he believes the UNIX software will be a major product for MSL, bundled as part of the standard Fujitsu UNIX package sold worldwide. Barnes also foresees a variety of products/options spinning off from the new development. Of note, the marketing rights to the UNIX product (including Japan) will be owned by Fujitsu Limited.

In terms of the MANASYS mainframe product, Barnes expects sales to be maintained or slightly decrease in the future. As product development is revenue-driven, the only potential for growth is if CEC sales grow significantly in Japan (as little new business is foreseen for Australia).

Relationship Issues.   While Barnes continues to see CEC as a relatively important strategic relationship for international growth, the Fujitsu relationship is of greater importance:

> That is the key. My goal is to strengthen that [Fujitsu] relationship . . . whatever Fujitsu wants us to do we will do . . . we went to CEC because Fujitsu told us to . . . that is not to say we are not conscious of other values, like diversification strategies and so on, but we do nothing here without informing Fujitsu, even forming our diversification strategies.

Key in this relationship is the future direction for MSL in the UNIX market, and Barnes notes that his goal is to produce what Fujitsu asks for, and in a budget better than they are expecting.

The terms of MSL's agreements range from a reasonably open-ended relationship with FAL, to more formal agreements with Fujitsu Japan and CEC. For example, the FJ agreement is effective until 1993, with reviews every six months. In all relationships, Barnes is solely responsible for negotiating the agreements and managing the relationships. He believes this is necessary, as the relationships are so critical that only he can manage them.

Overall, Barnes expects that with the company's move into the UNIX market, employee numbers could increase to 30–35 people in 1991. As the 1990–91 fiscal year draws to an end on March 31, Barnes is now faced with the issue of how best to manage MSL's relationships in order to maximize the long-term growth opportunities for the firm. Of some concern to Barnes is the degree of vagueness in the MSL–Fujitsu relationship. He states:

> In some ways we seem to be extremely lucky that we are part of Fujitsu's dream for the future, and they're feeding us a few bits and pieces of what that is. We don't actually have a blueprint of what we are going to be doing in five years' time—there's just no detail.

APPENDIX A   Partner Details

Fujitsu

- Japan's largest computer manufacturer, owning ICL and 49 percent of Amdahl.
- World's second largest computer manufacturer (after IBM).
- One of the world's leading producers of telecommunications equipment, semiconductors, and other electronic components.
- Fujitsu Australia (FAL) is the only major non-Japanese outlet for Fujitsu computers sold as Fujitsu computers (in distinction to products usually sold in an OEM arrangement, and badged as ICL, Amdahl, etc.).
- Given reasonable autonomy in developing own relationships.

Computer Engineering and Consulting Ltd. (CEC)

- Third largest Japanese software house, public as of 1989.
- Primary business is computer and engineering consulting, but also sells a range of software products unrelated to MANASYS.
- Approximately 1,400 employees.
- Totally independent of Fujitsu but a major reseller of Fujitsu equipment.

APPENDIX B MSL Company Objectives

We want MANA Systems Limited to be:

- A provider of high-quality product and service giving excellent value to our customers.
- A good corporate citizen.
- A great place to work.
- An excellent investment.
- A significant force in the international software market.
- A producer of innovative software products positioned toward the forefront of mainstream programming technology.

Source: *1990 MSL Corporate Document*, p. 2.

APPENDIX C Biographical Notes

Outlined in this appendix are brief biographical notes of the senior management at MSL (other than Robert Barnes). Barnes characterizes the company as young, with a high number of university graduates.

James Penfold: Software Development Manager (age 33).

Penfold joined MSL in 1982, and is currently responsible for the day-to-day operations of the company and management of the Mainframe department. He is also on the board of directors. His career began as a programmer with MSL after graduating in 1982 with a B.Sc. (Mathematics) and COP (Computer Science). Most of his programming and project management experience is with the mainframe product.

Mark Townsend: UNIX Prototyping Manager (age 28).

Townsend is the fourth-longest employee of MSL and was involved with the initial development of the Mainframe product. He has also spent two years in Australia, working on customer sites. Townsend has no tertiary degree, although he has a technical background. He is now responsible for providing product direction in the UNIX area, and coordinating the company's research function.

Paul McGlashan: UNIX Implementation Manager (age 31).

McGlashan joined MSL in 1989 following employment at Trilogy as support manager. He has an M.Sc. in Computer Science, and is experienced with UNIX. He is responsible for coordinating the new UNIX department in its product development.

IV MANAGING INTERNATIONAL GROWTH

CASE SUMMARIES

CASE 11: COGNEX CORPORATION

By Don Hopkins (Temple University, USA)

Cognex Corporation, headquartered in Needham, Massachusetts, manufactures and sells computerized vision systems for industrial robots. The firm was founded by Dr. Robert Shillman, a former M.I.T. professor, by selling directly to end users of robotic systems. This strategy failed, and the firm refocused on selling its vision systems to robot manufacturers. It was very successful, sometimes growing almost 50 percent per year during a period when U.S. robotic firms were failing completely. Four years later it went public, and within two years was the market leader with $29 million in revenue. Yet about half of Cognex's sales comes from only three firms, and most of its growth comes from sales to Japanese firms. At the end of the case, Dr. Shillman is concerned about future threats from existing and potential Japanese competitors, about the need to move from an entrepreneurial style of management to a mature style, and about opportunities to expand its product line and target market. Readers have an opportunity to consider alternative responses to these issues.

CASE 12: INTERNATIONAL UNP HOLDINGS, LTD.

By Kris Opalinski and Walter Good (both of University of Manitoba, Canada)

International UNP Holdings, Ltd. (IUNP) was established and headquartered in Canada in 1989 for the purpose of channeling equity investment into the Polish manufacturing sector. The case is set in 1994 and outlines the company's development to the point that it has raised $48 million and has acquired a majority interest in three medium-sized, state-owned, Polish manufacturers. The case concludes with the president and CEO of IUNP reviewing the operations of the three subsidiaries, with the primary focus on IBIS, a manufacturer of bakery production equipment. IBIS has experienced a recent drop in its sales. IUNP is concerned with the pace and direction of post-privatization changes taking place in IBIS and needs advice on how to respond.

CASE 13: MONAGHAN MUSHROOMS

By Barra O Cinneide (University of Limerick, Ireland)

This case concerns an Irish company's efforts to market agricultural products in the European Community. While the primary focus of the case is marketing, issues in business strategy and financial management also come into play.

CASE 14: NATURE ISLE HERBAL TEAS, LTD.

By Scott Field (University of Washington, USA)
and edited by Richard G. Linowes (American University, USA)

Nature Isle Herbal Teas, Ltd., from Dominica West Indies, is a producer of herbal teas and spices sold in retail-sized packages. As their sales increase, they face a number of production challenges, including dryer limitations, productivity limits in a manually intensive leaf-removing process, an inadequate inventory system, and a cut-off of the water supply. Pricing is done without accurate information about per item costs. The company is now attempting to export to the French Caribbean islands and is looking for ways to fill new orders with existing operations. Readers must determine whether the company has adequate capabilities for production and exporting. ■

CASE 11
COGNEX CORPORATION

In 1981, Dr. Robert Shillman, a professor at M.I.T., formed a company called Cognex Corporation located in Needham, Massachusetts. It was intended to build customized machine vision systems. These systems were meant to serve as inspection systems and be the "eyes" for industrial robots. The firm's first five years were a disaster.

Cognex got off to a rough start but learned from its early experiences. It had to walk away from some early contracts because it could not solve the customers' problems. For example, in 1985 American Cyanamid wanted Cognex to build a vision system to read expiration dates on packs of surgical sutures. The firm got the system to work in the lab, but it failed on-site in Cyanamid's plant in Puerto Rico.

The fatal problem was the strong tropical sun: The light in the plant was too bright. The Cognex system used a strobe light to freeze an image of the product. However, this system required that the surrounding light be significantly weaker than the strobe. This was not the case at midday in the Puerto Rican plant. The problem could have been solved by putting a cover over one part of the manufacturing floor, but the firm's specialized software engineers did not think of simple solutions like this.

"We had a bunch of people who knew a lot about software processing, but not much about conveyor belts," noted Allan Wallack, a consultant brought into Cognex to change its strategy. Cognex had to refund Cyanamid's money and walk away. Errors like this resulted in $5 million in total losses by 1986.

Wallack and Shillman soon decided that Cognex would have a hard time making a profit on customized systems like the one designed for Cyanamid. Instead, Cognex decided to focus on standarized, proprietary vision systems for OEMs (original equipment manufacturers) in the electronics and semiconductor markets. The primary customer would not be the end users who produce the chips or electronic devices but the firms that sold robots and testing equipment to the end user.

In 1986, Cognex implemented this new strategy. This required new products and restructed management, sales, marketing, manufacturing, and engineering departments. However, the strategy allowed the company to focus on new product development, rather than on the intensive service support required for customized systems sold to end users. In 1987, Cognex began shipping its new products.

Now the company thrives, growing about 50 percent a year. Most significantly, the bulk of its growth comes from Japan, where Japanese companies have a tradition of shunning American suppliers in favor of dealing with other Japanese companies. Shillman says, "In 10 or 15 years, we'll have hundreds of millions of dollars in

Source: This case was prepared by Don Hopkins, Temple University, USA. This case is intended for classroom discussion only, not to depict effective or ineffective handling of administrative situations. All rights reserved to the author and the North American Case Research Association.

revenue."[1] How was this turnaround possible in an industry where virtually every other American producer of robots or robotic subsystems has been driven out of business? The robot business is now one of a long list of industries dominated by the Japanese. How did this aberration come about, and will it continue?

THE INDUSTRIAL ROBOT INDUSTRY

The robotics business once was seen as having great potential. Two big mistakes happened along the way. First, the market was overestimated, resulting in vast overcapacity in the 1980s. Second, the industry was lost to the Japanese. American firms bet on the wrong technology, and the large American firms exited the industry. Westinghouse, GE, IMB, and Cincinnati Milacron have all left the business after being beaten by the Japanese. Many smaller American firms, such as Prab and Graco, have stopped making robots.

Westinghouse acquired Unimation Inc., the American firm that first developed industrial robots, in 1963. Westinghouse planned to build a billion-dollar business in factory automation. "It's absolutely sick. It breaks my heart to think of how we lost the industrial robot industry," said George Munson, former marketing vice president at Westinghouse Unimation. "Our basic approach was wrong. It was a classic case of trying to merge an entrepreneurial organization into a relatively slow-moving, large American corporation," commented Thomas Murrin, the manager in charge of Westinghouse's advanced technology group, which includes Unimation.[2]

In 1983, there were 62 American firms producing complete robots. Unimation was the leader with its Unimate hydraulic robot and had over 40 percent of the U.S. market. Unfortunately, Unimation and other U.S. firms bet on hydraulic robots, whereas the industry ultimately would be dominated by electric robots. Japanese firms, like Kawasaki Heavy Industries Ltd., hedged their bets and developed both hydraulic and electric robots.

"Unimate suffered from a design flaw that caused it to vibrate. Consequently, a coupling in the fluid line had to be slightly loose, lest it burst under pressure. The dripping that resulted couldn't be fixed, short of redesigning the robot at prohibitive expense. So, the devices were equipped with drip pans that overflowed unpredictably, sometimes halting the assembly lines where they were in use. When a robot broke down, it took two people to work on it—a plumber and an electrician."[3]

But Westinghouse liked its product because it could sell drip pans as options. "Our guys said why fix it when we were making money on the drip pan, not to mention the extra hydraulic fluid," said Mr. Weisel, a former Unimation manager.[4] However, customers like Chrysler started replacing hydraulic robots with electric

---

[1] *Forbes*, December 10, 1990, p. 284.
[2] *The Wall Street Journal*, November 6, 1990, p. A1.
[3] Ibid.
[4] Ibid.

ones. Out of the 2,000 robots now at the car company that weld, stamp, and assemble parts, only 15 percent are still hydraulic.

Westinghouse introduced PUMA in 1985. PUMA was a large electric robot capable of replacing Unimate, but the company was too late. In 1985, Unimation sales dropped 40 percent. PUMA was a me-too robot, too late to compete with the Japanese. Additionally, by the mid-1980s, customers were less interested in robots because these firms started to comprehend that their products would have to be extensively redesigned in order to effectively incorporate robots into the manufacturing process. Manufacturing and product development would have to work together in designing new products. This was not typical for many American firms at the time. Japanese robot makers aided their customers in redesigning their products to be "robot friendly." The Japanese stressed simple robots, keeping fixed costs low and in line with JIT (just-in-time) production. American firms stressed high-cost "smart" machines, exploiting their firms' software skills. For example, GE designed a four-arm robot that did many things simultaneously, but the machine was so taxed that it broke down frequently. One reason U.S. manufacturers were not in love with robots is because keeping them from breaking down was so much work. In some operations, American companies that once used robots have eliminated them completely.

The Japanese were able to build on their experience and develop comparable robots with 30 percent fewer components. Partly as a result, their robots have lower maintenance costs and are more reliable.

THE VISION THING

In spite of the failure of these large American firms, some small entrepreneurial firms were successful in certain niches. One of these niches was machine vision systems. Machine vision systems are used for machine guidance, part sorting, inspection, and gauging. For example, the inspection of package labels or semiconductor chips is a tedious, labor-intensive process that can be replaced with the use of a vision system, resulting in higher productivity. IBM has replaced its chip inspectors with a vision system made by Cognex. Many industry experts predict that robots with vision capability will be the next generation of robots as they become more sophisticated. Already, Ford and GM use vision systems to install auto windshields.

The basic idea behind a vision system is to digitize a picture and interpret its meaning through computer software. Systems range in complexity from simple camera–computer hookups to units with laser controls. Machine vision comes in unidimensional, two-dimensional, and three-dimensional forms. Pictures are made up of elements called pixels. The pixels are digitized and interpreted by a customized software package.

THE VISION SYSTEM INDUSTRY

In 1985 there were probably about 100 vision system firms (this number includes manufacturers and systems houses; systems houses combine hardware from different companies, design the software, install and debug the system, and then provide service). Today there are many fewer vision firms, probably about 20. Between 1985 and 1990, there was a huge shakeout as a result of too many firms entering the business because of overly optimistic forecasts and low entry barriers. Only the firms with a strategic commitment remained.

The industry was easy to enter. An industry expert commented, "There is no barrier to entry. None. Any halfway bright person could go to Digital Equipment Corporation and buy an original equipment manufacturer's [OEM] computer, say, for about $5,000, and from any number of companies buy an interface board that lets a camera 'talk' to the computer, and go to any video store and buy an off-the-shelf camera that's used for security surveillance or something, put it all in a cabinet that costs a couple hundred bucks, and he's got a vision system. It doesn't do much, and it's not very sophisticated, but he's a player in the market!"[5] As a result, the market was full of mom-and-pop companies, small players operating out of their garages.

Vision systems have been easier to sell than robots because unions apparently do not feel as threatened by them. Purchase decisions for vision systems are thus made at lower levels of management than for other robots. Part of this acceptance is because the vision systems do a better job than manual labor can. A manager with a vision firm noted, "A good example is label inspection. Picture dishwashing liquid bottles coming by. You are sitting in a chair in front of a conveyor and the bottles are coming by at a rate of five a second, 300 a minute. On the other side of the conveyor is a mirror, and your job is to look at both the front of the bottle, and in the mirror, at the back of the bottle. You are supposed to identify those bottles that have torn labels or labels that are misplaced by more than a sixteenth of an inch. That's a lousy job, and you probably aren't doing it very well."[6]

By 1988, machine vision sales were only $196 million, and about half of the firms making systems made them for their own use. By 1990 nearly half of the entire market was represented by the electronics and automotive industries. According to Bader Associates, the entire 1990 market was $477.8 million, broken down as follows: 10 percent from electronics, 38 percent from autos, 10 percent from machinery, 8 percent from fabricated metal products, 6 percent from fabricated commodities, and 28 percent from various small users (see Exhibit 1).

Competition between companies is based on software, computing speed and power, product functionality and performance under "real-world conditions," flexibility, programmability, and on-site engineering expertise and service.

Vision systems are used in two main ways. One is to recognize an object or pattern. An example would be the system used to scan bar codes on items at grocery store checkouts. The second is to measure specific characteristics of an object. This second function is more important to manufacturing operations. Systems that assess depth, surface orientation, and position are key to guiding robotic devices. This visual guidance is called "visual serving." For example, a

---

[5] David W. Rosenthal, *Robotics*, Multicon, Inc., NACRA, 1984.

[6] Ibid.

EXHIBIT 1 Forecasted Robot Use and Sales in the United States and Application by Industry

Industry	1985	1990	1995
Agriculture	1%	1%	1%
Mining and extractive	1	2	2
Construction	0	1	1
Electricity generation	1	1	1
Consumer consumables	2	5	5
Nonmetal commodities	2	4	5
Primary metals	3	4	5
Fabricated commodities	5	6	6
Fabricated metal products	10	8	8
Machinery	8	10	11
Electronics	8	10	16
Automotive	51	38	26
Aerospace	6	6	8
Other transport equipment	2	3	4
Total	100%	100%	100%

Forecasted Robot Sales in the United States, by Application

	1985	1990	1995
Machine tending	16%	15%	15%
Material transfer	16	15	15
Spot welding	26	15	10
Arc welding	10	10	9
Spray painting/coating	10	10	7
Machining	5	7	7
Electronic assembly	6	12	14
Other assembly	5	8	12
Inspection	5	7	10
Other	1	1	1
Total	100%	100%	100%

	1985		1990		1995	
Application	Units	Sales	Units	Sales	Units	Sales
Machine tending	800	$ 28.0	1,650	$ 61.1	2,250	$ 69.8
Material transfer	800	28.8	1,650	62.7	2,250	78.8
Spot welding	1,300	78.0	1,650	95.7	1,500	75.0
Arc welding	500	30.0	1,100	66.0	1,350	78.3
Spray painting	500	30.0	1,100	66.0	1,050	63.0
Electronics assembly	300	10.5	1,320	52.8	2,100	66.4
Other assembly	250	8.8	880	30.8	1,800	63.0
Inspection	250	13.0	770	38.5	1,500	75.0
Other	50	2.0	110	4.2	150	6.0
Total	4,750	$229.1	10,230	$477.8	13,950	$575.3

Source: Joseph F. Engelberger, *Robotics in Service,* MIT Press, 1989. (He criticizes the above forecasts for excluding service robots.)

camera may be placed on the end of a robotic arm and used to guide the arm to its destination. An example would be the SMD (surface mount device) industry where a vision system guides a robot in mounting an electronic component on the surface of a circuit board.

THE ROBOTICS INDUSTRY

In a technical sense, vision systems are not robots but are often a major robotic subsystem, so the success of the two industries is strongly linked. A robot, according to the Robot Institute of America (RIA), is a "reprogrammable multifunction manipulator designed to move material, parts, tools, or specialized devices through variable programmed motions for the performance of a variety of tasks." *Programmable* is the key word in this definition. Thus, a complicated but single-use piece of factory equipment would not qualify as a robot.

Robots were invented in the United States over 30 years ago. Significant growth in installation started in the 1980s. Forecasters had optimistically predicted sales of $2 billion by 1990. During the middle of the 1980s, it became clear that the industry would not live up to these expectations. In 1984 shipments by U.S.–based robot suppliers were 5.136 units and $332.5 million in sales. The U.S.–installed base was 14,500 units, mostly in the auto industry, as of 1984. Sales and units, respectively, were $443 million and 6,209 in 1985 and $441 million and 6,219 in 1986. RIA reported booked orders of about $500 million in 1990. Robotic exports equaled $100 million in 1990 and represented 6,000 complete units. This is twice the unit volume exported in 1989. Orders for 1991 were level, but shipments were expected to increase as the backlog was reduced.

The auto industry absorbs about 50 percent of the industry's sales, mostly by buying spot welders. As such, the bulk of U.S. robotic producers are located in the midwestern states of Illinois, Indiana, Iowa, Michigan, and Wisconsin, but particularly in Michigan, where about one-sixth of all U.S. robot producers are located.

The auto industry is, of course, very cyclical. The robotics industry is starting to diversify its customer base, however. Other applications include heavy machinery, aerospace, electronics, food, drugs, and service industries, as well as arc welding, spray painting, loading and unloading, machining, material transfer, assembly operations, and inspection. Almost 37,000 robots had been installed in the United States by 1990 and another 20,000 more by the end of 1991. Trends aiding this growth are an increasing labor shortage, a growing market for used robots, more emphasis on manufacturing, miniaturization in the electronics industry, the potential for service robots (for security, cleaning, and use in health care), and the new importance of product integrity in the pharmaceutical industry.

The advantage of a robot comes primarily from its ability to work at a constant pace and with high accuracy throughout a work shift. This results in lower hourly costs for the operation of an industrial robot relative to a blue-collar worker. In 1981 the direct hourly labor cost was about $17 in the auto industry, compared to a robot's hourly cost of about $5. Robots also increase flexibility, allowing plants to work on a batch basis involving a variety of products at the same site.

Growth in the market for robots is likely to be affected by several factors. First, the cost of robots may decrease as they slide down the experience curve. The average cost of a robot in 1990 was either $40,000 or $110,000, depending on whose estimate you accept. These figures are expected to decline significantly in the next 10 years. Second, sensing devices may improve. "Blind robots" are adequate only in very orderly manufacturing environments (not the norm), and thus the large amount of research being conducted on visual and tactile sensing devices may lead to a broader market. Third, robot size might be reduced. The size of robots has started to decline, increasing the potential for placing them in preexisting plants. Finally, systems integration and "building block designs" now being emphasized in the robotics industry are moving away from individual robots and toward complete systems of flexibile manufacturing and modules that comprise them.

THE JAPANESE ROBOTICS INDUSTRY

Japan is the leading producer, exporter, and market and has the largest installed base of robots in the world. However, it may also be the most saturated market for robots. There are about 300 Japanese robot firms, which provide about 50 percent of the world's demand for robots and generate sales of about $2.1 billion. Exhibit 2 shows the number of robots installed by country for 1980, 1984, 1989, and 1992.

Kawasaki Heavy Industries became the first Japanese entrant in 1968, when it signed a licensing agreement with Unimation. Kawasaki improved on the Unimation design, and other firms soon entered the market, including Hitachi, Toshiba, and Ishikawajima-Harima Heavy Industries. Many important competitors entered in the middle 1970s. Fanuc (pronounced "fan-nuke") entered in 1974 and is now considered the world's dominant robot firm. Their first units were made for

EXHIBIT 2   Robots Installed by Country

Country	1992	1989	1984	1980
Japan	274,000	220,000	67,300	15,250
United States	40,000	37,000	14,500	4,700
Germany	28,120	22,400	6,600	1,255
Italy	24,268	9,500	2,585	353
France	11,917	7,063	2,700	580
United Kingdom	9,634	5,908	2,623	371
Spain	5,476	2,000	516	284
Sweden	5,297	3,800	2,400	940
Belgium	3,221	1,800	775	58
Total	401,933	309,471	99,999	23,791

Note: Does not include manual manipulators and fixed-sequence control machines.
Source: Adapted from Japan Industrial Robot Association, July 1985.

their own use. Fanuc is well known for the totally automated noodle factory it produced and for its use of robots to build its own robots.

Robots using the Panasert brand name, produced by Matsushita, were critical in America's loss of the consumer electronics industry. The robots automated the insertion of components onto circuit boards for TVs. Matsushita sells products under the Panasonic brand name and is known for its world-class manufacturing expertise.

Japanese competitors can be placed into several strategic groups, including steelmakers (e.g., Kobe Steel and Daido Steel), machinery producers (e.g., Fanuc, Toyoda Machine Works, Komatsu, and Toshiba Seiki), electronics firms (e.g., Hitachi, Matsushita, NEC, Toshiba, Fuji Electric, and Mitsubishi Electric), and transportation equipment firms (e.g., Kawasaki and Mitsui Engineering and Shipbuilding). Japanese firms often utilized their robots in their own manufacturing process, perfecting them in the process before putting them on the market. Some Japanese firms also have the advantage of being in the electronics industry, allowing them to easily incorporate electronic components into their robots. However the Japanese have a definite disadvantage in software, which partly explains their emphasis on simpler robots.

There are several reasons that Japan became the biggest and earliest market for robots, including global dominance of the Japanese electronics industry, growth of their auto industry, a pronounced labor shortage, lifetime employment practices, a high proportion of engineers in management, less short-term financial pressure, emphasis on energy conservation, cooperation of unions, development of many Japanese companies as the premier manufacturing firms in the world, and government assistance and encouragement.

Japan represented 60 percent of the total installed base of robots by the early 1970s. In 1984, it represented 66 percent versus North America's 14.9 percent—and where the customers are, the producers are likely to be. "The total populations of robots in the United States is around 37,000," says John O'Hara, president of RIA. "The Japanese add that many in one year."[7]

Why have U.S. firms been so slow to incorporate robots into their manufacturing operations? "The companies selling robots plain lied about the capabilities of their equipment and the circumstances under which they could perform," says Roger Nagel, a former manager of automation technology at International Harvester.[8] "U.S. companies made robot hands that were so ungodly complex that in many cases, they had no chance of standing up in a real industrial environment," says Dennis Wisnosky, former vice president of GCA Industrial Systems Group, previously the second leading robot firm in the United States.[9] The Japanese started with simple machines and then used their experience to make more advanced robots.

The industries in Japan with the heaviest use of robots are as follows: electronics industry (36 percent of installed base), automotive industry (29 percent), plas-

---

[7] *Forbes*, April 16, 1990, p. 150.

[8] Ibid.

[9] Ibid.

tic processing industry (10 percent), general machinery industries (7 percent), and the metalworking industry (5 percent).

Japanese robotics firms held the dominant position in the 1980s by a large margin. As a spokesman for the Long Term Credit Bank stated, "It's only a matter of time before the industrial robot becomes one more piece of merchandise that symbolizes Japan."[10] According to Andrew Tanzer and Ruth Simon, writing in *Forbes* magazine, "It happened in consumer electronics, memory chip production, and machine tools. Now it's happening in robotics."[11]

Robots can make flexible manufacturing and JIT production and inventory easier to achieve. Japan's firms are in the forefront of these "lean" production methods. For example, though U.S. carmakers have robotized, they have done so mainly in the area of spot welding and spray painting. Japanese carmakers, on the other hand, have robotized in a way that allows them to shift quickly from the production of one model to another. In the United States, robots have not spread much beyond carmakers and their suppliers.

In 1991, America imported $300 million in robots and parts as part of a total demand of $350 million. The United States exported $210 million in robots or parts in 1991, mostly to Europe and Canada. America imports approximately 55 percent of its complete robot systems, 80 percent of them from Japan. Many American robotics firms produce entirely offshore, often in Japan.

The Japanese market has become highly saturated. It has been estimated, for example, that as much as 90 percent of Japan's auto assembly lines have already been automated. Japanese electronics firms are also considered to be highly saturated. Most electronics firms moved to automatic insertion in the early 1970s. Also, many of the electronic firms, like Matsushita, produced their own robots and were among the first to automate. But as electronic components are miniaturized further, a new wave of automation may develop in this industry. Saturation is leading to increased pressure to export and to find new applications.

GMF

The largest seller of robots in the United States was the joint venture between General Motors and Fanuc known as GMF. This venture had about 27 percent of the U.S. robot market in 1985. GMF produced painting and laser robots used for welding and cutting. It had 1991 sales exceeding $250 million. Fanuc altogether has about half the U.S. market, although in imports twice as many robots as it makes in the United States, and its U.S.–produced units are designed in Japan. Fanuc also entered a joint venture with GE. Many other Japanese companies forged links with U.S. firms mainly to provide distribution of Japanese hardware or gain access to U.S. software. Many U.S. robotics firms buy basic Japanese robot units and add refinements and peripherals such as software and vision systems. No Japanese firms, other than GMF, set up manufacturing in the United States. Japanese robot

---

[10] Daniel Hunt, *Industrial Robotics Handbook*, 1983, p. 298.
[11] *Forbes*, April 16, 1990, p. 150.

makers are making modest profits, at best, because of the intense competition, but most remain in robotics to help maintain their own manufacturing capability.

Fanuc is the world's leading producer of industrial robots. It is reported to be consistently profitable. Fanuc is the lowest-cost producer and yet has very high quality. Controls and robots account for about 75 percent of its business. The company believes in "*Weniger Teile*" (German engineering slogan for reducing the number of parts) as a way of driving down costs.

Since GM and GE threw in the towel and linked up with Fanuc, the company has had the U.S. market handed over to it. GM was the industry's single biggest customer. Says consultant Gordon Richardson, "U.S. manufacturers were caught napping. They were trumpeting all sorts of advances, but they had not done the underlying job of making reliable systems."[12] Fanuc has a reputation for making reliable systems. There is speculation that Fanuc will one day abandon its U.S. partners.

COGNEX CORPORATION

Cognex has managed to prosper, along with a few other machine vision firms such as Allen-Bradley and Itran in the United States and Israeli-based Optrotech and Orbot. Although about 100 firms have attempted to develop profitable machine vision businesses, Cognex is one of only a few to make it a viable business. Cognex earned $6.5 million on sales of $21 million in 1990. For the past several years, it has grown about 50 percent a year. Cognex had installed more than 7,500 vision systems by the end of July 1991, more than anyone else. Cognex management claims to have 10–20 percent of the machine vision market.

Cognex's focus on proprietary machine vision systems for the electronics industry struck gold when it began selling to General Signal's Electroglas division, which produces equipment to check the silicon wafers used for semiconductor chips (i.e., wafer probers). However, Cognex's strategy makes it highly dependent on a small number of specialized products in cyclical, closely related industries.

Customers.   Cognex's U.S. customers include AT&T, Digital Equipment, Electro Scientific Industries, GE, Hughes Aircraft, Merck Pharmaceuticals, Polaroid, Teradyne, Instruments, Xerox, IBM, Hewlett-Packard, and General Signal. Their Japanese customers include Ando, Micronics, Seiko Seiki, Shinkawa, Suziki, Tenryu, Toray, TSK, Yamaha, NEC, Tokyo Seimitsu, Matsushita, Sanyo, and Komatsu. Other international customers include Alphasem, Bobst, Elektronik and Technik, Fraunhofer Institut, Intertrade Scientific, Hiltcroft, Rolex, SGS-Thomson, and Trident Micro Systems.

However, in 1990 Cognex's top three customers represented 47 percent of its net revenues. In 1988 Cognex had two main customers: General Signal, representing 18 percent of total sales, and IBM, representing 9 percent. Its third major customer is Japan's Shinkawa Ltd., with whom Cognex signed a contract in 1989 for $9 million in products to be delivered over two years. Shinkawa is a leader in the manufacture of

---

[12] *Fortune*, May 25, 1987, p. 56.

wire bonding equipment (wire bonding machines attach chips to the ceramic packages inserted onto printed circuit boards) and in the use of machine vision systems. Shinkawa replaced its own vision systems with those of Cognex. Cognex is providing it with the Cognex 2000, as well as wire bonding software, and has given Shinkawa the right to manufacture the 2000 and its software under "certain circumstances."

In fact, most of Cognex's recent growth has come from Japan. For example, during the first quarter of 1991, sales grew 8 percent domestically, but 59 percent in Japan, compared to the same quarter of 1990. "In a world where companies are reporting earnings decreases, we're ecstatic. Compared to the general economy, we're doing extremely well," commented Shillman.[13]

Cognex has won about two-thirds of the business for vision systems of semiconductor and electronic equipment firms (excluding captive sales). Shillman says, "We really are the market leader in the country and maybe the world. It's still a small business, but we're growing nicely."[14] Cognex thinks of itself as being in the electronics and semiconductor business, rather than in the robotics industry.

Trends in the electronics industry (i.e., semiconductor chips, consumer electronics, and computers) favor machine vision, due to smaller components and higher-density circuits requiring accurate alignment, inspection, and placement. Cognex vision systems guide the placement of components onto integrated circuits (for instance, as applied in the SMD market) that go into consumer electronic products. A majority of these customers are in Japan and Korea. In 1990, Cognex signed sales agreements with leading manufacturers of SMD assembly equipment. Probably the biggest producer of SMD (or automatic insertion) equipment is Matsushita with its Panasert line. Other Japanese producers of SMD assembly equipment include Sanyo, TDK, and Fuji. Surface mounting is a new technology used in making circuit boards; the old approach, called "through-the-hole," involved placing a component in an opening in the circuit board. With surface mounting, the component sits on top of the board, and thus no holes are needed in the board. Other Cognex OEM markets include laser memory repair systems, package printers for integrated circuits, printing systems for the production of printed circuit boards, wire bonders, die bonders, semiconductor wafer dicers, and probers. In many of these applications, a vision system is used to locate the item accurately so it can be processed (e.g., probers rely on a vision system to align each chip prior to testing).

Cognex also sells to advanced manufacturing engineering companies that puchase multiple systems for internal use in their own manufacturing processes and to systems houses that packakage complete production systems.

Products.   Customers pay for each system they buy from Cognex, as well as a licensing fee per system for each software module. The software comes in modules organized by three function levels and according to tasks: (1) system software (tasks: image acquisition, compilation, communication, control, and math functions), (2) image processing (tasks: filtering, histogramming, projecting, spatial

---

[13] *The Wall Street Journal,* February 12, 1990, p. B4.
[14] *Electronic Business,* February 5, 1990, p. 26.

averaging, transforming coordinates, edge detecting, morphology, and auto-focus), and (3) image analysis software (tasks: search, reference feature selection, character recog-nition, inspection, and scene angle finder). Customers can build their own systems by using the C programming language to interconnect each of the three levels of software.

The firm also sells what it calls VAP (vision application programs). These are complete vision systems for targeted vision problems. For example, the company offers VAPs for high-speed character vertification and for the SMD market.

Cognex's products include the Cognex 2000, 3000, 3100, 3200, and 4000. Introduced in 1990, the 4000 is a vision system that can be plugged into a customer's computers. These products are designed to perform automatically inspection, identification, guidance, and gauging tasks. Of the $7.6 million increase in sales from 1989 to 1990, 66 percent came from growth of the 3000 and 17 percent from growth of the 2000. Income is also generated by such services as software development and licensing fees.

An advanced Cognex system sells for about $20,000. It typically includes a circuit board and vision software. The heart of its product consists of a printed circuit board run by a Motorola microprocessor (68000 or 68020) and a propri-etary coprocessor that Cognex refers to as its "vision engine" (a coprocessor is not included in the 2000 model). This hardware is controlled by proprietary software. Its model 2000 has 2 MB of memory, and its family of 3000 models have 2–8 MB.

Competition.   Cognex has little real competition in Japan from the Japanese because of their disadvantages in software. Customers want a minimum of hardware and a maximum of software, because it saves space. Space is very expensive in manufacturing environments requiring absolute cleanliness, such as in a semi-conductor fabrication facility. Cognex has a one-board system that saves space compared to the multiboard systems of competitors. The Japanese use primitive "binary" vision systems (black and white) compared with the better "gray-scale" vision systems used by Cognex. Gray-scale systems are more accurate and result in higher yields (i.e., fewer defective circuit boards). In some product types. Cognex competes against the Japanese firms Yaskawa and CSC (Creative Systems Corp.). But Cognex is pressured more by American firms, such as Itran, AISI, Imaging Technology Inc. (ITI), ICOS, View Engineering, International Robomation Intelligence (IRI), and Adept Technology. One of Cognex's main competitors, Intellidex, went bankrupt in 1991. Cognex has three types of competitors: other firms like itself that produce machine vision systems, firms that produce them for their own needs (and who might sell to the external market in the future), and producers of "board-level" processing systems, some of which have developed machine vision software recently. Several machine vision companies are profiled next.

- *Intellidex.* Founded in 1981, it was the number two U.S. firm in the niche of assembly robots for the electronics and semiconductor industries. But sales have been small and profit elusive. Sales were about $15 million in 1990. The firm went bankrupt in May 1991.

- *Adept Technology.* Intellidex's main competitor. The firm was formed when a group of West Coast engineers left Unimation. The firm has 70 percent of the market for small assembly robots. Sales have stagnated at about $40 million for several years. The company says it is profitable but will not talk about a rumor that it will delay going public because of a weak balance sheet.

- *Robotic Vision Systems.* Like many vision system survivors, RVS is focused on one narrow niche. It emphasizes the guidance of robots that apply sealants. The company has posted modest profits in the past but recently won a $3.6 million sale to Ford Motor Company for a system that sprays coatings on the lower part of car bodies to help them resist scratching from stones or other road debris.

- *Perceptron.* This firm makes sheet metal checking devices for the auto industry. Its latest generation is named Veristar. Sales were $10 million in 1988. Sales to European carmakers have skyrocketed, and Ford recently bought a new system. Foreign sales were about 35 percent of total sales in 1989.

- *Hitachi.* Hitachi America Ltd. manufactures robots for arc welding, material handling, and assembly; vision technology for robot guidance, product inspection and flow control, measurement, and security. However, it has not emphasized the external market for vision systems.

- *Panasonic Factory Automation.* PFA offers four distinct automation product lines: Panarobo assembly robots, welding equipment, Panasert electronic circuit assembly equipment, and Panasonic test and measurement instrumentation. This Japanese firm also has not emphasized the external market for vision systems.

- *Sony Corporation of America Factory Automation Equipment Division.* Sony Factory Automation Division provides robots, vision systems, compact table-top assembly units, odd-form component insertion and surface mount machines, flexible precision assembly cells, and systems integration services. An integrated robot vision system is available, as well as a stand-alone high-speed, gray-scale vision system, but it makes vision systems mainly for its own use.

- *Applied Intelligent Systems Inc.* AISI designs and manufactures a family of machine vision computers and software for automated recognition, measurement, and inspection tasks. The AISI computers, combined with applications and development software, provide OEMs, system integrators, and others with machine vision systems.

- *Itran Corp.* (pronounced "i-train"). Itran Corp. manufactures machine vision systems for the inspection and process control needs of manufacturers. Applications include pharmaceuticals, electronics, high-speed packaging, and automotive. Its products include I-Pak, a label verification system designed for the pharmaceutical market, and the MVP series, used for a wide variety of manufacturing applications.

The Japanese Threat.   One main concern is how long large Japanese electonic companies will refrain from entering or emphasizing Cognex's markets (the top 11 Japanese electronic firms are Matsushita, NEC, Toshiba, Hitachi, Fujitsu, Sony, Mitsubishi Electric, NTT, Canon, Sharp, and Sanyo). Sony and Hitachi already supply their own needs for advanced vision systems and might be the first to challenge Cognex's dominant position in its markets.

Cognex protects its technology mainly by keeping "trade secrets," rather than by patenting. The company's software is copyrighted, and the firm uses a number of security measures to protect its intellectual property. For example, Cognex uses nondisclosure agreements with employees, suppliers, consultants, and customers. However, "reverse engineering" is a constant threat for Cognex, and the firm's *Prospectus* (from when it went public in 1989) notes, "Effective patent, copyright, and secret protection may be unavailable in certain foreign countries."

Japanese customers are a major part of Cognex's sales, totaling about 40 percent. Revenues grew in Japan by 103 percent in 1990. The company's attitude is that by doing business in Japan, it "becomes Japanese." In 1990, Cognex established a Tokyo subsidiary, Cognex K.K., and terminated its relationship with its previous Japanese distributor.

In December 1990, Cognex signed its first contract with a Korean customer, a major Korean conglomerate. Cognex expects this agreement to lead to the use of Cognex vision systems in this customer's integrated circuit manufacturing plant.

Sales in Europe were up 191 percent in 1990, compared to 1989. European sales represented 7 percent, 5 percent, and 9 percent of total sales in 1988, 1989, and 1990, respectively. Domestic sales, as a percent of total sales, have been declining, with 79 percent, 64 percent, and 49 percent of total sales being domestic in 1988, 1989, and 1990, respectively. Japanese sales, as a percent of total, have been increasing, with 13 percent, 29 percent, and 40 percent, respectively, in 1988, 1989, and 1990. Cognex has offices in California, Germany, and now Tokyo, in addition to its headquarters in Massachusetts.

Manufacturing.   In-house manufacturing at Cognex includes final assembly, quality control, and final testing, as well as shipment of systems and board-based products. Parts for components are purchased from suppliers and sent to subcontractors for assembly and testing. Some subassemblies are made in-house. All commodity items like electronic parts and sheet metal are purchased, inspected, and warehoused. The firm has its own quality control inspectors, materials personnel, and purchasing agents. Some components are available only from a single source. Some final assembly of systems-level products is done outside by third parties. The third-party contractor assembles and does initial testing of the product, using fixtures and programs owned by the company, and returns the product to Cognex for quality inspection and final testing.

Technology.   "Engineers designing automated equipment demand machine vision technology that is extremely flexible, accurate, and easy to integrate. They also demand products that provide a well-planned growth path so that they can solve new and more difficult problems without completely reengineering their systems. Cognex Corporation is unique in offering a complete, compatible family of single-board vision systems designed for the OEM, system integrator, and advanced engineer. It offers a family of systems that provide accuracy, flexibility, and a range of performance levels in various industrial applications."[15]

Cognex's systems require that factory engineers use the C programming language. "You get eight-ring bound books of documentation with their systems. For somebody who's not a programmer, it's overwhelming," comments Jeffrey Johnson, who works for Square D Company as an expert in manufacturing engineering.[16]

Cognex plans to simplify the programming requirement by using a system of English phrases on a Macintosh computer. This new system, called On-Sight, has been sold on a test basis to several firms (known as beta sites) since October 1990. The company plans to incorporate customer comments in to the product design process.

Also in development is the VC-2, a vision chip intended to detect visual defects in manufactured products. This chip is known as an "ASIC" (application-specific integrated circuit). The VC-2, which will be proprietary, was expected to be completed in 1991. This chip, according to Cognex, will perform vision detection of flaws at a high rate of speed in new and more difficult applications, such as finding cracks on semiconductor dies and unintended ink streaks in printing processes. The firm believes the VC-1, an earlier version, was the world's first ASIC able to run both image analysis and image-processing functions at high speeds. A patent was applied for in 1987. All Cognex's vision chips are produced by outside contractors.

Finances and Management.   In spite of its rapid growth, the company has no outstanding long-term or short-term debt (though in August 1990, the firm was granted a line of credit equal to $1 million, or 80 percent of its receivables, whichever is less). It went public in the summer of 1989, offering shares at $11 and raising $6.6 million in this offering. As of August 16, 1991, its stock sold over the counter for $57 per share.

In a news release, Cognex announced net income of $4.3 million or $.99 per share for the first six months of 1991, compared to $2.9 million for the same period of 1990. Revenue was $14.5 million, compared to $10.9 million for the same period in 1990. Chairman Shillman said, "Business remains strong in our two principal markets, the United States and Japan. Shipments of our newest product, the Cognex 4000, increased from 2 percent of revenue in the first quarter to 15 percent in the second quarter, evidence of the growing acceptance and demand for this product."[17] See Exhibits 3 and 4 for financial statements.

Cognex's management consists of Shillman, four vice presidents, and a director of marketing. Shillman is a Ph.D. and former professor who wrote his thesis on how people recognize written characters. The board of directors consists of Shillman,

---

[15] Cognex product literature.

[16] *Forbes*, December 10, 1990.

[17] News release, July 23, 1991.

EXHIBIT 3   Cognex Income Statements

	1991	1990	1989
Revenue			
Product	$28,959,000	$20,932,995	$14,524,594
Other	2,589,000	2,624,774	1,385,701
Total	$31,548,000	$23,557,769	$15,910,295
Costs			
Product	$ 5,338,000	$ 3,977,884	$ 3,741,173
Other	541,000	308,683	222,208
Total	$ 5,879,000	$ 4,286,567	$ 3,963,381
Gross profit	$25,669,000	$19,271,202	$11,946,914
R&D and engineering expense	4,362,000	3,778,786	2,507,532
Selling, general, and administrative expense	8,694,000	6,768,649	4,873,359
Income from operations	12,613,000	8,723,767	4,566,023
Interest income	1,401,000	1,329,563	699,322
Interest expense	2,000	66,577	81,551
EBIT	14,012,000	9,986,753	5,183,794
Tax	4,520,000	3,466,000	1,469,000
Net income	$ 9,492,000	$ 6,520,753	$ 3,714,794

two representatives of venture capital firms, and two outsiders. The company had 224 common shareholders of record as of December 31, 1990, with 4,341,756 shares outstanding. It earned $1.50 per common share in 1990. One of its customers, General Signal, invested $3 million to ensure access to its technology.

Cognex has about 100 employees. The firm has 16 direct sales and service employees, 14 engineers involved in software development and four involved in hardware projects, and the balance of its employees are involved in product documentation, customer training, administration, and engineering support.

THE FUTURE

Cognex management summarizes its approach to the business in the following ways: "What's the key to our success? We believe it's innovation . . . our willingness and, oftentimes, our eagerness to do things differently than they have been done before. We don't want to be the same as everyone else. We want to be better."[18]

In terms of customer relations, Cognex pledges, "We will do whatever it takes to satisfy each customer. In return, we require the customer's firm commitment to an ongoing and profitable relationship." On corporate culture: "We have created an innovative corporate culture that is responsive to employees' needs, both personal and professional. We encourage creative dissent, and we reward both talent and perseverance in all aspects of our employees' daily endeavors."[19]

[18] Cognex, *Annual Report*, 1990.
[19] Ibid.

EXHIBIT 4   Cognex Balance Sheets

	1991	1990	1989
Assets			
Current assets			
Cash and equivalents	$13,449,000	$ 4,062,074	$ 5,973,139
Short-term investments	20,105,000	17,221,524	8,081,762
Accounts receivable less reserve	4,152,000	2,701,976	1,743,767
Other receivables	—	628,390	145,462
Inventories	1,051,000	944,501	854,497
Other current assets	764,000	208,989	80,431
Total current assets	$39,431,000	$25,767,454	$16,879,058
Equipment, furniture, and leaseholds at cost*			
Machinery and equipment	$ —	$ 3,531,991	$ 2,461,365
Furniture and fixtures	—	280,044	272,370
Leasehold improvements	—	268,361	260,511
	$3,925,000	$ 4,080,396	$2,994,246
Less accumulated depreciation and amortization	1,914,000	2,362,729	1,885,548
	$ 2,011,000	$ 1,717,667	$ 1,108,698
Other assets	270,000	333,655	174,239
Total assets	$41,712,000	$27,818,776	$18,161,995
Liabilities and Equity			
Current liabilities			
Current part of long-term debt		$ —	$ 21,395
Current part of deferred revenue	$ 258,000	683,825	369,200
Deferred credits		—	584,150
Accounts payable	303,000	295,458	173,699
Accrued expenses	2,626,000	1,095,818	764,143
Accrued income taxes	389,000	—	306,603
Customer deposits	1,682,000	1,907,805	1,627,758
Total current liabilities	$ 5,258,000	$ 3,982,906	$ 3,846,948
Stockholders' investment			
Common stock, $.002 par value—authorized 10,000,000 shares—issued 4,075,903 and 4,051,642 shares in 1990 and 1989, respectively	17,000	8,152	8,103
Additional paid-in capital	19,269,000	16,172,746	15,246,529
Deferred compensation	—	—	(15,000)
Cumulative translation adjustment	(1,000)	(22,508)	(21,312)
Accumulated earnings	17,169,000	7,677,480	1,156,727
Treasury stock, at cost, 250,000 shares in 1989		—	(2,060,000)
Total stockholders' investment	36,454,000	23,835,870	14,315,047
Total liabilities and equity	$41,712,000	$27,818,776	$18,161,995

Cognex's goals for 1991 include:

1. Initiate development of the next generation of vision engine.
2. Ship VC-2, proprietary vision chip.
3. Continue development of On-Sight.
4. Expand participation in the SMD market.
5. Sign at least one OEM in a new market or application.
6. Expand sales in Japan and Korea.
7. Continue growth in revenues and profits.

Robert Shillman's letter to stockholders concludes:

> Cognex's second decade promises to be as exciting as the first. The need for Cognex products is expected to grow in order to satisfy the increasing demand, worldwide, for highest quality goods selling at the lowest possible price. Faced with this demand, manufacturers of all kinds of products . . . from the simplest light bulb to the most complex computer chip . . . are increasingly turning to automated manufacturing, and, in many cases, automated manufacturing means machine vision.
>
> To continue to dominate the market for vision systems in this next decade, Cognex will focus its team on creating machine vision systems with the following four attributes:
>
> 1. *Capability:* Our products must be capable of solving a broad range of problems in a wide variety of industries. Our vision systems must be equally proficient in guiding robots inserting windshields at an automotive plant as they are in inspecting microscopic wire bonds in an integrated circuit.
> 2. *Reliability:* Our products must work reliably under difficult, factory-floor conditions, where everyday problems can include uncontrolled part placement, poor lighting, and noisy electrical environments.
> 3. *Useability:* Our products must be useable by a wide range of customers, from the experienced design engineer at an OEM to his factory-floor counterpart who oftentimes has no knowledge of machine vision or computer programming.
> 4. *Affordability:* Our products must be priced so that our customers can readily realize their payback potential.
>
> As we enter our second decade, we will continue the Cognex tradition of working hard, working smart, and using innovation whenever possible. We look forward to the challenges, and to the successes that are on the road ahead. And look forward to sharing the rewards of the journey with you.[20]

A key question is, Should Cognex try to expand its product line and target market? At present, it is dependent on two closely linked, cyclical industries and is dependent on three major customers for 49 percent of its business. New industries or applications would reduce this dependence. Or should Cognex make a thrust into the broader robotics market?

---

[20] Ibid.

Can the firm successfully make the transition from an entrepreneurial firm to one that is professionally managed? At present, the firm is made up mostly of engineers. As the firm grows, its administration may require professional management. History is replete with firms whose founders hung on too long in trying to manage their creations themselves (e.g., Ford). On the other hand, is Cognex vulnerable to losing key employees?

Another question for this successful firm is, Can it continue to be successful in markets where the bulk of customers are Japanese and where it has to complete against Japanese firms selling vision systems? Will customers like NEC, that uses Cognex systems in the production of semiconductors and incorporates these systems into its own robots, continue to buy from Cognex as Japanese firms start to emphasize machine vision products? How well will Cognex be able to compete if Sony and Hitachi start to focus on the external machine vision industry? How well are they protected from "reverse engineering," something the Japanese excel at?

Apparently, the firm thinks it will continue to succeed. It survived the huge shakeout of 1985–1990 because, according to Shillman, "Our technology was better."[21] Cognex believes it can continue to win the Japanese market by "becoming Japanese."

---

[21] *Fortune*, August 13, 1990.

CASE 12
INTERNATIONAL UNP HOLDINGS LTD. (1994)

In early October 1994, George Bonar, the president and CEO of International UNP Holdings Ltd. (IUNP) arrived in Poland to participate in the annual shareholders' meetings of IUNP's subsidiaries. During his visit he also planned to negotiate new investments and discuss his company's future role in the Mass Privatization Program with government representatives.

His first task on arriving in IUNP's Warsaw office was to analyze the most recent quarterly reports of Biawar, IBIS, and Unipak, the three subsidiaries his company had acquired over the preceding two years. George had already skimmed the documents, and was quite satisfied with the results presented by Biawar and Unipak. IBIS's performance, however, was disappointing. This was not entirely surprising to him because, for some time, he had been concerned with the pace and direction of post-privatization changes taking place in this subsidiary.

He had a clear view of what steps would be needed to bring IBIS back in line with IUNP's expectations. He also felt that by taking a closer look at all three companies he might be able to discern some patterns which could help him to avert similar situations in the future.

COMPANY HISTORY

IUNP was formed in Vancouver, Canada, to establish a pool of capital for investment in Poland's manufacturing sector.[1] The idea of creating an investment fund for this purpose had first crossed Stan Lis's mind in early 1989. Changes in the politics and the economies of central Europe had just begun but it seemed apparent to Stan that, as a result of a collapse of the communist system, countries of the region would increasingly open their doors to the West. Consequently, farsighted Western entrepreneurs and investors could capitalize on what might be enormous profit opportunities by getting an early foothold in these new markets. For Stan, it seemed natural to concentrate on Poland. Not only was it his native country, but it was at the forefront of the trend toward adopting the free market system.

Stan had settled in Canada in 1976 and had been involved in the Vancouver investment community since then. He presented his idea to Bill Hudson, a close friend and business associate who also committed himself to the venture.

The initial efforts of the partners to raise the capital for their investment fund were unsuccessful. Stan and Bill decided they needed to include a successful

---

[1]The start-up of IUNP was discussed in a 1990 business case study entitled "International UNP Holdings Ltd." available from the authors at the Faculty of Management, University of Manitoba.

Source: This case was prepared by Kris Opalinski and Walter Good of the University of Manitoba Canada as a basis for classroom discussion rather than to illustrate either effective or ineffective handling of an administrative situation. © Canadian Consortium of Management Schools, 1994.

business executive in their venture to work out the details of the company's business plan, contribute a higher level of professionalism to its operations, and lend more credibility to the concept. Their search led to George Bonar, a seasoned business executive, also of Polish decent.

George was initially somewhat skeptical of the opportunities described by Stan and Bill and wanted to investigate the viability of the idea himself before fully committing himself to the venture. He agreed to sign on as a consultant to investigate the situation before making a decision. The preliminary search George conducted in Canada indicated that investing in Poland had considerable merit. In order to confirm these initial findings, George continued his investigation in Poland. This visit confirmed his view that the country offered the opportunity of a lifetime for Western investors and, upon his return, he joined the company as president, CEO, and significant shareholder. One of his initial acts was to develop the following short-term organizational objectives for IUNP:

1. Improve the company's credibility (which he perceived as the major factor in attracting investment capital).
2. Raise $5 to 10 million in equity capital.
3. Develop UNP's overall strategy.
4. Develop procedures for the identification of investment opportunities and their subsequent screening, as well as guidelines for managing the company's investment portfolio.
5. Search for investment opportunities and allocate a portion of any acquired funds to Poland.

It took him more than a year and $1 million of his and his partner Bill Hudson's money to obtain the capital needed to implement his strategy. He later commented on the company's early days:

> At the beginning, IUNP was just a concept, a dream, the legitimacy of which had yet to be proved to potential investors. To sell this concept, we had to portray ourselves as a credible company. This was not easy for a one-person business operating out of a borrowed office. We had to build our credibility based on the reputation of people associated with us. We brought in some of the most reputable Canadian business executives on our board while retaining the services of legal and accounting advisors with names recognizable worldwide. This may have seemed an extravagant strategy, but it worked.

By 1991, the company had managed to raise $8.5 million in equity funding, an amount sufficient to finance the acquisition of two or three Polish subsidiaries. Large financial institutions, such as the British branch of U.S.–based Fidelity Investments, Murray Johnstone International Ltd. of Glasgow, and Fleming International Investment Ltd., were the major investors, who, in addition to their money, contributed additional credibility to the company.

With the newly obtained capital, IUNP could strengthen its operating base. In May 1991, the company founded a Dutch subsidiary, UNP Holdings B.V., that was to be used as the acquisition vehicle for making investments in Poland.[2] In the second half of 1991, IUNP opened a permanent office in Poland.

THE INVESTMENT PROCESS

By early 1992, George had scanned some 250 companies, of which he found 75 attractive enough to warrant a more detailed investigation. His approach to evaluating potential Polish investments followed a carefully designed set of guidelines (Exhibit 1) and procedures (Exhibit 2), which were to ensure the consistency and efficiency of the process.

Exhibit 1   IUNP Investment Guidelines*

IUNP generally intends to invest in businesses in Poland which are profitable and will only make an investment if an investee company meets any seven of the following Investment Guidelines:

1. It operates in the manufacturing sector.
2. It is operated by management which IUNP believes to be competent.
3. It manufactures goods that have a sizable demand in Poland and are competitive with domestic and imported products in Poland.
4. It has fewer than 1,000 employees.
5. It does not operate in an industrial sector which has a high visibility or social or environmental sensitivity.
6. It manufactures goods with a high labour content such that it takes advantage of current wage rates which are low relative to wage rates in similar industries in other developed countries.
7. It has a significant market share in its product area.
8. It manufactures goods that do not have a high brand visibility or a large marketing content.
9. It uses mature technologies instead of high technology unless the high technology is available in "packaged" form.
10. It has established and secured domestic access to supplies and materials.

---

* Quoted from the July 28, 1993 offering of IUNP shares.

Exhibit 2   IUNP Investment Procedure*

Sourcing of Investments
IUNP seeks potential investments through the use of existing contacts in Poland and contacts developed by management on an ongoing basis. The typical sources of information on investment opportunities include state administration, consultants, trade development offices of foreign embassies, international organizations operating in Poland, and commercial and investment banks.

(continued)

---

[2] Under the terms of the Netherlands–Poland Income Tax Convention, the withholding tax on dividends paid by a Polish company to a Netherlands-based investor (generally set at up to 15 percent) is waived if the investor holds more than 25 percent of the capital of the Polish company. This compares favourably with the terms of the Canada–Poland Income Tax Convention, which does not allow for such a waiver.

(Concluded)

Screening and Due Diligence of Investments

1. *Initial Screening.* A company identified as a potential investment opportunity is contacted personally by IUNP executives. Based on information provided by the management of the potential investee company and review of generally available sources of information, IUNP's management decides whether the prospective investment satisfies the Investment Guidelines.

2. *Initial Due Diligence.* Initial due diligence involves a review of legal, financial, and technical operations of the potential investee company. Outside expertise is used if required, particularly in translating the financial statements of the company into the Canadian format. If this stage results in a positive evaluation of the potential investment, the two sides enter into a letter of intent.

3. *Letter of Intent.* Generally, letters of intent entered into by IUNP include an agreement in principle as to IUNP's investment, a right for IUNP to conduct further due diligence of the investee company, and an agreement by the investee company not to consider investment proposals from any party other than IUNP for a specified period of time, usually six months.

4. *Due Diligence.* Due diligence is initiated by detailed discussions with the management and, if one exists, the Employees' Council of the investee company. If appropriate, the relevant Polish authority, usually the Ministry of Industry, is involved in the investment discussions at this point. Should these discussions proceed in a satisfactory manner, then the due diligence review is formally undertaken and pursued to completion. This review encompasses a review of the following aspects of operations of the investee company:

   - The business plan.
   - Historical operating results.
   - Financial and marketing projections.
   - Customer base and competition.
   - Technology, operations, and quality control.
   - Environmental impact (if deemed necessary).

IUNP's Investment Approval Process

Following a positive result of due diligence, an investment proposal is prepared by IUNP's management and submitted to the Board's Investment Committee for approval. The Investment Committee reviews each investment proposal and makes a recommendation to the IUNP Board of Directors to approve or reject the investment.

Negotiations with the Polish State

An investment proposal approved by the Board becomes the subject of negotiations with the Polish State. The valuation and capitalization of the prospective investee company are the major issues negotiated with the State. IUNP prefers to base its initial valuation of the investee company upon a multiple of not more than 1.5 times the historical annual earnings, after the payment of interest but prior to depreciation and any mandatory payments to the Polish State and excluding any changes to noncash working capital.

The actual negotiated value assigned to the assets and liabilities contributed by the Polish State to the new company may differ from IUNP's initial valuation. In addition, IUNP may choose to increase its contribution beyond ECU 2 million (Cdn. $3.2 million), the amount required to qualify an investment by a foreign company for a 3-year tax holiday. In such a case, IUNP would acquire a larger share of the new company.

Completion of Investment

The investment may be completed if the following requirements have been met:

1. Approval is obtained from the Polish Ministry of Privatization, the Anti-Monopoly Commission, and any other applicable authority (often the Ministry of Industry or a provincial governor).

2. The constituting documents of the newly formed investee company are signed before a notary and registered.

---

* Based on the relevant section of the June 28, 1993 offering of IUNP shares.

With his previous experience in dealing with prospective acquisitions, George had developed a fairly good feeling of what to look for. Obviously, the primary investment criteria had to be met in each case, but, in his direct dealings with the managers of his prospect companies, he was also looking for some indication of their openness to new ideas, a positive attitude, and a gleam in their eye suggesting their commitment to their companies, all intangible qualities. George stated:

> I know after five minutes of a conversation with a general manager of a company interested in joining us if there is common ground on which we can build our relationship. If there is not, I spend an hour with him just to be polite, but then let him know that I don't see us working together.

Two of these companies, Biawar Bialystok, a producer of water boilers, and IBIS Bydgoszcz, Poland's leader in the manufacture of baking equipment, were considered viable investments. However, negotiations regarding their privatization proved to be quite a challenge for IUNP. The management of Biawar and IBIS were wholeheartedly supportive of the idea of privatization with IUNP's participation but had to overcome resistance from their Employees' Councils to their privatization plans. This was readily overcome at IBIS, but came very close to derailing negotiations with Biawar and delayed the process significantly.

The approval process at the state level further delayed IUNP's investments. In the early 1990s, Poland had just begun implementing a newly designed privatization program. The idea of foreign participation in the privatization of State-Owned Enterprises (SOEs), although approved by several consecutive governments, was fiercely contested by nationalist parties viewing foreign money as a threat to the country's political and economic independence. This made government agencies involved in privatization very defensive in considering agreements involving foreign capital. On the other hand, state administrators did not have any experience in managing the process, which often resulted in uncertainties about the relevant regulations and implementation guidelines. Consequently, the approval process was riddled with confusion and uncertainty, both causing significant delays.

As a result of these circumstances, IUNP had to wait until 1992 to complete its first two investments. In April 1992, the IBIS agreement was finalized, while negotiations on the takeover of Biawar continued until November before all necessary approvals were obtained.

IUNP AS AN INVESTOR

With over $5 million (Cdn.) invested in IBIS and Biawar, George could be assured of IUNP's future as a holding company. To further enhance its credibility, he initiated the process to list IUNP's securities on the Toronto Stock Exchange (TSE). He then hired Justin Bonar, his son, with a background in computers and business administration, to take over the administrative duties at the Toronto office, including the handling of the company's application for the listing on the TSE. Later in the year, Marek Scibor-Rylski, a British-born venture capital executive of

Polish descent, joined the company as a full-time replacement for John Wleugel.[3] Mr. Scibor-Rylski, with an engineering and business background as well as fluency in Polish, was also to assist George in sourcing, selecting, and screening investments in Poland.

At the end of 1992 IUNP's long-term prospects seemed excellent, but, in the short run, the company faced a severe cash flow problem. Of the $8.5 million raised in 1991, $5 million was spent on the two acquisitions, more than $2.5 million on ongoing operations (in 1991 and 1992), $800,000 on securities issue costs, and some $800,000 on the partial repayment of liabilities. Although in April and May of 1992 George raised an additional $1 million through the private placement of 1.3 million IUNP shares, the company's cash position in early 1993 was very weak.

George, who always tried to ensure the long-term stability of his company, had anticipated this situation well in advance. However, he felt that the company's chances of raising new equity capital would be better after obtaining the listing of its shares on the TSE. The listing was approved in November 1992, which set the stage for a new offering of IUNP's securities.

This public offering was an anxious event for George, but in the end it was a real breakthrough for the company. After five months, during which IUNP ran out of cash, the first tranche of the offering was closed. J. P. Morgan and Morgan Stanley, two financial institutions of international stature, joined the roster of IUNP's shareholders, further validating the company's strategy. Subsequent closings came in quick succession in May, June, and September of 1993, bringing a total of $20 million (Cdn.) in gross proceeds.

George further exploited the momentum created by the success of the second offering, and, immediately after its closing, issued yet another offering, which closed in January 1994 bringing an additional $12.5 million in equity capital. In the end, the company's total capitalization reached $42 million, an amount firmly securing its future needs.

During 1993, IUNP continued its search for new investment opportunities. In the early part of the year it signed a letter of intent with Unipak Gniezno, Poland's leading manufacturer of packaging equipment. Six months later, the acquisition was completed, marking quite a significant improvement in the pace of the approval process.

With an increased level of activity in Europe, the company could no longer effectively operate from its Toronto headquarters. In August 1993, it moved its head office to London where its staff was expanded to six. The Warsaw office was also expanded by the addition of four employees. In George's view this structure could serve the company's needs for the next few years.

Throughout the second half of 1993 and 1994, George and Scibor-Rylski were busy identifying prospective investee companies in Poland, negotiating deals, and getting governmental approval. After securing the company's financial well-being, George had more time to explore some additional opportunities created by IUNP's

---

[3] John Wleugel, a retired executive from Bata Limited (the Czech shoe manufacturer reestablished in Canada after World War II) had previously performed the duties of vice president of finance on a part-time basis.

unique position as the only foreign holding company operating in Poland. He was particularly interested in the planned Mass Privatization Program, which would affect some 600 of Poland's SOEs. In anticipation of the final approval of the program, he teamed up with one of IUNP's shareholders, Murray Johnstone of Glasgow, and, with the additional participation of Bank Gdanski, formed Hevelius Management, a consortium hoping to become one of the managers of the National Investment Funds.

In August 1994, the new consortium was ranked (unofficially) as the 9th of the 19 candidates who applied to become NIF managers. This meant that its chances to become one of 15 managers to be selected were reasonably good. If, in fact, the consortium became a NIF manager, IUNP would have an additional growth opportunity. Beside receiving management fees for its services, Hevelius could also obtain up to 15 percent of its NIF's ownership. This latter component of the remuneration package could mean significant growth for IUNP which held a 65 percent share of Hevelius.

In mid-October 1994, IUNP was just a few steps from completing several new acquisitions. Negotiations with a glass container maker, Antoninek, and FADA, a Gniezno manufacturer of industrial lifts, were already completed and the acquisition agreements were awaiting approval from the Ministry of Privatization. Two other investment opportunities were being negotiated with companies from the timber processing and electronics industries. In addition, IUNP was close to completing an agreement with Polbita, a distributor of cosmetics and household chemicals. In this deal, IUNP was engaged in a complex arrangement involving a $5.5 million loan with an option to convert it into equity. Part of the capital to be provided to Polbita came from Wasserstein Emerging Markets, a New York–based financier. This transaction, once finalized, would signify IUNP's first foray into the service sector and first agreement with a private company.

INVESTMENT CLIMATE IN POLAND[4]

In the second half of 1994, Poland's economic prospects looked promising. It was the first country in post-communist East and Central Europe to have pulled out of the deep recession caused by the collapse of the region's previous regime. It was expected that its growth in 1994 would at least match the 4 percent achieved in 1993, while inflation would be reduced from 36 percent to 27 percent. With its 38.5 million population, a 1993 GDP of $85 billion (U.S.), and choice location (astride major east-west and north-south communication routes), Poland had emerged as the single most important market in Central Europe, ripe for treatment as a Big Emerging Market (BEM). However, experts agreed that this growth, largely fueled by domestic consumption, might be difficult to sustain without an increase in exports and investments. It was hoped that foreign capital would contribute significantly to both of these growth factors.

---

[4] Based on Colin Jones, "First over the Wall," *The Banker,* May 1994, pp. 58–60.

A more significant role for foreign investment in the country's expansion would become possible after its foreign debt had been significantly reduced in early 1994. An agreement with the Paris club on a 50 percent reduction of the $33 billion owed to its members was followed by an agreement with 300 commercial banks who had agreed to reduce the $13.2 billion owed to them by 42.5–45 percent.

As a result of these two debt-reduction agreements, Poland could reenter the international capital market on normal commercial terms instead of relying upon loans from foreign governments and international financial institutions like the World Bank. It was expected that the Polish government would be able to raise funds from the syndicated loan market on more favourable terms.

It was also anticipated that the improved financial situation would provide a more stable, less risky investment environment, increasing the attractiveness of equity investment in Poland. In the early 1990s, Poland was not very successful in attracting a proportionate share of Central Europe's relatively modest inflow of direct investment. By the end of 1993, the overall value of foreign investment in Poland did not exceed $2.8 billion (U.S.), with a further $4.6 billion in forward commitments. This compared unfavourably with the much smaller and more heavily indebted Hungary which attracted $7 billion.

Foreign direct investment in Poland was heavily skewed toward Italy and the United States as countries of origin. In 1993, Fiat and Coca-Cola, with their investments in new production facilities, accounted for this dominance. Interestingly, Germany, which accounted for one-third of Poland's external trade, provided only just above 7 percent of all foreign investment in 1993. Japan largely refrained from investing in Poland.

In particular need of equity capital was the country's fast-growing private sector, which accounted for 60 percent of national output in 1993 but attracted very little interest from foreign investors, who concentrated their interest on joint ventures with SOEs.

THE PRIVATIZATION PROGRAM

Poland's privatization program had two goals: first, to transform and redistribute property rights to different categories of economic agents (employees, managers, private and institutional investors, foreign companies, and banks) and, second, to restructure state-owned enterprises. It was initiated in 1990 by the Sejm (the lower chamber of Parliament) which adopted a series of laws defining the legally acceptable ways of transferring ownership of economic entities from the state to private investors.

The principal methods of privatization under the Law of 1990 on Privatization were as follows:

A. Individual privatization:

  1. *Capital privatization.* Sale of an enterprise through public offering, employee buyout, or trade sale by tender.

2. *Privatization by liquidation.* Winding up of a state enterprise in order to (*a*) sell its assets, (*b*) contribute its assets into a new company owned in whole or in part by private capital (foreign or domestic), or (*c*) lease its assets to employees and/or management. Privatization by liquidation was reserved for SOEs showing good profit performance and favorable growth prospects.

3. *Liquidation under bankruptcy.* The sale or leasing of assets of SOEs placed under bankruptcy proceedings due to their insolvency.

4. *Commercialization.* Transformation of an SOE into a joint-stock company owned by the State Treasury and managed through a Supervisory Board controlled by the state (⅔) and an Employees' Council (⅓). Commercialized enterprises could be viewed as hybrid firms, owned by the state, but managed for commercial purposes.

B. Mass Privatization:

5. *The Mass Privatization Program.* Provided for privatization of several hundred larger, relatively healthy SOEs. After preliminary selection, SOEs participating in the program were to be transformed into companies owned by the State Treasury. At the same time, a number (10–20) of "National Investment Funds" were to be set up (as joint-stock companies) to manage the portfolios of securities of the firms participating in the program. Each fund would then receive a small share (1–3 percent) in many of the privatized SOEs and a large share (33 percent) in a few (10–15). Ultimately, 33 percent of the shares of each SOE participating in the program would be owned by a single fund, 27 percent by all the remaining funds, 10 percent by employees, and the remaining 30 percent by the State Treasury. Authorized adult Polish citizens would receive investment certificates representing one share in each investment fund.

IUNP used "privatization by liquidation" to acquire its subsidiaries. From IUNP's perspective, this method provided several advantages over the alternative methods. First, as a result of the process, the newly established entity was legally separate from its predecessor, limiting IUNP's exposure to the liabilities of the old entity. Second, the approval process for privatization through liquidation was much simpler than for capital privatization. Third, and most important, by applying this method (a "money in" deal), IUNP could channel its investment to the new subsidiary instead of transferring it to the State Treasury.

MANAGEMENT OF IUNP SUBSIDIARIES

The relationship between IUNP and its subsidiaries was defined by the terms of their privatization agreements. These agreements provided IUNP with the power necessary to affect all major aspects of corporate governance in IBIS, Biawar, and Unipak. However, IUNP viewed these agreements primarily as a safeguard and did not want to use them to interfere with the ongoing management of its subsidiaries.

Of course, all company officers were always available to assist in resolving specific problems raised by the managers of these subsidiaries. Advice, discussion, and persuasion were the major methods applied by IUNP's executive staff.

IUNP was formally required to provide its subsidiaries with "the most far-reaching assistance in the organization and development of export products." It was also obliged to "ascertain that they receive assistance and training in management and the organization of production, marketing, and other expertise." IUNP was to receive $50,000 (Cdn.) per year from each company for its services subject to the company meeting its profit target for the year.

In 1993 and 1994, George was very active in negotiating licensing agreements on behalf of IUNP's subsidiaries. His international corporate experience was of tremendous help, especially in the early days, when Polish executives had to overcome their timidity in dealing with representatives of major international companies. One of these managers commented on George's role in forming his attitude toward business:

> Mr. Bonar has helped me a lot in changing my way of dealing with problems. He rarely gives you a direct solution to your problem, but puts you on the right track in analyzing it. I once asked him for advice on some technical problem. He answered, "Do you know who would know the answer?" I said, "Probably someone at a German company." "So, take your car and go there," he said. For me, it was an eye opener: Just go?!

Supervisory Boards[5] provided IUNP with a formal way of influencing the direction of its subsidiaries. Their composition reflected the relative share of each company held by IUNP and the state. George Bonar, Marek Scibor-Rylski, and the company's comptroller, Adam Michon, represented IUNP, in some cases complemented by Polish business executives. The state was represented by members nominated by the Ministry of Industry or appropriate government authority.

These boards met quarterly to review the company's operating results and deal with other matters of significance. They had the power to preapprove all fixed asset transactions, capital investment plans, credit facilities, and changes in banks and banking arrangements. The boards also nominated members to the company's Management Board (for a two-year period), and approved annual business plans and quarterly performance reports.

Since one of the principal factors used by IUNP in assessing investment prospects was the competency of their management, it was assumed that the change in ownership would not lead to any major changes in their managerial staff. This was consistent with George's view that IUNP could not afford to fire the managers of its subsidiaries as it would discourage the management of other prospective investee companies from seeking his involvement.

The company provided some training in areas crucial to the growth of its subsidiaries, such as marketing, information systems, and general management. Managers of IBIS, Biawar, and Unipak had participated in corporate seminars

---

[5] The management structure of private companies in Poland typically consisted of nonexecutive supervisory boards (the equivalent of boards of directors) and management boards consisting of company executives.

where they shared information and experience on organizing their operations in these crucial areas. IUNP also invited keynote speakers who discussed areas of particular interest to the companies.

IUNP planned to implement a common financial reporting system in all three of its subsidiaries. This system was to be based on a MIS package adapted to Polish accounting regulations. IBIS and Unipak were chosen as the pilot sites with scheduled January 1995 implementation. Biawar, which had already adopted a locally developed system, was to switch to the new system later. Production planning and reporting modules were to be implemented once the core accounting modules/functions had been fully adopted.

By mid-1994, IUNP had also implemented a corporatewide e-mail communications system and distributed database. Lotus Notes was the core of this system. It enabled IUNP corporate offices in London and Warsaw and the three investee companies to automatically replicate and exchange information on sales, costs, and orders.

IUNP's staff were in constant communication with their subsidiaries. Their major concern was with translating financial results from Polish to Canadian (international) standards. The new reporting system, which was designed to produce two sets of records (in both the Polish and Canadian format), was intended to relieve the Warsaw staff of the bulk of these tasks.

TRANSITION GOALS

IUNP's investment in each of its Polish subsidiaries was expected to contribute to their transformation from production-oriented entities operating in a planned economy to market-driven businesses functioning in a competitive environment. Obviously, the primary objective for each subsidiary was to increase its profits to a level sufficient to provide a superior return on IUNP's investment. Considering the risk involved in investing in Poland, IUNP required a cash payback of 2–3 years.

It was felt that, in order to meet this primary objective, all three companies had to adjust their mode of operations in three major areas:

1. *Developing a market orientation.* This goal was common for all three subsidiaries and presupposed both the organizational and cultural changes required to improve responsiveness to market signals. A better customer service system, improved market research capabilities, and, most of all, closer alignment of corporate activities with marketing objectives were the practical measures of progress in this area.

2. *Upgrading production technology, modernizing and expanding product lines.* Capital contributed by IUNP was expected to address the most immediate investment needs of each company. Further, the technological gap between IUNP's subsidiaries and its Western competitors was to be closed through the acquisition of licences from leading manufacturers. Therefore, the ability of each subsidiary to adopt foreign licences and accelerate the new product development process was viewed as a primary success factor.

3. *Changing corporate culture.* IUNP viewed internal communication as a primary factor determining a business's ability to achieve its goals. Improved communication was fundamental in fostering the culture of shared goals, open discussions, and transparent responsibilities among the company's staff. Information technology was considered a major factor in opening up communication routes, and a company's ability to adopt it was considered an important measure of its success in the transition process.

IUNP did not develop a formal policy for managing the transition in each of its subsidiaries. It was felt that this would be difficult, if not impossible, for a diverse set of entities operating in different industries, markets, and with different histories. Consequently, no formal compliance requirements or evaluation criteria were set. The evaluation process was expected to come naturally as part of the ongoing supervision of the three entities.

THE GENERAL IMPACT OF PRIVATIZATION

IUNP's investments had a profound impact on all three subsidiaries. The most important change resulted from the fact that private ownership put an end to the question of who was in charge of the company. This relieved management from having to satisfy multiple conflicting objectives set by various stakeholders, which included the state administration, trade unions, and the workers' councils.

The new ownership set the stage for implementing a rational management system in which corporate goals, responsibilities, and evaluation criteria were clearly defined and well understood by all parties involved. Under the new system, managers had their hands untied and could set goals for their subordinates and demand performance while being responsible for their own decisions. This also allowed for a more rational human resource policy. Qualifications and performance were becoming the determinants of an employee's place in the corporate hierarchy, which was also reflected in a compensation structure which favoured skills, responsibility, and achievement.

These managerial changes induced a markedly different attitude toward work among employees. Better discipline as expressed by a willingness to follow orders and established procedures, decreased absenteeism and tardiness, and greater attention to the quality of work performed were just a few qualities of the new spirit brought about by the change. Obviously, the fear of losing relatively well-paying jobs in a country affected by high unemployment was certainly a factor in enforcing these new attitudes as well. However, it was generally agreed that the major impact could be attributed to the introduction of a sensible and fair management system.

Organizational changes emphasized the new strategic direction embraced by the three companies. The driving force behind their activities switched from production to marketing. This was reflected in the leading position given to the marketing and sales departments relative to their production and administrative counterparts. The marketing departments were the only ones that grew in size, despite a general trend to reduce employment in other areas due to increased productivity. Business plans, marketing research, customer satisfaction, product positioning, and distribution channels were being quickly adopted as part of management's vocabulary.

In addition, increased foreign competition stressed the importance of quality of production and customer service. Foreign licenses obtained with the funds contributed by IUNP addressed this problem, but were not sufficient to entirely change a system which traditionally turned out goods generally below international standards. In response to this challenge, all three companies implemented quality management programs which concentrated on developing production systems with built-in quality. They were also developing a system of rewards and penalties tied to the quality of output at each stage of the production process.

Privatization had an immediate effect on the subsidiaries' financial position. Equity capital provided by IUNP was used to reduce their significant debt burden, which immediately improved profitability. In addition, the privatized companies were relieved from the surtax on excessive salaries and wages (*popiwek*), and the tax on fixed assets (*dywidenda*). In addition, foreign investment above 2 million ECU qualified investee companies for a three-year tax holiday.

George was generally satisfied with the transition process taking place in Unipak and Biawar (Exhibits 3 and 4). Within a relatively short time, these two companies were able to meet the objectives established by IUNP. They could now be viewed as truly market-oriented manufacturers of significantly improved products. Also, their manufacturing, although still less productive than their foreign counterparts, was no longer inferior technologically. Most important, their corporate cultures fostered a spirit of achievement, cooperation, and openness to new ideas.

At the same time, George was seriously concerned with the developments taking place at IBIS. This company, which was initially considered a jewel among his acquisition targets, could not shake off its past. Although it implemented many changes consistent with IUNP's expectations, George and his colleagues felt that IBIS's employees only paid lip service to the new system, while still continuing to act in the old manner. Their marketing, although consuming the same proportion of sales as in the other two companies, did not produce the expected results as measured by the quality of their market analysis and, foremost, the company's ability to align its production activities with its marketing objectives.

THE SITUATION AT IBIS

Overview of the Business.   IBIS had traditionally occupied a dominant position in the manufacture of bakery production equipment in Poland. Over the post-war period, bakery production in Poland was dominated by large, state-owned producers, often serving entire urban centres with a limited range of basic products. Under the centralized structure of the Polish economy, IBIS (then part of the Spomasz group, an industrial combine for manufacturing food processing

EXHIBIT 3   **Biawar—Corporate Profile**
Before and after Privatization

	1991	1994
IUNP investment and share	SOE	IUNP investment (1992)—Zl 37 bln. ($2.8 mln.) Ownership (1994)*: IUNP—86% State—10% Employees—4%
Rank and size	Medium-sized manufacturer Zl 68 billion sales Zl 1 billion after-tax profit 275 employees	Medium-sized manufacturer Zl 220 billion sales Zl 35 billion net profit 285 employees
Culture	Confrontation	Collegiality
Product line	Water heating tanks—100%	Water heating tanks—75% Instant water heaters—25% Kitchen oven hoods—< 0.5% Hot-dog cookers—< 0.5%
Geographic coverage	Poland—99% Export—1%	Poland—99% Export—1%
Evolution	SOE with no future	Dynamic private company
Organization	Four departments Four layers of management	Three departments Three layers of management
Performance goals	Survival Cash-flow maintenance	Domination of domestic market Profit growth New-product development
Strengths	Good quality of products Low cost	Strong distribution network Good quality of products Broad product line Collegial management style
Weaknesses	Financial instability No marketing capabilities Poor morale	Production bottlenecks Inadequate working capital
Strategy	Maintenance of market share	Market leadership

*After the employee buyout of 4 percent of the Biawar shares.

equipment) was assigned a monopolistic position for the manufacture of bakery equipment.

With the introduction of market forces into the food processing sector, large bakeries began to lose market share to small, local, more responsive bakeries offering a greater variety of products of superior freshness. Consequently, by the early 1990s the demand for equipment for large bakeries was significantly reduced. At the same time, thousands of small bakeries were opening, each requiring bakery equipment. Obviously, these small bakeries required equipment suited for small production volumes and specific types of bakery products, such as baguettes and croissants, which were becoming increasingly popular.

EXHIBIT 4   **Unipak—Corporate Profile**
Before and after Privatization

	1992	1994 (projected)
IUNP investment and share	SOE	IUNP investment (1993)—Zl 45 bln. ($3.75 mln.): IUNP—51% State—49%
Rank and size	Medium-sized batch manufacturer Zl 80 billion sales Zl 15 billion after-tax profit 600 employees	Medium-sized batch manufacturer Zl 135 billion sales Zl 24 billion net profit 578 employees
Product line	Based on technology from the 1970s: packaging machines—70% milk separators—6% spare parts, services—24%	15% sales —new or modernized products: packaging machines—79% milk separators—4% spare parts, services—17%
Culture	Indifference Strong departmentalization	Motivation Collegiality
Geographic coverage	Poland—95% Export—5%	Poland—90% Export—10%
Evolution	Stagnating SOE	Growing private company
Organization	Five departments (directors) Five layers of management	Three departments Three layers of management
Performance goals	Survival	Profit growth Technological improvement Market-share growth
Strengths	Strong production base Relatively good product quality Low cost	Knowledge of the market place Low cost Strong financial base Customer franchise
Weaknesses	No clear mandate for management Internal conflicts Lack of working capital Obsolete product line	Low productivity Shortage of specialized marketing skills Narrow product line
Strategy	Price leadership	Value leadership

IBIS was in a relatively good position and made an effort to introduce a new product line responding to these needs. However, its success was limited as Poland became the target of a number of foreign manufacturers of bakery equipment. Their products, although more expensive, were superior in aesthetics, reliability, and durability, and—most importantly—labour-saving controls. Faced with this competition, IBIS's products, although less expensive, could not obtain a significant market share. Although the company was able to survive, it could not prosper without new products and technologies. This, of course, was impossible without additional capital, not readily available to a company generating hardly any profit. Consequently, for IBIS, privatization, with its potential for bringing in additional equity capital, was the only real chance for long-term survival.

Management and Employees.   The management of IBIS included a core group of 15 to 20-year company veterans supported by recent appointees recruited from outside of the company. The group was dominated by engineers with degrees from Bydgoszcz Technical University. In terms of age, it was a balanced mix of people in their mid-50s and those in their early 40s.

Jerzy Gorzynski, the company's president (in his mid-50s) was an economist with a long career in management even prior to joining IBIS in 1979 as economic director. He was appointed to his current post in 1990. His management style was a little autocratic, emphasizing the importance of corporate hierarchy and formal organization. His central role was indispensable in dealing with problems, but his domination over his team members may have limited their ability to make their own decisions.

The Privatization Process.   The lack of growth prospects under state ownership made the company's management consider privatization. It was initially felt that "strategic investors," that is, foreign manufacturers of bakery equipment, would be the best match for the company. However, not one of a number of strategic investors contacted by IBIS in 1990 wanted to transfer technology to a potential competitor. They were more interested in converting the Polish company into a supplier of components for their own products. This method of privatization was rejected.

Although this attempt at privatization was unsuccessful, it caused members of the Employees' Council and the trade unions to accept the general idea of privatization with foreign capital. This proved quite important when, in early 1991, IUNP contacted the company and decided that its situation merited further review.

The results of this review were positive and in July 1991 IUNP and IBIS signed a standstill agreement which set the stage for subsequent negotiations. Over the next five months, IUNP conducted its due diligence while negotiating the monetary terms of its investment with the state administration. By November 1991, the negotiations were completed, and their results awaited final approval from the ministries of privatization and industry. That this stage was completed in only five months was later attributed by Mr. Gorzynski, IBIS's president, to his persistent lobbying of the ministries involved, culminated by a visit of a busload of his workers to the ministerial offices in Warsaw. This action apparently eliminated all the existing barriers, and resulted in an immediate approval of the privatization deal.

The Effects of Privatization.   The funds invested by IUNP were largely used to pay off most of IBIS's existing debt burden. However, the most significant impact on the company's situation came as a result of its newly obtained ability to acquire foreign technology and new machinery for those processes with the most impact on the quality of its products. In 1992, with George's participation, IBIS negotiated a licensing agreement with Zucchelli Forni SPA and Sancassiano SPA, two major Italian manufacturers of bakery equipment. With these licenses, IBIS could add modern ovens and mixers to its offering, significantly improving its product line for small bakeries.

With its expanded financial and technological capabilities, IBIS's management could concentrate on improving operations. Their efforts focused on three areas: marketing, corporate organization, and production quality.

In marketing, top priority was assigned to changing the corporate image. IBIS was generally perceived as an unresponsive, low-quality producer, a picture quite inconsistent with the company's new orientation. The task of changing this negative image was assigned to the newly created Marketing and Sales Department. Significant resources were allocated to a promotional campaign featuring a new corporate logo and licensed products, and providinng information on the expanding network of regional sales and service offices (four in Poland, one in Russia, and one in Germany).

As part of its overall attempt to rebuild the company's image, Mr. Gorzynski decided to refurbish IBIS's corporate offices. He began with his own office, which was substantially expanded and equipped with expensive furniture, all intended to communicate a new corporate style to his visitors. The Marketing and Sales Department was next in line for upgrading of its facilities. By late 1994, however, only a visitors' room in the section of the corporate headquarters housing the marketing department had been rebuilt.

These steps were accompanied by changes in the company's organizational structure, which became less fragmented and flattened. Some departments were consolidated, most notably production and technology, while the number of management levels was reduced from five to four.

IBIS also put a great deal of effort into bringing the quality of its products up to international standards. In 1992, the company initiated an application for the ISO 9000 certification, a process typically taking two years. A number of technological processes were also upgraded in order to match the quality offered by foreign competitors.

The changes brought significant results (Exhibit 5). IBIS's sales in 1993 increased almost threefold, with a further 60 percent increase planned for 1994. At the same time, its profits rose from the 1992 figure of Zl 4.5 billion to almost Zl 13 billion in 1993, and Zl 28 billion budgeted for 1994. The geographic orientation of the company's sales pattern shifted from east to southwest, with close to 50 percent coming from Germany, the Czech Republic, Slovakia, Hungary, and Lithuania.

Problem Areas.   Although the above facts would suggest a healthy operation poised for further expansion, by 1994 some disquieting signs had begun to appear. There seemed to be a problem with the company's management style, which was characterized by secrecy, fragmentation, and a lack of direction. Each department appeared to be driven independently, with only limited communication with the rest of the company. Access to information on corporate performance as well as other issues affecting the entire company was confined within departmental lines. For example, the corporate business plan was kept confidential, the individual copies locked in the desks of a privileged few. Communication with IUNP suffered from this lack of openness, sometimes resulting in delays, distortions, and conflicting information.

EXHIBIT 5   IBIS—Corporate Profile
Before and after Privatization

	1991	1994
IUNP investment and share	SOE	IUNP investment (1992)—Zl 30 bln. ($2.9 mln.) Ownership: IUNP—53% State—47%
Rank and size	Medium-sized manufacturer Zl 47 billion sales Zl 1 billion after-tax profit 540 employees	Medium-sized batch manufacturer Zl 200 billion sales Zl 20 billion net profit 420 employees
Culture	Autocratic	Autocratic
Product line	Full line of bakery equipment: ovens—27% mixers—22% formers/dividers—16% trolleys—13% parts/service—22% Majority of products technologically outdated	Full line of bakery equipment: ovens—32% mixers—28% formers/dividers—7% trolleys—19% parts/service—14% 25% of sales from licensed products (ovens, mixers, and trolleys); most products modernized
Geographic coverage	Poland—90% Export—10%	Poland—60% Export—40%
Evolution	Deteriorating SOE	Growing private company
Organization	Five departments Five layers of management	Three departments Four layers of management
Performance goals	Maintenance of cash flow Sustaining sales levels	Sales/profit growth Development of marketing Quality improvement
Strengths	Low cost/price Large capacity Technical competence	Good quality of products Product-market fit Financial stability Low cost
Weaknesses	Marketing capabilities Lack of product-market fit Product quality/aesthetics Low productivity	Deficient marketing Poor internal communication
Strategy	Price leadership	Value leadership

Beside general managerial problems, George also identified marketing as a functional area with major weaknesses. There was no clear direction in IBIS's overall marketing program. The company's understanding of the forces shaping the market in Poland seemed to be inadequate. George also suspected that the departmental divisions within the company adversely affected IBIS's responsiveness to market signals, even when they were accurately interpreted by their marketing people.

These problems were further evidenced by IBIS's management views on IUNP's involvement in the company's operations. They felt that IUNP interfered too frequently in their internal operations while providing too little support in areas which could directly affect IBIS's results, such as developing international distribution for IBIS's products.

All these symptoms caught IUNP's attention within the first year after the acquisition. However, at that time, they were difficult to validate. The company's 1992 and 1993 results were excellent and IUNP's policy not to interfere in the ongoing operations of its subsidiaries made it very difficult to influence these mostly intangible aspects of IBIS's corporate governance. This was not made any easier by the reluctance of IBIS's officers to openly discuss their problems. For the time being, IUNP limited its action to communicating its concern to IBIS's management.

However, as the company's revenues plummeted in the third quarter of 1994, it became obvious that the situation required IUNP to take immediate steps. IBIS's management attributed this to the overall decline in demand for bakery equipment in the Polish market, a situation precipitated by the low prices for bakery products which made new investments in equipment unprofitable. This was not a convincing argument to IUNP especially since there had been no hint of this possibility in the company's 1994 business plan.

In October 1994, IBIS's marketing director resigned. A new director was to be appointed by the supervisory board at its next meeting. Further changes in the company's top management could be undertaken following the board's recommendations.

FINAL CONSIDERATIONS

George attributed IBIS's situation to a communication problem stemming from a deeply rooted culture of interdepartmental competition, secrecy, and fear of reprisal for going against the established ways. His concern was not only with addressing this problem at this particular company, but also with adjusting IUNP's policies in such a way that similar situations could be avoided at other acquired companies. His options included the following:

1. A more active role by his company in assigning management staff within its subsidiaries. He regarded this option as undesirable in view of his long-term acquisition goals, which could be jeopardized if managers of his prospective investee companies were to receive a chilling message of possible management dismissals following an acquisition agreement.

2. Assignment of on-site advisors to top management of problem subsidiaries. This approach could be difficult to implement due to its cost and the problem of finding consultants with the required level of expertise and language capabilities. Moreover, the effectiveness of an outside advisor in companies with internal communication problems could be limited.

3. Developing a set of clearly defined transition goals for each company and the evaluation of management based on their ability to meet those goals. This would also be a costly approach, particularly considering the growing number of IUNP's subsidiaries. It would have to be applied indiscriminately, because problems with transition related mainly to intangible aspects of corporate governance and were difficult to identify before the acquisition was completed. On the other hand, IUNP's own expertise could allow it to deal with a variety of specialized industries. This would require hiring external consultants for each acquisition once it has been effected, with all the related costs and uncertainties.

4. Maintaining the status quo. IBIS's performance could well improve with the overall growth of the Polish economy. Possibly, it was simply a matter of time for the cultural change to take effect. The existing means of influence through the supervisory board could be used more effectively while IUNP's contacts with its problem-ridden subsidiaries could be extended and increased. Later on, more emphasis could be put on analyzing corporate culture as a significant predictive factor in the due diligence phase leading to an acquisition.

George felt that the current problems at IBIS could be addressed within the existing set of guidelines and policies. However, he realized that with an increasing number of subsidiaries, the company would have to identify the most effective way of directing and handling their transition to private companies.

CASE 13
MONAGHAN MUSHROOMS

INTRODUCTION

Co. Monaghan, situated in the North East of the Republic of Ireland, is one of the country's smallest counties in terms of size and population. It borders Northern Ireland and retains many features of the traditional culture/lifestyle of the historic province of Ulster, of which it is a constituent part. The agricultural holdings, averaging 15–20 hectares, are well below the E.U. level and the whole of Co. Monaghan has been classified as "disadvantaged" in European Community terms, therefore entitling farmers to maximum support funding for agricultural and regional development. The principal source of income is agriculture—the mainstays of the local economy being dairying and beef production but, traditionally, the county has been a prime contributor, also, to white meat (pig and poultry) production in Ireland. In recent decades, however, the North East of Ireland has become a significant base for horticulture, gearing most of its output to export markets, particularly the United Kingdom. One firm in particular, Monaghan Mushrooms, located at Tyholland, five kilometers from Monaghan town, has been influential in developing this sector of agribusiness activity.

In the early 1980s, against the background of small-sized, marginal farms, a young VEC (Vocational Educational Committee) schoolteacher in Co. Monaghan, Ronnie Wilson, explored the potential for developing alternative indigenous enterprises.[1] One of his initial interests concerned the prospects for profitable use of agricultural "waste," such as farmyard manure. Ronnie Wilson, without any specialized agricultural or horticultural expertise, decided to establish a new venture in Tyholland that would help to encourage neighbouring farmers participate in a new initiative which, though run on a private enterprise basis, would rely on community effort. Monaghan Mushrooms Ltd., a wholly owned subsidiary of the Pleroma group, is now one of the leading mushroom companies in the U.K./Ireland. Through 1995, the enterprise can claim to have created employment for over 1,100 people, on either a full-time or part-time basis (see Exhibit 1).

Excluding its growing operations, Monaghan Mushrooms maintains a payroll for more than 300 employees, including over 100 dedicated to collection and distribution, 65 in composting operations, more than 50 within the Fresh Division and on processing activities, 10 specialist advisors to growers, and up to 90 personnel involved in marketing, administration, and management. A diagram, representing the management roles within Monaghan Mushrooms, at year-end 1993, is contained in Exhibit 2.

---

[1] Paul O'Kane, "Mushrooming Millions" (Profile of Ronnie Wilson), Business This Week, *The Irish Times*, October 14, 1994.

Source: This case study was prepared by Barra O' Cinneide, College of Business, University of Limerick, Ireland, with the intention of providing a basis for class discussion rather than illustrating either good or bad management practices.© 1995 Barra O' Cinneide, University of Limerick, Limerick, Ireland.

Exhibit 1	On-Farm Employment (combined full-time and part-time), Monaghan Mushrooms, 1994	

Location	Employers	Number of Employees
Republic of Ireland	Independent growers	945
Northern Ireland	Kernans (MM) subsidiary	135
Scotland	Monaghan Mushrooms (MM), Fenton Barnes, Edinburgh	65*
Total		1,145

* Mostly full-time, contract employees of Monaghan Mushrooms.

Note: A member of Monaghan Mushrooms estimates that on-farm employment can be apportioned 15 percent full-time and 85 percent part-time, approximately.

THE IRISH MUSHROOM SECTOR

Pre-1980 the Irish mushroom sector was comprised mainly of a few large production units. Their operations were based on the traditional British system of growing in large wooden trays, stacked four or five high in the cropping houses. The farms were fully self-contained in that, in addition to growing mushrooms, they produced their own compost and each company undertook the task of marketing its own output. These companies were remarkably innovative and enterprising for their time, but they suffered from several serious drawbacks. These included high capital investment and the difficulty of achieving a sufficient quantity of high-quality products, together with attendant management problems because of the large-sized units and high labour costs. In addition, the concept of individual marketing made it difficult to penetrate the upper end of the market where quality and continuity of supply are necessities. These farms were thus in a weak position to compete successfully on the British market, while the home market had proved to be too small to warrant significant further expansion. However, integrated corporate groups, like Monaghan Mushrooms, emerged that began to apply the benefits of R&D (research and development) and "best practice" promoted by Teagasc, the Irish Agriculture & Food Development Authority, while adopting new strategic business approaches.

THE ROLE OF RESEARCH AND DEVELOPMENT

During the 1970s, research workers at the Kinsealy Research Centre of Teagasc, the Irish Agriculture & Food Development Authority, were examining alternative systems of mushroom production. These included the use of plastic bags placed on the floor of insulated plastic tunnels. Every aspect of the system was investigated, including type of compost, size of bags, and general crop management. The result was the prototyping and development of a new system of mushroom production suited to Irish circumstances. One of its main features was the low capital cost. This new system proved to be attractive, commercially, in that it

EXHIBIT 2   Monaghan Mushrooms Organisation Chart

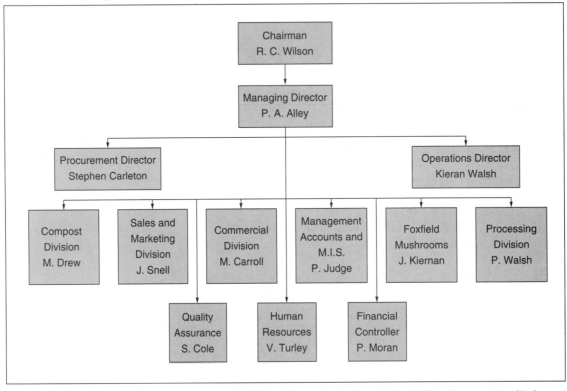

Note: Functional Reporting: J. Stanley, finance director and P. E. Monaghan, secretary; Executive Board: All positions except quality, human, and financial.

allowed people with little capital to develop a small mushroom enterprise. From such research activities, and subsequent exploitation, this particular aspect of Irish horticulture has literally "mushroomed"!

The R&D (research and development) undertaken at Teagasc gave rise to the concept of central compost facilities supplying spawned compost to many small satellite growing units. Additionally, in order to ensure the new system would function effectively and efficiently, an integrated organisational structure was proposed as the model, with central marketing of the mushrooms as a critical core activity. The researchers mainly responsible for this innovative thinking at the time were Cathal MacCanna and Jim Flanagan at Kinsealy. The *Kinsealy model* was successfully commercialised with the adoption of the system described, above, by a number of entrepreneurs such as Ronnie Wilson of Tyholland, Co. Monaghan, and Pat Walsh of Gorey, Co. Wexford. They set about constructing compost facilities to the required high standards, arranging networks of small growing units, and establishing appropriate marketing systems. This was done with considerable back-up from the research and advisory personnel of the relevant state bodies.

ORIGINS OF MONAGHAN MUSHROOMS

In recent decades, the North East of Ireland has become a significant base for horticulture, gearing most of its output to export markets, particularly the United Kingdom. One firm in particular, Monaghan Mushrooms, has been influential in developing this sector of agribusiness activity and exploiting marketing opportunities in the United Kingdom.

Monaghan Mushrooms in 1981 set up its franchised network of mushroom growers—a group of enterprising small farmers dedicated to production of quality mushrooms. By establishing its satellite system of mushroom production, the Tyholland firm encouraged the participation of neighbouring farmers in a new initiative which, although run on a private enterprise basis, would rely on community effort. The system that evolved fitted very well into the socioeconomic structure of Irish agriculture which is mainly based on small farms. Many of these farms, being on marginal land, were looking for a means of supplementing family farm income and the Kinsealy model provided such an opportunity, with the relatively low cost of establishing viable small mushroom units. Training in mushroom growing was provided by the advisory services and, within a short time, most of the new growers became technically proficient, while quickly developing their business expertise on the job. The company's control systems were devised to align as effectively as possible with the growers' commitment to grow and hand pick mushrooms, in order to keep pace with market requirements. Monaghan Mushrooms now has a wide range of activities.

COMPOST MANUFACTURE AND THE GROWING PROCESS

All the main players within the Irish mushroom sector have a strong commitment to invest in facilities, including cold stores, (work areas that are environmentally controlled), packing and labeling machinery, and transportation systems. For instance, in production of one of the basic inputs, compost, advanced technology is employed. Today's composters have developed reliable systems for producing compost to the quality level needed for yielding firm white mushrooms with high dry matter content. As all the inputs of mushroom compost are natural materials, mainly straw and animal manure, there can be significant variations in their nutrient properties. The composters have imposed stringent monitoring of raw materials to ensure that the production processes give a consistent formula and, consequently, reliable results at the individual farm level.

It is claimed by Monaghan Mushrooms that its grower franchise network, using the bag growing system, offers many advantages as it has been designed to ensure:

- The supply of firm white mushrooms with a high dry matter content and long shelf-life.
- The dedication of specific growers to selectively harvest mushrooms for individual customers to their specifications and packaging requirements.
- The segregated grower network curtails the spread of disease.
- The individual quality control of product, with the features of a "cottage industry" environment. Mushrooms are picked when ready, immediately

placed in the grower's cold store, the first link in the "cool chain" distribution system.

• The flexibility to increase mushroom production as market conditions dictate.

RANGE OF MONAGHAN MUSHROOMS' OPERATIONS

The Tyholland plant is the focus for "adding value," either through the Fresh Division or within processing operations (e.g., canning). Monaghan Mushrooms' operations now include:

• Mushroom compost production.
• Supply and erection of growing facilities to mushroom farms.
• Mushroom growing.
• Organising and controlling a franchised growing network.
• Servicing the U.K. retail and food processing markets with quality fresh mushrooms.
• Processing mushrooms in cans and jars for the European market.

FRESH MUSHROOMS

Monaghan Mushrooms has an impressive portfolio of customers for its fresh products, including all the major retailers. It supplies, mostly on a nonexclusive basis, the Big Five chains in Britain: Sainsbury, Tesco, Safeway, Asda and Somerfield, formerly Gateway, (see Exhibit 3, U.K. Retail Mushroom Market). The company offers an extensive range of fresh mushrooms, sized and graded to customer requirements. Monaghan Mushrooms has its own specialist transport fleet that collects the output from contracted growers, concentrating its operations at five depots. In addition to its operations at Tyholland, where indigenous production is aggregated, Monaghan Mushrooms has 30 large growing units, or "houses," in the U.K. at Fenton Barnes, where the Irish group has an integrated centre combining production, collection, packaging, sales, and distribution in Scotland (see Exhibit 4). The Co. Monaghan plant remains the focus for "adding value," either through the Fresh Division or within processing operations (see below). In addition to the collection fleet, Monaghan Mushrooms operates a "mixed" delivery system (50–50, company owned/contract hauliers) to their customers, the U.K. multiple retailers.

PROCESSING DIVISION

As well as being, now, one of the leading suppliers of quality fresh products to the U.K. market, Monaghan Mushrooms is also a strong force in the food processing sector. In conjunction with its Fresh Division, the processing operation at Monaghan Mushrooms gives the company flexibility in the production and supply of quality mushrooms to many markets. Processing takes place within a "stainless steel environment" and, in line with its policy of continuously updating

EXHIBIT 3 U.K. Retail Mushroom Market, August 1994

UK RETAIL MUSHROOM MARKET
(SEPT '93—AUG '94)
VALU-PACK CULTURE A WORRYING TREND

The U.K. mushroom market can be divided into a number of segments: retail, catering, and processing sectors. All these sectors are important outlets for Irish mushrooms particularly the retail market which is responsible for just under half of the total fresh mushroom sales in the U.K. Thus developments and trends in this sector are of critical importance to the Irish industry.

The retail sector is made up of multiple grocers, co-operative stores, symbol and independent grocers, farm shops/stalls and other miscellaneous outlets. The multiple grocers have the major share of the retail mushroom market as they do with all fresh produce. The major multiple grocers include Sainsbury, Tesco, Safeway, Asda, and Gateway.

A continuous market measurement of mushrooms in the U.K. retail market is carried out and for the purpose of this market research, mushrooms are included as a salad vegetable (with cucumbers, celery, peppers, tomatoes, and lettuce). In the year ending August 1994 expenditure on salad vegetables showed a 4% increase (3% by volume) on the previous year. The majority of the salad vegetables are sold through the multiple outlets with a 62% share of the volume, an increase of 7% on the previous year. Tesco and Sainsbury lead the way in terms of market share having now achieved between them 34% (volume) of the retail sales for salad vegetables.

Expenditure on mushrooms in the year ending August '94 was £189m, a 10% increase on the previous year. This in volume terms is equal to 83,000t, a 7% increase on the previous 12 months. In relation to the loose Vs prepack share of the market, the volume

of mushrooms sold loose makes up 65% of the market, prepacked sales (including valu-packs) 33%, and the remaining 1% is made up of sales of exotic mushroom types (e.g., browns, oysters, shiitake, etc.).

Looking at this more closely and keeping in mind that the overall retail market grew by 7% year after year to August '94, the percentage share of the total retail market held by loose mushrooms dropped by 3%. The share of the market held by pre-packed mushrooms (including valu-packs) has increased in volume by 3%. Closed loose mushrooms have dropped 1% and open loose mushrooms by 2% in market share. In contrast the closed pre-pack and open pre-pack/valu-pack segments have each increased their market share (volume) by $1\frac{1}{2}$%. The valu-pack segment is estimated to have an 8% share of the total retail market. In summary, within the last year the consumer has purchased more prepack mushrooms than in the previous year with a resultant loss in market share by loose mushrooms. The repercussions of this trend will be discussed later.

The multiple supermarkets continue to dominate the retail market with 66% of all expenditure on mushrooms taking place in these outlets. In volume terms this is equal to 61%, an

increase of 9% on the previous year. This was achieved at the expense of the other varied outlets. This had led to gain in market share by all the major multiples. Sainsbury is presently recording the highest volume sales of mushrooms with 18% (up 3%), Tesco 15% (up 3%), Gateway 3.3% (up 1%), Safeway 8.2% (up 1%) and Asda 9% (up 1%). Thus because of the increasing power of the major multiples and the share of business the Irish mushroom industry has within the multiple sector, developments and trends which occur on the supermarket shelf will directly impinge on the Irish industry and how it develops in the future.

1994 U.K. Retail Market Data— Observations

While the overall growth in the retail market is obviously a positive sign a closer examination of the data throws up a worrying trend. In the past year the major multiple supermarkets have been engaged in an ongoing promotional campaign to win market share from their competitors. Fresh produce including mushrooms has been a prime target. The promotions are leading to an overall downward pressure on the price of mushrooms on the supermarket shelf. The phenomenon of the valu-pack has developed at an alarming rate, and this development is not in the long-term interest of the Irish industry. A valu-pack is where a specific pre-packed quantity of mushrooms of a lower quality are sold at a lower price than loose produce. The data clearly shows that the retail market is being driven forward and that the valu-pack content of the pre-pack sector is primarily responsible for this. Loose mushrooms as a share of the total retail market have lost share while the pre-pack sector (including valu-packs) has gained.

Source : *Mushroom News*, published by An Bord Glas, October 1994, vol. 2, no. 3.

(*continued*)

EXHIBIT 3 (*continued*)

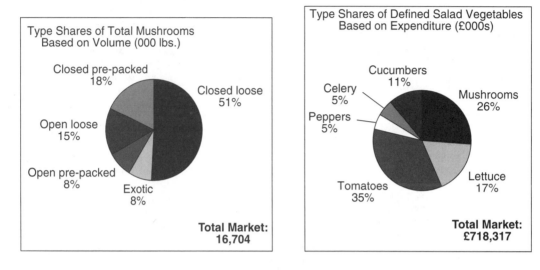

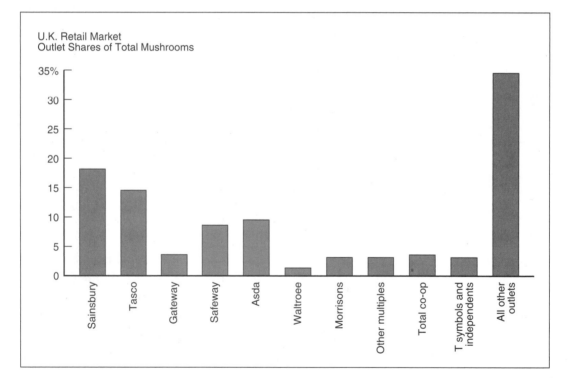

(*continued*)

EXHIBIT 3 (*concluded*)

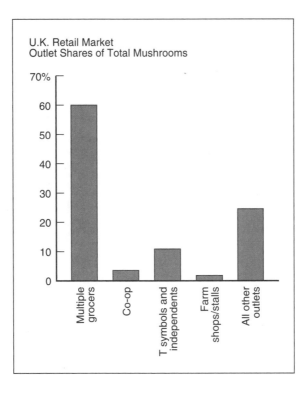

One of the main strengths of the Irish industry to date has been its ability to produce uniform chips of prime quality, graded mushrooms. While loose mushrooms still have the greater share of the market, present indications are that the valu-pack line is beginning to eat into this share. The quality requirement of this line is not as high as the prime loose product and thus from a marketing point of view the major quality advantage that the Irish industry has had to date is now being eroded. Ireland's competitors in the marketplace will look on this development as an opportunity for them, as the production of this valu-pack line is more suitable to their production system. The sales of the valu-packs are resulting in an overall downward pressure on the retail price of mushrooms and at a time when input costs for producers are rising, this is an unfavourable development as it makes the likelihood of receiving a price increase back from the marketplace more difficult. Over the coming months the retail market will be watched closely, particularly in relation to the development of the overall market but more especially in relation to the ongoing progress of the valu-pack sector.

Wholesale Markets

The U.K. wholesale markets, despite going through a state of decline at the present time, are an important outlet for mushroom sales and have a major influence on the price of mushrooms in the overall market. The first quarter of 1994 evidenced a good supply/demand situation resulting in satisfactory returns. The second quarter saw a deterioration in the market with supply outstripping demand for a number of weeks. The reason for this included a drop in demand, increased producer yields, change in weather conditions (higher temperatures) bringing volumes of mushrooms on stream, and also extra produce from additional houses.

The summer months generally saw the markets in a state of over-supply. The normal dip in demand was further accelerated by very warm weather conditions experienced in the U.K. this summer. Recent reports from the wholesale markets are showing a reasonably tight supply/demand situation. Some of the reasons contributing to this situation included in increased demand following the summer months and an overall reduction in producer yields (reportedly due to straw quality).

Predictions are that in the short term this tight supply/demand situation will prevail.

EXHIBIT 4   **Monaghan Mushrooms Depots/Growers ("houses")**

Depot	Number of Growers	("Houses")
1. Tyholland, Co. Monaghan	132	(590)
2. Glenveagh, Co. Donegal	29	(118)
3. Foxfield, Kilnaleck, Co. Cavan	49	(218)
4. Benburb, Co. Tyrone, N. Ireland	38	(166)
5. Fenton Barnes, Scotland—all large "houses"	3	(30)
Total	275	(1,122)

its plant, the company has recently installed modern profile-slicing and sterilization equipment, undertaking laboratory testing and analysis throughout the process. The product range of whole and profile-sliced mushrooms is packed in a comprehensive range of sizes (cans and glass jars) for the retail, catering, and food processing markets. Fresh sliced and semiprocessed products are now supplied in large packs to food processors.

MAINTAINING STANDARDS/COMPETITIVENESS

New satellite growers are selected following an interview by the management of the contracting central organisation, that is, Monaghan Mushrooms. When selected, they are supplied with a total mushroom growing package incorporating a well defined code of practice for producing and harvesting the product. The growers are supported by professional advisory staff and quality assurance personnel who monitor and audit their performances. Incentive and award programs motivate the growers to produce mushrooms to the required quality and hygiene standards. A stringent quality assurance program has been adopted within the sector, with control systems operating throughout the chain—from the growers through to customer delivery. Only the highest quality mushrooms are delivered to meet the demands of "today's consumer, today!" Mechanical harvesting of the mushrooms is avoided in order to ensure a standard high quality end product.

The increasing popularity of mushrooms in today's fresh produce market is the result of changing consumer attitudes toward healthier eating lifestyles. Mushrooms are supplied to specification, in a comprehensive range of sizes in both metric and imperial weights. Monaghan's product range covers the whole spectrum of customer requirements and currently includes baby buttons, buttons, closed cups, open cups, and flats in white and brown varieties, as well as canned products. Mushrooms are supplied to specification, in a comprehensive range of sizes in both metric and imperial weights. Monaghan Mushrooms operate a JIT (just-in-time) system of deliveries, with "window slot" timing at multiple retail depots. The temperature-controlled transport fleets, cushioned with air suspension, collect the mushrooms from the growers and, after sorting, packing, and cooling, the mushrooms are delivered daily to customers throughout the U.K. (see Exhibit 5).

EXHIBIT 5   Monaghan Mushrooms—Production and Distribution

ADVANTAGES OF THE IRISH SYSTEM

In recent years, the performance of the mushroom sector in competing success-fully on export markets indicates that the Irish system has a number of advantages, including:

- The central composter, by specialisation, can supply a compost material of the highest quality.
- The grower with a relatively small unit and personal incentive can give great attention to detail.

- The system of production in plastic bags on one level with a large air-to-bed ratio facilitates production of very high quality mushrooms with reasonable capital outlay.
- The central marketing system guarantees a continuity of supply of high quality product and access to major customers.

As indicated, above, one of the main benefits, undoubtedly, has been the central marketing system developed by enterprises such as Monaghan Mushrooms.[2]

ATTEMPTING TO STAY AT THE FOREFRONT

Through attention to quality, customer service, investment in technology, and R&D, Monaghan Mushrooms has attempted to become a trendsetter for the industry (see Exhibits 6 and 7), through:

- Investing in technology and enhancing the quality of its product/service to customers.
- Promoting mushrooms as a health food.
- Maintaining its leading position within the European mushroom sector through development, acquisitions, and diversification.

EXHIBIT 6   Kabeyun Ltd.: Compost Manufacture

Kabeyun Ltd., a wholly owned subsidiary of Pleroma, the holding company of the Monaghan Mushrooms group, is the largest producer of mushroom compost in Britain or Ireland. Using advanced technology the company produces quality compost needed to yield firm white mushrooms with high dry matter content. As all the inputs of mushroom compost are natural materials, mainly straw and animal manure, there are consequent variations in their nutrient properties. The company imposes stringent monitoring of raw materials to ensure that the production processes give a consistent formula.

The Kabeyun enterprise strives to achieve consistency, through providing a wide range of expertise and other back-up resources, such as the following:

- Sophisticated blending equipment which mixes the raw materials in their correct proportions.
- Computerised environmental control throughout the sterilisation process.
- Laboratory analysis of raw materials and finished product.
- Special facilities for filling and sealing the compost for the bag growing system.
- An efficient fleet of distribution vehicles equipped with forklift trucks giving prompt delivery of the bagged compost to the growing units with minimum exposure to the elements.

The group has compost-making facilities at four locations, including Scotland, and it has indicated that one of its prime missions is to be at the forefront of development in compost manufacture.

---

[2] Monaghan is so oriented to international marketing that it has refrained consistently from supplying the domestic Irish market.

EXHIBIT 7   Clonkeen Mushroom Developments Ltd.: Mushroom Technology and Horticultural Equipment

---

The Pleroma group also owns Clonkeen Mushroom Developments Ltd. Founded to service the expanding mushroom industry with growing units, the company's product range has expanded significantly in recent years. The firm is now a major supplier of growing tunnels, control technology, and ancillary supplies to the mushroom and horticultural sectors in Ireland. The company's R&D team is available to assist in the design and development of custom-designed facilities.

The current product range offered by Clonkeen Mushroom Developments includes the following facilities and equipment:

- Growing tunnels constructed from quality heavy wall (2 mm) steel tubing which has been hot dipped galvanised for lasting protection against corrosion. Units are insulated with 120 mm fibre glass between two 1,000 gram polythene covers.
- Twin fan ventilation systems designed to give accurate and fully automatic environmental control in the growing tunnels.
- Cooling systems with specially designed six-row cooling coil.
- Control equipment giving temperature and humidity readings on a digital display unit.
- CO_2 meters complete with water separator, piping, and filters.
- Production supplies—thermometers, watering, and harvesting equipment.

A breakdown of Monaghan's projected sales is given in Exhibit 8, while the latest data on European production are contained in Exhibit 9. Details of recent acquisitions and corporate development at Monaghan Mushrooms are contained in Exhibit 10.

COORDINATION/ORGANIZATIONAL DEVELOPMENT

An umbrella body representing composting/marketing companies, growers, and associated firms, for example, spawn suppliers, the Irish Mushroom Growers Association, IMGA, was established several years ago and includes most of the major players such as: Monaghan Mushrooms, Tyholland, Co. Monaghan; Carbury Mushrooms, Co. Kildare; Connaught Mushrooms, Galway; Greenhill Compost, Carnagh, Kilogy, Co. Longford; Marley Compost, Crush, Carrickroe, Co. Monaghan; and Walsh Mushrooms, Wexford. In addition, regional groups representing individual mushroom growers have IMGA membership. The industry, through IMGA, has devised a voluntary levy scheme on the basis of a IR£0.5 contribution per ton of compost. Approximately 10 percent of this levy is devoted to IMGA's administration and the remainder to funding R&D projects. Basic and applied research is carried out for the industry, on an ongoing basis, by Teagasc, both through its horticultural division at Kinsealy Research Centre and through its food research centre in Dunsinea, Co. Dublin. There is, also, a Mushroom Research Group at the National Agricultural and Veterinary Biotechnology Centre, University College, Dublin.

In addition to the advisory services provided by the industry's major firms, short intensive courses, both for new mushroom growers and to assist the transfer of technology to existing farm enterprises, are organised under the

---

EXHIBIT 8   Projected Sales, Monaghan Mushrooms, 1994

Fresh Division	IR£36.5 million
Processed products	IR£6.5 million
Total:	IR£43.0 million

EXHIBIT 9   E.U. Mushroom Production, 1992

Country	('000 Tons)
France	220
Netherlands	190
United Kingdom	118
Italy	115
Germany	60
Ireland	41
Belgium	31*
Denmark	na
Spain	na
Luxembourg	na
Portugal	na
Greece	na
Total:	780[†]

* = 1991 figure.

[†]Estimated global production for the E.U.

Source: *Mushroom News*, vol. 1, no. 3 (December 1993); vol. 2, no.1, An Bord Glas, Dublin, March 1994.

aegis of Teagasc. An Bord Glas operates a National Auditing program and in 1993 instituted its National Hygiene Awards for the mushroom industry. It recently announced incorporation of its awards program (organised on a regional basis), within the auditing program (see An Bord Glas Hygiene Awards in Exhibit 11).

IRISH MUSHROOMS: PERFORMANCE/PROSPECTIVE FUTURE

It has been acknowledged, generally, that the mushroom sector has been the main success story of Irish horticulture (see Exhibit 12). The sector doubled full-time jobs to 1,400 and increased part-time employment to 4,000 in the period

---

EXHIBIT 10   Profile of Ronnie Wilson

In October 1994, Monaghan Mushrooms purchased Britain's second largest mushroom producer, Middlebrook Farms, for an undisclosed sum. The deal should increase Monaghan Mushrooms' annual turnover, currently estimated at £50 million, by about 40 percent, and its successful completion has transformed Ronnie Wilson into one of the major players in the £400 million British and Irish mushroom market. Most Irish companies would have made quite a hullabaloo about such a deal, but that is not Mr. Wilson's style. The negotiations and sale of Middlebrook, which has its headquarters at Avon, south of Bristol, were completed in secret and when news of the deal broke, Mr. Wilson declined to comment. Some Irish agriculture sources were surprised by the Middlebrook deal as the U.K. company is a direct employer, and operates large commercial farms. It would appear to be exactly the sort of operation that Mr. Wilson and Monaghan outmaneuvered in the 1980s.

In stereotypical, Ulsterman fashion Ronnie Wilson says very little and generally keeps to himself. He is reputed to be a straight talker and a shrewd but tough negotiator. According to colleagues, he is a workaholic who adopts a hands-on approach to everything. One said that his only problem may be delegating responsibility, and letting go sufficiently to allow himself time to explore other directions. Until quite recently the soft-spoken Mr. Wilson met his growers on a regular basis, but he has now handed over the day-to-day running of the mushroom business to his management team. While the humble mushroom has made him a great deal of money, the former schoolteacher has a lifestyle that belies his wealth. Ronnie Wilson is rarely interviewed, even more rarely photographed, and could conceivably be termed Ireland's most reclusive businessman. He still lives in Tyholland, Co. Monaghan with the company's compost and processing facilities within sight of his front door.

During its 15 years in business the turnover and profits of Monaghan Mushrooms have never been revealed. With annual sales of £50 million, market analysts believe that the company generates profits of about £3 million a year. The actual ownership of Pleroma, the holding company which owns Monaghan and Middlebrook, is also a matter of some conjecture. It is known that Mr. Wilson, who is its chief executive, holds a majority stake in the company, while a substantial minority stake, thought to be about 30 percent, is held by Mercury Asset Management, the investment arm of the British merchant bank, S.G. Warburg. The Scottish businessman, Mr. Joe Barber, who is the chairman of Pleroma, is also believed to have a stake in the company.

In early 1990 Monaghan bought competitors Foxfield of Cavan and Kernans of Armagh which had a combined turnover of £21 million. Ronnie Wilson entered the pig processing market in February 1994 with the purchase of the troubled Uniport group and he now spends most of his time at its headquarters in Cookstown, Co. Tyrone. Mr. Wilson has a strategic vision to expand Pleroma into a broad-based food company, and he is reported to be interested in purchasing the former Tunney meat plant in Clones. He was also part of a consortium that made a failed bid for Leckpatrick Dairies which was bought by Golden Vale.

Source: Adaptation of Paul O'Kane, "Mushrooming Millions," Business This Week, *The Irish Times,* October 14, 1994.

1988/1992. Its sales, the majority in the U.K., have doubled to IR£54 million in the past seven years.[3]

A potential for controlled, market-led expansion in the mushroom industry, leading to additional employment of 3,000 (880 full-time and 2,200 part-time) is foreseen by Teagasc.[4] Significantly, the mushroom industry has been targeted as

---

[3] Colm Murphy, "Horticulture Plan Looks to U.K. Market," *Sunday Tribune,* June 5, 1994.

[4] "A Strategy for Horticultural Development," September 1994, Teagasc, Kinsealy.

Exhibit 11   **An Bord Glas Hygiene Awards**

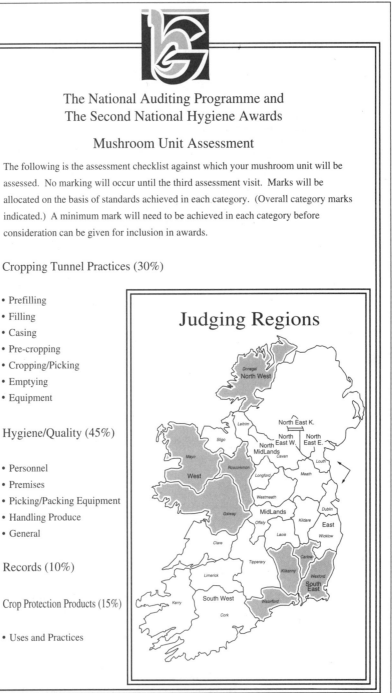

The National Auditing Programme and
The Second National Hygiene Awards

Mushroom Unit Assessment

The following is the assessment checklist against which your mushroom unit will be assessed. No marking will occur until the third assessment visit. Marks will be allocated on the basis of standards achieved in each category. (Overall category marks indicated.) A minimum mark will need to be achieved in each category before consideration can be given for inclusion in awards.

Cropping Tunnel Practices (30%)

• Prefilling
• Filling
• Casing
• Pre-cropping
• Cropping/Picking
• Emptying
• Equipment

Hygiene/Quality (45%)

• Personnel
• Premises
• Picking/Packing Equipment
• Handling Produce
• General

Records (10%)

Crop Protection Products (15%)

• Uses and Practices

Judging Regions

EXHIBIT 12   Ireland, Mushroom Production, 1980/93
('000 Tonnes)

Year	Fresh Home Market	Fresh U.K. Exports	Processed Exports	Total Production
1980	1.8	5.0	—	6.8
1981	1.7	5.4	0.6	7.7
1982	2.4	5.2	1.8	9.4
1983	3.2	5.4	2.5	11.1
1984	4.6	6.0	3.3	13.9
1985	4.8	9.4	4.1	18.3
1986	6.2	8.5	3.4	18.1
1987	6.2	12.1	2.7	21.0
1988	7.0	13.1	2.2	22.4
1989	9.1	18.0	3.5	30.6
1990	7.6	26.2	3.0	36.8
1991	7.7	27.0	4.5	39.2
1992	8.7	29.1	3.2	41.0
1993	9.5	32.5	2.0	44.0

Note: While the average annual rate of growth of production within the E.U. was 5.5% (compound), Irish producers achieved an average of 16.3% per annum over this period.
Source: *Mushroom News*, vol. 2, no. 1, March 1994, p. 4., An Bord Glas, Dublin.

the main plank in a new five-year plan,[5] presented to the government in June 1994 by An Bord Glas (literally "The Green Board" in the Irish language), the Horticultural Development Board. Brendan O'Donnell, chief executive, An Bord Glas, believes that:

> The U.K. market provides the main opportunity—a study of the German market, the largest in Europe, has shown it is not commercially viable to export fresh horticultural products to it.

The state board has been given comparatively extensive powers and funding to develop and promote the Irish horticultural sector, with statutory powers to impose levies within the horticultural industry but, to date, it has preferred to encourage cooperative efforts in undertaking initiatives in training and R&D for the mushroom sector.

APPARENT DANGERS ON THE HORIZON

However, in spite of optimistic projections of future growth, several potentially serious threats to the Irish mushroom sector have arisen:

---

[5] *Mushroom News*, vol. 2, nos. 1, 2, and 3, March, June, and October 1994, An Bord Glas, Dublin.

1. The first five months of 1992 had represented a period of relative exchange rate stability, with reserves rising and interest rate differentials vis-a-vis other Exchange Rate Mechanism (ERM), countries narrowing to historically low levels. Conditions began to deteriorate in June, however, when the prospect of steady progress towards Economic and Monetary Union (EMU) was questioned, following rejection of provisions of the Maastricht Treaty in the first Danish referendum on further integration of the EU.

The following statement describes the ensuing events, from the Irish perspective :

> Pressures intensified in September 1992 and remained for the rest of the year. Liquidity conditions deteriorated sharply and money market interest rates rose to unprecedented levels as the Central Bank utilised increases in its overnight support rate to defend the currency. Difficulties persisted in early 1993 and, eventually, the Irish pound's central rate was realigned within the ERM on 30 January 1993.[6]

After an expensive defense of the Irish currency over five months, in the latter half of 1992 and the beginning of 1993, the IR£ was devalued in line with sterling but, later, became one of the strongest currencies within the European Monetary System (EMS) "upper band" (see Exhibits 13 and 14), raising fears of a prospective drastic decline in profit margins for Irish horticulture and the mushroom industry, in particular. Fluctuations in exchange rates, particularly pressures on the Irish "punt" vis-à-vis U.K. sterling, can pose major problems for the Irish mushroom industry, as occurred during the major upheaval on European financial markets in Autumn 1992. This instability on the money markets resulted in devaluation of most of the E.U. currencies including U.K. sterling, to a more significant degree than initially occurred in the case of the IR£. Consequently, it was widely reported that many of the elements of the Irish economy, including the mushroom sector, suffered heavily in terms of export competitiveness.

2. Since the late 1950s the Irish government has been anxious to provide as many incentives as possible to encourage development of the industrial sector—in particular by attracting overseas firms to establish manufacturing facilities to serve European markets. Up to the 1980s a benign fiscal system designated that all profits on exports were tax free. However, as a result of joining the European Community in 1973, the Irish government was forced to eliminate any discrimination in its tax policy in relation to firms selling on the domestic versus export markets.

Due to provisions for derogation from the European regulations, the Irish government had a lengthy period in which to develop an appropriate response strategy. Mushroom production was deemed to be manufacturing until recently, and so qualified for the preferential rate of 10 percent corporate tax that the Irish government had applied to the manufacturing sector of the economy. However, in 1993, following pressure from its own mushroom growers, the British government

---

[6] Central Bank of Ireland, *Annual Report*, 1992 (incorporating *Quarterly Bulletin*, Summer 1993), Central Bank, Dublin.

Exhibit 13   IR£'s Performance on Financial Markets, 1992–1993

EMS stability was dramatically shaken in September 1992 when sterling and the lira left the Exchange Rate Mechanism (ERM) and, along with the Spanish peseta, were devalued. It is estimated that well over a billion pounds left Irish financial markets in a few days. The Central Bank's external reserves fell nearly £2 billion, from £3.05 billion at the end of August to £1.07 billion at the end of September.

There were four distinct phases in the management of the Irish pound exchange rate during 1992 and the early part of 1993. The first, from January to May, was a period of relative exchange rate stability. During the second phase, from June to mid-September, tensions in the European Monetary System (EMS) resulted in sizable negative foreign exchange interventions and higher interest rates in support of the Irish currency. The third phase was from mid-September to January 1993, during which time there was intermittent severe pressure on the Irish pound. Over this period, the external reserves were depleted, the EMS support system was extensively utilised, and domestic liquidity conditions tightened significantly as pressures on the currency culminated in a realignment of the Irish pound within the ERM on January 30, 1993. The final phase—February to April 1993—was marked by a significant improvement in sentiment in the foreign exchange and money markets. Before the end of March, interest rates were reduced below pre-crisis levels, outstanding debts for market support were repaid, and the external reserves were rebuilt.

Sterling had always been the Achilles' heel of Ireland's EMS policy. The view of foreign investors was that the Irish pound was susceptible to devaluation during periods of sterling weakness—the devaluation of the IR£ in 1983 and 1986 provided ample justification. Hence, when sterling devalued in September 1992, foreign investors withdrew their funds from Ireland in order to avoid incurring a capital loss. However, contrary to the earlier episodes, the Central Bank decided in September 1992 not to devalue but, instead, to raise interest rates to defend the exchange rate.

Since a devaluation in 1986, the Irish government had pursued a policy of fixing the IR£ in the EMS band in order to keep interest rates and inflation close to the German levels. The government was intent on sticking to this policy despite the sterling depreciation. There was a danger, of course, that the loss of competitiveness associated with the sterling devaluation would reduce Irish exports and increase imports.

In order to compensate for this, the government introduced a "market development fund" which paid IR£50 per job per week to firms affected by the devaluation of sterling. This fund was intended to be only a temporary measure as it was expected that sterling would appreciate in the near future and the trading difficulties facing Irish firms would disappear.

In the event, the UK£ did not appreciate within the expected time span, leading to the forecast by one commentator that the market development fund was destined to "prove unworkable and effective."*

* Anthony J. Leddin, "Unemployment and EMS Membership," *Labor Market Review,* Winter 1992, FAS, Training & Employment Authority, Dublin.

submitted a formal complaint to the European Commission concerning the Irish preferential rate, claiming "unfair competition"—since a standard rate of corporate tax, 27 percent, was applied across the U.K. embracing all industries, the horticultural sector included. The Dublin government was forced by Brussels to declassify mushroom production as "manufacturing," and, under the Finance Bill of 1994, imposed the standard 40 percent corporation profit tax rate on mushroom producing companies, with composting companies retaining their 10 percent tax status.

EXHIBIT 14   Exchange Rates in Dublin Market, 1992/1994 Period Averages

	v. UK£		v. UK£	v. DM	ECU	Effective Index*
1992						
January	0.9323					
February	0.9275					
March	0.9312	Qtr 1, 1992	0.9304	2.6662	1.3053	67.98
April	0.9209					
May	0.9101					
June	0.9158	Qtr 2, 1992	0.9155	2.6692	1.3013	67.63
July	0.9320					
August	0.9434					
September	0.9861	Qtr 3, 1992	0.9538	2.6530	1.3087	69.81
October	1.0705					
November	1.0892					
December	1.0753	Qtr 4, 1992	1.0784	2.6363	1.3426	72.50
1993						
January	1.0673					
February	0.9622[†]					
March	0.9677	Qtr 1, 1993	1.0353	2.4995	1.2834	68.85
April	0.9882					
May	0.9800					
June	0.9772	Qtr 2, 1993	0.9817	2.4386	1.2486	66.40
July	0.9425					
August	0.9324					
September	0.9421	Qtr 3, 1993	0.9391	2.3676	1.2283	64.00
October	0.9542					
November	0.9491					
December	0.9516	Qtr 4, 1993	0.9516	2.3881	1.2442	64.72
1994						
January	0.9597					
February	0.9603					
March	0.9619	Qtr 1, 1994	0.9607	2.4625	1.2706	65.50

* Trade-weighted exchange rate index for the IR£ (base 1971 = 100).

† Realignment of the EMS (European Monetary System) occurred on January 30, 1993, resulting in an effective 10% devaluation of the IR£.

Source: Central Bank of Ireland, *Quarterly Report.*

3. One can see some storm clouds gathering due to a claimed increase in production capacity in Holland. Mushrooms are among the most important horticultural crops in The Netherlands with 190,000 tons harvested in 1993.

Exports of fresh mushrooms have grown to 50,000 tons, with the U.K. being the second largest customer of Dutch fresh mushrooms in 1993—British sales representing 19 percent, or 9,500 tons of mushroom exports from The Netherlands.

4. In the U.K., multiple supermarkets continue to predominate as the main channels for the household purchase of fresh produce. The multiples' share of the market is still growing, having control of in excess of 60 percent of the retail market segment (in terms of volume). The major chains are continually competing aggressively with each other to increase their individual market shares. Currently, the multiple chains are involved in a "price war" with fresh produce, including mushrooms, being a prime target. Loose mushrooms which up to recently had achieved a selling price of £1.53/lb., without seemingly having any negative adverse effect on consumption, are now being sold below this price level. On the other hand, the consumer can purchase more mushrooms at a reduced cost by choosing from the valu-pack ranges (e.g., 750 grams retailing at £1.59, or l lb. packs retailing at £0.89, and so on). It is known that Irish mushroom producers are attempting to gauge the likely effects of these developments on the sector and to develop appropriate strategies to guard their respective market shares.

5. In the medium to long term, availability of straw could prove to be a critical factor. Increased "Setaside" provisions under the CAP (Common Agricultural Policy) program, will release over 86,500 acres of land from cereal production in Ireland in the course of 1994. When the prospective effects of this EU measure are combined with the potentially increased demand for straw from the thriving Northern Ireland export market, there is the threat of a significant increase in the price of straw to Irish mushroom growers, who may be forced to import straw from the U.K. On the other hand, there could be an increase in the indigenous supply of this critical raw material due to production of longer straw, as a result of E.U. prohibition of growth regulators under REPS (the Rural Environment Protection Scheme).

6. Ireland is probably the only country where mushrooms are entirely hand picked. The work is done mainly by women who work hours which suit their personal and domestic situations. The introduction of the new Workers' Protection Act by the Irish government means that new rates of PRSI (Pay Related Social Insurance) now apply to part-time workers. Some pickers are now saying they will quit because of the risk of losing social welfare benefits, since if, "at the margin," part-time earnings from mushroom picking are added to existing family income, they and their families may lose some entitlements. It is feared that the mushroom sector will find it difficult to survive without a plentiful supply of part-time labour, and a strong case has been made for retention of the Farm Casual Scheme, allowing farmers to take on workers for purposes such as harvest cropping.

CASE 14
NATURE ISLE HERBAL TEAS, LIMITED
Dominica, West Indies

It was a typical June day in Dominica. There was powerful sun, tropical heat, high humidity, sporadic downpours, and a stunning rainbow in the distance over the mountains of the rain forest. Alvin Paul, production manager for Nature Isle Herbal Teas, stood in the open double doors of the factory as dark clouds approached. He reflected on the changes the company had weathered over the last few years, and wondered if management would steer the company well into the future. The management team was about to meet to determine the company's strategy. They had all worked hard to develop the company over the years, but now, with a potentially huge export market within their reach, Alvin had misgivings. Were they ready to handle this new level of growth? If they lost the confidence of their new distributors in Guadeloupe and Martinique, would they get another chance? There was so much to gain—and everything to lose. They would probably only get this one shot at success.

THE COMMONWEALTH OF DOMINICA

Dominica is a small island in the West Indies between the French islands of Guadeloupe and Martinique. The east shore faces the Atlantic Ocean, the west the Caribbean Sea. Dominica gained its independence in 1980 from the British Commonwealth. Its 72,000 local inhabitants are largely descendants of slaves brought to the island by the British some 200 years ago. While English is the official language, French Creole (or "patois"[1]) is promoted as part of Dominica's cultural heritage. The island is very mountainous, and the mountains are covered with the lush green vegetation of rain forests. It is said that there are 365 rivers on the island—one for every day of the year.

Dominica was not a typical Caribbean island. The tourist industry, like the rest of the economy, was not highly developed. (There are few sandy beaches and most of the coast is rocky, with sheer drop-offs leading to very deep water; the seas around the island offer some of the finest diving and snorkeling in the world.) The government had not approved any large scale hotel projects in order to protect Dominica's natural setting. Cruise ships had recently visited more frequently, but

---

[1] Patois is a combination of French and African languages. Dominicans are proud of their local language, and it now even appears in print. Original inhabitants of the island were the once warlike Caribs, whose descendants still live in the Carib Territory in the northeast. Some Carib words have become common terms in Dominica, but it is no longer spoken as a language. The Creole of Dominica is easily understood by the Creoles of Guadeloupe, Martinique, St. Lucia, Grenada, Trinidad, and Haiti, but it is not identical to any of them, and, even within Dominica, it varies slightly.

Source: This case was written by Scott Field of the University of Washington, USA and edited by Richard G. Linowes, American University, USA. This case is written as a basis for class discussion rather than to illustrate either effective or ineffective handling of an administrative situation.

since they stopped only for a few hours, their contributions to the local economy were limited. The areas that seemed to show the most economic promise were specialty crops (including tropical fruits), ecotourism, and scuba diving. The government had preserved almost a third of the island as national parks. There was little industrial pollution since there was not much industry on the island. In the agricultural sector, however, soil erosion from clear-cutting and the increased use of herbicides and pesticides were posing ecological threats. Furthermore, as consumption increased, Dominica had begun to experience waste disposal problems.

Because of the incredible fertility of the island, hunger was not a problem. The temperature never dropped below 60 degrees and could reach well above 90 degrees during the day. It often rained, but rarely for very long periods of time. Even though most people were poor by the standards of developed countries, many had televisions and most city dwellers had electricity, running water, and indoor plumbing. Vehicle ownership was on the rise, but most citizens relied on a minibus transportation system when traveling inland.

Inland transportation was a development challenge. Most of the main interior roads were paved and in good condition. Because of the history of British influence, cars drove on the left side of the road. Local minibus drivers provided the only means of public transportation. They negotiated blind curves on narrow, steep mountain roads with great finesse at speeds that often frightened visitors. Although the island was only 16 miles wide, the drive from Melville Hall (in the North) to Roseau (the capital in the South) usually took an hour and a half. There were a limited number of large trucks available for hauling, and freight rates were high. Duties were imposed on most goods coming into the country, and the duties on vehicles and parts made vehicle ownership expensive.

Another transportation challenge was the lack of a lighted airport facility or one capable of handling large airplanes. There were two airports on the island—Canefield (near Roseau) and Melville Hall. Melville Hall was more accessible to larger planes than Canefield, but the runway was not long enough to allow for passenger jets or large cargo carriers. Canefield was more convenient to Roseau, but it could only accommodate small propeller planes. Despite frequent turbulence and an alarmingly steep descent, pilots deftly landed their small planes on its perilously short runways. With no night landing facilities, it often took two days to reach Dominica from the United States. These inconveniences discouraged tourism and trade.

Dominica faced many of the uncertainties and inconveniences common to Third World countries: cash and credit shortages, political instability (manifested through surprising outcomes in elections), high costs associated with importing capital equipment, disadvantageous economies of scale, and poor domestic infrastructure. The nation's economy was heavily dependent on agriculture. Local farmers had historically developed a dependence on whatever crop was most in demand at the time. This led to economic upheavals when the demand for selected crops declined. For example, many hillsides were covered with untended lime trees that were once harvested to supply the Rose's Lime Juice plant in Roseau.

When Rose's operations relocated, Dominica lost its market for limes, and the trees went unattended. Coffee, cocoa, grapefruit, and oranges were also once main export crops, but they had all lost most of their markets.

Banana exports now accounted for about 70 percent of the island's desperately needed foreign exchange earnings. Unfortunately, the subsidized price that Great Britain and France paid for bananas was higher than what German housewives were willing to pay, and the European Community had recently negotiated a gradual reduction in the price of Caribbean bananas. Dominican farmers rightly claimed that they could not produce bananas with the same economies of scale enjoyed by Latin American producers. Compounding these worries were concerns that the NAFTA agreement would divert the little investment capital Dominica now received to Mexico.

The largest private employer and exporter in Dominica was Dominica Coconut Products (DCP). DCP manufactured soaps, lotions, and hair care products under its own brand names and under license for Dial and Palmolive. DCP was currently paying more than the world market price for Dominican coconuts to help prop up the economy. Its owner warned that DCP could not compete effectively in the world market paying such high prices indefinitely. Bellot Products was another Dominican firm that processed the island's agricultural products. It produced specialty products such as juice concentrates and hot sauces. These products were sold domestically and abroad, and marketing efforts were being made to increase their presence in the United States.

There were a few small manufacturing firms. Despite the assistance that was available to small businesses, most failed within a few years. Remnants of expensive equipment (usually financed through international development agencies) could be seen rusting near various buildings. While seldom lacking in good intentions, the would-be managers of these businesses needed more than business financing; they required technical assistance in business development to complement their loans for capital equipment. Since the local economy was so small, few businesses could reach significant size without exporting. Exporting could be extremely complicated and costly. A small business owner was not likely to have the expertise required to deal with the range of issues key to exporting, such as financing, regulations, tariffs, shipping expenses, and advertising in a foreign language.

Retailers were among the oldest and most successful businesses in Dominica. The largest retail businesses were owned by a few prominent families. Restaurants, bottling operations, and gift shops composed a significant portion of the economy.

On weekends everyone flocked to local markets in the larger villages and cities to buy and sell food and other items. This was a major social event. Through bartering and negotiating people stocked up on supplies in the open air markets. Among the exotic produce available were plantains, christophenes, pawpaws, dasheen, and breadfruit. Nonfood items, such as beautiful straw baskets, mats, and wood carvings produced on the Carib Reserve, were treasured by Dominicans and tourists alike.

The local currency, the Eastern Caribbean dollar, was shared by the several member countries of the Eastern Caribbean Development Bank. It was pegged to the U.S. dollar.[2] While it enjoyed the stability of the U.S. dollar, some Dominicans were calling for it to float freely to help make export prices more competitive in world markets.

DOMINICAN CULTURE

Dominicans were very social people. They typically greeted everyone on a bus when they boarded. If they made eye contact with someone on the street, they were expected to greet the person or risk being considered unfriendly. Outsiders occasionally went out of their way to visit with people for the same reason. Word of mouth traveled fast, and it was essential to leave a good impression wherever possible. Dominicans were very friendly and helpful, but somewhat guarded in business and personal dealings until the other party was known and accepted.

Dominicans were fascinated with Americans and all things American. Nonetheless, the pace of life in the Caribbean was considerably slower than in the United States. People could speak for a long time before getting down to the business at hand. It could take considerable time to complete even the most common tasks and errands. Local citizens advised visitors not to express too much impatience or irritation with the status quo.

Even the government of the island moved slowly compared to what citizens of developed countries would consider reasonable. Nature Isle recently experienced an unexpected water shutdown. The prior owner of an adjacent business closed down his operation without paying his water bill. Nature Isle's water line was connected through his property. Nature Isle leased this facility from the government. Since the government was also in arrears on its own water bill, the water utility used Nature Isle as leverage to receive payment from the government before restoring service. After negotiations, prodding, and countless phone calls, Nature Isle's managers finally regained their access to water some six months after its disconnection. In the meantime, they had to hand carry all the water they needed from a water line at the neighboring National Development Corporation, some 100 feet away.

The people of Dominica practiced the "early to bed, early to rise" ethic, except when there was a party. They are an industrious and hard working people. Most of the villagers around the island supported themselves through fishing and agriculture. Dominicans enjoyed social events and there were many widely celebrated feasts and holidays during the year. Often celebrations were scattered over a period of weeks so that it was possible for "fête-lovers" ("fête" is the Creole word for party) to drift from village to village following the revelry. Colorful costumes were worn at special festivities celebrating local culture.

---

[2]The exchange rate was fixed, with the Eastern Caribbean dollar equaling 37 cents in U.S. currency (EC$1 = US$.37).

THE COMPANY

Nature Isle Herbal Teas was a small firm that began as a one man operation seven years ago. The company had received support from DEXIA (Dominica Export Import Agency), other development agencies, the government, and local media. The brand name was well-known and the products popular in Dominica. The company experienced rapid growth over the preceding few years as the managers improved the packaging and the production process. Annual sales revenues exceeded EC$120,000 (see Exhibit 4). Nature Isle produced retail-sized packages of herbal teas and spices; there were 20 different products in their line. Although these herbs and spices were widely used in the Caribbean, only about 30 percent of revenues came from exports. Marketing efforts to date had focused largely on the Dominica market, but recent promotions in Guadeloupe and Martinique revealed that there were excellent opportunities in the export market.

The building that housed operations was a corrugated metal structure with a cement floor. Some of the equipment from the previous owner still occupied space at one end of the 2,000 sq. ft. building. There were no screens on the windows or doors, and no air conditioning. As was typical of Dominica, mosquitoes and other insects added to the misery of hot, humid days. Fortunately, there was often a breeze off the mountains behind the building to help make the heat bearable. Inventory was stored in an area where the roof above had no major problems. Nature Isle kept a leased solar dryer next to the factory and held 8.5 acres of farmland in the countryside.

The company's management team consisted of four partners. None of them had had any university training; they had all acquired their management skills through experience and at various seminars provided by development organizations working in the Caribbean region. All four partners were deeply committed to the success of the company. They had all lived on meager salaries to meet the cash flow demands of the business. They had all sacrificed their own salaries many times in order to pay their employees.

Glen Martin was the founder and chairman of the company. He recognized that Dominicans loved infusions made from local herbs.[3] Due to their increasingly busy lifestyles, however, they might like the convenience of local herbs packaged in tea bags. Glen saw this as a potential market, and he started the business selling single serving bags of herbal tea. He began by grinding the herbs and spices by hand. He would purchase boxes of Red Rose tea and empty the tea bags, filling them with his own product. Glen established a reputation for being quite knowledgeable about herbs.

Although reading and writing were difficult for him, Glen had an extensive vocabulary and a grasp of many fundamental business concepts. Over the next seven years, he recruited three partners to help him expand the business. He hoped to further the development of Dominica by providing more employment opportunities and new markets for its diversified crops.

---

[3]Although most contain no tea leaves, these infusions were widely known as herb teas.

Alvin was Glen's first partner. George Charles was brought in next as general manager. Both invested many years of effort for minimal compensation in return for equity positions in the company. The latest partner was the new marketing manager, Joey Alleyne. So far, Joey had concentrated only on local markets but he was anxious to learn more about capitalizing on export opportunities. As the company grew, they hired additional workers. There were now four full-time production workers and an office manager.

As is common to fledgling companies in developing nations, Nature Isle Herbal Teas relied heavily on revenue grants and assistance from a variety of development agencies. This was how initial growth was financed. The company was now at a crossroads. Development assistance had become limited and the company held a great deal of short-term debt, making the timing of cash flows a critical management issue. The company had not established strong banking relationships or adequate equity to enable them to consolidate loans.

Although Nature Isle had not yet saturated the market in Dominica, Glen Martin and his management team perceived diminishing returns for local large-scale marketing efforts. The island population was small, there was little disposable income,[4] and many grew their own fresh herbs for cooking and teas.

The company produced two distinct lines of products: herbal teas and spices. The herbal teas and most of the spices were organically grown and solar dried. They were all natural and had no preservatives.

THE PRODUCTION PROCESS

Farmers grew herbs and spices for the company. As raw materials were received they were examined for quality and weighed for payment. Herbs and spices were usually washed before passing on to the next phase, the solar dryer. Products to be solar dried were placed in the dryer for five to seven days until they reached the correct moisture content level. The dried herbs were hand sorted to remove twigs and other debris. One employee could sort about 15 lbs. (1 lb. equals 454 grams) of leaves during a workday. Sorted product was then milled into a fine powder by a milling machine before packaging. Alvin took charge of the milling process since he was the only one who knew how to run the machine.

Milled raw materials for tea were then placed in the tea bagging equipment that packaged the tea together with the thread and tag, and then boxed it in batches of 20 sachets (each sachet weighed approximately 1.5 grams). Boxes were opened and folded before they were loaded into the tea bagging machine. This process took about 20 seconds per box and it was performed in batches. Without breakdowns, the bagging machine could fill six boxes per minute, with each box containing 20 1.5-gram tea bags. The new tea bagger could produce 10,800 boxes per week when running at 75 percent capacity. Boxes of tea were closed and placed

---

[4]Annual per capita GNP was approximately US$2,000. Even though food was relatively inexpensive, many other imported items were expensive for Dominican citizens.

EXHIBIT 1   Nature Isle Herbal Teas, Ltd., Product Lines

Herbal Teas

Peppermint

Spearmint

Cinnamon

Ginger

Basilic

Bergamot

Citronelle

Anise

Spices

Cinnamon (ground and bark)

Nutmeg (ground and whole)

Ginger (ground and whole)

Anise (ground)

Bay Leaf (ground)

Tumeric (ground)

Cloves (ground and whole)

---

in a tub and then taken to the shrink-wrap machine operator. Samples of the boxes were weighed intermittently to verify consistency in weights. Boxes transferred to the shrink-wrap machine were wrapped and placed into cartons, each containing 24 boxes.

Spices were placed in a filling machine after the milling process and bagged in polypropylene bags in quantities of 20 to 40 grams each. Spice bags were then sealed with a foot-operated heat sealer and packaged individually in cartons for shipping and delivery.

Operations were contained in an oblong-shaped, steel frame building with galvanized zinc sheet sidings and roof with dimensions of 90 ft. × 20 ft. (see Exhibit 2). The solar dryer was located about 15 feet away from the main entrance to the building and measured 20 ft. × 14 ft. The solar dryer had a capacity of 1,000 lbs. of fresh product per week with an average yield of 130 lbs. of dried herbs. Given the present capacity of the solar dryer, Nature Isle could produce about 1,967 boxes of herbal teas each week. The site was conveniently located on the outskirts of the city, approximately 2.5 miles from the seaport and seven miles from the airport at Canefield.

Most of the herbs required for production were supplied by about 15 farmers who each converted about 2.5 acres of land for growing herbs. Spices such as cinnamon and ginger were supplied by a variety of farmers, while nutmeg and

EXHIBIT 2   Plant Layout

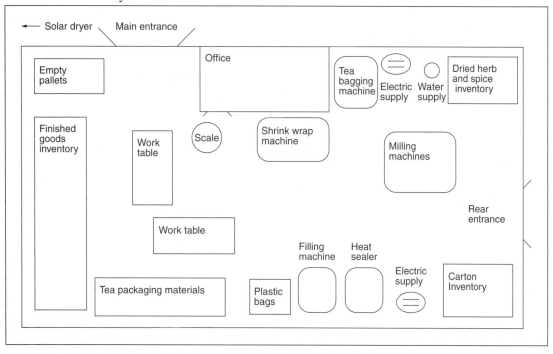

cloves were imported from an island far to the south and then milled or reexported in their original form. There was an additional 8.5 acres of land available for cultivation. Nature Isle agreed to assist farmers who supplied them by providing them needed tools and fertilizer in exchange for paying prices slightly less than market price.

Glen Martin regularly drove out to the countryside to talk with farmers about his raw material needs. He often encouraged farmers to plant a particular crop by offering to pay a high price for the first order. Most herbs could be grown in three months. Return trips were required to pick up many of the orders (not all farmers had trucks or vans for transporting their crops). Packaging materials had been ordered in large quantities a year before. They were expected to last for at least the next several months.

THE COMPETITION AND LOCAL DISTRIBUTION

Local imports of herb teas originated primarily from the United States and Great Britain. Lipton's (England) mint herbal tea sold at EC$6.36 retail for 32 grams. Heathway (U.S.) retailed a peppermint tea for EC$15 for 56 grams. Lion Cross (U.S.) had a spearmint tea retailing for EC$7.21 for 30 grams. Nature Isle mint teas retailed at EC$6.50 for 30 grams.

EXHIBIT 3   Raw Materials Requirements

	Product Mix	Boxes Required	Pounds Required
Teas			
Peppermint	25%	14,423	5,344
Bergamint	12	6,923	2,922
Spearmint	15	8,654	3,660
Basil	12	8,229	3,467
Anise	5	3,429	902
Ginger	12	8,229	2,178
Citronelle	12	8,229	1,525
Cinnamon	7	4,800	253
Total	100%	62,916 units	20,251 lbs.
Spices			
Cinnamon	15%	15,600	1,040
Nutmeg	15	9,375	830
Ginger	10	7,784	2,595
Anise Bay	5	5,556	3,658
Tumeric	18	14,012	4,695
Other	37	28,802	1,930
Total	100%	81,129 units	14,748 lbs.

The major competitor of spice products was Chief's from Trinidad with bottled cinnamon, nutmeg, and ginger retailing at EC$3.55, $3.20, and $4.30, respectively.

Competitor packaging was more sophisticated. In taste tests, however, many consumers indicated that Nature Isle products had a much stronger aroma and fresher flavor. Nature Isle had a 15 percent price advantage at the retail level for spice products due to the simple packaging style they had adopted.

THE MANAGEMENT MEETING

Nature Isle Herbal Teas had been selling almost exclusively in the domestic market. In the previous year the company entered into an exclusive distribution agreement with a distributor in Guadeloupe, a French island just to the north of Dominica. They sent a small shipment of their product for sale in several retail stores, and unfortunately, most of the products did not sell well during the few months they were available. The distributor, Mr. Tichy, had advised them that in Guadeloupe there was a negative perception of Dominica. This was due to Dominicans' willingness to work for low wages and for their undercutting Guadeloupe's market prices on agricultural products. The distributor suggested some changes in packaging to aid in the promotion of Nature Isle products in

Guadeloupe. Nature Isle spices were sold in nonresealable plastic packets. Labeling on the tea boxes was designed for the Dominica market, but also included some French translation of key information. There were complaints that the stylized font depicting the brand name and the type of tea was not clearly legible. It was also suggested that name recognition should be increased through promotion and advertising. Production of a commercial for television would cost about 10,000 French francs.[5] Running the ad at least three times a day for a week would cost 9,000 French francs over and above production. Mr. Tichy also suggested that since teas and spices were products in different markets, they should be marketed separately. With these changes, he was certain that the products could be successfully sold in the Guadeloupe market.

Glen Martin believed that a cost-effective promotion campaign was essential if products were to be marketed effectively in the French market. Products were already on the shelves in Guadeloupe and Mr. Tichy had invested a good deal of his own time and money in placing these products with certain retailers.

While Mr. Tichy was busy in Guadeloupe, the Nature Isle management team signed an exclusive distribution agreement with Mrs. Lionis in Martinique (a French island to the south). An order for 75,000 French francs of assorted teas was submitted and hopes were running high that there would be subsequent orders in the near future. The Martinique order was to be divided equally among four teas: peppermint, spearmint, bay, and basil. The teas are being sold to Mrs. Lionis for 288 francs per carton (24 boxes per carton).

THE BUSINESS STRATEGY MEETING

All four partners were present. Alvin started the discussion by acknowledging the Martinique order. "I'm really glad you got this order, George, but I wish you hadn't promised delivery in just one week. I'm not certain that we can fill it that quickly. I know we need the money, but if we sell too fast I don't know if we can keep up."

"The staff just needs to be more disciplined," George Charles replied. "Right now, I don't know if they'll be on time in the morning or after lunch. We lose as much as two hours of production time some days."

Joey broke in, "The timing of this order is really bad since I have another order for six cartons of peppermint tea for our best customer right here in Roseau. We only have four cartons in stock. We need to think about ways to expand our production capability to meet the new orders coming in."

"Before we go any further, we need to assess our situation. Alvin and George, you take a look at our production capabilities and come up with a plan to increase our capacity. Joey and I will work on a marketing plan for exporting products into Guadeloupe and Martinique at a pace we can keep, and at a price we can afford," Glen concluded. "Let's meet in one week to compare our plans and decide on future tactics."

---

[5]There were 5.2 French francs to the U.S. dollar.

CASE DISCUSSION

1. Identify the production bottlenecks and recommend potential solutions.
2. What inventory issues can you identify? Suggest how you would deal with these issues if you were part of the Nature Isle management team.
3. Develop an export strategy for the company. What time frame is reasonable? How would you go about identifying potential competitors? What questions must be addressed before a full-scale export strategy is implemented?
4. Given Nature Isle's current product lines and packaging, what ideas would you pose to them for new product development?
5. The most recent financial statements for Nature Isle are contained in Exhibits 4 and 5. What is your opinion of the current state of their financial affairs? What financial management strategy should they follow?

EXHIBIT 4   **Nature Isle Herbal Teas, Ltd., Income Statement**
All Amounts Are in Eastern Caribbean Dollars (EC$)

	1989	1990	1991
Sales	**32,735**	**75,836**	**123,300**
Cost of sales	24,875	41,411	63,176
Gross margin	7,860	34,425	60,133
Operating Expenses:			
General/administrative	56,967	123,641	107,899
Depreciation	5,252	8,102	19,867
Operating profit/loss	(54,349)	(97,318)	(67,633)
Revenue grants	83,862	109,734	57,264
Amortization of grants	2,351	5,869	13,747
Net Profit/Loss	31,864	18,285	3,378

EXHIBIT 5   Nature Isle Herbal Teas, Ltd. Balance Sheet
All Amounts Are in Eastern Caribbean Dollars (EC$)

	1989	1990	1991
Assets			
Cash	12,322	18,643	25,159
Receivables	2,200	2,680	3,338
Inventories:			
Packaging	5,217	14,146	58,642
Raw materials	21,181	33,214	38,503
Current assets	40,920	68,683	125,642
Factory equipment	32,741	67,387	163,529
Depreciation	(6,569)	(13,525)	(26,802)
Vehicles		27,505	27,505
Depreciation		(1,146)	(7,726)
Total assets	67,092	148,904	282,138
Liabilities and Equity			
Accrued expense	750	3,726	7,420
Loans/notes	3,240	14,940	31,580
Deferred interest		(7,848)	(11,867)
Loans payable	6,725	25,403	57,534
Total liabilities	10,715	36,221	84,667
Capital grants	17,244	55,265	136,675
Owners' equity	7,269	7,269	7,269
Accumulated funds	31,864	50,149	53,527
Total liabilities and equity	67,092	148,904	282,138

C H A P T E R

V Cultural, Ethical, and Legal Issues

CASE SUMMARIES

The case chronicles the experience of Greg Hucek, a first-generation American with roots in Central Europe. Hucek is attempting to build a business supplying upscale shopping bags to Czech Republic specialty and department stores. Hucek's business is a premium-priced, fashion differentiated business attempting to position itself in an economy long accustomed to low-cost, low-quality commodity goods and services. Much of the case describes Hucek's efforts to acquire material, financial, and informational resources and the major impediments posed by the Czech legal, business, and governmental infrastructure. An issue with his Slovak supplier is considered in some depth. The case also describes the impact of his prior entrepreneurial failure in New York and the impact of his family background as Hucek attempts to build his bag business. ■

CASE 15
RIVERDANCE

*"I am of Ireland, ...come and dance with me in Ireland."**

INTRODUCTION

This study looks at the development of *Riverdance*—a brief musical and dance sequence specially commissioned by RTE, the Irish Broadcasting Authority, for the Eurovision Song Contest held in Dublin, Ireland, in 1994. It aims to explore the innovatory aspects of *Riverdance* and attempts to analyze what lessons might be learned in relation to "generating success from a new idea," in the world of the performing arts. It also seeks analogues, in terms of innovation and entrepreneurship, that relate to mega TV broadcasted events, such as "Italia 90" World Cup Finals and the 1992 Olympic Games in Barcelona, Spain.

EUROVISION SONG CONTEST

Traditionally, the annual three-hour Eurovision Song Contest broadcast is divided into two main sections—the first relates to presentation of 23 or 24 songs from nations which are members of the European Broadcasting Union (EBU), and the second section comprises voting by each of the countries in turn on the songs. An intermission of seven or eight minutes' entertainment is provided by the host television authority—*Riverdance* being the RTE presentation at the Point Theatre, Dublin, in 1994 (see Exhibit 1). *Riverdance*, as one commentator reported, rather irreverently, was:

> Originally meant to be a European space filler—an entertaining diversion while the judges made up their minds which piece of sub-pop drivel would be given the exaggerated title of "best song."

Prior to 1994, Ireland had hosted the Eurovision Song Contest on four previous occasions, 1971, 1981, 1988, and 1993, with the capital city, Dublin, as the venue for all but the last year when Millstreet, Co. Cork became the first nonurban center ever, to stage the song contest (O'Cinneide, 1993). Ironically, although over 3,500 people attended the 1993 competition held in the equestrian arena in Millstreet, the population of the town itself is just 1,500.

IRELAND HOSTS EUROVISION, 1993–1995

Funding for the song contests held in Ireland came from several sources. First, the EBU, European Broadcasting Union, contributed a certain amount; RTE obtained

---

*From *"Ich am of Irlaunde,"* Middle English dancing song, written around the year 1300, quoted in Breathnach, 1983. This case is intended as a basis for class discussion rather than to illustrate either effective or ineffective handling of an administrative situation.

Source: This case was written by Barra O'Cinneide, University of Limerick, Ireland.

EXHIBIT 1   *Riverdance* **Eurovision Song Contest**
The Point Theatre, Dublin, April 30, 1994

Credits

Music composed and produced by: **Bill Whelan**

Guest dancers and Irish dance choreography: **Michael Flatley/Jean Butler**

Dance troupe: **The Eurovision Irish Dancers**

Choreography: **Mavis Ascott**

Assistant choreographer: **Belinda Murphy**

Choir: **Anuna**—lead singer: **Katie McMahon;** directed/conducted by **Michael McGlynn**

Orchestra: **RTE Concert Orchestra**—led by **Michael d'Arcy;** conducted by **Noel Keleghan**

Eurovision production: **Moya Doherty**

Source: Listed credits for *Riverdance* video, augmented with acknowledgment to Katie McMahon, Anuna.

---

significant sponsorship and financed the balance. Ireland is a very small country, with a small audience base—the total (annual) national funding for national radio and television production is on the order of IR£115 million. Out of this amount, RTE has to provide two television and three radio channel services to the entire country. So, the European Broadcasting Union, with its demands for special international communications and state of the art technology, creates huge pressures, measured in financial terms, alone, at approximately £2.5 million. There is an obvious in-built challenge to the host broadcaster to demonstrate its technical and creative abilities to the vast viewership the program attracts.

As it has been seen by RTE's management as "a matter of huge national pride," a high level of technical and artistic planning, in addition to special logistical support, was required in the production of the contest. After Ireland's Eurovision win at Millstreet, particular attention was given to creating *Riverdance* as the interval item. *Riverdance* was something in which RTE invested a significant part of its program budgeting. In turn, this led to a very commercially viable and successful product from RTE, providing a handsome return to RTE on its investment. Much of RTE's output, like many other TV stations, conforms to well-understood patterns whose budgets can be set with some degree of certainty. With an event like the Eurovision Song Contest both the size and the impact of external forces make control far less certain. The popularity of *Riverdance*, however, and the resulting commercial success created for the first time the prospect that managing the Eurovision Song Contest could do more than drain the host organization of resources.

Management of the project became a real-time challenge, balancing costs with creativity. In measuring the success of the production's management we can judge, eventually, the final judgment, in terms of the value for money, must be in the eyes of the beholders, the audiences—the Eurovision fans, in particular, but also in the media critics.

PROBLEMATIC ESTIMATES OF THE EUROVISION AUDIENCE

It is claimed that over 300 million viewers tuned in, worldwide, to the 1994 Eurovision broadcast at some point during the three-hour schedule. This would seem to provide an extremely favorable scenario for further development of the interlude piece as product "derivatives." However, one of the more interesting side issues concerning *Riverdance* is the little recognized fact that, according to this author's calculations, it is likely that no more than 10 percent of this number, that is, 30 million TV viewers, saw the interlude live on that particular Saturday evening. This resulted from two important factors:

1. As far as can be ascertained, only a handful of broadcasting channels, including BBC and RTE, screened the entire Eurovision program. In many countries other than Britain and Ireland, the intermission time was utilized to show advertising since the format of Eurovision allows only a seven or eight minute window of opportunity for commercial revenue generation.

BBC, being a public broadcasting authority, does not transmit advertising and RTE, being the host station, had to transmit the interlude entertainment. The Irish station thereby lost its normal advertising screening time which added further to the enormous cost of staging the song contest, estimated to have cost RTE over IR£1.5 million, net of commercial sponsorship and a special contribution from the EBU.

2. Even among viewers that were tuned into Eurovision during the interlude, there was the inevitable temptation (one might even say necessity) to respond to either the calls of nature or the opportunity of making/consuming beverages, and so on, since the first section of the song contest was of more than 100 minutes duration, with nearly an equivalent viewing time to follow!

THE GREAT IRISH DIASPORA

As against the necessity to overcome the comparative lack of knowledge or understanding of *Riverdance,* discussed above, there is a potentialy large ethnic Irish pool of prospective customers for *Riverdance* and its derivatives (including the ensuing *Riverdance—The Show*) through networking into what is called the "Great Irish Diaspora" of over 70 million people who claim Irish descent or affinity, mostly in the English speaking world, for example, in the United States (with a reputed 44 million Irish population), Canada, United Kingdom, Australia, New Zealand, South Africa, and so on.[1]

---

[1]An interesting feature of the *Riverdance* story is that, at the time of writing, a video of *Riverdance—The Show* had not yet been released on the North American market even though the European VHS standard version has been on sale for over a year. No doubt, this is because the Irish promoters do not wish to release the video within North America before the launch of *Riverdance—The Show* in New York in Spring 1996. This has been facilitated by the different videotape formats in use in Europe and the United States.

Moya Doherty, producer. The *Riverdance* sequence at the Eurovision Song Contest 1994 was conceived by Moya Doherty. She was born in Co. Donegal, moving later with her family to Dublin. After joining RTE in the late 1970s as a radio broadcast assistant, she attended RADA, the Royal Academy of Directing & Acting, in London where she pursued a course in classical and Shakespearean acting and directing. She returned to RTE as a production assistant, this time in television. By 1984 she was presenting *The Live Arts* series and fronting RTE's first-ever breakfast TV programs, on the Los Angeles Olympics.

Moya Doherty moved again to London in 1985 working with the emergent TVAM breakfast television team, reporting and presenting news features. In 1989 she returned to RTE, working on a range of productions—embracing features, variety, current affairs, and young people's programs. In July 1993 she commenced thinking about her Eurovision assignment, as producer. She remembered that several months previously she had seen Michael Flately and Jean Butler dance as part of the *Mayo 5,000* events—her husband, John McColgan, was producer of the RTE broadcast of the celebration concert (Battersby, 1995):

> It was the first I had seen either of them dance. That night in the National Concert Hall, Dublin, I was struck by Michael Flately's innovative approach to Irish dancing. He has introduced an entire series of new steps and rhythms. I think he has, single-handedly, changed the face of Irish dancing. I knew I wanted Irish dancing to feature in the Eurovision show. We were following 26 songs and I did not want another singer. There is something about the rhythms that is elemental to me, it's just a personal thing. I have been planning, for a long time, to do a documentary on the history of Irish dance—and I will do it, sometime.

Bill Whelan, composer. Bill Whelan, the Limerick-born originator of the *Riverdance* music, is an internationally recognized composer. He collaborated with Andy Irvine in the production of *East Wind,* an album of Bulgarian music, and has acted as arranger for a host of stars, from "U2" to Kate Bush. He wrote the musical sound track for the film *Lamb* and in the Spring of 1995 developed the score for *Trinity*—a Broadway adaptation of the work of Leon Uris on revolutionary Ireland.

In 1992 Ireland participated in the World's Fair held in Seville, Spain. The Irish government was committed to presenting an appealing national image to the world, but more particularly to a Spanish audience! A program of cultural events was staged at the Irish Pavilion, including a new musical piece, *Seville Suite,* composed by Bill Whelan. It is not surprising, perhaps, that Spanish strains were entwined in the *Seville Suite* and the theatrical production became a fusion of flamenco and Irish dance styles. One of the dancers was Jean Butler who was to feature subsequently in *Riverdance*. In 1993 Bill Whelan composed *The Spirit of Mayo,* a work for full orchestra as part of the *Mayo 5,000* celebrations referred to above.

In planning for the Eurovision intermission feature, Moya Doherty discussed with Bill Whelan the possibility of composing an original musical piece illustrating Irish dance for an international audience, while ensuring a high entertainment value. It was hoped that it would prove possible to capture an aquatic theme, as it had been decided to interlace the first half of the three-hour long Eurovision program with several video montages of riverside aspects of Dublin, bearing in mind the Point Theatre's location on the banks of the River Liffey. The result was Whelan's composition, *Riverdance*, which was performed by the RTE Concert Orchestra, conducted by Noel Kelaghan (see Exhibit 2).

The "Riverdancers."   Although the Eurovision feature item contained a troupe of twenty dancers, most attention has been directed at the performances of the lead duo, Jean Butler and Michael Flatley, as in the following media comments (Corr, 1994):

> Combined with Bill Whelan's music, the machine-gun feet of Michael Flatley and Jean Butler conjured up visions of a mystic and proud nationality, and reawakened a Celtic revival, providing a fast, sexy link between our dissolving heritage and the

---

Exhibit 2

Riverdance—The Music

Extract from the Program Note for *Riverdance—The Show,* by Dr. Micheal O'Suilleabhain, Professor of Music, University of Limerick.

So what of *Riverdance*—the music? I think it significant that it found its premiere on Eurovision before a vast European audience. Here was music, not for a new Ireland alone but for a new emerging Europe. The Eastern European rhythms which had been drifting around within Irish tradition since 1968, when Andy Irvine literally brought them home after a journey there, form an important part of the soundscape. The Bulgarian/Macedonian sounds blew, now and then, like a gentle wind through the music of *Planxty* throughout the seventies. In 1980, Bill Whelan caught the bug when he worked with the group, and over ten years later, in 1993, he closed the circle by producing a recording entitled *East Wind* (Tara Records) by Andy Irvine and Davy Spillane. This was an album on which I played piano for one of the tracks, and I remember the creative terror I felt as I followed Irvine, Spillane, and some visiting Bulgarian musicians down the helter-skelter of rhythmic intricacy. After all of the laid back, "how's your father"/"could be worse" jiggling of a West Clare jig, jumping constantly between 9/16, 11/16, and 15/16 time patterns of the Bulgarian musical mind left us all breathless. It was like doing a Clare set dance on fast forward!

It seems to me that Irish traditional musicians have always had that strength of purpose to allow them to assimilate no end of outside influences. In fact, the tradition itself as it came down to us over the past three centuries emerged from the Scots/English/Irish cultural melting pot of the 18th century. The second half of this century now ending has seen a return to this appetite for new sounds, and the Eastern European influence Bill Whelan has chosen to highlight at times in *Riverdance* is one of the more challenging of these.

Riverdance is part of the contemporary stories of Irish music flowing into the sea of world music. The real wonder is that, for this part of the story, it has met a sister from which it has been separated for far too long. Music and dance are the same word in our tradition. Now as we stamp the ground in life-giving affirmation, our hands are rising up even of their own accord—just as the *sean-nos* dancers had it in embryo—calling everyone to the celebration of a culture broken free.

---

genius of a pure pop moment. So, *Riverdance* has taken its place in Irish folk history, with a rush of national pride—up there with "U2" who conquered the globe in the eighties. Besides the attractions of *Riverdance's* supercharged dance routines and Whelan's twilight music, there's also the sexual chemistry on stage between Flatley and Butler. Back at Eurovision, their open interpretation of Irish dancing won acclaim, but the smouldering intensity of parts of the performance was also applauded.

Flatley says:

When Jean and I saw the piece, we started to realize that that energy was here and we tried to go ahead and develop it. It just seemed to happen. We didn't purposefully go out and say, "let's look sexy." It came out a lot more sexy that night than we'd ever planned, that's for sure, and I think it will be developed to a further extent with the upcoming *Riverdance—The Show*. I think people need that chemistry: They want to see a show that's exciting and entertaining, that has a little bit of sex, a little bit of lovingness, and a little bit of everything. Most of all, they need to come away feeling they've been entertained, and go home happy.

Similarly, in an otherwise controversial piece, an *Irish Times* journalist extols the artistry of *Riverdance* (Courtney, 1994):

The dancing is breathtaking, and from the moment that Jean Butler emerges in her sexy black number and makes those precisely placed kicks, you're hooked. When Michael Flatley bounds onstage like a dervish, playing the mischievous Pan, tempting the dancers out of their static routines and into something altogether more devilish, you feel a mixture of fear and liberation. By the end of the dance, nothing less than wild abandon could be the appropriate response.

Born in Chicago, Illinois—his father was from Co. Sligo and his mother from Carlow—Michael Flatley was credited in the *Guinness Book of Records* with being the fastest tap dancer in the world, at 28 taps per second. He has won over 120 dance titles of every kind, in 13 countries and almost every U.S. state. He was the first American to win the World Championships in Irish Dancing. He was described by the National Geographic Society following his appearance in New York with The Chieftains, as "a living treasure." He has been a world champion Irish flute player on two occasions, a Golden Gloves boxing champion, a master-level chess player, a member of Mensa (with an IQ of 170), and the youngest ever recipient of the U.S. National Heritage Fellowship.[2]

New York-born Jean Butler has been involved in Irish dancing since the age of four. Although she trained in ballet and tap, Irish dancing became her specialty and she has won innumerable regional and international championships. In addition to performing at the Irish Pavilion in Seville during Expo 1992, as mentioned previously, she danced at the *Mayo 5,000* celebrations

---

[2]A repertoire of Flatley's flute music was released recently on Son Records. A bronze statue (49 cm. high and sculpted by an unknown artist, 1985), which represents Michael Flatley in a traditional step-dance pose, is on permanent exhibition in the Hunt Museum at the University of Limerick.

at the National Concert Hall, Dublin. Michael Flately also performed at *Mayo 5,000*, but *Riverdance* was the first occasion on which Flately and Butler danced together. A theater studies graduate, Jean Butler plans to combine acting with her dancing career.

Anuna.   For most viewers, perhaps, the orchestral music and the dance sequences overshadowed the performance of the other main artistic contributors to the Eurovision interlude, Anuna, the Celtic Chamber Choir, formed in Dublin in 1993. The group, whose name is derived from the Gaelic language, is committed to raising interest in the vast quantity of Irish music which is ignored by the general listener (Jackson, 1994). Although the group's repertoire draws on a millennium of Irish music, Anuna has worked with performers such as Sting, The Chieftains, Sinead O'Connor, and Barry Manilow.

Eurovision provided an unexpected promotional breakthrough for the group. At the National Entertainment Awards ceremony held in Dublin in December 1994, Anuna were adjudicated to be the top "classical" artistes for their performances during 1994, including their choral contribution to *Riverdance*. Several media observers have referred to the fact that the euphoric analyses of the Eurovision intermission piece gave Anuna's contribution, particularly the part played by the lead singer, Katie McMahon, insufficient acknowledgment (see, for instance, Jackson, 1994):

> Now and then, amid the morass of mediocrity that these days passes for music, there surfaces a sound which is so sublime, it immediately reminds one of poetry, purity, and perfection. As *Riverdance* evolved, the relatively sparse vocal lines created by Anuna were undoubtedly overshadowed by the more "sexy" and spectacular talents of dancers Jean Butler and Michael Flatley.

Referring to the group's Eurovision appearance, Michael McGlynn, *Anuna's* 30-year-old founder, arranger, and composer, explains (Jackson, 1994):

> In some respects, people now think of Anuna only in terms of *Riverdance*. Yet when you're carried along on something as positive as that, you can't really complain, can you? I mean, let's face it, our work is highly specialized and, compared with similar groups in other countries, we now sell huge amounts of product, directly as a result of *Riverdance*.

POST-MORTA ON *RIVERDANCE*

Post-Eurovision, most critiques, even Courtney's controversial piece, referred to above, were effusive in their praise of the actual *Riverdance* performance, for example (Corr, 1994):

> This year, *Riverdance* came to represent all things to all Irishmen and Irishwomen. Could it be the unofficial national anthem? Well why not, considering some of the claims made on behalf of the piece's potency? It stemmed the Great Irish Diaspora, embracing our ethnic communities, worldwide; it has done more for national pride than a generation of political leaders; and it might even settle the national debt!

Theater producer Cameron Mackintosh, the main guiding force behind the transfer of *Les Miserables* and *Miss Saigon* from London's West End to Broadway, has stamped his imprimatur on *Riverdance* (Corr, 1994), hailing it as:

> One of the most exciting mixtures of folk dance and music combined with Broadway pizazz I have ever seen.

Riverdance's popularity has been reflected in audio and video sales of the Eurovision performance. Immediately on its release, soon after Eurovision, *Riverdance* became the best-selling single in Ireland for 18 weeks and, up to year-end, it had been charted in the "top 30" ratings continuously for 33 weeks during 1994. Following the end of year presentation of *Riverdance* at the Royal Command Performance in London, it reached the no. 17 position in the U.K. singles' rankings at the beginning of 1995, having entered the charts a few weeks before Christmas. It was broadcast on *Top of the Pops* on BBC1 television, on January 12, 1995, charted as no. 13. It attained its highest position, no. 9, on February 2, and was still ranked no. 14 on February 16. All proceeds from video sales were donated to Irish Rwanda Relief.

ADVERSARIAL COMMENTS ON *RIVERDANCE*

Not all observers responded enthusiastically to *Riverdance* (Courtney, 1994):

> I've had *Riverdance* up to my neck. There has been a deluge of wildly sycophantic articles discussing the possible ripple effects of *Riverdance* on Irish dancing in particular, and Irish culture in general. If the papers, including the *Irish Times*, were to be believed, *Riverdance* had dragged a once-staid art form kicking and screaming into the modern world. Might I respectfully suggest that *Riverdance* has also shoved Irish dancing, unceremoniously, into the realm of showbiz? Nobody could possibly have been thinking, while watching the piece, that they were witnessing a seismic event in Irish cultural history, could they? Nobody sat there, dizzy from watching Michael Flatley's startling dance routine and shouted: "All is changed, changed utterly!" I suspect all that came later, when the scribes sat down and dampened their quills for the big cultural rewrite. Don't get me wrong, *Riverdance* is an excellent piece which is well written, well choreographed and perfectly paced, with a superbly executed climax. It's a fine piece of popular entertainment, and certainly deserves its place in modern Irish culture. It's certainly a lot better than "Rock 'n Roll Kids" (Eurovision winner).
>
> But let's get our feet back on the ground, here. Just because something is well performed—and *Riverdance* is among the best performances you'll see in any genre this year—doesn't mean we should adopt it as some national symbol of artistry freedom, a metaphor for a changing vision of Ireland at the millennium's close. It's Irish dancing with a dash of Broadway, or Broadway with a dash of Irish dancing, and it's done as well as you would expect from two of the finest professionals in the business. Irish- Americans Flatley and Butler have not returned to Ireland to find their roots, but to borrow a piece of national history and incorporate it into a clever dance routine. They haven't exactly plundered our heritage, but neither do they advance it. They are slick, professional, showy and hugely talented, but with a marked showbiz streak.

EXHIBIT 3   *Riverdance* **Reviews**

Extracts in *The Sunday Times* advertisement, June 25, 1995 for Labatt's Apollo
Theatre, Hammersmith. "Returning by Enormous Demand from October 3
for 3 weeks only."

"Thrilling—intoxicating—it succeeds triumphantly."

Financial Times

"Dance does not often get so good."

The Guardian

"Electifying—a spectacular success. Routines of impossible syncopation and
irresistible rhythm. All you can do is surrender to the primeval urge and
scream and shout."

Mail on Sunday

"The audience roars its approval."

Observer

RIVERDANCE'S ACCEPTABILITY TO THE TRADITIONAL IRISH DANCING FRATERNITY

Post-*Riverdance*, a major controversy arose regarding the challenges it posed for traditional Irish dancing (see Exhibit 3).[3]

Toward the end of the last century, dancing had become an increasingly important component of Irish folk culture as a result of popularization of nationalist traditions with the "Gaelic revival," but this particular indigenous art form had been developing in an unorganized, nonregulated manner (see Exhibit 4). In 1929, Conradh na Gaeilge (the Gaelic League), which had been responsible for much of the earlier cultural renaissance, established Coimisiun le Rinci Gaelacha (the Irish Dance Commission), to regulate the then "lawless" Irish dance world. This organization laid down strict rules in relation to teaching practices and standards. It is now the controlling body in regard to all official Irish dancing championships and it has more than 700 dance teachers, not just in Ireland but in North America, Britain, and Australasia where there are many major events among the global ethnic communities. Each year, the Coimisiun organizes the World Championships in Irish dancing, with competitions extending over more than a week. Although the Coimisiun is the only organization controlling and promoting Irish dancing worldwide, another body, Comhdhail Muinteoiri na Rinci Gaelacha (the Association of Irish Dance Teachers), has existed since 1969 as a result of an acrimonious teacher-led rift within the Coimisiun. By comparison with the latter organization, the Comhdhail's membership is confined mostly to Ireland. Among the Irish dancing fraternity there were divided opinions on aspects of the staging of *Riverdance*, even if the artistry of the Eurovision spectacle was acclaimed, generally.

---

[3]For an account of the evolution of Irish dancing and of its role in the indigenous (folk) culture, readers are referred to the author's background note to *Riverdance*, entitled *Irish Dance* (O'Cinneide, 1995).

EXHIBIT 4

The Arts Council, Dublin, recently published *The Public and the Arts—A Survey of Behaviour and Attitudes in Ireland,* which provides data comparative to their last attitudinal survey carried out twelve years ago. The intervening period was one that coincided with the demise of both the Irish National Ballet and the Dublin Contemporary Dance Theatre. It was also the period where the dance portfolio within the Arts Council was increasingly eroded, witnessed by the fact that, for the past five years, there has been no dance officer in the Arts Council itself.

Is it any wonder, then, that this unhealthy state of affairs is reflected in public attitudes? According to the survey of all the arts disciplines:

> Only one art form, that of dance, shows no growth in attendance between 1981 and 1994. It seems clear from the attendance figures, and from the attitudes and priorities of the public, that dance is barely present on the public arts agenda.

There is, of course, a final element to be addressed, that of the response of the dance community, and of individual dancers, choreographers et al. I would suggest that the recent performance of *Riverdance* is a useful paradigm for the current situation. The public loved it, raved about it, were proud of it. The theatre dance purists pooh-poohed the simplistic notion that simply dressing, long-legged Irish dancers in short black numbers and long wigs was doing anything for dance in Ireland. But was this not an example of dance addressing "the continuing market failure"? If getting dance onto the public agenda is to be achieved, it looks like we need all the legs we can get!

Source: Emer McNamara, "Dancing on Thin Ice," *Dance News Ireland*, Winter 1994, p. 12.

GALA EVENTS AS SPRINGBOARDS FOR ARTISTIC/CULTURAL PROMOTION

In seeking some explanation for what has transpired following the Point Theatre performance, it is interesting to note that in recent times, at globally screened events such as the World Cup Finals (*Italia 90,* for example), and the 1992 Barcelona Olympic Games, host nations have introduced indigenous forms of the performing arts which have tried to illustrate features of their countries' cultures, for example, the much extolled performance by Jose Carreras, Placido Domingo, and Luciano Pavarotti on July 7, 1990 to celebrate the World Cup Finals in Rome.

With TV mega events, such as *Italia 90,* the producers have devised attractive settings and presentations for the specially commissioned items, and the involvement of "super star" performers is, undoubtedly, an attempt to ensure that the mass audience will find the theatrical piece appealing, thereby providing a form of risk insurance, as it were, for the novelty of the presentation. It could be said that in such instances, perhaps, the "halo effect" of television operates, whereby the medium is so powerful that audiences can come to accept that if a star performer is involved, the artistic piece itself must be high caliber!

Strategy literature indicates that two broad categories of stimulatory infuences, "push" and "pull" factors, can be the inspiration for initiating ventures. In the case of the *Seville Suite* production, it was an instance, undoubtedly, of the push factors at play, since the Irish government was committed to presenting an appealing national image to the world, but more particularly to a Spanish audience. The fact that Ireland had hosted a song contest in Millstreet the preceding year could have been another push feature relating to the conception of *Riverdance*. There was an obvious challenge to produce an innovative intermission piece, the second time around.

Although there have been many instances of new ventures being developed from push influences, there is general agreement among the marketing fraternity that pull factors emanating from the marketplace are the most likely to lead to traditional business success. Responding to the pull factors of the market is the philosophy underlying one of marketing's basic tenets, the marketing concept, which extols customer orientation, as distinct from doing what is considered best from the producer's viewpoint.

Usually, however, the organizers of major events such as *Italia 90* do not undertake market research to discover customer preferences and do not seem to have availed of opportunities to pretest the prospective product with sample audiences. So it might be claimed, justifiably, that the push orientation normally predominates, often with the rationale that little is really known about the "dark side" of performing arts—the pull (demand) factors.[4]

The World Cup Finals "musical intermission" spawned a series of highly successful operatic audio and video recordings. The audio recording of what has become known as *The 3 Tenors in Concert* has popularized the talents of Carreras, Domingo, and Pavarotti to an unprecedented level, with the *Italia 90* performance becoming the world's number one classical best-seller, attaining sales of over 12 million. This was followed by a highly successful companion *3 Tenors* album, which by year-end 1994 had sold 7 million copies.

ENTREPRENEURSHIP IN THE ARTS: ART OR ENTREPRENEURSHIP?

Riverdance provokes questions on the application of entrepreneurship principles to cultural/art forms, and consideration of topics such as *"Entrepreneurship in the Arts"*: *Is it more a matter of Art rather than Entrepreneurship?* where "Art" is considered to be a surrogate for creativity/artistic talent. This could lead to an analysis of attempts, in recent times, by many nations to preserve and develop unique aspects of their culture, in particular efforts to introduce (perhaps to "invent" even), new indigenous forms of the performing arts illustrating features of their countries' cultures. An additional discussion point raised by *Riverdance* is the evolution of new cultural products, and the figurative tightrope that has to be walked by the arts/culture sector when developing new enterprises. While maximum commercial success must be sought for new products, this must not be at the expense of artistic values which can be demeaned by mass market over-exploitation.

---

[4]The difficulties of pretesting gala performances, intended as one-time spectacular events can be understood. However, in the case of traditional theater, it is quite common for new productions to be tested first, "in the provinces" or, as our American colleagues might say, "off-Broadway," before bringing the final versions to the major venues, for example in the West End.

RTE'S INNOVATION CAPABILITIES

The Eurovision Song Contest provided the canvas, as it were, from which *Riverdance* could emerge as an original artistic creation. The ability of a small public broadcasting station to take on the world's giants in the field of gala television is one of the kernel issues, since the reported TV audience for Eurovision is in the region of 300 million. But how can RTE best balance its need to look for new initiatives against the widely accepted maxim "you should stick to your knitting" (see Peters & Waterman, *In Search of Excellence*), and avoid veering too far from its core business?

To what extent might Moya Doherty be classified as an entrepreneur, as distinct from being a creative TV producer? Is there evidence that she had a carefully thought-through approach to creation of the 1994 television spectacular, particularly in relation to risk taking, or was she merely a fortunate opportunist, "in the right place, at the right time"?

FUTURE SCENARIO FOR *RIVERDANCE?*

Several interested parties need to assess the prospects for expanding the *Riverdance* concept. Likely interested individuals and groups include the original principals involved in the Eurovision presentation: Moya Doherty, Bill Whelan (composer), the U.S. dancers, Anuna, and, of course, RTE.

Prospective long-term development of *Riverdance* begs the question:

> Is it possible for an Irish cultural presentation (managed and controlled by Irish interests) to challenge the international market leaders?

Combined together, the original players in the development of *Riverdance*, including the largest stakeholder, RTE, must be considered to be a "minnow" in world entertainment terms. So what strategies can the Irish interests develop in their search for international success? Can they dare to mount a major challenge to well-financed and highly promoted theatrical productions on Broadway and in London's West End? To what degree should the *Riverdance* promoters consider, in this regard, the significance of the Great Irish Diaspora (estimated to number over 70 million, worldwide).

REFERENCES

Battersby, Eileen. "Mother of *Riverdance*," *Irish Times*, February 9, 1995.

Breathnach, Breandan. *Dancing in Ireland*, Dal gCais Publications (in association with the Folklore and Folk Music Society of Clare), 1983, p. 11.

Corr, Alan. "*Riverdance*—The Musical," *RTE Guide*, December 30, 1994, pp. 8–9.

Courtney, Kevin. "Go Jump in the Lake, *Riverdance*," in the Second Opinion column, *Irish Times*, December 20, 1994.

Jackson, Joe. Anuna: *Riverdance's* River of Sound," *Irish Times*, December 23, 1994.

O'Cinneide, Barra. "Noel C. Duggan—The Best Is Yet to Come?" paper presented at European Foundation for Management Development Case Development Workshop, Paris, September 1993; published also at the European Case Clearing House, Cranfield, U.K., with Teaching Note (393-144-1/8).

O'Cinneide, Barra. "Irish Dance," background note to *Riverdance* case study, University of Limerick, March 1995.

CASE 16
SHOPPING AT THE BURJUMAN CENTER
THE CASE OF A SHADY BUYER

A beautiful lady came into the French Gallery, a small specialty shop located in a large mall in the United Arab Emirates (U.A.E.). The store sells colognes, cosmetics, jewelry, watches, sunglasses, and gift items for men and women. There are five employees working at any one time in the shop. Both men and women are employed as retail clerks in the store. Sales representatives from cosmetic and perfume companies also work in the shop on a varying schedule. Most of these representatives work between one and three days per week. A few representatives work every day but Friday. Friday is honored as a Holy Day, although retail stores stay open in the U.A.E. on Fridays since most people are off work. The sales representative's wages are shared by the local distributors and the retail store.

A salesman, Mr. Ali, believed he saw a female shopper put something under her jacket, but he was not positive. He told the store manager, Mr. Faheem, about the incident. A couple of weeks later, the same woman returned to the store. This time the salesman immediately alerted the manager. Mr. Faheem and Mr. Ali both watched her. She didn't notice. She tried on various sunglasses. She picked up three at a time to try on instead of trying them on individually. She slipped some pairs of sunglasses into her purse. When the store manager, Mr. Faheem, and the salesman, Mr. Ali, approached her and accused her of stealing, she started crying. Then she proceeded to accuse Mr. Ali of sexual harassment in a screaming voice. She said he accused her of stealing because she refused his advances. When Mr. Faheem attempted to detain her until the police arrived, she darted to another entrance. The store manager did not want to create a scene by chasing the woman in front of the customers. This would have created a negative image for the store because it is against the culture as well as the religious norms of the Middle East to physically restrain a woman. The manager ran to the door and locked it in time. The mall security arrived within a matter of minutes and waited for the police. The customers continued to shop. The door was locked so they couldn't leave anyway. This incident happened on Friday, the busiest day of the week for the store. There were fewer employees working that day because some of the cosmetic and perfume company sales representatives were off.

When the police came, they discovered that the suspected shoplifter was a woman, so they went back to the station and returned with a female police officer. After they completed the initial investigation at the store, the officers took the

Note: Fictional names have been used in the case. This real incident occurred at a trading company in Saudi Arabia in 1993. This case is intended as a basis for class discussion rather than to illustrate either effective or ineffective handling of an administrative situation.
Source: This case was written by Dianne H. B. Welsh and Ibrahim Al-Fahim, both of Eastern Washington University, USA.

suspected shoplifter back to the station. She vehemently denied stealing any sunglasses even though Mr. Faheem and Mr. Ali had taken them out of her purse. The police officer searched her purse at the station. He found another pair of sunglasses with the French Gallery price tag on them, a two-week tourist visa, and a passport from Lebanon. The police later searched her hotel room and found more stolen property. The woman was convicted of theft and sentenced to three months in jail. After serving her time, she was sent back to Lebanon.

Later, she was identified as part of an organized crime ring. The ring hired beautiful women with tourist visas to steal. In the Middle Eastern countries where Islam is the predominant religion it is against the culture as well as the religious norms for a woman to be stopped or held. They leave the country with a large amount of stolen goods when their visas are up. There are many of these rings operating now.

Note.   Security devices are seldom used in the U.A.E. because most people consider it offensive to be monitored for theft. Compared to most western countries, shoplifting and other misdemeanor thefts are relatively infrequent. However, in recent years theft has become more common. Retailers are beginning to explore options available to reduce shoplifting and employee theft.

CASE 17
TAŠKY HUCEK

THE ORIGIN OF A BUSINESS CONCEPT

Greg Hucek's eyes glazed over as he lunched with his father and a friend in a warm restaurant in Vienna, the city from which his dad had originally emigrated to America. Young Hucek was musing over what he had done over the past few years and what he might do over the next few. Across the table, a jovial family friend spoke in German punctuated by the exaggerated facial and hand gestures common among Viennese, about how he had successfully expanded his Austrian chain of home centers into Hungary. Hucek had been interested in moving to Europe and now saw the transitional economies in East Central Europe as a new frontier for entrepreneurs with determination and resourcefulness.

For two years after graduating in 1984 from Emory University in Atlanta with a bachelor's degree in history, he opted for the secure environment of a job in his grandfather's real estate business in Baltimore. He then found the self-confidence to follow his heart into a career in the fashion industry which had long been one of his interests. He moved to New York and took a production management job in a clothing firm to learn the ins and outs of the business. After a year and a half, using savings and some of an inheritance he had recently received, he started his own company designing and manufacturing a line of women's clothing. After several missteps and losing a large amount of money, he closed down the business, believing he had learned a lot about what not to do in starting and running a business. He later reminisced, "After that I took six months off. I was really bummed out. I couldn't decide what I wanted to do next. It was an emotional setback because I had put so much into it. I was 26 when I started the business and I had all my energy. I had everything: I was positive, I was sharp, I knew what I wanted and I was doing it. When all that vanishes in front of your eyes, you really grow up, mature, and learn about yourself, when you have a failure like that."

The clinking of dessert dishes by the Viennese waiter "Meine Herren, Ihre Nachspeise," brought Hucek back to the conversation with his father and their Austrian friend. They were now discussing the Czech Republic, which is in central Europe between Austria, Germany, Poland, and Slovakia. The friend explained how, until the autumn of 1989, this country had been communist and all legal businesses were owned by the national government and directed by several layers of bureaucrats. Now the Czech Republic was in transition from a planned economy to a market economy in which the state enterprises were to be largely privatized or closed and in which an ever increasing number of new entrepreneurs were creating new businesses to help take up the slack. Under communism people had grown

Source: This case was written by Charles Wankel of St. John's University, USA and Robert DeFillippi of Suffolk University, USA. Copyright ©1996 by Charles Wankel and Robert DeFillippi. This case is intended as a basis for class discussion rather than to illustrate either effective or ineffective handling of an administrative situation.

accustomed to providing and receiving indifferent and often poor service. Wages were low and did not vary with the quality of one's work or with the level of customer satisfaction. Products and services were offered in very limited styles and typically only with a set of standard features. Western products were infrequently on the market. Listening, it became clear to Hucek what career move to make next. He decided he would go to Prague, the capital and largest city in the Czech Republic, and seek out business opportunities. Although his father was originally from Austria, his surname was a legacy of a Czech great-great-grandfather who had moved in the last century to Vienna. He saw this connection as a good omen.

Prague is a thousand-year-old city replete with ancient architecture, art, and legends. It is alluring, beautiful, and yet relatively inexpensive for the legions of American and West European youths who flock to the newly liberated city. Hucek spent his first two months in Prague looking for a favorable market niche that he might profitably exploit. He was uncertain what problems he might encounter in setting up a business there. He purchased an apartment building that had street-level commercial space and which would provide a place to live, as well as being a promising real estate investment. This enabled him to put what remained of an inheritance into "something concrete." Half of the loan was financed by an American friend and was to be repaid from the revenues generated from tenant rent over the next four years. So, in early 1992, Hucek moved into the top floor apartment of the largely residential six-story apartment building he had purchased, a short distance from Wenceslas Square, Prague's shopping hub. After his New York experience, he wanted to start a business that was not capital intensive and whose growth would be predicated on his own sweat. As he explained, "I would be counting on myself."

Keeping his eyes open for a business opportunity, Hucek noticed that upscale stores in Prague used prosaic, even unattractive, plastic bags for packaging customer purchases. He saw it as incongruous that customers who bought expensive dresses and suits had them shoved in cheap plastic bags. He thought that the showy type of laminated paper bags used in quality shops from New York to Honolulu to Paris would soon be demanded and used by Prague stores to help them frame world-class quality images. Also, his uncle was in the bag business in Vienna and could provide him with any needed technical advice.

BUSINESS START-UP

In an effort to get his footing in this new environment, he went to the American consulate. His parents had suggested that the consulate would provide great contacts and invite him to many exclusive embassy functions. His parents' image of the American community in Prague was something akin to the chummy upscale foreign group hanging out in Rick's Place in *Casablanca*. Hucek arrived at the consulate, went past the marine on duty, and told the receptionist that he would like to meet with one of the consuls to get information on doing business in the Czech Republic and some useful contacts. As the receptionist phoned upstairs, Hucek assumed she was informing one of the economic attachés that

Hucek would be right up. Indeed, she then informed Hucek that everything was OK and that he would have to wait but a minute. After about five or ten minutes a clerk came down to the reception area with about forty photocopied pages of information which he swiftly handed to Hucek. That was it. Hucek related that "I didn't have the expectation that they set you up in business. However, this certainly deflated the vision of support that my parents had communicated to me." The material turned out to include some stimulating and useful items, though. Hucek was particularly intrigued by a five-page essay that presented one person's ideas on doing business in, what was then, Czechoslovakia. A list of English-speaking lawyers was also provided. All told, it was not a panacea for the many problems that embroiled an American entrepreneur in Prague.

Hucek's legal fees for getting his business going came to be about $700. Combining his living space and office enabled considerable tax deductions.

Very little equipment was required to run the bag supply business. Hucek considered his telephone and fax machine to be his key items. He had a computer but did not seem to see that as critical, off-handedly mentioning in August 1992 that "I had gotten it before coming to Prague." However, as the business grew, he found it more important and useful.

He said that his business did not require much previous knowledge. You had to understand color printing enough to deal with printers and to help explain technical requirements to customers. Also, a knowledge of manufacturers' offerings was needed.

Hucek came to the Czech Republic with no knowledge of the Czech language. He hired a 17-year-old woman in 1992 to assist him in interacting with customers and other business contacts. By the Spring of 1994 he was able to converse well in Czech, though still short of fluency, so he continued to use an assistant for interpretation. His first assistant had spent some time in the United States and Hucek said she understood American thinking and actions. "I do not pay a U.S. salary, but a good wage by local comparison. Wages are going up because there is a shortage of labor. 3,000 crowns [$120] per month is not a high salary, as it used to be." She left the firm in August 1993 to work with her fiancé in a new business he had started.

Hucek had also hired a second full-time employee to assist with the business phone calls and office work. However, the young woman left after two months for a better employment opportunity. "It's very hard to find good people. Unemployment is below one percent in Prague. No one is desperate for a job in this city. It is hard to find and keep anyone who is any good. Many of the young people I interview are not well groomed. They slouch and they don't look at you when they shake your hand. Some display shocking manners for an interview. But without experience in a market economy, these young people just don't know any better."

Hucek found the experience of day-to-day living in the Czech Republic was quite different than living in New York, Baltimore, and Atlanta had been. Relations among and with Czech people were often more formal and conducted with different rules and expectations. Many people still maintained some of the gruffness that almost a half century of socialism had engendered. "You say *dobrý den* [good day] and they just don't even react to you. You can look them right in the face, walk up, and say *dobrý den* and they ignore you completely. And that's very surprising. You run into that a lot. You can go into stores, and they are really rude and such. Mostly in state shops, but even in some private stores, they are still not customer-oriented. They still come to you without a smile, like you are intruding in their space because you walked into their store. This is still pretty prevalent here." Hucek said it was almost startling to encounter good service, saying "I went to an eyeglass shop today. This lady was astoundingly friendly. She came up and said, '*Dobrý den*, how can I help you?' and smiled. I mean just something so simple is rare." Good service was increasingly found in Czech enterprises and some run by foreigners, such as Prague's McDonald's restaurants, but overcoming the legacy of socialist disincentives took time.

In the nascent business climate of the Czech Republic, obtaining payment from customers could be problematic. Even in 1995, the commercial code had not been fully developed and the courts were perceived to be clogged with several years' backlog of lawsuits. Evaluating the creditworthiness of potential customers was problematic given the brief life of all private firms. Like many other businesspeople in the Czech Republic, Hucek required either a letter of credit or payment in full in advance. Needless to say, he had lost some potential customers due to these requirements. In 1993 it became illegal in the Czech Republic to demand payment in cash. However, when dealing with potentially troublesome customers there were ways for suppliers to use loopholes in the law to protect themselves.

Hucek had some particularly difficult times in implementing customer sales through intermediary agents. In one instance, an advertising agency had ordered a large quantity of laminated paper bags with a colorfully drawn map of a golf course for promotional distribution at an important golf tournament in an ancient spa town across the border in Germany. When the bags were delivered, the agency's head (Mr. B.) was outraged to notice that on the outside bottom of the bags was imprinted Hucek's logo, which was approximately three square centimeters in size. It featured a shopping bag with "Tašky Hucek" on it, below which was printed "Praha" (Prague) and a phone number. The right to imprint this logo had been one of only four prominently listed points in the straightforward business contract used by Hucek and signed by one of Mr. B.'s junior associates. This unfortunate fellow was fired on the spot by Mr. B. for having signed a contract with such a clause in it. Mr. B. contacted Hucek and demanded a 30 percent discount because of the inclusion of the Hucek identification on the bag. Hucek refused to grant this. Sensing that Mr. B. might seek to avoid payment after the bags were in his possession, Hucek told Mr. B. that full payment in cash would be required at the time of delivery. Mr. B. rejected that, citing a recently enacted Czech law on payments in business transactions: "You can't force me to pay cash. So I can't pay cash. It's against Czech law!" Hucek responded: "You're right. I can't force you and I'm not forcing you. But I'm saying if you would like the bags tomorrow, you can get cash. There's no law saying you can't go to the bank and get cash if you want it." After 45 minutes of heated conversation, Mr. B. agreed to pay the originally contracted price in cash the next day.

When Hucek arrived at the agency's office the next day to deliver the bags for the imminent golf tournament and receive payment, he was met by a young female employee who accepted the shipment. Hucek noticed that one man who appeared to be the agency director with whom he had argued on the phone was working at a nearby desk and acted totally oblivious to Hucek's presence. Hucek went over and said "Mr. B., I'm sorry that we had this problem but I think . . ." At this point, Mr. B. interrupted Hucek, saying, "If you have anything to say, say it to Mr. C. [an employee of the agency]. Do you know what we are going to do this weekend, Mr. Hucek? I've ordered stickers with my agency's name on them and we are going to put our stickers on all of your bags to conceal your logo. Do you think for a minute that we're going to give these bags out at the tournament with your name on them?"

Some months later Hucek reflected on the incident: "I suppose all the hostility was because Mr. B. was the middleman for the golf tournament. Mr. B. wanted people to call him for bags in the future and not call me. It seems that middlemen in this country want their fingers in everybody's pie. That advertising agency doesn't think of itself as an agency providing a specialized service for their clients, such as the best advertising. Here in the Czech Republic, such a business doesn't concentrate on doing one thing well and getting a good reputation for its expertise. Instead, it looks for opportunities to make profit any way it can. Doing business in the Czech Republic is a kind of free-for-all where everybody is stepping on everybody else. The business courtesies that we are used to in the United States are not prevalent here."

RELATIONS WITH SUPPLIERS IN ITALY AND SLOVAKIA

After considering many of Europe's bag suppliers, Hucek decided to purchase upscale laminated paper shopping bags from GPS, a well-regarded Italy-based manufacturer with distributors in most West European nations. He decided to acquire inexpensive plastic bags from a Slovak firm. Although Slovakia had become independent of the Czech Republic, goods still went across the border with the Czech Republic duty-free. Thus, a Slovak supplier was equivalent to a Czech one with respect to the lack of import duties. Hucek's company Tasky Hucek became GPS's exclusive distributor in the Czech Republic. He wanted to distribute the gamut of bags: whatever a customer might desire, from inexpensive to pricey. Since he was initially working out of his apartment he had the bags come first to a shipping agent where they sat a few days. Hucek then selected a few samples from the shipment. Next he judged whether they were done properly and, finally, arranged to have them delivered to the customer's address.

Although Hucek was generally satisfied with his sources of supply, he experienced some difficulties with a Slovak supplier of plastic bags. Once a customer rightly complained about a printing error of a black bar on 30 percent of the bags in one order produced by that supplier. Hucek agreed not to charge the customer for the misprinted bags. However, when Hucek attempted to obtain a similar credit from the Slovak bag firm he was offered only half the cost of the misprinted bags.

A second area of difficulty with this supplier concerned price quotations. The supplier only provided Hucek with a partial price list. Hucek would frequently have to phone the supplier to obtain prices of sizes or items not included on the price list. Sometimes, this supplier would take up to three days to respond to Hucek's request for a price quotation, which once resulted in the loss of a customer for Hucek. On other occasions, the Slovak supplier would quote one price to Hucek over the phone but then, after Hucek submitted an order, demand a higher price. Hucek might have already negotiated a price with his own customers based on the supplier's original price quotation and would have to stand by it.

A third area of difficulty that Hucek had with the Slovak supplier was in the timeliness of delivery. Once, a major customer who had already paid a 50 percent deposit to Hucek complained of nondelivery of the bags. When Hucek phoned the supplier, the person with whom he spoke there assured him that the order had been sent. One week later, the customer still had not received delivery. When Hucek phoned back the supplier, he was informed that there had been a mix-up and the bags had yet to be shipped to Hucek's customer.

Hucek summarized his dilemmas with his Slovak supplier: "I want to go to a long-term supplier relationship. I currently give them all my plastic bag business. They have good quality and I'm happy with their prices. However, I cannot afford to continue my business with them if these problems continue. I have to decide if I can persuade them to change their methods of business practice or if I should simply take my business elsewhere."

ESTABLISHING A CUSTOMER BASE AND CUSTOMER RELATIONS

Hucek's business grew steadily, though not as quickly as he had anticipated. He placed an advertisement in the classified pages of the Prague telephone book. He landed a few important accounts. One was the Dům Elegance store. This had been considered the most fashionable store in Prague for many years, but had become somewhat lax in its merchandising. A large British real estate firm bought it along with its building and placed a tremendously large order for Hucek's bags in August 1992, seemingly enough to last it for eight years. This unusual over-ordering apparently was indicative of other management decisions, however, and in June 1993 the store folded. However, the liquidation of Dům Elegance occurred after the store had made payment on six years' worth of Hucek's bags.

A key Hucek strategy was to convince department stores to switch from plastic bags to paper ones. Accordingly, he targeted five department stores in particular. He had early success with only one, the Maj department store. Hucek characterized the purchasing practices of the five department stores as follows, "All they see is the price and they do not think about image and how it is perceived." Maj decided upon a pleasant paper bag that cost them about 6 crowns [25 cents]. Although this was not considered very expensive by Hucek, it was four times more than they had been paying. Hucek calculated his prices by simply adding a 40 percent markup. Unfortunately Kmart, an American department store chain, purchased the Maj in 1993 and the new owner did not think that upscale shopping bags were needed.

Marketing knowledge was at a very low level in the Czech Republic. Indeed, it was the rare Czech manager who had read or taken courses in marketing. During the four decades of communism shops were owned by the state, consumer goods were relatively scarce, and people generally purchased whatever was available when things of interest appeared on the market. Prices tended to be very low which also encouraged such distortions in buying and selling. Thus, in an economy in which goods were rationed by scarcity rather than price, building a quality image was something alien to business. However, as marketing sophistication developed in the Czech Republic, Hucek's quality bags might be more in demand.

Hucek was patient. He explained, "It is going OK, but I guess like any entrepreneur I wish it would go faster. But it's going to take a while before all those stores start to see that these plastic bags are really so ubiquitous that they really should have something a little nicer, especially the nicer stores." However, in 1993, many upscale stores still did not see any benefit in upscale bags. As Hucek observed, "As a matter of fact, I went into this expensive men's store, men's suits and the like, and I thought for sure that they would have at least some interest in a nicer paper bag. And they had absolutely none. They had black plastic bags with an ad printed just on one side, which is what most of the Czech companies print, just on one side. You're really paying for a bag and getting half the advertising. They just weren't interested. It just takes time."

OPTIONS

Hucek hoped his bag business would be a steppingstone. "Ideally, I would like to spend a few years developing this business and when it does very well—well enough to make a decent living—maybe other opportunities will open for something, another business. I will see. I always have a lot of other ideas but I am not going to spread myself out too thinly."

Greg was in the process of reassessing his original strategy of depending upon large Czech department stores as the primary customer base for his upscale shopping bags. "The large department stores around Prague are not upscale enough to be interested in our Italian supplier's high-quality paper bags. There is simply not enough demand at these large stores. Our large department stores are not like Nordstrom's or Bloomingdale's in the United States, where our paper bags would be more in demand by their fashion-conscious clientele."

However, a newly emerging market niche suggested a potential opportunity for upscale shopping bags. Greg had begun to observe the proliferation of smaller boutique shops around Prague. These specialty shops, selling a limited line of clothing apparel or cosmetics, included a growing number of branches of Western companies with well-established brand names and upscale quality reputations. Christian Dior had sold its wares in Prague long before the 1989 revolution. Lancôme and Nina Ricci boutiques had opened shortly after the 1989 events, and Elizabeth Arden debuted in 1992. More recent entries included Guerlain boutiques and Estée Lauder. The smaller size and scale of operation of such boutiques prohibited the opportunity for large bulk orders (25,000 bags annually) that Hucek had received from Dům Elegance and the Maj department store. Greg estimated that each of the Prague specialty boutique stores would require no more than between 2,000 to 5,000 bags annually for their customer needs. Moreover, these stores had exceedingly high quality and on-time delivery requirements.

A second trend Greg observed in Prague was an increasing number of industrial trade shows, at which both Czech and foreign firms displayed their wares through exhibition booths and promotional displays. It occurred to Greg that his paper bag designs might complement each exhibitor's overall promotion displays. Although the anticipated direct sales to trade show exhibitors was modest (less than several hundred per exhibitor per show), the promotion of the Greg Hucek/GPS trademark might well result in useful leads for follow-up sales to exhibitors and to trade show attendees, who included retailers and wholesalers of the goods and services being promoted at the exhibit.

In 1995, Hucek still had no competitors in the top market niche of upscale, stylish bags. Greg found his plastic bags represented approximately 50 percent of Tašky Hucek's annual sales but contributed only 25 percent to the firm's net profits. Moreover, Greg was concerned that the low-quality, commodity nature of the plastic bag market, compounded by the poor quality and on-time unreliability of his own plastic bag supplier, would undermine the upscale, quality image Greg was attempting to build for Tašky Hucek.

By contrast, the upscale paper bag segment of Tašky Hucek's product line was still an emerging market. This was most helpful to his enterprise. In the fall of 1993, Tašky Hucek still had no competitors in the top market niche of upscale, stylish bags. However, sales in this segment were more uncertain and of lower volume. To solicit prospective buyers among the boutique specialty shops required personal contacts and the offer of sample bags demonstrating the quality and fashion appeal of Tašky Hucek. Such relationship building would take time and energy and each small-volume sale would have to be repeated over many boutiques in order to realize sales volumes comparable to a single department store order for more conventional plastic bags. However, at least the shopping bag buyers in the boutique stores were not purchasing agents who viewed bags as a commodity, cost item. The buyers in this segment were fashion-conscious, entrepreneur/managers who needed to be convinced that the Tašky Hucek shopping bag was an aesthetically appropriate complement to the fashionable goods sold at their boutiques.

Although Greg considered the risks of the upscale paper bag market to be considerable, he was additionally drawn to paper bags as an environmentally superior business option. "I personally want my business to emphasize the ecological benefits of paper bags in our country. As the Czech Republic seeks to enter the European Union, the Czech Republic will have to develop an environmental consciousness similar to that of Western Europe. My business is one example of such environmental consciousness and I would like to develop advertising materials that promote the environmental advantages of paper bags as well as the higher quality of Tašky Hucek paper bags."

VI Cross-Border Finance Issues

CASE SUMMARIES

CASE 18:   CAROLINA FURNITURE COMPANY

By A. Qayyum Khan (University of North Carolina at Charlotte, USA)

Thirty years after the founding of this family business, president and CEO George Fishburn, son of the founder, had expanded the firm nationwide and produced more than $42 million in sales revenue. The firm then began exporting; within two years, between 12 and 15 percent of revenue was derived from exports to Germany, Japan, and Singapore. However, Mr. Fishburn is concerned about recent transaction losses due to fluctuating exchange rates. This short case focuses on devising a financial hedging strategy to deal with the exchange rate risks of this small but expanding firm.

CASE 19:   DOKA CORPORATION: AN ENTREPRENEURIAL RUSSIAN HIGH-TECHNOLOGY VENTURE

By Mikhail Gratchev, Robert D. Hisrich (both of Case Western Reserve University, USA), Zakhar Bolshakov, Dmitri A. Popov, and Alexei B. Ilyin (all of Zelenograd Business College, Russia)

This case focuses on the development and operationalization of a Russian high-technology private venture. The basic problems are general business strategy, marketing, and development of international business in the European Community and the United States. ∎

CASE 18
CAROLINA FURNITURE COMPANY

George Fishburn, president and CEO of Carolina Furniture Company, sat leisurely in his office on a Friday afternoon reviewing the German sales figures for the second quarter of 1991. He was very pleased with his firm's exporting activities. Two years ago his company had no foreign customers and today it had several big customers in Germany, Japan, and Singapore. About 12 to 15 percent of the firm's revenues came from export sales. Although sales to Germany had dropped somewhat from the previous year, they would still amount to about $2 million in 1991. As he reviewed the figures he noticed that in one instance, the deutsche mark (DM) had declined in value from $0.6693/DM to $0.5824/DM, from the time the sale to the German customer was booked to the time the firm received payment. The decline in the value of the deutsche mark resulted in a transaction loss of almost $26,000 on an invoice of $200,000. Because export sales had a margin of 15 percent, it still left the firm with a profit of $4,000; however, George wondered if the company could afford to lose this kind of money from the vagaries of financial markets.

His thoughts began to stray as he scrutinized the numbers. He had worked hard for the past 12 years and the business had prospered under his leadership. He remembered that fall day in 1979 when he received a call from his mother at his dormitory at the University of North Carolina–Chapel Hill informing him that his father had just had a stroke and the prognosis was rather dim. He had rushed back to the family home in High Point, North Carolina. Albert Fishburn died the following week, leaving the reins of the business to his son. George Fishburn did not return to college after that, and never became the foreign correspondent for *Time* magazine that he had always wanted to be.

The Carolina Furniture Company was formed in 1958 by Albert Fishburn and his army buddy Leroy Brown. Initially, the company manufactured early American furniture that emphasized simple styles and high quality. The economic growth of the 1960s and 1970s, accompanied by an increase in home ownership, helped the company grow by leaps and bounds. By 1973, sales had grown to $5 million and total assets rose to almost $1.5 million. On the average, the firm maintained a healthy profit margin of 7 percent of sales, making the two army buddies quite affluent in a short period of time. In 1974, Leroy Brown sold his share of the business to Albert Fishburn and moved to Florida.

The initial days after his father died were difficult for George; he had to learn the furniture business and deal with the recession. For the first time in its history, Carolina Furniture Company suffered a loss in the 1981–82 fiscal year. During the next three years George learned the business and instituted major changes in the company. First, he modernized the plant with new machines which reduced

Source: This case was prepared by A. Qayyum Khan, of the University of North Carolina at Charlotte, whose cooperation is acknowledged with appreciation. This case is intended as a basis for class discussion rather than to illustrate either effective or ineffective handling of an administrative situation.

dependence on manual labor, improved productivity, and most importantly, achieved substantial cost savings. Equipment holdings were reviewed annually, and as much as possible, the firm tried to remain on top of new technology. Outdated or obsolete equipment was sold to smaller furniture manufacturers. The improved productivity increased the profit margin to 12 percent, the highest in the industry.

Second, he implemented an aggressive marketing strategy. In the past, Carolina Furniture Company had depended entirely on wholesale furniture distributors for orders. Under George's direction, the company opened its first display booth in the furniture mart at Hickory, North Carolina. This allowed the firm to be more responsive to customers and to achieve a greater market exposure. The booth was a great success. Within three years, major furniture outlets and retail chains (like J.C. Penney's) on the East Coast carried the Carolina Furniture line. In 1985, another display booth was opened in the Merchandise Mart at Dallas, Texas. The third display booth was opened in 1987 in San Francisco, California. With three display booths, the company achieved national coverage, and by 1989, annual sales had grown to $42 million.

The third major change that George instituted was the expansion of the product line. In addition to the Early American styles, the company introduced several avant-garde lines that the baby boomer generation found attractive. An in-house design team was recruited that worked closely with the marketing personnel and salespeople at the three display booth locations. Every spring the new designs were introduced and displayed in the major furniture shows and at the display booths.

In spite of these successes, George always remembered the recession of the early 80s. He recognized that the furniture business was essentially a cyclical business, and the next recession could have an adverse consequence on his business unless he diversified to new markets in other countries. The accessibility of the factory to several seaports in North Carolina and South Carolina, along with the presence of several major banks in the area, offered Carolina Furniture many advantages that domestic furniture manufacturers elsewhere did not have. In late 1988 George embarked on an export strategy. After preliminary research and consultation with bankers and the export promotion office at the North Carolina Department of Commerce, George Fishburn and Lisa Hammonds, vice president of marketing, decided that export markets should be targeted in countries that had a trade surplus with the United States and were expected to experience a faster economic growth than the United States. In June 1989, George and Lisa traveled to Germany, Japan, and Singapore to explore export markets and seek customers in those countries.

The trip was a great success. Several German retailers expressed interest, and two major furniture outlets signed firm purchase contracts worth $250,000. However, the German customers insisted that the orders be invoiced in deutsche marks. George knew that it wasn't difficult to convert deutsche marks to dollars and he readily agreed. Given the prevailing exchange rate of $0.5122/DM, he signed the sales contract for DM488,091. Delivery and payment were scheduled for the third week of September 1989. When payment was received in 1989 the deutsche mark had increased in value to $0.5353/DM, yielding an inflow of $261,275, a gain of $11,275. George was very pleased with this outcome. Economic forecasts indicated that the dollar was expected to remain weak against all major currencies. Therefore, Carolina Furniture adopted a policy of invoicing all its foreign customers in their respective currencies.

Now that the dollar had begun to strengthen, George thought the time might have come to change the denomination of the firm's export invoices. He called Lisa for her views, and she reminded him of the difficult negotiations they had experienced with Japanese and Singapore importers to agree on the denomination of the sale. A request for a change in terms, especially when the dollar was showing signs of strength, might not be acceptable to the importers and could result in a decline in orders. Lisa, therefore, felt that the denomination of the export sales should not be changed.

Allen Bradley, corporate treasurer and vice president of finance, was looking forward to some rest and relaxation over the weekend when George Fishburn called him. George was very concerned about the transaction loss from the German sale and he wanted to meet with Allen on Monday to discuss the alternatives for hedging foreign exchange transactions. The firm's bank, Nationsbank, had earlier offered its services to Carolina Furniture Company for hedging foreign exchange risk. "It just may be the time to take Nationsbank up on its offer," said George as he hung up. After he got off the phone, R&R was the last thing on Allen's mind as he began to compile the necessary information.

As Allen checked the records, he found that Carolina Furniture Company had the following foreign exchange transactions under contract. Unless these transactions were hedged, the dollar cash flow from these transactions would depend on the spot rate of the foreign currency at the time payment was received.

Germany.   A sale of DM2,000,000 to the Hamburg International Hotel which is opening for business in January 1992. Parts of this order have already been shipped. The last consignment will be shipped in the second week of October and payment will be received on November 14, 1991.

Japan.   A payment of ¥150,000,000,000 will be received from Sakado Enterprises, a large trading company in Tokyo, on September 18, 1991. The furniture against this order was shipped in the second week of August 1991.

Singapore.   1. Two hundred and fifty thousand Singapore dollars (S$) are due on November 23, 1991 from Patusan Brothers, a furniture retailer. The furniture against this invoice was shipped in the last week of July.

2. Another S$250,000 would be due from Patusan Brothers on February 17, 1992. The shipment against this invoice will be made in the last week of December 1991.

Next, Allen began outlining the alternative hedging strategies. Basically, he had two alternatives. First, he could recommend the use of forward contracts which allow the purchase or sale of foreign currencies in future periods.

International banks make forward markets in the major currencies. However, no forward contracts were available for the S$ in the United States. Forward contracts could be tailor-made with respect to amount and maturity. Typically, banks did not offer forward contracts to speculators, and preferred to deal with hedgers only. The transaction amount of forward contracts' size is usually large, a million dollars or more. If Carolina Furniture chose to use the forward market alternative, it would have to execute a short hedge (i.e., sell foreign currency forward) since it is expecting foreign currency inflows.

The second alternative would be a money market hedge. This technique is especially suitable for those currencies that do not have forward contracts. A short hedge in the money market involves borrowing the foreign currency with the same maturity as the expected inflow. The borrowed foreign currency is then converted in the spot market and usually invested in the domestic money market. Since the foreign currency loan and inflow have the same maturity, the loan is paid with the foreign currency inflow.

While reviewing this information, Allen realized that the same hedging instrument may not be suitable for all the foreign exchange transactions and a different hedging instrument may have to be used for each transaction. Therefore, the problem, as he saw it, was to find the appropriate hedging strategy for a given foreign exchange transaction.

EXHIBIT 1   CAROLINA FURNITURE COMPANY
Exchange Rates—U.S. $ Equivalent
Friday, August 16, 1991

	DM	¥	S$
Spot	$0.5824	$0.007474	$0.5748
30-day forward	0.5796	0.007470	N/A
90-day forward	0.5733	0.007454	N/A
180-day forward	0.5700	0.007435	N/A

EXHIBIT 2   CAROLINA FURNITURE COMPANY
Selected Interest Rates
Friday, August 16, 1991

	1-Month	3-Months	6-Months
United States			
Prime rate	5.70%	5.85%	5.95%
LIBOR (London)	5.55	5.70	5.80
Germany			
Prime rate	11.47	12.10	10.21
LIBOR (London)	11.32	11.95	10.06
Japan			
Prime rate	6.40	6.95	6.95
LIBOR (London)	6.19	6.75	6.75
Singapore			
Prime rate	4.67	5.23	5.58

CASE 19
DOKA CORPORATION
AN ENTREPRENEURIAL RUSSIAN HIGH-TECHNOLOGY VENTURE

Russia is a radically changing country. Russian entrepreneurship is on the leading edge of the radical economic and political transformation of society that should lead to new business developments, improved quality of life, and a decline and eventual defeat of the Mafia structures. The economic vitality of Russia rests heavily on flourishing small businesses, transformed large industrial complexes, the development of financial infrastructure, and the internationalization of present businesses. This development requires high quality of management and entrepreneurship, creative thinking, and strong business ethics.

INTRODUCTION AND BACKGROUND

Russian entrepreneurship as a phenomena is not radically different from other countries' experiences. In Russia, entrepreneurs desire economic freedom, innovations, and organizational creativity. Research indicates that the transition to a full-fledged market economy will result in an even greater diversity of entrepreneurial profiles and organizational cultures, different property forms, and a variety of corporate strategies. Not surprisingly, most Russian entrepreneurs are young, allowing a new generation to achieve economic well-being. Their business activity and business mentality have been strongly influenced by: (1) the country's historic heritage (state-centered state, multi-cultural society, and weak middle class); (2) the communist ideology; and (3) the absence of reliable business laws and market-oriented economic education. In spite of this, Russian entrepreneurs have much courage, and the ability to implement large-scale projects, to fight bureaucracy, to survive and be patient, and are also loyal personal friends.

After official acceptance of the need for economic changes for national survival and economic success in the mid-1980s and the adoption of related laws in the perestroika years, entrepreneurship in the form of cooperatives, individual labor activity, and joint ventures with foreign capital led to unprecedented growth of business activity in the former U.S.S.R. However, the absence of modern business practices and institutions resulted not only in the commodity exchange rush but also in the total breakdown of traditional economic ties. The financial speculations initiated by state-owned structures made the bankers and traders appear as super entrepreneurs in their role in economic development when compared to the industrialists.

Post-perestroika developments created a new national industrial structure. There is a fast-growing number of privatized enterprises and new start-ups, as

Source: This case was written by Mikhail Gratchev, Robert D. Hisrich, (both of Case Western Reserve University, USA) and Zakhar Bolshakov, Dmitri A. Popov, and Alexei B. Ilyin (all of Zelenograd Business College, Russia). This case is intended as a basis for class discussion rather than to illustrate either effective or ineffective handling of an administrative situation.

well as joint ventures and foreign-owned establishments. Within post-Socialist Russia in the 1990s there is emerging a new level of economic and administrative freedom, and attempts for more healthy cooperation between business companies and with the state, based on partnership and consensus in the national interests. At the same time demonopolization of the economy has facilitated the development of entrepreneurship. Contemporary economic creativity to a great extent relates to new businesses either in the start-ups, or within "incorporation by privatization" of large-scale amalgamations. Intensive networking has emerged within the entrepreneurial community. While most of the business miracles occur in trade, finance, and banking, new developments also take place in selected industries that shape the backbone of national competitiveness, such as construction, oil and gas, and aerospace. More and more private and publicly owned producers are overcoming serious economic and legal problems and benefiting from the new economy.

THE COMPANY AND LOCATION

One of the visible phenomena of such an entrepreneurial breakthrough is the fast growth of new companies in high-tech sectors of the economy, such as microelectronics, biotechnology, new materials, and software development. Doka Company, founded on May 6, 1987 in Zelenograd (Moscow), became one of the first Russian independent high-tech companies. Its founder and since that time chairman of the board and director general is Alexander Chuenko. The company was started and continues to be located in Zelenograd, a city near Moscow with a population of about 300,000 and administratively a part of Moscow city.

The characteristics of Zelenograd as a center of the microelectronics industry of the Soviet Union (the so-called Russian Silicon Valley) was its industry-related focus and special status as a closed city (restricted to foreigners) controlled by state security officials. Zelenograd satisfied 60 percent of the demand for electronic devices in the U.S.S.R and 70 percent of demand for many types of computer chips. Zelenograd's leading industrial facility, Angstrem, built the first satellite in the world, "Sputnik."

Having been founded in the late 1950s, Zelenograd for decades remained under direct control of the state and Party leaders. For a long period of time, Zelenograd was famous for its high standards of living and concentration of intellectual elite. After the breakdown of the Soviet Union and collapse of economic ties with former republics, the level of industrial production in Zelenograd dropped by more than 50 percent, thus reflecting the situation in the Russian economy in general. Having lost economic ties and many trade opportunities within the former U.S.S.R., many enterprises started seeking new international contacts. Today several Zelenograd companies have contracts with Samsung, Gold Star, IBM, and other international companies. Their experiences confirm the acceptable level of technology, quality standards, and skills required for high-tech developments.

Zelenograd itself is a technological center connecting business, production facilities, research, and higher education institutions with its Technological

University (previously known as the Moscow Institute of Electronic Engineering). The Technological University focuses on preparing highly qualified young specialists in microelectronics and is ranked among the top five engineering schools in Russia. The aggressive and ambitious graduates developed a highly competitive spirit in Zelenograd even prior to perestroika. In 1987, when the government of the Soviet Union officially permitted new forms of business entities other than state-owned enterprises, many people were ready to become entrepreneurs.

May 6, 1987 is celebrated yearly by Doka as its birthday. On this date the company was officially registered as one of the first independent R&D firms in Russia, at the very beginning of free market and private business revival in the country. This company was initiated based on the "Four Vs": volition, vitality, verve, and vigor. The founders were advanced, innovative young engineers who previously worked at state-owned enterprises. Doka was originally established as the independent "center for scientific and technical creativity of young people." This unusual form had a legal framework that allowed the company to open a banking account and act as an independent contractor. It could also establish its own guidelines in hiring people and paying individual's salaries.

This new organizational concept was totally different from the traditions of the communist state. Two years before the parliament had adopted the Law on Entrepreneurship, the first Decree was signed by the deputy prime minister allowing new independent economic firms to collaborate with the state-owned enterprises. This caused many such firms to be established by young people willing to take risks.

BUSINESS AND INVESTMENT STRATEGY

Innovations are central to the core strategy of Doka. In the current Russian high-tech environment there are many "unoccupied zones" in advancing technologies. From its start, Doka has followed a policy encouraging innovations, some of which hopefully would turn into excellent marketable products. With many new ideas and projects, Doka was in a position to launch risky initiatives.

Headquartered in Zelenograd, at the start-up Doka focused on microelectronics, applied hardware/software systems, special components, and instruments. The project groups concentrated on projects in these fields while extending their research into new multidisciplinary areas. This strategy fit well with the conditions and available experience, as well as the intellectual and industrial abilities nearby. The company had quick financial returns and further strengthened its technological position for further growth by positioning itself when there were few competitors in the market. The revenue breakdown in 1990 is indicated in Exhibit 1, with the majority of revenue coming from telecommunications and information technologies (39 percent) and financial operations (34 percent).

Doka has always had a strong strategic vision of the industry and technology development. The company saw the need for establishing reliable links in the business environment and developing effective information systems and telecommunication networks. Besides developing effective products in the telecommunications and

EXHIBIT 1   Doka's Revenue Breakdown, 1990

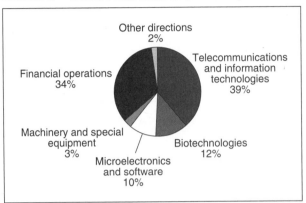

information technologies as well as in engines, the company started a project that later produced original state-of-the-art machines. In the area of high-productive virus-free agriculture plants, Doka, with a group of leading scientists in biology, algology, and chemistry, developed original biotechnology and new equipment. By investing money in other innovations similar results were achieved in pioneer investigations. These new business opportunities were approached by the company through high-tech expertise and risks were reduced through a narrowly focused strategy in the unstable Russian economy.

One area in the Russian economy needed by the entrepreneurs was a free banking system to facilitate innovations and business transactions in the new market economy. Doka helped fill the void by creating a banking system in the region of Zelenograd. Doka was one of the founders of Technopolis Innovation Bank, the first independent commercial bank in the region. This liaison made it easier for Doka to manage financial policy, develop investment strategy, and direct and administer funds more efficiently.

In 1991, Doka had an annual turnover of 247 million rubles ($6 million), with most of the key R&D projects and divisions being reorganized as business units under the Doka Group (see Exhibit 2). Doka was transformed into a multilateral business center with associated subsidiaries and affiliates. Each of these was engaged in separate and related innovative projects, with a clear level of autonomy and responsibility.

The affiliate members and spinoffs of the Doka Group maintain their relations with the parent company as well as each other. This type of alliance benefits each separate group as well as the parent company. Doka was developing into a prosperous company of R&D, manufacturing, investment, and a trade system that dealt with thousands of partners and customers in different regions of Russia, other republics in the former U.S.S.R., and Western economies. According to President Alexander Chuenko, "Business is developing fast and the numbers (sales volume)

EXHIBIT 2   **Doka's Investment Patterns**

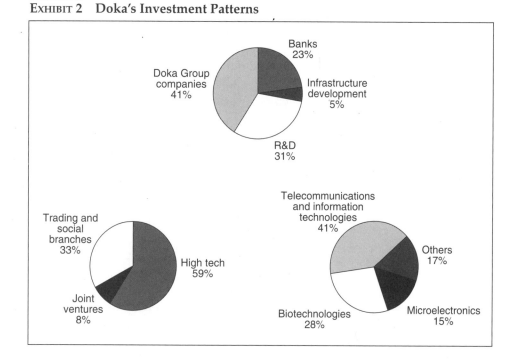

of today do not really tell the whole story about tomorrow." In 1995, Doka's sales increased, for example, in lighting equipment by 300 percent and in software by 200 percent. In addition to being one of the leading Russian software exporters, Doka is the biggest producer of virus-free potato plants in the world, with total annual production of 3,000,000 minitubers.

CURRENT LINES OF BUSINESS

In order to be successful in business in the current unstable situation in Russia, a fast-growing business like Doka has to be extremely flexible in management and coordination. Doka had to prove its organization, marketing, analyzing, and financial potential while persisting in the core high-tech projects. A careful assessment of the developing lines of business led to the benchmarking of priorities, resulting in a number of narrowly specialized companies being detached from the Doka Group and becoming completely autonomous. Presently, Doka has several directions slated for expansion: telecommunications, software, biotechnology, lighting equipment, and culture.

Telecommunications.   Doka's top management know the importance of developing and accessing high-quality communication networks. This understanding initially led to the development of the original telecommunication system that facilitates the internal exchange of information between Doka and its suppliers, customers, and partners. It also generates additional revenues, thus reducing the costs of maintaining and operating the system. For Doka, telecommunications facilitates internal information exchange and the effective use of a database that contains information on 4,000 customers.

One result of this effort is the Remart Telecommunication System, which the company started to develop a few years ago. Doka and its partners heavily invested in Remart, which is a world-class jointly shared information media combining a great number of separate data transferring systems and connecting them with different domestic and international networks.

Remart is a multipurpose hardware/software complex. The system has: A host computer which can serve up to 256 end users simultaneously; an electronic switching unit; data transmitters; and a remote workplace. Software packages include the distributed SQL-standard database support. Remart can operate as a communication server-preprocessor. The Remart database on a Sybase SQL Server is able to process a large number of simultaneous users' queries. Both hardware and software are adopted and certified for the level of quality of the telephone lines throughout the territory of the former U.S.S.R. The various data processing and communicating processes available include: Electronic Mail, Telex/Telefax, Databases, Seminars and Conferences for the remote participants, and Computer Advertising. One of the most important parts of the system is the Banking and Stock Exchange (Globex-analogue) module allowing bankers and dealers unlimited opportunities for contact and making monetary transactions. There is also the Electronics Supermarket module providing remote clients with sale/purchase information. Soon hundreds of supermarket departments all over Russia will be managed from Doka's headquarters. Today it operates in the cities of Kaluga, Kemerovo, Krasnoyarsk, Ekaterinburg, Orenburg, and St. Petersburg. The hosts of the Remart System have been installed in different regions and institutions of Russia such as the Central Bank of Russia, with the center being Doka. It also has nodes to various electronic communication networks such as Relcom e-mail, Sovam Teleport, and Sprintnet. The Remart System is technically designed and organized so that it will not be significantly impacted by any changes in the political situation. This helps Doka make sure that political cataclysms or economic turmoil do not directly affect this project.

Software.   Doka is the leading Russian educational and leisure software developer and exporter. The company was one of the first Russian companies selling proprietary software products, entering international markets in 1989 with the *Welltris* game. Over 200,000 copies of this game have been already sold in Western Europe, the United States, and Japan. Subsequent products have gained a broad international recognition for their original ideas as well as their eloquent and intelligible graphic design. In 1992–93, Doka created and introduced the Windows Games Set including *Magic Eraser* and a modified Welltris-clone game named *Tubis*.

The growing interest of mass consumers in computer dictionaries, testing, and training and educational programs led Doka to the development of easily operated multilingual software with mobile pop-up screens and mouse support. The *Doka-Tutor* program is a guide to master foreign languages, either to train in the lexica to check one's knowledge, or to customize the training mode to fit personal preferences. *Doka World Map* is a unique dictionary-in-pictures educational and reference package, where users can look through as many as 3,000 words and expressions traveling across the world map from one picture to another and select images on the screen. And *Baby-Type* is a simple program making it possible to cope with keyboard operations playfully. About 30 of the company's educational and game titles are distributed worldwide today.

Doka is continuously expanding into new software areas. In 1994 it started a multimedia software development, resulting in the creation of a number of CD-ROM and CD-i titles. Doka Software has regularly exhibited at CeBIT International Fairs since 1990, and year after year several novel programs or packages are presented at this show.

Biotechnology.   The management at Doka feels that biotechnology is a classic example of putting together advances in several different fields, such as microelectronics, machine building, and agriculture, resulting in a unique first-class product that few in the world can develop.

The significant pollution and deterioration of the environment sparked the company's efforts to: work on the agricultural problems; provide future generations sufficient food free of chemical admixture and viruses; ameliorate plantation conditions; accelerate plant growth; protect plants from diseases; and generally improve the quality of agricultural products. To fulfill this mission, Doka has cooperated with the scientists of the Institute of Plant Physiology of the Russian Academy of Sciences. This collaboration has led to the development of original technology and equipment for biosynthesis, cultivation and reproduction of plants, extension of plantation output, and other aspects of fertile bioprocessing. Some techniques for industrial photosynthesis and virus-free plants have been created, manufactured, certified, and commissioned. The industrial system for designing virus-free seed material production for potato minitubers has been developed. This has resulted in the annual production of about 500,000 minitubers, providing well-conditioned seedlings for the plantation of 1,500 hectares.

In April 1993, the Federal Program for Virus-Free Potato Minitubers Producing Development was approved by the government of the Russian federation. This program allowed technological systems like Potato Tree or Microclone designed by Doka to be purchased and used by agroindustries and farmers everywhere in Russia.

Doka's achievements in agricultural cultivation have occurred in such areas of biotechnology as microclonal propagation, regeneration "in vitro," plant acclimatization, and hydroponics growth optimization. Minivit-type industrial sets were developed to make assorted greeneries (i.e., fennel, celery, parsley) rich in vitamins and other elements good for human consumption. Microalgae cultivating and organic compounds biosynthesis are also being investigated by the company. Valuable metabolites produced by their unique photobioreactor are important for medicine, pharmacology, biology, and chemistry.

The company's biotechnological devices have been exhibited at the world's fairs and workshops in Hannover and Potsdam, Germany and expositions in a number of countries. These have attracted the strong interest of international experts. Since 1992, Doka has worked closely with the Price Edward Island Potato Board of Canada, one of the world leaders in potato growing and processing. The company is looking at other international proposals on cooperation and contracts.

Lighting.   Different types of leisure activities are developing rapidly in Russia. Hundreds of theaters, dance halls, night clubs, and casinos are being started throughout the country, from Moscow to the remote sites of Siberia and the Far East. The Russian people want the shows to be better and better. There is a demand in the Russian market for special stage and performance lighting systems. In 1988, Doka started production, distribution, and servicing of lighting equipment and developed its own long-term lighting program. The company developed systems and devices like lighting panels and control desks and manufactured lamps, motors, and filters at a quality level comparable to European standards, at about half the cost.

The first Doka lighting products were purchased and installed in the Moscow Ostankino TV Company. They were then installed in different clubs and discotheques in Russia and other republics of the former U.S.S.R. This lighting equipment is still not perfected or versatile enough to satisfy the advanced requirements of more than 10,000 show-centers to be reconstructed or reequipped throughout Russia. This is an opportunity, according to company managers, for Doka to import the products of Western lighting manufacturers. When Doka participated for the first time abroad as a lighting manufacturer at the specialized international forum Siel/Paris in February 1993, people were surprised by the quality of their products displayed. This quality allowed the company to develop relationships with such firms as FAL, ADB, and JEM. Acting as their exclusive dealer within the former U.S.S.R, Doka has extended the range of lighting items available in Russia, and enhanced its position as one of the leading Russian lighting companies. Doka's Western partners have obtained access to the Commonwealth of Independent States (C.I.S.) market without facing any legal, financial, or promotional problems. These Western companies have also used the opportunity to combine their products with some of the cheaper, high-quality accessories produced by Doka.

Doka decided to operate as a universal distributor carrying a variety of products from simple, small, and cheap units to complicated expensive automated systems, complying with clients' lighting needs for shows, discotheques, theaters, as well as entire lighting systems. This approach is unique among Russian lighting companies. In order to show all the lighting items to its customers, Doka has opened a special showroom in Zelenograd.

The lighting installations made by Doka and its foreign partners have been used by the TV Studio of the Russian State Parliament—Duma; Sergei Obraztsov's Central State Puppet Theater; Solaris Nightclub at Cosmos Hotel in Moscow; and the Mobile Lighting System of Russian State TV. Lighting systems have also been delivered to European Russia, Ural, Siberia, Ukraine, Uzbekistan, and other republics of the former U.S.S.R. International partnerships with the lighting manufacturers in

England, United States, Germany, and Taiwan have been developed. Doka's extended dealership and service network is able to reach most of the Russian regions.

Culture. Not only technology, but creative spheres such as those of architecture, theater, and music are being developed and promoted by Doka. The cultural domain provides an opportunity for cultivating and enhancing international contacts and understanding between foreign countries and Doka.

Doka's Architectural Studio professionals represent a "new wave" of modern Russian architecture and design. Besides serving as a model for good area arrangement, this architecture is used to decorate any interior. Its highest level was recognized at a special UNESCO competition and at many exhibitions in Japan, France, England, Germany, Italy, Norway, and the United States.

Doka is also sponsoring and equipping the Municipal Theater named Vedogon. This young theater has succeeded in combining the traditions of Russian realistic acting schools with the principles of medieval European *comedia del arte*. The theater company does local performances and has also toured.

Doka has also cooperated with Marina Tarasova, a well-known violin-cellist whose mastery has been highly appreciated by audiences in Russia, France, Italy, Germany, Czechoslovakia, Finland, Portugal, Hungary, Poland, Turkey, and China. The company has promoted her LPs and CDs in Europe.

INTERNATIONALIZATION STRATEGY

Doka Company is well known in Russia as an innovative and reliable manufacturer and partner. New clients and customers are constantly being developed, as are new partners in business. Doka is willing to develop initial relations on the basis of trust and friendship. This same approach is used in the company's international strategy. During the last few years, the company's products and services have been widespread throughout Russia and other territories of the former U.S.S.R., from Byelarus to the Far East, as indicated in Exhibit 3. The company's goal is to match its technologies, equipment, and services to customers' requirements and expectations.

One of the features of Doka's international strategy is the development of its international dealer network. Many wholesale buyers have volunteered to become distributors of Doka in the C.I.S., thereby assisting the company to enlarge its network of qualified mounting, installing, and service outlets. By 1994 the company had established dealerships and was selling its products and services in Russia, Ukraine, Byelarus, Kazakhstan, Kirghizstan, Tajikistan, Uzbekistan, Turkmenistan, and Georgia.

Doka is recognized by many as one of "the most aggressive" private R&D companies in the former U.S.S.R. As is indicated in Exhibit 4, the company is trying to expand its business around the world.

Doka has contacts with companies on all the continents except Antarctica. Since entering international markets, a number of projects have been completed with partners from Poland, Finland, Sweden, Germany, Denmark, Belgium, France,

**EXHIBIT 3   Map of Sales and Dealership within Russia and the C.I.S.
Republics, 1994**

EXHIBIT 4   Doka's Worldwide Partnership in 1994

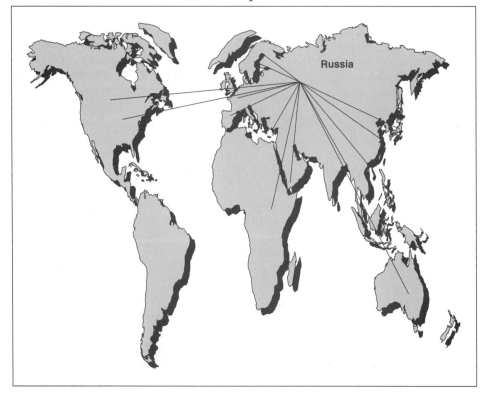

Switzerland, Slovenia, Italy, Spain, United Kingdom, United States, Canada, South Africa, Israel, Saudi Arabia, Hong Kong, Singapore, Taiwan, Australia, and Japan. After its foreign exhibition debut at CeBIT-1990 in Hannover, Doka continues to participate in different international fairs and meetings, such as ECTS (London, software); Frankfurter Buch Messe (Frankfurter/Main, publishing); Biotechnica (Hannover, biotechnology); World Potato Congress (England, agriculture); SIB (Italy, lighting); and PLASA (London, leisure industries).

These provide Doka the opportunity to multiply its international contacts and strengthen cooperative partnerships. That is also one reason the company promotes products made in Italy, Belgium, England, United States, Taiwan, and other countries in the Russian market. The products and technologies developed by Doka are distributed worldwide by Doka's dealers in the United States, Canada, Japan, Germany, France, and Australia. Doka's innovations have been patented in the United States, Germany, U.K., Japan, France, and Sweden.

The international market plays a vital role for the company, especially in software development. The company's strategy for international expansion in software development is a pressing problem.

Until 1993, personnel computers were not common in Russia. Companies' workstations were bought only for business purposes, and the domestic market of home and personnel computers did not exist. In 1994, a Russian market for software started as a result of large sales of personnel computers (see Exhibit 5). At the end of 1994, the company started distributing its products in Russia.

At this time, the Russian government started its official fight against piracy, because in 1994 70 percent of all software distributed in Russia was illegal. According to Deputy General Director Alexey Gritsay, "The difference between the Russian and international markets is going away, and the company now has a global strategy that includes both domestic and international markets." A new game called *Total Control* was presented in Russia in December 1995, in Europe in January 1996, and in the United States in May 1996. The game could be bought in any of four languages: Russian, German, English, and French. In Russia, Doka will publish and distribute the game, and the world rights were sold to the German company Software 2000.

Doka concentrates its efforts on applied, educational programs and games for IBM-compatible computers, as Apple computers represent only 2 percent of

---

EXHIBIT 5   Russian PC Market Estimate (units × 000)

	1990	1991	1992	1993	1994	1995E
New sales	310	350	420	570	816	1,170
Growth rate	9%	13%	20%	36%	43%	44%
Retirements	15	20	25	35	45	60
Installed base	795	1,125	1,520	2,055	2,825	3,935

Source: "East European Semiconductor Market Overview," *Future Horizons* (May 1996), p. 8.

EXHIBIT 6   Worldwide Multimedia Market, 1992–1996
(in 000s of units shipped except as noted)

Item	92	93*	Percent Change (1992–96) 92–93	Percent Change (1992–96) 94–96[†]
Total	4,815.4	10,315.1	114.2	26.9
Multimedia products	1,065.4	3,465.6	225.3	25.1
Authorizing software	728.9	1,726.1	136.8	16.2
Multimedia PCs and workstations	325.0	1,690.5	420.2	31.2
Networks	11.6	49.0	322.4	72.2
Upgrade kits	675.0	1,109.5	64.4	−4.7
Peripherals	3,075.0	5,740.0	86.7	32.5
CD-ROM drivers	825.0	1,720.0	108.5	27.6
Sound boards	1,800.0	3,200.0	77.8	28.6
Video boards	450.0	820.0	82.2	539.0

* Estimate.

[†] Forecast of annual compound rate of exchange.

Source: Dataquest, Inc. Sighted in *U.S. Industrial Outlook 1994*, U.S. Department of Commerce, International Trade Administration, p. 27.

computers in Russia. Internationally, the multimedia segment is growing very rapidly, which is especially attractive for Doka. The multimedia segment should increase to almost $12.0 billion by 1996 and will increase an average of 17.3 percent a year until the year 2000 (see Exhibit 6).

Lacking a developed sales network and international marketing experience Doka works through reliable partnerships. These partnerships include Spectrum HoloByte (U.S.), Bullet Proof Software (Japan), VIF and Infogames (France), Sybex Verlag, ZYX, and Hi/Tec (Germany), Lexicon Software (U.S.), Peruzzo Informatica (Italy), and Scandinavian CD-ROM Publishers (Denmark). Doka supplies each partner with master disks and the appropriate license to publish selected products within an agreed-upon territory. The company can also supply the packaged products on diskettes or CD-ROMs. Doka can also customize programs. All products are sold under the Doka brand name.

Working through partners helps Doka offset the Cold War and country-of-origin effect. The propaganda during the Cold War made Russia and Russians look very strange and wild to the world. After one presentation of Doka's products and projects in Germany, two businessmen from South Africa asked the Doka representatives if it was true that all Russians drink a glass of vodka during breakfast. While the West usually does not doubt the quality of Russian weapons and space technologies, many people in Western countries feel that Russians cannot produce any other quality high-tech products. Some Western businessmen actually offered a small amount of money for the copyright to all Doka's products for the entire world and forever.

While in 1990 Doka was the first Russian software company to take part in the CeBIT International Fair and through displaying its products there it started searching for reliable partners, it was not until late 1991 that the first contract was signed. By 1995, Doka had one hundred products and one of the highest overseas sales volumes by a Russian software company. Not all Doka's ideas and products find their customers in the West. *Lingua,* a unique program that gives the user the opportunity to choose out of the eight native languages the language he or she wants to learn by interacting with different people in different situations and hearing voices of native speakers, was not approved by the education committee in Finland. The committee complained about the unequal treatment of men and women, as all the executives simulated by the computer were men and all the tellers were women.

Doka also promotes software products made by other Russian firms that do not have the experience or the financial capability to work directly with the West. The company offers about 10 to 15 new software products each year.

ORGANIZATIONAL STRUCTURE OF THE COMPANY

According to its statute, Doka is a closed share capital company doing its own R&D business, and arranging a network of branch offices, associates, cooperation manufacturers, authorized dealers, and remarketers. The company is overseen by a board of directors which is responsible for the company's general directions and financial policy determination. The managing board implements the decisions of the board of directors, and manages the overall current businesses and affairs of the company. The auditing committee provides the control of the company's finances and economy and reports to the shareholders at the shareholders' meeting. The company's organizational chart is indicated in Exhibit 7 and a description of the key individuals is shown in Exhibit 8.

Exhibits 9 and 10 present the financial operations of Doka and the change in the contribution of different lines of business in the company operations for the period 1990 through 1995. The company experienced strong growth from its well-defined strategy, diversification into several high-tech areas, and access to some government-sponsored programs. The sales volume increased nearly 20 times in five years, from $1,850,000 (1990) to $34,680,000 (1995). While all the main businesses—telecommunications, biotechnologies, microelectronics/software, machinery/special equipment, and financial operations—had steady growth during these years (except for the decrease in financial operations in 1994–1995 due to the crisis in the Russian banking system in 1994), the role of each of the lines has changed.

In 1990, the highest sales were from telecommunications and information technologies. Their $734,000 sales volume was 39.7 percent of all the company's sales. While the sales in this area grew over the next five years to $1,491,000, its share of total company sales dropped to 4.3 percent. This market was difficult for the company, with the larger former state-owned and now privatized companies dominating the market.

During this time, Doka developed other innovative areas. In biotechnology, sales grew from $218,000 (1990) to $9,969,000 (1995); in microelectronics and soft-

EXHIBIT 7   Doka Organizational Chart

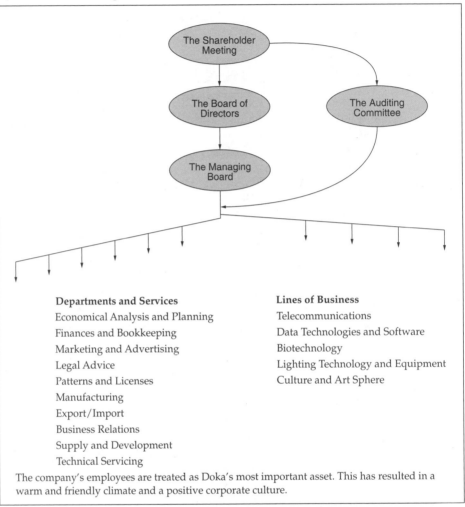

Departments and Services
Economical Analysis and Planning
Finances and Bookkeeping
Marketing and Advertising
Legal Advice
Patterns and Licenses
Manufacturing
Export/Import
Business Relations
Supply and Development
Technical Servicing

Lines of Business
Telecommunications
Data Technologies and Software
Biotechnology
Lighting Technology and Equipment
Culture and Art Sphere

The company's employees are treated as Doka's most important asset. This has resulted in a warm and friendly climate and a positive corporate culture.

ware, sales grew from $179,000 (1990) to $10,023,000 (1995); and in machinery and special equipment, sales grew from $63,000 (1990) to $12,173,000 (1995).

Another indicator of the company's success is its steady growth in total assets. Total assets reached 18,394,500,000 rubles in the first nine months of 1995. Net property was assessed ⅔—12,024,800,000 rubles and total current assets of 6,369,700,000 rubles.

One general principle is assumed in the employees' collaboration at Doka: Everyone has his or her own personality with specific characteristics, abilities, potentialities, and interests that should be taken into account and used for the welfare of everyone and the company as a whole. The company's personnel policy keeps pace with the changing concerns and needs of its employees. This

---

EXHIBIT 8   **Members of the Board**

ALEXANDER M. CHUENKO, Chairman of the Board and General Director

---

Chuenko was born in 1957 and graduated from the Moscow Institute of Electronic Engineering in 1979 with a Diploma degree in automatics and electronics. After graduation from the Institute he worked as a technology engineer at the Angstorm Microelectronics Plant in Zelenograd, which in the mid-1980s was the leading free market business establishment in the region. He was the main initiator and founder of Doka Company and has been its general director since the first day of the company's existence.

ALEXEY M. GRITSAY, Deputy General Director—International Business

---

Gritsay was born in 1957 and graduated from the Moscow Institute of Electronic Engineering in 1980 with a Diploma degree in automatics and electronics. In the period of 1980–1990 he worked as an engineer and officer at high-tech institutions in Zelenograd and Moscow. Since 1987 he had cooperated with Doka Company as a consultant. In 1990 he took the position of international business director at Doka.

EVGENY S. ZAYCHENKO, Deputy General Director, Development and Manufacturing

---

Zaychenko was born in 1958 and graduated from the Moscow Institute of Electronic Engineering in 1981 with a Diploma degree in machinery technologies. After graduating from the Institute he worked at the Elion Machinery Plant in Zelenograd. In 1988 he took a position at the Doka Company in development and manufacturing.

VYACHESLAV A. KARTASHEV, Executive Director

Kartashev was born in 1937 and graduated from the State Polytechnic Institute in 1966 with a Diploma degree in radiotechnics. After graduating from the Institute he worked as an engineer and department chief at microelectronics institutions and plants in Zelenograd. He elaborated the problems on economics and management in the fields of microelectronics. Since 1989 he has held the position of Doka Company executive director.

---

policy has minimized the company personnel turnover, which is a real problem for many other Russian companies.

Joint activities and parties help facilitate a favorable corporate climate. Events like holidays and Doka's birthday are celebrated together by employees.

Doka is an equal opportunity employer and gives all employees the same chance to succeed. Each person's opportunity to advance depends on his or her performance.

Many of Doka's managers have engineering backgrounds. These top managers do not feel that the lack of formal marketing knowledge is a disadvantage. They think business education alone does not provide the logical thinking that is so vital in a high-tech business. However, managers at Doka are taking development courses in business. Alexander Chuenko attended classes at the London School of Business, and Alexey Gritsay took some business courses at the Russian University in Germany.

Everyone in the company works hard to achieve success. Programming specialists, for example, do not complain about the lack of advanced computers. They say,

Exhibit 9   Doka's Assets (millions of rubles)

	1991	1992	1993	1994	1995 (9 months)
Total current assets	328.1	392.0	794.1	3201.1	6369.7
Net property, plant, and equipment	27.1	29.3	500.6	3575.7	12024.8
Total assets	355.2	421.3	1294.7	6776.8	18394.5

Exhibit 10   Doka's Turnover Analysis

Directions	1990 Value	%	1991 Value	%	1992 Value	%	1993 Value	%	1994 Value	%	1995 Value	%
Total	1.850	100.0	2.735	100.0	4.661	100.0	9.120	100.0	18.937	100.0	34.680	100.0
Telecommunications and information technologies	0.734	39.7	0.845	30.9	1.100	23.6	1.578	17.3	1.648	8.7	1.491	4.3
Biotechnologies	0.218	11.8	0.429	15.7	0.834	17.9	1.842	20.2	4.734	25.0	9.606	27.7
Microelectronics and software	0.179	9.7	0.336	12.3	0.853	18.3	1.915	21.0	5.302	28.0	10.023	28.9
Machinery and special equipment lighting systems	0.063	3.4	0.328	12.3	0.942	20.2	2.371	26.0	5.492	29.0	12.173	35.1
Financial operations	0.623	33.7	0.755	27.6	0.872	18.7	1.286	14.1	1.534	8.2	1.144	3.3
Other directions	0.031	1.7	0.041	1.5	0.061	1.3	0.128	1.4	0.227	1.2	0.243	0.7

"In the West, 10 specialists are writing one thing, and 10 others are writing another. We have to do everything by ourselves—what is done abroad by 10 people, here is done by only one. We have to spend more time and work harder creatively."

Executives of Doka believe in the economic success of Russia. It is just a question of time. When looking at the future, the company sees changes in Russian opportunities. The company plans to remain the leading player in three of its lines of business: software development, biotechnology, and lighting equipment, and is ready to develop new lines of business as new opportunities emerge. For example, Doka is working with some roots of different plants that can be developed to be used as a substitute for insulin. Using its competitive advantage of high scientific and technological potential, Doka wants to become a major global player in any field it enters.

VII HUMAN RESOURCE ISSUES

CASE SUMMARIES

CASE 20: CRISIS AT WRENTHAM CORPORATION
A CASE OF EXECUTIVE SELECTION AFTER MERGER

By George W. Danforth (GulfNet,Inc., USA), James J. Chrisman (University of Calgary, Canada), and David M. Schweiger (University of South Carolina, USA)

The principal issue in the case is selecting a new division president of Wrentham Corporation, because the current president has resigned to accept a position with a rival firm. There are three candidates being considered for the position. Before selecting the new president, the decision makers must also consider the future strategic direction of the division and a number of immediate pressing concerns. One strategic issue is whether or not Wrentham should expand outside of the United States. The case contains brief descriptions of each of the candidates and memoranda from three of them. It also includes a debate among the decision makers concerning the needs of the division and the relative merits of each of the candidates. Only one candidate has international business experience.

CASE 21: DIAMOND POWER: CAPITALISM IN CHINA (A)

By Richard C. Scamehorn (Ohio University, USA)

This case concerns a medium-sized U.S. company and its formation of a joint venture to manufacture and sell boiler maintenance equipment in a remote area of the People's Republic of China (PRC). A U.S. citizen, along with his wife, moves to the PRC as the managing director of the joint venture. The case describes the complexities of operating a manufacturing business in the PRC and the problems that the manager and his wife have with living in a very foreign culture. Fearing the violence in Tiananmen Square might spread to a civil war, the general manager and his wife flee China at the end of Part A, and the manager is left questioning the value of all their effort.

Case 22:   The Hit and Run Expatriate Employees

By Diane H. B. Welsh and Ibrahim Al-Fahim (both of Eastern Washington University, USA)

The case is set in Saudi Arabia and deals with laws regarding expatriate employees. Saudi Arabian law dictates that when an expatriate leaves a firm for any reason, the person cannot work for another Saudi firm for at least three years unless he or she has written permission from the former employer. Two Egyptian expatriates have changed employment. However, they do not inform the government of that fact, nor do they request written permission from their employer. Subsequently, their former employer learns that they are working for a competitor with whom the company has always enjoyed an excellent relationship. The new employer wants to retain the workers and asks the former employer to give them permission to work for another employer. The former employer must decide how to handle the situation. ■

CASE 20
CRISIS AT WRENTHAM CORPORATION
A CASE OF EXECUTIVE SELECTION AFTER MERGER

On the morning of August 1, 1991, Hal Benning, chief executive officer of Wrentham Corporation, a large diversified manufacturing company located in Houston, Texas, picked up the phone and punched in the number of Frank Powell, chairman of the board and longtime friend and associate. The news would not be good.

"What's up, Hal?" Frank asked. "You sound troubled."

"The quarterly numbers are in and Computerstat is going to show another net loss, about $2.5 million. What's more, I've just learned that George Steele will be stepping down as division head at the end of the month to take a position with one of our competitors. He wants to move on while he is still marketable. George feels that if he stays and the division's merger with Microstat fails, his career will be damaged."

"I'm sorry to hear that but I can't say I altogether blame him," said Frank. "This merger has been an awfully messy business."

"It's been rough for all of us," interjected Hal, "but we told the stockholders when we decided on the acquisition that we could make the new combined division profitable."

"That we did, Hal," agreed Frank. "Obviously, we have quite a task in front of us. Where do we stand today?"

"We are still well behind the planned integration schedule and our costs are way over budget. I know both the Microstat people and our folks from Home Computer are trying to work together, but they just don't share a common vision for the business." Hal continued, "For example, no one seems to agree about our international strategy. The Home Computer managers view the domestic market as our bread and butter and see foreign markets as only an incremental opportunity. On the other hand, Microstat's position is that penetrating foreign markets is the key to our future growth, profitability, and even survival. Operationally, we have the same sorts of problems. R&D has not made significant headway on any project requiring cooperation between Wrentham and Microstat people. My feeling is that we are to a large extent still managing two separate organizations."

"I noticed that many of the manufacturing and financial reports are still segregated," stated Frank.

"Integrating MIS remains a problem," acknowledged Hal, "but what concerns me most is a lack of unity and trust that extends all the way down to the factory floor. Out at the Santa Clara plant, Microstat people won't follow the advice of our process engineers because they don't trust our knowledge of their products and

Source: This case was written by George W. Danforth of GulfNet, Inc., USA; James J. Chrisman of the University of Calgary, Canada; and David M. Schweiger of the University of South Carolina, USA. This case is intended as a basis for class discussion rather than to illustrate either effective or ineffective handling of an administrative situation.

markets, and some of the Home Computer managers are blaming Microstat for our performance problems. This type of divisiveness has to go. If it continues, we'll never achieve greater economies of scale or improve our product line."

"The competition *is* getting ferocious," observed Frank. "The low-end marketers are beating us on price and the market leaders have superior products. If that isn't bad enough, getting access to distribution channels has never been tougher and some of our customers believe we may not be around much longer. Our dealers are getting nervous. If we don't take some action soon we'll really be in trouble."

"True enough, but the real problem is here at home, Frank. People are getting burnt out on the integration program; all those task forces and meetings divert their attention from the problems facing the business in the marketplace. We have to find someone who is strong enough to turn this division around."

"You're quite right, Hal. I think we need to bring in someone to help us with this one. Why don't you see if Bill is available?"

"Agreed. I'll take care of it right away."

BACKGROUND

Wrentham Corporation was founded in 1936 by William Wrentham as an office equipment firm. In 1978, it entered the microcomputer industry and two years later was restructured into three autonomous divisions: Wrentham Office Supply, Wrentham Communications, and Home Computer, now called Computerstat. Before the merger, Home Computer, with its headquarters and manufacturing facilities located in Houston, Texas, designed and produced relatively unsophisticated, low-priced microcomputers for both the home user and business market segments. Its key strength was in the home user market, a segment that represented nearly 80 percent of Computerstat's total sales. It also sold machines to small and medium-sized businesses. With annual sales of $214 million per year, Home Computer was one of the larger microcomputer manufacturers in the United States. The division survived an industry shakeout in the mid-80s but had been unable to establish a leadership position in the PC industry.

Starting in 1988, Home Computer made some tentative attempts to sell PCs in Europe, particulary in France, Italy, and the United Kingdom, but had not been particularly successful. The great majority of its sales were still concentrated in the continental United States and distributed through mass market channels.

Although Home Computer was marginally profitable in 1989, management began to realize that its future hinged largely on its ability to adapt to a new set of opportunities and threats emerging in the industry. Demand in the home user market segment had begun to level off while the business market was showing higher growth. Furthermore, the domestic market was beginning to show signs of maturation while international demand for microcomputers still offered significant opportunities for expansion. Price competition was also intensifying, requiring greater economies of scale and cost reductions to remain competitive in all but the most specialized market segments. Finally, both home and business users were demanding microcomputers with greater storage capacity, processing speed, and software and systems capability, making effective R&D and marketing even more crucial to keep pace with technological change, shifting customer preferences, and increasing competition.

In response to these opportunities and threats, the president of Home Computer and his staff mapped out specific strategic objectives: (1) decrease dependence on the home computer market, (2) significantly increase sales to the business sector, (3) penetrate selected foreign markets such as Canada, Western Europe, Australia, and New Zealand as the first step toward securing a strong international presence, and (4) improve both product and process R&D. Management concluded, however, that it was not possible to implement the required changes rapidly enough from within the division to keep pace. Therefore, it was decided to seek an acquisition in order to achieve its objectives.

About that time, Microstat, a comparably sized firm located in Santa Clara, California, announced that it was looking for a buyer. It had experienced declining sales and profit margins had been driven down by price-slashing competitors. Microstat was strapped with far too much inventory and its cash position was weak. Faced with an approaching deadline to repay a $24 million long-term loan, it had looked without success for another lender and a buyer for its unsold inventory. To make matters worse, the company was betting its future on a new product that had yet to make it out of the design phase. Although Microstat was in trouble, Home Computer's management believed its strengths were consistent with the needs of the division.

Microstat focused on the small to medium-sized business market segment. Sales to home users accounted for only 16 percent of total sales. Moreover, Microstat had established strong distribution channels in Europe; international sales accounted for over a third of its total sales. The company was particularly strong in Germany, France, and the Benelux countries (Belgium, The Netherlands, and Luxembourg). It was also in the process of negotiating an agreement with a large Japanese electronics firm to produce computers under that company's label. Wrentham's corporate and divisional management agreed that with more emphasis on process engineering to reduce costs, and its strengths in product R&D and international marketing, Microstat would make an ideal acquisition for Home Computer.

When the acquisition was announced in January 1991, a number of teams made up of both Home Computer and Microstat managers were put together to work out the many aspects of the merger. A top management team was tasked to oversee a comprehensive integration program and to build a cohesive, unified division. Functional teams worked on the specifics of melding various operations and systems, such as R&D, sales, manufacturing, and human resource and information systems.

Six months later, it was apparent to management that the integration program had not progressed as far as it had hoped. A number of critical, technical problems remain unresolved. The human resource team was finding it difficult to develop a system to determine positions, compensation, and seniority that would be perceived as fair by all employees. Management had yet to develop a usable information system, making it nearly impossible to access usable financial data in a timely fashion. Efforts to reorganize the R&D function were meeting stiff resistance; the department remained polarized along old company lines with Home Computer engineers arguing for cost control and Microstat people unwilling to budge on product design features. In addition, R&D suffered from a lack of leadership and direction as the vice presidents of R&D from both the merged businesses left after the merger. Manufacturing had experienced a similar ongoing debate over quality assurance and on-time delivery standards.

THE CANDIDATES

Two weeks later, Bill Brandt reported the results of his search for a new president for Computerstat to Hal Benning and Frank Powell. He had been instructed to conduct his search without soliciting the input of George Steele, the departing president of the Computerstat division. Brandt had retired from his position as Wrentham's director of human resources the previous year but was kept on retainer as a part-time management consultant due to his experience and perspective accumulated over a career of 43 years with the corporation. Bill began:

> I've narrowed the list down to three candidates, the first of whom I'm sure you are both familiar with—Tom Banks. As you know, Tom worked for one of the largest firms in the computer industry for 17 years before coming to work at Wrentham 10 years ago. For the last eight years, he has been Home Computer's vice president of manufacturing, a position he holds today in the combined operation. He has a bachelor's degree in Electrical Engineering from Texas Tech and an M.B.A. from Texas A&M. He's 54 years old, and is married with three children. What makes Tom an attractive candidate is his years of experience in the computer industry and his ability to manage operations efficiently. Although Home Computer's products have not fared as well in the market the past few years, Tom has helped keep the division afloat by squeezing costs so that it could remain competitive with the larger companies.
>
> Tom is known for his passionate involvement on the factory floor. It's not unusual to see Tom, sleeves rolled up, walking the manufacturing line, or talking with line supervisors about part specifications or equipment maintenance. But behind the facade of a spirited, blue-collar team player is a technical genius. Tom's intellectual grasp of the intricacies of each step in the production process is without equal. What's more, he has an intuitive ability to recognize how any change will affect the entire process, and his overriding bottom line, cost.
>
> Tom is known as upbeat, energetic, and good-natured; however, when he feels his goals are being compromised, he has been known to be very aggressive in defending his views. Some may even say that he is dogmatic and inflexible when challenged. I consider him to be a forceful advocate for quality and efficiency. In fact, many of the standards and procedures in force at the plants today were developed and implemented by Tom. He simply loves to make computers.
>
> The second candidate is Sheila Covington. Sheila was with Microstat when it started up in 1981. Before the acquisition, she had been its vice president of marketing for three years, a position she now holds with Computerstat. She received both her bachelor's degree in Marketing and M.B.A. from the University of California. Sheila is only 39

years old and still single, but she has a fiancé who is a partner in a high-powered San Francisco law firm.

Sheila is known as a risk taker and an internationalist. While at Microstat before the acquisition, she was able to push through her program for headlong international expansion at a time when other smaller companies were hesitant to commit quickly and heavily to overseas markets. Her success in winning solid distribution agreements in Europe accounted for much of Microstat's success. She speaks fluent German and can hold her own in French. In fact, she was an exchange student in Frankfurt during one of her undergraduate years. She enjoys traveling and likes to mix business with pleasure during her many trips. For instance, during her 1990 vacation in Switzerland, Sheila was introduced to an executive of the Yokohama Company which led to Microstat's negotiations to sell private label computers in Japan. Although talks have stalled since the merger, whatever hope we have of building a presence there in the next several years rests on her shoulders.

During my two weeks talking to people in the company, it became apparent that she retains quite a following from the Microstat crowd, not only in sales, but also in R&D and manufacturing. While at Microstat, Sheila worked very closely with both of these functions to facilitate the production of a greater mix of products.

Sheila is a zealot for customer satisfaction and it is this orientation that probably accounts for much of her success in opening up and expanding markets. She has not been without her detractors though. Some would say that she is either ignorant of or unconcerned with cost control. I believe this view is a gross oversimplification. Sheila understands the need to control costs as well as anyone, but she's always been more of a revenue-oriented manager. She has always tried to attack new market segments, both foreign and domestic, and has advocated increasing market share through greater product differentiation and value-added features. To Sheila, short-term inefficiencies are a necessary evil when you are creating a larger revenue base in a growth industry.

The final candidate is Carl Ferris, who I am sure you are aware is credited with much of the success of the Dynasis–Culver merger in Wrentham's communications division. He is 57 years old and although best known for his five years at Dynasis, his real background is in network communications. Before jumping to Dynasis, he had worked for Electron Equipment Company for 25 years where he attained the status of vice president of R&D.

Carl was known as somewhat of a rogue at Electron. He spent as much time dabbling in other functions as he did in his own. Surprisingly, for someone with such a technical background, including a Master's degree in Computer Information Systems from M.I.T., he has always been a seller of ideas, a charismatic sort. I've heard comments that Carl could sell you the sole of your own shoe and you'd thank him for it. The truth is that Carl is a leader. He has a knack for galvanizing people and gathering support.

I was able to talk to a number of my contacts at the Dynasis division over the past week, and I think I've been able to put together a pretty good picture of what has happened there. It seems that at the outset, Carl pulled together many of the best managers from both companies and formed a tightly knit team. They say that Carl presented his ideas powerfully and enthusiastically, yet listened to his people with equal intensity. He cajoled top managers to advocate views different from his own. He was open and willing to compromise, and absolutely demanded the same from his staff. His one firm rule was that once the team had hammered out a decision, every member was to support it 100 percent. Carl does not tolerate excessive individualism, divisiveness, or half-hearted loyalty. You're either with the team or you're not. It's been rumored that he heard one senior vice president complaining about a policy one too many times to a staff member and Carl sent him packing on the spot.

But I don't regard Carl as a hard man. He treats people with the highest dignity and respect. His praise is quick and sincere, and he abhors finger pointing. Sure, some hard decisions had to be made at Dynasis, and Carl shouldered the responsibility. One plant in South Korea was closed, other operations consolidated, and countless jobs redefined. He publicly told employees up front exactly what was going to happen and why. It was a painful transition, but Carl's reputation for integrity and his keen leadership enabled Dynasis to redirect its efforts quickly and effectively. The only problem I see is that taking over Computerstat would represent a lateral move for Carl. He has been training several men as possible successors and appears to believe he is in line to replace Jim Hamilton as COO of the corporation in a year or two. Carl is not a young man so if you want him to take on this challenge it will be necessary to be up front with him regarding his future here, and perhaps offer him a position on the board, as well as a substantial increase in salary.

There was a pause as each man reflected on what had been said. Hal spoke up first. "I think that each of these individuals is highly capable. However, the success of the new president will be largely determined by how his or her skills and vision serve to meet Computerstat's particular strategic and operational needs."

"Whoever is chosen is going to have to get a quick handle on the situation," chimed in Frank. "There are a number of issues that must be dealt with immediately. Market demand has been lagging. The economy is in a recession, and this recent string of unprofitable quarters must be arrested and turned around in short order. This company is depending on Computerstat to generate some cash flow. Our stance has been in the past, and I believe should continue to be, that Computerstat must be able to operate successfully on its own without looking to the corporation to bail it out. The plan was that Computerstat would be in the black by the end of the year. That was the commitment George made to us and that we made to our stockholders. I am not amenable to changing these expectations at this juncture."

"I understand your position, Frank," Hal responded, "but much of Computerstat's poor performance can be explained by Microstat's initial overestimation of sales and profit projections. The company was not in the shape that we were led to believe. That said, I agree with you in substance. The turnaround must be quick. Yet the pressing short-term demands must somehow be reconciled with the implementation of a new strategic direction. I question whether either Home Computer or Microstat could have gained and held onto a competitive edge on their own. George Steele had his ideas on where this division was headed, but they haven't panned out. The new president of Computerstat will want to implement his or her own plan, regardless of what has been done in the past. I see that as a good thing."

"Well, time is short," lamented Frank, "and we are not going to get any closer to a decision by drinking coffee and speculating. We have a pool of three outstanding candidates here and we must make a decision quickly. I suggest we notify the candidates today, and ask each of them to submit a memorandum within three days outlining what actions they would take to turn Computerstat around and how they see the division competing in the future." (See Exhibits 1 through 3 for the memorandums submitted by each candidate.)

"Good idea," nodded Hal, "By the way, Bill, Frank and I have reconsidered our decision to keep George out of this process. Although we still have our concerns, we now think that it's best to get as much input as we can, including George's. I know you would have preferred to talk to George at the outset. Nevertheless, your work here reflects your customary thoroughness. I've asked George to join us here for a meeting on Friday at eight.

"That'll be fine."

Exhibit 1

From: Tom Banks
To: Hal Benning

It was with great satisfaction that I received your phone call telling me that I was to be considered for the position of president of Computerstat. I wholeheartedly appreciate your confidence and recognition of my past contributions to the company. Although I enjoy my present position immensely, I would readily welcome the challenge and opportunity that the position of president would offer.

As you are well aware, Computerstat has suffered losses since our acquisition of Microstat six months ago. Before the acquisition, we were maintaining marginal profitability in a tight economy and weakening market conditions. Our losses over the past two quarters can be partly explained by the company's hesitance to quickly consolidate a sufficient number of manufacturing operations to achieve the necessary lower unit costs. If such an action plan had been aggressively pursued, we could have enjoyed significant and immediate savings, and been able to position ourselves to realize an adequate per-unit profit margin by now. I would implement such a plan, and anticipate that Computerstat would return to profitability in two quarters, three at the most.

A second and related factor is that we are still producing the same mix of Home Computer and Microstat machines that each made before the merger. If we plan to gain a competitive edge, we can no longer afford to fragment our efforts by making a wide range of machines aimed at every market segment in the industry. We simply cannot produce the same number of models as we do now and do it at a competitive cost. We also need to be patient. I would like to see Computerstat sell more products overseas someday. But we simply cannot afford to be expending our efforts on expansion in Europe or Japan, or any other foreign market for that matter, until we have put our U.S. operations in order. While those other markets are attractive, our success or failure today, and for the foreseeable future, depends on how well we do at home.

The keys to Computerstat's success in the future are: (1) strictly defining what we do best and adhering to it, and (2) understanding where the industry is headed and how Computerstat fits into that picture. What Computerstat does best is make quality, low-cost microcomputers. Microstat should be assimilated into the division so as to enhance that capability. Furthermore, such a strategy positions the company to survive and grow with the industry. Our low-cost stance enabled us to ride out the earlier industry shake-out. The industry is now approaching maturity. The days of double-digit sales growth are about over and probably will never return. The market is approaching saturation, and price competition is accelerating. A second shake-out in the near future is not unlikely. The survivors will be those companies that are structured and focused on efficiency. If I should be chosen as president of Computerstat, this is the precise direction I would take.

EXHIBIT 2

From: Sheila Covington
To: Hal Benning

I am very excited at the prospect of serving as president of Computerstat, and offer my sincere gratitude to you and to the board for selecting me for consideration.

As outlined in Home Computer's original contacts with Microstat's managers and supported to some extent by the ongoing work of the top management team, the primary aim of the Home Computer–Microstat merger was to bring Microstat's marketing strength to bear on Home Computer's line of low-end computers, and to continue to push forward with the enhancement of higher-end Microstat models.

The common element shared by the effective companies in the industry is that they aggressively pursue and capture market share wherever the opportunity presents itself. Concerning higher-end machines, market characteristics are changing as fast as technological advances both create and meet new needs. The range of uses for microcomputers is unlimited and expanding (e.g., multimedia, home banking, and communications). Running concurrent with this technological explosion is a greater demand for peripherals, specific capabilities, and various value-added items including service. In order to compete in this market, Computerstat must offer the customer a choice of models and assorted enhancements.

There is also considerable potential for Computerstat to sell products overseas. Our research department tells me that with our high end machines we could achieve substantially greater penetration in Western Europe and capture a significant market share in Japan if we put forth a concerted effort.

The market for simpler machines still offers relatively untapped opportunities in many foreign areas, particularly developing countries and the emergent Eastern European states. Quick entrance will enable Computerstat to establish a firm base from which we can grow with these advancing countries; the first to the market often prevails over late arrivals, even those with better or less expensive products.

In summary, Computerstat's recent drift from profitability is due to its failure to attack new and emergent market segments. Consistent with this reasoning, I would pursue greater product differentiation of high-end models, and penetration of high potential foreign markets with our low-end machines. Not only will this strategy set Computerstat on a highly competitive course, but it will build a larger revenue base from which the company can begin to shortly realize real and sustainable profits.

EXHIBIT 3

From: Carl Ferris
  To: Hal Benning

I must say I was quite surprised when you called the other day to ask me if I would be interested in
   taking over the helm of Computerstat. After much thought, I have decided that if you share my
   vision for the company, then I would welcome such an invitation. Let me tell you how I view this
   challenge, and precisely what I believe I can do for the firm.

My Dynasis experience has confirmed to me what I have suspected for some time. As general manager,
   I cannot direct the activities of an organization as a field marshal does his cavalry. I am neither that
   commanding nor that clever. Joining two organizations greatly disrupts conventional management
   processes, making the role of general manager all the more difficult. Consequently, merger situations
   offer a hazardous and utterly frustrating road to anyone intent on unilaterally implementing even the
   most ingenious strategic plan.

The fundamental purpose of any merger is to create synergies which enable one large unified firm to
   perform certain activities cheaper and more effectively than the two firms did apart. The reason
   why most companies' post-merger performance is poor is that they underestimate not only the
   technical difficulty associated with achieving certain synergies but also the substantial inertia
   demonstrated by employees of all echelons when confronted with change. The key then is to
   unfreeze people from the dictums and scripts of the past and to encourage and facilitate new modes
   of thinking and doing. This is not a matter of selling the Microstat people on the Home Computer
   way of thinking or vice versa. What I want to do is create a new meaning for all employees that they
   will feel is superior to either of the old ways; the effectiveness of any major strategic reorientation
   will be both dependent upon, and a consequence of this.

Because future performance will be determined by the relative success of integrating the two
   companies, the dominant and overriding standard which Computerstat must measure itself against
   must be a set of goals associated with the integration program rather than those related to short-
   term performance. The implication of this is that if Computerstat is going to emerge as a viable and
   profitable going concern, it can no longer afford to continue to emphasize short-term profits at the
   expense of efforts that will create a long-term enhancement in competitiveness. Given the current
   state of the division, these objectives are not reconcilable.

As an outsider from another division, I offer the distinct advantage of not being constrained by
   any prior alliances or mind-set. Two polarized groups of employees are also more likely to
   follow my lead than that of an insider who will inevitably be associated with one of the two
   organizations. In sum, what I offer Computerstat is a unique set of proven skills and experience
   that can meld the two organizations into a stronger and more profitable company in 12 to
   18 months.

  "And Bill," added Frank, "Hal and I don't want to walk out of this room on
Friday without a recommendation for a new president for Computerstat that we
can present to the full board. Time *is* of the essence here."

THE MEETING

Hal Benning closed the door to his office, and turned to address the three men
seated at the conference table. "First, I'd like to thank George for coming. I'm sure
his insights will be quite helpful. Before we get to the matter, I'd like to tell you

about an incident that occurred yesterday afternoon. Leo Hainsworth, the manager of our Houston plant, called. It appears that there's been a lot of speculation about who the next president will be. Anyway, Leo made it quite clear that both he and John Stearns, Computerstat's new vice president of R&D, feel they can work well with Tom Banks, but that if someone else is chosen all hell may break loose. He didn't put it that way, but his tone was clear."

"I don't know that we are going to make everyone happy here or that we should necessarily try," interjected Frank. "After reviewing the files, I'm leaning toward Sheila Covington. I think she offers a fresh and proactive strategy for Computerstat that will enable the company to compete effectively into the next decade. She seeks out opportunity aggressively, and is the only candidate who seems to understand that we are competing in an international rather than a national market. That's the sort of vision this company needs if it is to grow in this industry."

"I disagree, Frank," said Hal. "We've differed before and have come to some pretty good decisions."

"That's true, but only after I brought you to your senses," needled Frank. "You like Tom Banks."

"Yes I do. Am I that predictable?"

"Only to me," Frank laughed.

"Don't get me wrong, I like Covington, but after six months, she still owns her house in California. She rents an apartment here, but flies back every weekend to be with her fiancé. Tom Banks is stable. His track record reflects a highly competent and balanced manager. He's conservative and he doesn't make mistakes. His abilities and approach largely determined Home Computer's past success and I think the course he advocates is the most responsible and reasonable for the future. Tom Banks talks about what he knows, and I trust him with the company. He's not oblivious to the changes and globalization of the marketplace, but he does understand that you can't put the cart before the horse. I sense we might be at an impasse on this one, Frank."

"Bill, what do you think?" prodded Frank, his voice rising uncharacteristically.

"Well gentlemen, I'm not sure I'm going to be of much help because my inclination is to go with Carl Ferris. I think you need to consider the priorities of the merger. Carl is the most qualified to see the integration through. He's proven he's capable of pulling off a merger, and his selection would send a clear signal that Computerstat is no longer about either the old Home Computer or Microstat." Until the two companies are truly unified, all this talk about product rationalization, costs, technological innovation, or expansion in foreign markets is meaningless.

"But look at Tom's track record! Anyway, Ferris is not committed to the original schedule," growled Hal.

"He may be the only candidate with either enough foresight or courage to give the bad news," Bill responded.

"I don't see how either Banks or Ferris can provide a viable long-term focus for the company," argued Frank. "Only Sheila Covington has a clear vision for growth."

"OK, OK," called Hal. "We all agree that we disagree. George, we still haven't heard from you. How do you see it?"

"From what I've heard, I'm convinced that the reason for the lack of consensus is that the right person is not in this group of three." George cleared his throat, and continued in a low but impassioned voice. "Ellis Ross has been groomed for this position for the past six years. He not only expects the position, but has refused some attractive offers from the competition with the expectation that he would succeed me. Since joining us eleven years ago, Ellis has served five years as comptroller, four years heading up our strategic planning staff, and the past two as our chief financial officer."

"But Ellis is a staff man; he doesn't have any line experience," Hal challenged.

"That's true. On the other hand, he's extremely intelligent and is very well read. His analytical skills are extraordinary, and he's able to synthesize his knowledge of finance, operations, and strategic planning into cohesive action plans. That's what this division needs—a solid generalist with experience at the top, someone who understands the big picture. I'm convinced that Ellis is this person.

It was his idea to buy out Microstat, and it was a good idea. He knows both companies intimately and he knows how all the pieces should fit together. Any problems we've had with implementing Ellis's plan are my doing. Perhaps if I had let him run with the ball we would be faring better."

"If he knew you were off course, then why didn't Ross assert himself more?" probed Hal.

"It's not in his nature to push his superiors toward his position, but he certainly isn't weak-willed either. He's a company man. He fully exercises the authority given him, but he respects the word of his superiors. He's a quiet, analytic type, but given the responsibility, he will see this thing through. Anyway, I told Ellis a year ago that if he stayed, he would succeed me as president."

"You did what?!" Frank scowled.

"The recommendation of the president has always been followed in the past," explained George, "but the point is that Ellis is the only one who really understands Computerstat as a whole. If he's passed over, you'll lose him. Besides, this is a job for a younger man," confessed George. "Ellis is 43 and in excellent health. He's divorced, you know. No children. He's got the vitality, drive, and singular commitment needed for this job."

"We certainly don't want to lose Ross," said Hal, "but I question whether his reserved manner makes him ideally suited for this job."

"If this discussion has shed light on anything, it's that none of the candidates can claim that distinction," Frank mused. "But I just don't feel comfortable with Ross. We need to signal to both the employees and the shareholders that we're taking a new tack."

"Computerstat needs a fresh start," conceded George, "but it also needs continuity. Ellis would serve as an effective linchpin to guide the division through transition."

"Okay, maybe you're right and we should have considered Ross from the outset, but that doesn't change the fact that we need to find some common ground if we are going to be able to come to a consensus," complained Hal.

"I think you've pointed out a key issue here," observed Bill. "As things are, we could debate the merits of each candidate for a month, but one of the crucial elements of this process is that it has to be quick." Bill slid back in his chair and continued. "What I perceive is that each of us is working with a different set of assumptions. Hal, you consider past performance critical. Hence, you chose Tom Banks. Frank, you, on the other hand, believe that Sheila Covington is most capable of achieving what you think is most important, future growth. From my perspective, the overriding concern is the integration program, and, as I said, Carl Ferris is uniquely qualified in that respect. Now, we must seriously consider Ellis Ross; what he can contribute in the way of general management skills and continuity, and whether you are willing to lose him. Anyway, if we are going to reach an agreement it will be necessary to identify some common ground, as Hal put it. To find this common ground maybe we should focus less on the candidates and more on the criteria by which they should be evaluated. If we can come to agreement on that, then the logical choice should become clear."

"The best predictor of future performance is past performance," argued Hal. "Talk about vision for the future is good but it is nothing to bet the company on. It's not real. The past we know with certainty."·

"I think you're missing the point, Hal," retorted Frank. "It's a changing world and the only thing we know with certainty is that it will continue to change. Old Man Wrentham was a legend in his time, but he would be lost today. The future is uncertain and that implies risk. A vision for the future addresses *that reality*."

"And what of the merger, gentlemen?" began Bill. "I say the ability to manage this merger is most important. If Computerstat is unable to jump this first hurdle, neither a solid track record nor a vision for future growth is going to make much difference."

"True enough, but without some solid continuity at the top, the division will muddle along regardless of what 'tack' you choose," argued George.

"Frank and I hoped to make our selection today, but it's now apparent that this decision is more difficult than we foresaw," observed Hal. "Perhaps we should think about this some more and get back together in a couple of days to decide what selection criteria are most important, why, and which candidate best fits those criteria."

CONCLUSION

What then is the most important criterion for the selection of the president of Computerstat? Is it past performance, vision for future growth, the ability to integrate the two merged companies, or a balance between top management skills and the ability to provide continuity? Given this assessment, who should be the next president of Computerstat?

Case 21
Diamond Power
Capitalism in China (A)

THE FOUNDING OF AN INDUSTRY

A German immigrant, inventor, and engineer named Raphael Herman created Diamond Power Specialty Company in 1903 at Detroit, Michigan, with his invention: the sootblower. His original product isn't recognizable today; there has been a lot of change to the product and even more in the marketplace. Even with all the changes, the basic purpose of the sootblower remained the same; to clean the inside of a boiler while it remained on-line, producing steam. Those small turn-of-the-century boilers were as different from today's 14-story-tall leviathans as was Herman's original hand-cranked sootblower compared to today's computer-controlled systems.

Cleaning a boiler during its operation had become quite a task. The gas flows in the boiler's superheater section could reach 2,300 degrees Fahrenheit. To "reach" into that section and clean the ash and slag deposits was a bit tricky, since the probe, or lance tube, could easily melt away if there were any interruption in the airflow pumped along the inside of the lance tube. The airflow actually served two functions: the airflow coled the lance and saved it from melting, and then as it exited from a nozzle near the end, the airblast would knock loose the ash and slag from the outer surfaces of the boiler tubes.

This was a critical process in power generation. If the slag were unrestricted in its buildup, it would start to form an insulating coating on the exterior of the boiler tubes (where steam was being created on the inside), thus making the steam generating process highly inefficient. But when the sootblowers were run and the tubes were blown clean, the hot gas temperatures made steam generation a highly efficient process.

Diamond's two largest customers were the two largest boilermakers in the world: Combustion Engineering Company of Hartford, Connecticut, and Babcock and Wilcox of New York City. Babcock and Wilcox had standardized on Diamond's sootblowers and attempted to purchase Diamond's stock. They were able to purchase a majority of the stock from the descendants of Raphael Herman, but a few holdouts prevented total ownership.

The sootblower was Diamond's bread-and-butter product line. Over the years, Diamond developed several new products, but nothing else became a big money-maker like the sootblower. After an absence of competition for many years, two competitors finally sprang up: Copes-Vulcan, located in Lake City, Pennsylvania, and the Bayer Company of St. Louis, Missouri. All maintained profitable opera-

Source: This case was written by Richard C. Scamehorn of Ohio University, USA. The author gratefully acknowledges the invaluable assistance of the personnel at Diamond Power Specialty Company, in particular, the late William C. Clark, James Arens, and Charles Paugh. Copyright © 1996 Richard C. Scamehorn. This case is intended as a basis for class discussion rather than to illustrate either effective or ineffective handling of an administrative situation.

tions through World War II when the heavy demand for U.S. Navy ships made the industry a seller's market.

CHANGES AFTER THE WAR

After World War II, Diamond relocated its headquarters to Lancaster, Ohio, to escape the high Detroit wages of the United Auto Workers. The steam generation industry changed considerably. Demand for rotary sootblowers used on the relatively small ship's boilers declined dramatically. As the country's postwar economy expanded, the nation's utility companies constructed larger and wider boilers that required the newer "retractable" sootblowers. The Bayer Company could not keep up with this change in product technology, and its market share fell to less than one percent.

Copes-Vulcan, unlike Bayer, pursued the development of new products such as the retractable sootblower as well as high pressure and temperature fluid-handling valves, which became their major product line.

In 1963 Diamond developed the world's longest sootblower, with a "reach" inside the boiler of 55 feet. Copes also developed a 55-foot design to compete with Diamond. This product development was a direct response to customer demand, as the size of the largest boilers reached a width of 110 feet. This peak development in technology also represented a peak in business when an order for 200 sootblowers might total $10,000,000. During the 1970s, market volumes became erratic.

As the power-generation industry evolved into the nuclear era, Copes commanded a lion's share of the high-tech commercial nuclear valve business, in addition to nuclear applications for the U.S. Navy. Diamond, on the other hand, became the world's leading manufacturer of the roller-nut design of control rod drive mechanisms for commercial nuclear power reactors.

Despite these changes, sootblowers remained Diamond's major product line, with nuclear control rod drive mechanisms its secondary line. Copes's number one product was valves, with sootblowers their secondary product line.

There were other major differences between the two companies.

1. Diamond vigorously pursued overseas markets, first by export, and then by establishment of wholly owned subsidiary or joint-venture manufacturing operations in the United Kingdom, Korea, Sweden, South Africa, Canada, Finland, Mexico, and Australia. Two operations, in the United States and the United Kingdom, were 100 percent autonomous with complete machine-shop facilities, that is, they could manufacture all the components needed to assemble a sootblower. Sweden, Canada, and Australia were semiautonomous, with limited machining capability, that is, they could manufacture all of the necessary components except for the drive-train. The others were only assembly shops, utilizing components from the United States, United Kingdom, or in some cases, from the semiautonomous plants.

Copes, on the other hand, had a small number of foreign licenses, and occasionally competed for large international sootblower projects through export offerings.

2. Diamond had a large, well organized, professional field sales force, staffed primarily with full-time sales engineers. There were a few manufacturers' representatives, mostly a holdover from the pre-WW II era. Copes, to the contrary, had few company sales staff in the field. They relied on a network of manufacturers' representatives, all of whom represented other principals that manufactured equipment for the power industry.

3. Diamond's product design, neither hi-tech nor patented, incorporated both proprietary design components with moderate levels of technology. In particular, the power drive-train, a critical subsystem of the sootblower, represented the highest level of technology in the product. Copes, however, tended to utilize more standardized components in their drive-train. Although not off-the-shelf, many components were commercially available and compatible with different product-models, length being the only difference from product to product.

4. Diamond developed an extensive aftermarket support activity consisting of a "service" organization, a key element of the marketing vice president's staff. This service unit consisted of a network of "mini-factory" service centers located in New Jersey, Georgia, Ohio, Texas, Colorado, North Dakota, California, and Washington.

Each of the autonomous service centers had limited manufacturing capability to produce lance tubes, feed-tubes, replacement seals, drive-train and electrical components and thousands of other commonly needed replacement parts with only a few hours notice. Copes generally relied on their factory to produce the necessary proprietary parts while commercial suppliers provided a source for the nonproprietary parts.

5. Diamond's domestic sootblower market share averaged about 70 percent, with Copes capturing virtually all of the balance. Because of this high market share and the attendant economies of scale, Diamond could afford to selectively cut their new equipment prices and recoup the profit margin in the replacement parts market which was certain to follow. It was like giving away the razors to make the profit later on the razor blades.

6. Diamond's nondomestic markets were quite different; nationalism was the major reason. In the countries where Diamond had manufacturing operations, they were able to capture more than 50 percent market share (similar to the U.S.). In the rest of the world, Bergamann (in Germany) and Forrest (in France) competed with severe intensity. However, Diamond remained the only multinational manufacturing company.

NEW COMPETITION

By the late 70s, new orders for the domestic commercial nuclear industry had vanished with the shock of Three Mile Island and the aftershock of Chernobyl. It was even worse than no orders; there were cancellations of existing orders. What once looked like a comfortable backlog of long-term production of nuclear orders was shrinking so fast that commitments to purchase materials actually had to be canceled.

To make matters even worse, the conventional power generation market had lost its luster. In 1982, there was not a single new boiler order in the United States.

The orders for new sootblowers in the United States shrunk, but it was even worse in the Western European markets. This prompted Bergamann of Germany, the leading European sootblower manufacturer, to become interested in the U.S. market, a fact not known by Diamond until much later.

A DEVELOPING NEW MARKET

The officials from the People's Republic of China had actually sought out the meeting with Diamond Power Specialty Company in 1983. In some respects, that wasn't surprising since Diamond Power was the largest manufacturer of sootblowers in the world. In addition, it had the most modern and reliable equipment, better than any competitor and much better than anything currently being manufactured in China. The design of the Chinese boiler cleaning equipment was several decades old and provided both limited cleaning capability as well as limited durability in the hostile environment of a power generation boiler house. Because of the increasingly severe duty requirements that the Chinese now required with larger, higher output boilers, the Chinese wanted a linkage with a company that had better technology.

Jim Arens, as international vice president, had the responsibility to host the official representatives from the Chinese sootblower manufacturing company. Only after they arrived was it determined that just one manager of the Chinese company had made the journey. The rest were politicians, from the local level all the way to the Central Government in Beijing. A tour of the main plant at Diamond's headquarters in Ohio was followed by a Chinese luncheon with all the formalities. After returning to the plant, they discretely inquired about Diamond's possible interest in an operation in China. They had opened the door and Jim Arens was going to go through it.

Jim responded by stating they would not be interested in issuing a license for manufacture in China. He was pleasantly surprised when the Chinese officials responded by saying they also were not interested in such an arrangement. They also wanted a joint venture.

LENGTHY NEGOTIATIONS

With some awareness of the slow and careful pace by which these matters were usually undertaken by the Chinese, Jim advised he would determine the acceptability of pursuing matters further. The Chinese already had a factory, albeit less than modern, to make their equipment. Since the same type of product was made by both companies, the Chinese felt most of the building and equipment could be utilized to manufacture Diamond's equipment. As soon as the Chinese delegation departed, he talked with the vice president of marketing and the company president. Both expressed a definite interest, along with some specific requirements and limitations.

These could be summarized as:

1. A native Chinese as the managing director (M.D.), based on Diamond's previous extensive management of overseas ventures.

2. At least 50 percent ownership.

3. Use of Diamond's cash outlays to the joint venture company must be restricted to capital equipment, not to working capital.

4. Diamond's Ohio headquarters factory would buy component parts (for assembly into their products made in the United States and elsewhere) from the joint venture company. Payment to the joint venture company in U.S. dollars should furnish most of the foreign currency requirements other than for capital equipment.

5. Diamond would license its technology to the joint venture company for a minimum of ten years.

6. The value placed on the existing Chinese factory must be evaluated in Chinese replacement costs; the value placed on Diamond's technology must be at Western values.

It would be difficult to obtain agreement on most of these items. A 10-year license agreement was the maximum time period allowed by law. Chinese law also limited foreign ownership in a joint venture to 50 percent (this restriction has subsequently been relaxed). The Bank of China would not establish local currency credit for any venture capitalized at less than US$1,000,000. Diamond's position on all of these categories was at the maximum allowed under Chinese law. It left room for the Chinese to negotiate, but scant room for Jim Arens to yield. The Diamond position sounded a lot like a "take-it-or-leave-it" offer.

Negotiations dragged on for a total of thirty-seven months. There were sixteen negotiating sessions, averaging six days each. Every time one of these sessions was over, it took three days to get back in a reasonable frame of mind. To complicate matters, Mr. Fhu, the managing director of the existing Chinese company, categorically refused to accept the concept of a Chinese managing director. This issue of an indigenous managing director stayed on the table right up to the last week. They were difficult days.

The issue of the managing director's residence was typical of the frustrations in these negotiations. The Chinese kept saying that a financial provision would be made for a managing director's house, but they steadfastly refused to specifically state that it would in fact be built. Jim's concern was that the money would somehow find its way into the government's (or worse, some individual's) pockets, and that a house would never be built.

Over the time span of four sessions, with perhaps twenty hours spent on this one subject, they finally affirmed it would be built. To make matters even more complicated, all but two of these sessions were held at the location of the existing Chinese factory, in Jingshan. Jingshan was halfway around the world—remotely located in Hubei Province, about 175 km north of the capital, Wuhan, and the Yangtze River, 1,400 km west of Shanghai. Although there was a hotel in Jingshan, it was no joy to stay there. The rooms were Spartan, with paper-thin walls and paper tasting food in the dining room. There was no TV in the rooms because the closest transmitter was too far away. The town of Jingshan was Spartan also. The town was so poor that many of the homes had only dirt floors.

After returning home from these negotiating sessions it always seemed like top management was disappointed that such little progress had been made.

About once a year a high-powered delegation from either Wuhan or Beijing would arrive at Diamond's headquarters. They knew Americans expected faster progress so they showed up to make certain Diamond's top management knew the negotiations were serious. Those were difficult negotiations—physically and mentally.

THE COMPETITION INTENSIFIES

While the negotiations in China were continuing, some important market changes were starting to unfold in the United States that would later make a dramatic impact on the industry. Unrelated to all the prior events, a small, independent company in Atlanta, called Blalock, Inc., started to show some interest in supplying sootblower parts in the mid-1980s. The owner, Bill Blalock, supplied "mill-supply components" to power plants in Georgia. Bill could locate many of Copes's parts, like bearings and chain, as "off-the-shelf" items at mill-supply houses. The sootblower parts markup looked like a gravy train to Bill Blalock, but he was keenly aware that Copes had less than one-third of the installed base of operating sootblowers. He could sell more than twice the amount of parts for Diamond blowers, perhaps with little additional effort. The engineer in Bill knew he could easily "reverse-engineer" the proprietary, unpatented Diamond parts. With help from a good foundry, Bill could machine the castings to Diamond's finished dimensions, assemble the parts, and sell a complete power drive-train, one of the highest value-added replacement assemblies. With low overhead and no R&D expense, Bill thought he would be the low-cost producer.

He followed this plan to the letter, and was producing Diamond parts, selling them at prices 15–25 percent below Diamond and still reaping handsome profits in the process. He was happy, but now both Copes and Diamond were unhappy.

During 1988, the Bergamann division of Deutsche Babcock, A.G. in the Federal Republic of Germany saw Bill Blalock's small operation as a natural entrée into the American sootblower market. Bergamann quickly closed a deal to acquire Bill Blalock's parts business, giving them a toehold on the North American sootblower market for the price of Blalock's small operation. With this toehold, Bergamann could now also offer their equipment on new projects. This fortuitous event allowed them to offset their new equipment start-up costs with a built-in profit from the sale of both Diamond and Copes replacement parts. It had the markings of a textbook win for Bergamann and a matched pair of blunders for Diamond and Copes.

In the meantime, new power projects were few and far between. The competition for these multimillion-dollar orders grew even more intense with the entry of Bergamann. Profitability in the industry was eroding, although faster in the United States where Bergamann had initially focused (see Exhibit 1, Diamond Power Statement of Operations). Although the international margins were also eroding, the deterioration was not as severe as the U.S. market.

CHINESE NEGOTIATIONS FINALIZED

The final terms of the joint-venture agreement were explicit. The joint venture would be structured with 50 percent ownership by Diamond Power and 50 percent ownership by the People's Republic of China. The joint-venture company would pay US$350,000 for Diamond's license of technology plus an initial 5½ percent royalty on the value of shipments. This royalty would decline on a sliding scale down to 3½ percent by the end of the ten-year license period (with equal adjustments evey two years). The old Chinese company's property, plant, and equipment was valued in China at US$1,000,000. Diamond's headquarters would match this value with US$1,000,000 cash to the joint venture company, with the covenant that this money could only be used to pay for capital equipment or for fees/royalties owed to Diamond.

The issue of a native Chinese managing director was something else. Mr. Fhu, after nearly three years of negotiations, finally revealed his true thoughts on the subject. He wanted the prestige of the managing director's job, but feared an encounter with the government. He said if there was an issue that came to a showdown with the government, if he stood contrary to the government, he would be replaced and the company would lose. On the other hand, if there were an American managing director, the government could not fire him, and he might win the issue for the joint-venture company.

At the request of Governor Gao, governor general of Hubei Province, the joint venture would be named The Boiler Aided Machinery Company of Hubei, Pty. Ltd.

THE NEW MANAGING DIRECTOR

Diamond had no previous experience in China and Jim Arens flatly stated he had no interest in becoming the managing director. After an intensive personnel search, Diamond hired Tom Prebola for the job of managing director. At the time, Tom was in South America, selling belting and other rubber-based products for UniRoyal, Inc. A native of Boston and a B.B.A. graduate of Boston University, he had worked for several years in China and spoke Mandarin fluently. During a business trip to British Guyana, Tom met Julianna, who was destined to become his wife. Julianna, a Chinese born in The Netherlands, moved to Latin America during her primary school days and was also multilingual.

Becoming the new managing director was a significant career advancement for Tom. To be a managing director of a foreign company of nearly 400 people while still in his early 30s was a coup. Success in this job could lead to a major executive assignment before he was 40. But, it was halfway around the world. Before he could convince his wife to live there for two or three years, he had to convince himself.

"Tom, I want to know what the house will be like," Julianna asked of her husband.

"I saw the plans," Tom responded. "It's situated on the corner of the company property, away from the main gate, so the site is not too glamorous." Julianna cut in, "I was more interested in what the inside will be like."

"Well, from the plans, there are two bedrooms." Tom was less than assertive at this point, since he wasn't absolutely certain of the degree to which the plans rep-

Exhibit 1   Diamond Power Statement of Operations ($000)*

	1985	1986	1987	1988	1989	1990	1991
				Domestic Operations			
Sales	70900	71497	73585	73169	75004	75444	74400
Cost of sales	43922	43902	45074	45830	48751	50426	51920
Gross margin	26978	27595	28511	27339	26253	25018	22480
General and admin. exp.	12596	12974	13363	13764	14177	14602	15040
Operating income	14382	14621	15148	13575	12076	10416	7440
Taxes	7191	7311	7574	6788	6038	5208	3720
Net income	7191	7311	7574	6788	6038	5208	3720
				International Operations			
Sales	30608	31225	31822	32184	32977	33285	33965
Cost of sales	19909	20132	20467	21167	22506	23360	24888
Gross margin	10699	11093	11355	11017	10471	9925	9077
General and admin. exp.	4078	4250	4334	4541	4675	4832	5150
Operating income	6620	6843	7021	6477	5796	5094	3928
Taxes	3310	3422	3510	3238	2898	2547	1964
Net income	3310	3422	3510	3238	2898	2547	1964
				Consolidated Global Operations			
Sales	101508	102722	105407	105353	107981	108729	108365
Cost of sales	63831	64034	65541	66997	71257	73786	76808
Gross margin	37677	38688	39866	38356	36724	34786	76808
General and admin. exp.	16674	17224	17697	18305	18852	19434	20190
Operating income	21002	21464	22169	20052	17872	15510	11368
Taxes	10501	10732	11084	10026	8936	7755	56845
Net income	10501	10732	11084	10026	8936	7755	5684
				As a Percentage of Sales Domestic Operations			
Sales	100.0	100.0	100.0	100.0	100.0	100.0	100.0
Cost of sales	61.9	61.4	61.3	62.6	65.0	66.8	69.8
Gross margin	38.1	38.6	38.7	37.4	35.0	33.2	30.2
General and admin. exp.	17.8	18.1	18.2	18.8	18.9	19.4	20.2
Operating income	20.3	20.4	20.6	18.6	16.1	13.8	10.0
Taxes	10.1	10.2	10.3	9.3	8.1	6.9	5.0
Net income	10.1	10.2	10.3	9.3	8.1	6.9	5.0
				International Operations			
Sales	100.0	100.0	100.0	100.0	100.0	100.0	100.0
Cost of sales	65.0	64.5	64.3	65.8	68.2	70.2	73.3
Gross margin	35.0	35.5	35.7	34.2	31.8	29.8	26.7

(*continued*)

(concluded)

	1985	1986	1987	1988	1989	1990	1991
			International Operations				
General and admin. exp.	13.3	13.6	13.6	14.1	14.2	14.5	15.2
Operating income	21.6	21.9	22.1	20.1	17.6	15.3	11.6
Taxes	10.8	11.0	11.0	10.1	8.8	7.7	5.8
Net income	10.8	11.0	11.0	10.1	8.8	7.7	5.8
			Consolidated Global Operations				
Sales	100.0	100.0	100.0	100.0	100.0	100.0	100.0
Cost of sales	62.9	62.3	62.2	63.6	66.0	67.9	70.9
Gross margin	37.1	37.7	37.8	36.4	34.0	32.1	29.1
General and admin. exp.	16.4	16.8	16.8	17.4	17.5	17.9	18.6
Operating income	20.7	20.9	21.0	19.0	16.6	14.3	10.5
Taxes	10.3	10.4	10.5	9.5	8.3	7.1	5.2
Net income	10.3	10.4	10.5	9.5	8.3	7.1	5.2

*Note: All figures have been disguised.

resented the final product, although he felt the basic concept would be followed. "There's a central living area, sort of like a great room, and a kitchen and eating area which separates the great room from the sleeping area."

"Why," asked Julianna, "did it have to be built on the factory grounds?" Tom's response was specific, "So that running water and sewers would be available."

Although Tom wasn't attempting to overstate the character of the managing director's house, he knew it would be a far cry from their customary standard of living. On the other hand, by local Chinese standards, it would be the most expensive house in the city. Anything larger would be an ostentatious extravagance.

Julianna was aware of the career advancement potential that this assignment offered her husband. American executives with solid operating experience in China were few and far between, and Tom wanted to become one of the few. The appeal of becoming a managing director of a multimillion dollar company was of prime interest to both Tom and Julianna.

"Well, I'm game if you are," she said. "But if it's really hideous, I want to be able to come back to the States off and on, even if I have to do that by myself." "It's a deal," Tom replied, "and if you need a break, you can come back, either here, or to Hong Kong ... whichever you want. I don't want you to feel constrained before we even arrive there." She smiled as they knew their minds were made up.

Everything seemed to happen so slowly in China. Even after Jim Arens delivered the contract, signed by all the Diamond officials, it still took thirteen more months before it was signed by the Chinese goverment officials. Eight of these months were consumed by the Jingshan and provincial government officials, even though China's Ministry of Foreign Relations & Trade (MOFRT) had already studied it in detail and approved its contents.

In the Spring of 1988, with suitcases packed, loaded into the cab, Tom and his wife were off to the airport for the long trip to Jingshan. As Tom looked out the window, for the first time he expressed to Julianna his doubts about the new job: Could he be successful in this assignment? And, would it be fun trying?

MANAGING IN CHINA

After more than a year in Jingshan, Tom's doubts remained. Although the job was an exceptional assignment for a manager in his early 30s, it was also exceptional in its frustrations.

It seemed that when a decision had been made it never applied to any subsequent, related issue; a whole new decision process was always required. There was no concept of precedent to be applied to the next similar situation. The Chinese culture believed that since different people would be involved in a different set of circumstances that the same logic could result in a contrary outcome; or at least an inconsistent conclusion to the previous similar issue. Policy would not remain consistent from one decision-making process to another. Each time, hour after hour was required to hash out the details.

There was another aspect that Tom disliked personally and organizationally. As time went on, more and more operational details required his approval before action would be taken. Mr. Fhu was right about one thing: If he were managing director, he would have been replaced by now.

Frequently, this syndrome seemingly had nothing to do with the work scene. Tom felt as though he had become everyone's Godfather. One of the young shop workers had recently married. He and his bride routinely applied for married government housing. After several months of repeated complaints to the officials, the young couple still had no housing and were rapidly becoming unhappy. It was at this point they came to Tom to ask for his assistance in approaching officials of the government housing bureau.

Tom could not send them away, but on the other hand, there was no one in the bureau that he knew that could help them. Another day lost to a fruitless search for an efficiency apartment in a high-rise walk-up.

Then there were communications. After months of negotiations that seemed more like arguments, the government finally gave permission to install a Telex machine. Now, when headquarters needed to communicate, routine messages could be received on the Telex instead of a phone call, waking Tom in the middle of the night. Efforts to obtain approval for either a fax machine or a computer were rebuffed by the government on the basis that neither was required for the operation. Tom doubted if that was the real reason; but without facts to make an argument, he didn't want to raise a highly controversial issue based only upon the opinions of a "Western foreigner."

There was no privacy with the Telex machine. Mr. Fhu, via the Telex operator, had access to every communication sent or received. Anything that headquarters sent to Tom was known to all the partners, their directors, and their government; sometimes even before Tom had a chance to read the Telex.

Unexpectedly, there was a subtle benefit to this Telex situation, but, it had to be played very carefully. Because of the Asian concept of "saving face," none of the partners would ever admit to having read a Telex addressed to Tom. As a result, cleverly worded Telexes from headquarters could send a more pointed message, indirectly, to the partners than would be acceptable in direct conversation. Yet, even after they read the pointed Telex, they were forced to act as if they had not read it. It was an interesting situation: one of those where, "They knew, you knew, they knew." To use this situation effectively required both skill and patience. Nevertheless, Tom resented not being able to communicate with headquarters in confidence. It was one more of those irritating thorns that made the job frustrating.

Another unanticipated problem was the shortage of raw materials. Because of this, materials sometimes cost 50 percent more than originally expected and no one could predict their availability. It was the antithesis of JIT. If needed materials could be found, it was necessary to hoard them. As a result, hundreds of thousands of dollars worth of inventory was hoarded, depressing the cash flow.

The receivables problem added more misery. Cash was tight throughout China. Vendors were paid late according to the "customer daily chain." Customer A would promise to pay as soon as customer B paid them. However, customer B promised to pay only after customer C paid them, and so on down the "customer daisy chain." Although the joint venture company's terms were net 30 days, accounts receivable averaged 187 days outstanding, and some customers were 285 days outstanding. Threats were unacceptable and it seemed that customer concessions only led to further concessions.

Finally, there was the standard of business ethics. The Chinese ethics were neither better nor worse than Western standards; but, they were different. Their loyalty to the organization was central in their business life. That meant loyalty to the People's Republic of China. Often there were statements made that could not be factual, but they were sworn-to out of the sense of loyalty to country. This bothered Tom a lot, yet there was seemingly nothing he could do about it.

Another situation was the discovery that a man on his senior staff was stealing documents. Having caught the culprit in the act with the smoking gun in his hand, Tom was about to fire him when it was pointed out that the board of directors hired and fired all senior staff.

This was a 50–50 ownership joint venture, and the directors were lined up four and four. A straw vote indicated that if the firing issue were brought to the board, it would result in a 4–4 tie, meaning no action would be taken. Powerless to fire the culprit, Tom was determined to suspend him from his senior staff position. This sort of "unilateral" executive action shocked the Chinese partners, but they saw no way to force Tom to place him back on the senior staff. So, it was finally agreed to reassign him to another function, no longer reporting on the senior staff. Tom had made his point by suspending him, but the partners made their point by keeping him on the payroll.

All of these factors were adding up to a highly frustrating job.

Unexpectedly, in early June, the night watchman at the factory was pounding on the front door of the managing director's house. Julianna was the first to wake, and after realizing that the man had a important message for Tom, she woke him from a deep sleep. Tom rushed to his office phone, realizing that such an unusual call in the middle of the night must be urgent.

CIVIL UNREST

Jim Arens was on the phone. "Are you aware of what's going on in Beijing?" "I don't know what you're talking about," responded Tom, in a voice half asleep.

"There's civil war in Beijing," Jim declared, "and there's no way to tell how far it will spread or how serious it will become." All the signs of sleep had left Tom's voice. "When did this start? What's it all about? What's the problem, anyway?"

Jim told him all he knew, and that was from watching CNN. There was a demonstration by liberal students in Tianamen Square. Large crowds had developed, and there were some scuffles as the crowd increased. A strong antigovernment sentiment had developed. A symbolic replica of the Statue of Liberty had been sculpted and several fires were ignited to display it during the night. At that point, army troops moved in and opened fire on the defenseless demonstrators.

"Wow, that sounds gruesome!" Tom's voice was clearly shaken at this point. Jim went on about the brutality and murders of students in Tiananmen Square. Jim wanted to know if there had been any threats in Jingshan.

"No, nothing at all like that around here, Jim. Before your call, I didn't know that there was a problem. Some students had been demanding civil liberties, but it was pretty much isolated and the government didn't seem to give them any recognition."

Jim's voice suddenly became unusually firm. "I want you to get out now! Leave everything except what you can take as carry-on luggage and get to Hong Kong today. Don't take a flight that connects via Beijing. Being a foreigner, they might detain you there. Even if they don't, the turmoil may force closing of the airport. Get a flight to Hong Kong and you can get reorganized there. Do you think you can manage that?"

Tom had no source of information and probably couldn't get any valid reporting for at least a day. Realizing he was in an "information blackout" he immediately decided to move fast. "Jim, we'll be on a plane at daybreak. I'll call you the minute we are out of China."

"Safe journey and good night," were Jim's final words of encouragement.

When he returned to the managing director's house, Julianna was waiting for him with a cup of coffee. "What's so important this time," she wanted to know. Tom explained the situation. He already had the night guard getting the company car and driver ready for the trip to Wuhan where they could get a jet flight to Hong Kong. "We've got to go now, if we want to make the morning flight. We've got nearly 200 km to cover before sunup." Tom didn't want to frighten Julinna, but his stomach was reacting to the stress. Taking some direct action seemed like the right thing to do.

With two tote bags, they scrambled into the company car, drove through the darkness of Jingshan, and headed down the road for the trip to Wuhan.

In the faint light of predawn, they made out the bridge which crossed the Yangtze River. They could also make out the mob of people at the bridge entrance, with several fires burning alongside the road. The bridge was barricaded by a couple of busses along with the mob.

The airport was on the other side. Tom told the company driver, "Park two blocks away from the bridge and you walk up and find out whether we can get across in the car. If not, can we walk across? Are they arresting foreigners or especially, Americans? Get all the information you can. Whether we get to the airport or not depends on whether you can get us across this bridge. One way or another!"

After what seemed like hours, the driver returned and told Tom it would be better if they made the crossing inside the car, since fewer people would recognize them as foreigners. The crowd was nearly all younger people, mostly students at the university in Wuhan. He said they were demonstrating against the government, not foreigners. But, emotions were high. One of the students, who seemed to exercise an element of leadership, told the driver that he would move one of the busses to let their car pass.

That was good enough for Tom. "Let's do it," he told the driver. "Let's keep our heads lowered and don't peer out the windows as we cross," he said to Julianna. As they approached the bridge entrance, the bus on the left side of the road pulled forward as promised and they slowly drove past hundreds of onlookers. "Thank God!" Julianna breathed as they crossed to the other side and took the road to the airport.

When they arrived in Hong Kong and saw the television news they were finally able to comprehend what was going on in Beijing and some of the larger Chinese cities. The trip to the States was routine.

Back home, Tom thought about returning to China. Would it be safe? Even if it was, he wondered about all the arguments, anxiety, lack of privacy, and conflict with the ethical standards. Was it worth it?

CASE 22
THE HIT AND RUN EXPATRIATE EMPLOYEES

Salam Wholesalers is a trading company that handles consumer personal goods, such as sunglasses, cosmetics, colognes, and various sundries. Saudi Arabian law dictates that when an expatriate leaves a firm for any reason, the person cannot work for another firm unless they have written permission from their former employer. The person is prohibited from working for another Saudi Arabian firm for three years. It is permissible to resign and return to their home country. Two salesmen, Badr and Jalil, got a better job offer at Zag Company and they decided to leave Salam Wholesalers. These two employees were from Egypt. They did not tell the government they were changing employment nor did they request written permission.

Subsequently, their former general manager, Mr. Hadad, found out that they were working for a competitor. They had defrauded Salam Wholesalers, and broken Saudi Arabian law. Therefore, they would be sent back to Egypt. Mr. Kamal, the owner of Zag Company, enjoyed a good relationship with the owner of Salam Wholesalers. This was despite the fact that they were direct competitors. After the Zag Company found out that Mr. Hadad had taken action against the former employees, Mr. Kamal called Mr. Hashim. He asked him to give Badr and Jalil written permission to work for Zag Company. They were excellent salesmen and Mr. Kamal did not want to lose them.

Salam Wholesalers has invested a great deal of time and money to train the salesmen. In addition, they had incurred relocation expenses as well as other expenses. Salam Wholesalers had trained them well by providing them with on-the-job training and experience. Within six months from their point-of-hire, Badr and Jalil had found a better opportunity and left. It is important to understand that Saudi Arabian companies traditionally do not pay expatriate employees as well as natural born citizens. Oftentimes, once expatriate employees acquire on-the-job experience, they want to change jobs because they can earn more money at another firm.

When the Zag Company found out that Mr. Hadad, the general manager, had taken legal action and had informed the government, Mr. Kamal tried to convince Mr. Hashim to reverse the actions of his general manager. The owner of Salam Wholesalers felt he needed to support his general manager. He did not want these two expatriate employees to break the law and have the other employees see that they could get away with it. Mr. Hashim had a major dilemma to solve.

Note: Fictional names have been used in this case.

Source: This case was written by Diane H. B. Welsh and Ismael Al-Fahim, both of Eastern Washington University, USA. This case is intended as a basis for class discussion rather than to illustrate either effective or ineffective handling of an administrative situation.

Notes

Notes

Notes

Notes

Notes

Notes

Notes

Notes